M000204528

ANATOMY OF THE SOUL

by
Chaim Kramer

with
Avraham Sutton

Published by
BRESLOV RESEARCH INSTITUTE
Jerusalem/New York

Copyright © Breslov Research Institute 1998
ISBN 0-930213-51-3

No part of this publication may be translated,
reproduced, stored in any retrieval system or transmitted,
in any form or by any means,
electronic, mechanical, photocopying, recording or otherwise,
without prior permission in writing from the publishers.

We gratefully acknowledge Moznaim Publishers of Brooklyn, NY,
for their permission to print excerpts
from *Innerspace*, by Rabbi Aryeh Kaplan.

First Edition

For further information:
Breslov Research Institute
POB 5370
Jerusalem, Israel

or:
Breslov Research Institute
POB 587
Monsey, NY 10952-0587

e-mail: info@breslov.org
Internet: http//www.breslov.org

Printed in Israel

This book is dedicated

in memory of

Jonathan Levin

son, brother, teacher and friend

who, through his life's example,
touched deeply into the hearts
of those who knew him

and who inspired others
to reach out beyond their grasp
and attain that which seemed unattainable

In loving memory of my dear parents

Louis Israel Rosen *z'l*
and
Marion Ida Rosen *z'l*

who gave me life,
who inspired and assisted me,
in following the ways of God,
and in pursuing the path of healing,
and, who, most of all, were my best friends.

Riphael Avraham Rosen

Guide to the Book

Anatomy of the Soul explores the Bible's depiction of man as having been created in a "Godly image." The principle ideas in the book are drawn from the teachings of the great Chassidic master Rebbe Nachman of Breslov (1772–1810) and his closest follower, Reb Noson (1780–1844). It presents a description of the human anatomy with its essential spiritual parallels in order to encourage the reader to realize his or her full potential through perceiving the body as a temple for the soul. We have followed the standard practice of dividing the body according to physiological systems, as do most books on anatomy. However, because our intent is to explore the spiritual essence of the human anatomy, we have structured our particular approach accordingly.

Part One introduces the concept of "spiritual anatomy," taking the biblical representation of Adam as the prototype for all mankind. It also discusses the concepts of Adam in the Garden of Eden, his partaking of the forbidden fruit of the Tree of Knowledge of Good and Evil, his subsequent expulsion from the Garden and its contemporary meaning for us.

Part Two details the necessity for the body and soul to function together in harmony. The creation of a soul and a body, their interdependence and their major characteristics are then discussed. Many of the Kabbalistic concepts incorporated within our text are introduced in this section.

In Part Three we begin to explore the internal systems of the body. As will be clearly demonstrated, a person's character is rooted in his bloodstream and digestive system. These systems and organs are thus examined first so that we can understand how our basic character traits develop during childhood. We will explain, for example, the roots of anger and arrogance and how avarice, gluttony and lust evolve.

Following this, in Parts Four through Six, we discuss the organs that can be employed to counter man's baser desires. These include the central nervous system and the organs contained within the thoracic cavity (the heart and lungs — the seats of the intellect and emotions), which contain the means through which a person can learn to understand himself.

Part Seven discusses the peripheral nervous system, branches of intellect which endow us with the potential to master our desires and sublimate them for our spiritual benefit.

In Part Eight, the discussion centers on the skeletal and muscular systems, which enable us to ascend the spiritual ladder, each individual according to his own unique abilities.

In Part Nine, we discuss the reproductive system, along with a spiritual approach to sexual purity, marital relations, conception, pregnancy and birth.

Finally, Part Ten deals with the issues of why God saw a need to create man with a physical body and physical needs, the purpose served by death, and the idea of the ultimate reward, the World to Come, which *can* be experienced even in This World, simply by directing one's efforts towards transcending the pursuit of the material.

Appendix A contains the unabridged version of Rebbe Nachman's story "The Exchanged Children," which Reb Noson uses as a guide for understanding the respective roles of our physical and spiritual natures. Appendix B lists specific mitzvot that are associated with the various organs, quoted from the *Sefer Charedim*. Appendix C defines which of man's characteristics are rooted in which *Sefirot*, in order to better be able to strive for one's Godly image, quoted from the *Tomer Devorah*. Appendix D contains charts and visual aids to illustrate the Kabbalistic concepts introduced in our work.

* * *

Table of Contents

Preface

"All my limbs shall declare, 'God! Who is like You?'" (Psalms 35:10).

"I envy a sincerely devout person. He may appear to have hands and feet and a body like everyone else, but he is really something more. Such a person is very precious indeed" (*Rabbi Nachman's Wisdom* #14).

Rebbe Nachman of Breslov (1772–1810) was a leading Chassidic master of the late eighteenth and early nineteenth centuries. His *magnum opus* is the *Likutey Moharan*, a two-volume work comprising over four hundred lessons. Acclaimed by leading scholars the world over, from Chassidic masters and religious lay leaders to university professors, it is a masterful collection of discourses which span the entire spectrum of Torah literature. The material presented in *Anatomy of the Soul* has been culled mainly from the *Likutey Moharan* and from some of Rebbe Nachman's conversations, as well as from *Likutey Halakhot*, the discourses of Rebbe Nachman's closest disciple, Reb Noson (1780–1844).

The Bible, Talmud and Zohar are replete with stories of people who rose above their material circumstances and even mastered their physical bodies. In doing so, they became worthy of sanctifying their physicality, making themselves into "chariots" or "temples" of God's presence in the world. Nowhere is there such a wealth of material explaining how to master and transcend the physical as in Rebbe Nachman's teachings. Beginning with his first lesson, virtually every discourse includes a discussion of some part of the human anatomy, describing the inherent spiritual power of each organ.

Rebbe Nachman makes it abundantly clear: *Everyone* — no matter who — according to the effort he expends, can immediately begin to effect change in his life. He *can* ascend the spiritual ladder and internalize ever greater enlightenment. One of Rebbe Nachman's unique approaches expressed through his teachings was the principle that the functions of the physical body and their soul counterparts are inextricably interrelated, and, as we shall see, the parallels between body and soul are truly amazing. Rebbe Nachman's teachings range from the mundane to the sublime, representing the human anatomy as a reflection of the spiritual and showing how one can succeed in acquiring truly spiritual traits. Quite a few of the Rebbe's ideas, once explained, seem so simple that one may wonder why one never thought of them before.

The interface between spiritual and physical concepts is extremely difficult to present if a reader has only a limited background in Kabbalistic teachings. Thus, we are very grateful to Moznaim Publishers of Brooklyn, New York, who have given us permission to quote from *Innerspace* by Rabbi Aryeh Kaplan. Rabbi Kaplan's ability to present the most esoteric concepts in simple terms has greatly enhanced our presentation.

My deepest appreciation is extended to Avraham Sutton, who examined, diagnosed, operated and successfully treated the malaised anatomy of the original manuscript. His unique ability to get to the heart of the "matter" brought forth the "form" of this book.

More than heartfelt thanks are due to C. Safran, S. C. Mizrahi, S. Brand and C. Raphael for reviewing and editing this work. Incomprehensible as the "body" of my presentation was, their ability to reach into the "soul" of the matter was remarkable. May God bestow His blessings upon them, their anatomies and their families for good health and prosperity. Many thanks to Drs. Riphael Rosen and Robert Friedman. Their guidance and suggestions have proven invaluable. Thanks also to Dr. Noach Bittleman for his insights into oriental medicine. Thanks also to my colleagues at Breslov Research Institute for their patience and assistance in getting this book through its "purification process," making it reader-palatable.

Special note of profound gratitude is for Seymour Stein who has stood by me throughout the years. Our relationship covers several decades, to when Seymour was a student of my late father-in-law, Rabbi Zvi Aryeh Rosenfeld, while his parents extended their kindness and friendship to me. His earnest dedication and unstinting contributions to the Breslov Research Institute, have helped bring this work, along with many others, to completion. With his sincere encouragement and honest direction, we are fortunate that he is a real friend. May God bestow His kindness upon him and his family, in the merit of Rebbe Nachman for whom Seymour has sacrificed so much, for good health and prosperity, and that his dear parents receive true *nachas* from Seymour, his sister Ann, and all their offspring, Amen.

And last, but not least, I thank my wife who, though "taken from my rib," has nevertheless remained faithfully by my side. When I began this book she took ill and required several months of convalescence. I thank God Who, in His Infinite kindness, has returned her health. This book is thus an expression of my appreciation as I attempt to return the great favor God has shown us, by presenting Rebbe Nachman's teachings on anatomy. May the wisdom of the Rebbe be our guide as we yearn and search for Godliness, until we merit to experience it.

When speaking of the preciousness of a sincere person, Rebbe Nachman concluded: "Although desire for spirituality is very great, this alone is not enough. One must continually yearn in order to bring this good desire to fruition. Then, even if a person cannot fully complete his task, still, with his good desire alone he has accomplished something worthy" (*Rabbi Nachman's Wisdom* #14). Rebbe Nachman also taught that the soul is always finding new and wondrous spiritual delights. A person must have compassion on his body and share with it the soul's accomplishments (*Likutey Moharan* I, 22:5).

May God grant us the clarity to yearn and long for spiritual fulfillment, enlightening our bodies with our souls' attainments. By virtue of this, may peace come to the world, as we merit to see the Coming of the Mashiach, the Ingathering of the Exiles and the Rebuilding of the Holy Temple, speedily in our days, Amen.

Chaim Kramer
Jerusalem, *Tevet*, 5758

Part One

The Soul of the Anatomy

1

"In a Godly Image"

Midrashic and Kabbalistic tradition state that when prophecy existed, God's existence was much more evident than it is nowadays. God spoke in man's heart, heaven was on earth, spirit permeated matter. The truth is that this is still true. Man is still connected to God, earth is still connected to heaven, and matter is still permeated by spirit or energy. Today it is even known that matter is undoubtedly just another form of energy. Still, this phenomenon is deeply hidden, and mankind is searching desperately for a way to reconnect to God.

What connects God and man, heaven and earth, spirit and matter? Is there a bridge to God? Is there a ladder we can climb to heaven and bring its light back down into our lives?

There is a bridge and a ladder. It is called Torah.

What is Torah?

Torah is the written document received and transmitted by Moses at Sinai a little over 3,300 years ago. It is also the oral tradition that accompanied that document, including instructions on how to understand the basic meaning of the Torah (for it is an extremely terse text that says much more than meets the eye) and fulfill its commandments.

The Oral Torah dovetails with the written Torah in four primary ways encoded in the Hebrew word *Pardes*. *Pardes* is the source for the English word *Paradise*, which refers to the Garden of Eden. *PaRDeS* is also an acronym for four different levels of understanding the Torah: *P'shat* (simple meaning), *Remez* (allusion), *Drush* (homiletical meaning), and *Sod* (Kabbalah; secret meaning). All together these four levels are the keys needed to enter the Paradise of the Torah.

With these four keys, the Torah opens up and reveals not only its own secrets, but the secrets of the universe, the secrets of matter (space), history (time) and man (soul and consciousness). If we wish to go behind the scenes, and probe the mysteries of creation and human existence, the Torah is the address. The reason for this is that the Torah preceded creation. In truth, the Torah is nothing less than an illumination of what we call God's Mind. It is the conceptual link between Him and His world, between Him and us.

*

Torah and Anatomy

This is the Torah, man...

Numbers 19:14

It is well known that the Torah contains 613 *mitzvot* (commandments; plural of *mitzvah*) (Makkot 23b). The root meaning of the verb *leTZaVot* (to command) is "to bind." When we perform a *miTZVah* we bind ourselves and the world around us to God.

The 613 mitzvot divide into 248 positive commandments and 365 prohibitions. These commandments encompass every aspect of our relationship with God, with our fellow human beings, and with all existence. Through these commandments, God provided every necessary tool with which man could connect to God and bring all of creation to its ultimate perfection.

The human form also has 248 limbs, corresponding to the 248 positive commandments of the Torah, and 365 connecting tissues, veins or sinews, corresponding to the 365 prohibitions of the Torah (Zohar I, 170b). Thus, man was fashioned in the pattern of the Torah. Not only his soul, but the very body that seemingly prevents him from rising above the physical limitations of this world, is itself "a Torah." Through this connection, he can utilize all that is contained in the world to recognize and serve God with his body. With his soul he can ascend beyond the material world and enter the realm of the spirit. With his body he can channel the spiritual down into the material, creating the perfection that human life on earth was meant to be.

The Torah is the link that allows man to do this. Reb Noson writes about the link between the Torah and man's body:

> In order to effect a remedy, a physician must have complete knowledge of the human anatomy. He must know *all* the parts of the body — the limbs, arteries, veins, etc. He must know how each and every organ is interconnected and interdependent with the others. He must be aware of how each organ can be affected by every other. Then, and only then, can a physician understand the nature of the illness he seeks to cure. In the same vein the Torah is a body of law with each individual mitzvah representing an "organ" of that "body". To be able to fathom the true value of the Torah, a person must know its "anatomy" — its laws and ideals — how each mitzvah is interconnected with the others, as an individual, integral part of an entire Torah (*Likutey Halakhot, Rosh Chodesh* 5:6).

Reb Noson continues his discourse explaining the parallels between the Torah's "anatomy" and the human anatomy. This is a major theme found in the Kabbalah, which describes the connection between certain parts of the body and certain mitzvot. Reb Noson writes elsewhere that one who understands the writings of the Zohar and the ARI will realize that all the mysteries of the Kabbalah speak about this (*Likutey Halakhot, Minchah* 7:22). Two works mentioned in this book, *Sha'arey Kedushah* and *Sefer Charedim*, have this idea as a major theme (see also Appendices B–C).

*

Though corporeal, the human form corresponds to the Torah and reflects the highest levels of spirituality. Each part of the body corresponds to a different spiritual concept, a different mitzvah. Each organ and every vein contains its own spiritual power. When harnessed, these powers can elevate man above the material form that houses his soul. Moses is the paradigm for this elevation. He purified his physical body to such an extent that his corporeality was transformed into spirituality. The Torah bears witness to this when it relates that Moses ascended to heaven and remained there forty days and forty nights without eating or drinking (Deuteronomy 9:9). Another verse states, "This is the blessing with which Moses, the *man of God*, blessed the people of Israel" (*ibid.* 33:1) Moses is called a "man of God" because he succeeded in transforming his physical body into a Godly temple for his spirit (*Devarim Rabbah* 11:4).

It is thus written (Exodus 34:30), "When Moses came down from Mount Sinai with the two Tablets of the Testimony in his hand... he did not realize that the skin of his face had become luminous because of [God's] having spoken with him. When Aaron and all the children of Israel saw that the skin of Moses' face shone with a brilliant light, they were afraid to come near him."

* * *

2

In the Garden of Eden

One of the first steps we can take towards attaining true spirituality is to become more aware of the spiritual significance of the human anatomy. In order to do this, we must first recognize the greatness of the soul and learn how it relates to the body.

In the Zohar (III, 105a, 281a; *Tikkuney Zohar* #26, p.72a), the soul is said to tower so high above the body, that the body is called a "shoe" relative to the soul. Only the lowest extremity of the soul "fits" into the body. Through our desire to come close to God, through our thoughts, emotions, speech and actions, we can bring down greater and greater illuminations of our own souls. In this manner, anyone has the ability to make his physical body a chariot or a temple for the highest parts of the soul, as did Moses.

The human body was not always what we know it to be. Adam's body was a body of light. He radiated Godliness (*Bereishit Rabbah* 20:12). He was so awesome that the angels erred and contemplated worshiping him (*ibid.* 8:10). Even after he sinned, he remained a spiritual being clothed in a physical body and radiating spirituality. Still, relative to his level before the sin, and certainly relative to the level he was intended to have attained, his actions caused an occlusion of God's Light. His body of light (*kotnot or*, where *or* is spelled *aleph-vav-resh*, אור), which revealed the soul, congealed into a body of skin and hide (*kotnot or*, where *or* is spelled *ayin-vav-resh*, עור) which hid the soul (*ibid.* 20:12).

Light (*or* with an *aleph*) and skin (*or* with an *ayin*) correspond to the two specific trees in the Garden of Eden. In the Torah it is written (Genesis 2:8–9), "God planted a garden in Eden to the east. There He placed the man that He had formed. God made grow out of the ground every tree that is pleasant to look at and good to eat, [including] the Tree of Life in the middle of the garden, and the Tree of Knowledge of Good and Evil." Shortly after this is written God's warning (*ibid.* 2:17), "But from the Tree of Knowledge of Good and Evil do not eat, for on the day you eat from it, you will surely die."

The Torah explicitly states that Adam was commanded not to eat from the Tree of Knowledge. According to the Kabbalah, the prohibition included the Tree of Life, but only until sundown, the advent of the first Sabbath (cf. *Sefer HaLikutim* #3, pp.25–27). At that point eating from the Tree of Life would have become a mitzvah. And once Adam had eaten from the Tree of Life, he would have been allowed to eat of the Tree of Knowledge as well, for he would have had the ability to elevate the Tree of Knowledge back into its source in the Tree of Life (for the greater level always includes the lower level).

Thus, it was only in order to give Adam the opportunity to attain the highest spirituality that God placed him in the Garden with these two trees. Both of these trees were made by God, but, as with everything in creation, God fashioned them to represent potentially opposing or potentially complementary energies — depending on man's use of them. The Tree of Life corresponded to the soul, to spirituality. The Tree of Knowledge of Good and Evil corresponded to the body, specifically to the body's potential either to reveal the soul and radiate its holiness, or to conceal and smother the soul. Adam's mission was to transform the Tree of Knowledge into the Tree of Life, to irradiate the body with the *or* (light) of the soul. Instead he caused the soul to be obscured by the *or* (skin) of the body (see *Likutey Halakhot, Orlah* 4:2).

Adam was created with the ability to discern between good and evil. Why, then, was he so tempted by evil? He yearned for his spiritual source. He wanted to know God and discern His presence in and through everything in the world, even through evil.

But man was brash. He was subtly conceited. He wanted to be like God, to create worlds. So he was lured into thinking it was God's will that he transgress. *Then* he would appreciate God! Or so he thought...

If only he had endured the pain of temptation. If only he had perceived the experience of temptation as an opportunity to cling to God, to yearn and cry out to be saved from temptation... If only he had seen God hiding in the pain of that temptation, seen the Tree of Life hidden inside the Tree of Knowledge...

But no, the God consciousness that had been awaiting actualization was now actively constricted. Adam lost his exalted level of prophecy. Cut off from the higher levels of his soul, he experienced the sensation of "death" — "for on the day you eat from it, you will surely die." Ever since that moment, man's mission has been to seek the spiritual and return to his original level (see *The Breslov Haggadah*, p.12).

*

Man's essence is his soul. Had Adam not sinned, man would have been able to live a purely spiritual life — a full life of happiness, contentment and purity. He was to have lived forever — death was decreed only after he sinned. But Adam ate from the Tree of Knowledge of Good and Evil and thereby tainted his pure soul. Having succumbed to his physical desires, he fell from his level, was banished from the Garden of Eden and prevented from returning to it by the Revolving Sword (Genesis 3:24). We, his descendants, must pay the price for his actions, that price being the ever-present conflict between the body's needs and wants and the soul's yearnings.

The conflict between body and soul is beautifully illustrated in one of Rebbe Nachman's classic stories, "The Exchanged Children," in which it is told that a queen and her maidservant gave birth at the same time. The midwife switched the children so that the servant's son grew up as a prince while the prince was raised in the servant's house. Rumors spread that the children had been switched at birth, and so the true prince was banished from his kingdom by the pretender. He roamed the world, indulging his heart's desires, but eventually began to ponder his situation and to question his lifestyle. "If I am not the prince, should I have been banished from my kingdom? And if I truly am a prince, does it behoove me to live such a life?" The prince began searching for himself — for his true identity — and eventually became king over a kingdom greater than that which had been his previously. In an interesting twist, the servant, who had been raised as the prince, became his royal servant. (The story in its entirety appears in Appendix A.)

Reb Noson comments that the Revolving Sword which kept Adam from reentering the Garden of Eden corresponds to the *Heikhaley HaTemurot*, the "Chambers of Exchanges." While in these Chambers, one is continually faced with conflicts between good and evil, between light and darkness, between sweet and bitter (cf. Isaiah 5:20), because each presents itself as the correct choice. In short, these Chambers are represented by our conflicts over life itself — should we choose a material life or a spiritual life? Evil seems to be good, what is truly dark appears light and proper and what tastes bitter can become sweet and wonderful. Is the material evil or can the physical be good? Is the spiritual too bitter for the palate or can the spiritual experience be sweet?

Reb Noson explains that the obscurity of right and wrong found in these Chambers symbolizes the exchange of the prince for the servant. It is this obscurity that led to the conflicts between Isaac and Ishmael, between Jacob and Esau, between Joseph and his brothers, between the Jews and the Nations; and this is the source of the ongoing battle between body and soul.

Adam, by eating from the Tree of Knowledge of Good and Evil, descended into these Chambers and exchanged what was truly good — a life of eternal spiritual delight — for the temporal material life upon which our existence now depends. It is man's mission to seek spirituality, to discern between good and evil, so that he can end his personal exile and reenter the Garden. This is the ongoing struggle of each and every soul, in each and every generation.

More often than not, the soul — which is so elevated at its source — assumes the identity of its material surroundings. It surrenders and becomes captive, as did the prince in the story, to the materialistic drives that are in power at the time. The soul completely forgets its royal origins, becoming entrapped in physicality and deluding itself about the truth of its existence.

But is this the way it has to be?

* * *

Part Two

Body and Soul

3

God and the Soul

In our Preface, we wrote that, according to Rebbe Nachman, the functions of the physical body and their soul counterparts are totally interrelated. Rebbe Nachman literally saw the soul in every aspect of the anatomy. His entire treatment of the body was therefore spiritual-Kabbalistic. This being the case, this chapter is devoted to providing a Kabbalistic background to many of the teachings that will be mentioned in this work.

The word *kabbalah* means "received." It designates a body of knowledge that has been received prophetically and carefully transmitted from generation to generation. One of the basic tenets of Kabbalah is that everything in the physical dimension is paralleled in the spiritual dimension. Indeed, one of the cognates of the word *KaBbaLaH* is *haK'BaLaH*, meaning "parallelism" or "correspondence." This follows the ancient Kabbalistic teaching, "As above, so below; as below, so above." In order to grasp this principle, the initial stage of Kabbalah learning is usually devoted to mastering its complex system of correspondences. These correspondences are in no way to be thought of as mechanical. Rather, they afford us an inside view of the interrelationships that govern all existence, and lead us back to the root and source of all complexity in the Infinite Being Himself Who created and continues to sustain the entire interdimensional hologram we call "The Universe."

We thus begin our overview of the Kabbalistic system with a look at God Himself, the unitary Source of all existence. We follow this with an exposition on the four (which are really five) levels of the Tetragrammaton, the five levels of the soul, the five levels of universes, and the five elements of the physical world. Following this, we show the relationship of the Ten *Sefirot* to all of the above.

*

God and His Names

> Master of the worlds! You are the Hidden One Whose Unity is infinite and absolute, and therefore indivisible.
>
> *Petichat Eliyahu, Tikkuney Zohar*, Second Introduction

It is not by chance that the principle of God's indivisible Unity is at the beginning of the *Tikkuney Zohar*, one of the most important Kabbalistic texts in existence. This first statement of Eliyahu (Elijah the Prophet) stands as a signpost and a warning for anyone who wishes to understand who and what God is. Unlike everything He created, God Himself is not subject to the laws of division, categorization, quantification and qualification which characterize His creation. He transcends all dichotomies, polarities and paradoxes. All of these are part of Creation. God transcends Creation. He is outside the "system" He created. He cannot be judged by, nor is He subject to, its rules.

This bi-polar nature of reality is alluded to in the Talmudic statement (*Bava Batra* 74b), "All that the Holy One created in His world He created male and female." "Male and female" refer primarily to pairs of conceptual opposites such as heaven and earth, transcendence and immanence, revelation and concealment, mercy and justice, Divine omniscience and human free will, daytime and nighttime, sun and moon, soul and body, next world and this world, etc. Our experience and perception of God involve a number of these basic dichotomies or paradoxes which are built into the system of creation and exist only from our point of view, from the point of view of the system itself. They do not define God, but rather the double lens through which we perceive Him. In the words of the Maharal of Prague (*Derekh Chaim*, p.14b): "The intention [of the Talmud (loc. cit.)] is that the universe was created according to the principle of opposites. The Unity of the Blessed Name, however, is utterly unique."

This is also what the Psalmist meant when he sang (Psalms 113:4–6), "God is beyond the conception of all the nations; His glory is above the most spiritual heavens. Who is like God our Lord, Whose throne is so high? He looks down to see both heaven and earth alike!"

Kabbalistic tradition is unequivocal. God Himself is beyond all description. He is called *Ein Sof* (The Infinite One) because there is no finite category with which we can describe Him or His Essence. Only His Light, the Light of *Ein Sof*, flows in constricted form throughout the entire system of *Olamot* (Universes). As we shall see, the term *OLaM* derives from the root *ELeM* or *he'ELeM*, "hiddenness" and "concealment." In essence, the Olam (Universe) is God's "secret hiding place." God is *Melech HaOlam*, "the King of the Universe" or "the King Who hides Himself in His world." The various universes that God created are nothing but filters that screen out the powerful radiation of His Infinite Light. We call these filters by different names — Divine Names, *Sefirot*, Worlds, Universes, Dimensions, or, altogether, the Spiritual Dimension.

But, again, why do we need a system of channels, a spiritual dimension, between us and the Infinite? Why can't we relate directly to God? Because the energy would be too hot—like an atomic reactor. You can't plug a lightbulb into the reactor, unless, that is, you want it to disintegrate. You need a power station that reduces the electrical power so that you can use it and not get hurt by it.

Ein Sof is The Infinite, with a capital *T* and a capital *I*. By definition, *Ein Sof* does not allow for the existence of anything else. In order for anything else to exist, in order for the world and everything in it, and all of us, to exist, the *Ein Sof* had to create a step-down system. This system is like a limiting medium or a ladder, or, as the Kabbalists call it, a system of "garments" that conceals and diminishes God's light. The highest of these "garments" is the Name *YHVH* (pronounced *Yod-Heh-Vav-Heh* or *HaVaYaH*, for it is forbidden to pronounce the Tetragrammaton as it is written).

Before we go into this Name, let us point out the difference between God and His Names. It is known that we have different relationships with all kinds of people. We have a father and mother. We have spouses and friends and teachers. Sometimes we even have different names for the same person depending on the circumstances. This is because we can have different relationships with the same person. Depending on whether we find ourselves in a formal setting or a more casual or even an intimate setting, we might call the same person by different appellations. This can even be extended to using different inflections with our voices. Sometimes it doesn't matter what we say as much as how we say it. Generally speaking, as we get closer to someone, we speak to them differently, and the names and inflections become more intimate. For instance, say you meet a person named Martin Cohen. In a formal setting, you call him Mr. Cohen. When you get to know him better, he becomes Martin, then Marty; then you reach a level where there are no names. That is, although a person's name is a very deep thing, can we say that he or she is his or her name?

The same is true of God. A verse in Psalms says (65:2) "*Lekha dumiyah tehillah* — To You, silence is praise." We call God "our King," "our Father." In the Zohar we even call Him "our Grandfather." Moses calls God "the One with the Long Face." God Himself tells Moses that He is called, "*Ehyeh asher Ehyeh*" — "I will be what I will be," "I am what I am," or "I am the One Whose existence can only be expressed as Being." Daniel calls God "the Ancient of Days." We call God "Merciful and Loving, Wise and Righteous." We call Him "*Adonay*" (Master); "*Elohim*" (Ruler or Judge); "*Shadai*" (the Almighty). On the deepest level we call Him "*Havayah*", Being itself, and the Being who transcends space and time, Who was, is and will be forever, Who is above and beyond conception, the Source of all existence. All these names express different interactions that God has with His creation.

Although all these names are very deep, God is more than any name we can call Him. This is because even the highest name is finite compared to the Infinite Light that fills it. A name is a creation that expresses a certain relationship, that creates the possibility of a relationship between God and anything that He creates. God Himself, the Infinite, is above this — He transcends any relationship. This is why *"Lekha dumiyah tehillah* — To You, silence is praise."* So when we say or think or meditate on a Divine Name we are essentially relating to God The Infinite through this Name. As the Zohar (II, 42a) says, these Divine Names are like channels or conduits through which water flows. The only difference is that a physical channel exists even when there is no water flowing through it. These Divine channels and everything else would not exist for a moment if the Divine flow of energy stopped.

Let's come down a little. One of the most important tenets of Judaism is that God is One. The Torah says (Deuteronomy 6:4), *"Shema Yisrael Adonay Eloheinu Adonay Echad."* This is the *Shema.* We say these words at least twice a day. They are among the first words a Jew learns as a child and the last words he utters before he dies. On every Jewish doorpost there is a *mezuzah* proclaiming these words. They are found in the *tefilin* that we bind to our heart and mind daily. All these proclaim this most basic principle of Judaism.

What this tells us is that all things come from One Ultimate Source. All creation is bound together by God. There is One unifying Force in the universe, God alone, the *Ein Sof.* The Torah thus tells us (Deuteronomy 4:39), "Know it this day, and bring it into your heart, *YHVH Hu HaElohim* [God is the Supreme Power], in the heavens above and on the earth below; there is no other."

Open a Hebrew *Chumash* (Five Books of Moses) or *siddur* (prayer book) and contemplate the name *YHVH.* As noted, we don't pronounce it as it is written. This teaches us something too

— that God's highest Name, and all the more so His Infiniteness that permeates this Name, is beyond our ability to grasp. YHVH is the Holy of Holies of existence. It contains the secret of God's relationship with the world He created. By not speaking the Name, or even pronouncing its letters out loud, we acknowledge this holiness. We acknowledge that if there is one thing in the entire world which should never be misused or misappropriated it is the very Essence of Being and Existence itself, the Holy Name of God. Out of reverence, therefore, and as a sign that we are sensitive to that which is completely whole and holy, we may only think of its letters and what they mean, but never speak them as they are written.

The Tetragrammaton consists of four letters, *Yod, Heh, Vav* and *Heh*, plus a fifth level which transcends and includes the other four, the apex of the *Yod* (יהוה). According to the Kabbalists, these five levels encompass everything. This is the Name that represents the totality of everything that exists. And for our purposes, the only difference between this Name and the *Ein Sof* that fills and permeates it is that it is through this Name that God wills creation into existence. As we said, on the level of pure *Ein Sof*, we don't exist. God, however, wants us to exist. Let's see how this works.

This Name is related to the past, present and future tense of the Hebrew word "to be." In Hebrew, "was" is *hayah* (היה), "is" is *hoveh* (הוה) and "will be" is *yihyeh* (יהיה). This tells us something about God. It tells us He created time and that He is utterly beyond and above time. It tells us that in order to create, He hid His Infiniteness and brought the universe into existence in such a way that He would permeate it and yet not overwhelm it. Again, it tells us that God Himself is Existence, but that nothing could exist until He brought it into existence.

We can understand this better on the basis of an ancient Kabbalistic teaching which states that these four letters contain the secret of charity. According to this teaching the *Yod* is like a coin, simple and small. The *Heh* is like the hand that gives the coin. The *Vav* is the arm that reaches out to give. The last *Heh* is the hand of the person receiving the coin.

This is charity on a mundane level. It can also be understood on a Divine level. The *Yod* is existence. Existence is what God wants to give. On this level, however, existence is so powerful that we can't receive it. So the *Heh*, like a hand, represents the concept of something that can hold existence. The *Vav* is a further extension of this, something that reduces the power sufficiently to allow us to exist. The last *Heh* is our ability to receive the existence that God wants to give us (see *Innerspace*, pp.11–12).

God and the Human Soul

The ARI (Rabbi Isaac Luria, 1534–1572) explains that these five levels of the Tetragrammaton correspond to the five levels of the soul (*Etz Chaim* 42:3). The soul is actually one unit, attached to the One God, yet graduated into separate levels representing different aspects of its relationship to the body. These five parts are known (in descending order) as:

Yechidah	—	unique essence
Chayah	—	living essence
Neshamah	—	divine soul
Ruach	—	spirit
Nefesh	—	indwelling soul

They correspond as well to five levels of universes, *Adam Kadmon* (Primordial Man), *Atzilut* (Nearness or Emanation), *Beriyah* (Creation), *Yetzirah* (Formation) and *Asiyah* (Action or Completion).

All these sets of five can be described in terms of their parallels at the human level. A person's innermost will corresponds to the apex of the *Yod*, *Yechidah* and *Adam Kadmon*. The level of preconceptual or undifferentiated mind corresponds to *Yod*, *Chayah* and *Atzilut*. The process of thought corresponds to the letter *Heh*, *Neshamah* and *Beriyah*. Speech and communication parallel the *Vav, Ruach* and *Yetzirah*. Action corresponds to the final *Heh, Nefesh* and *Asiyah*.

Tetragrammaton	Universe	Soul parallel	Human manifestation
apex of *Yod*	Adam Kadmon	Yechidah	will
Yod	Atzilut	Chayah	mind
Heh	Beriyah	Neshamah	thought
Vav	Yetzirah	Ruach	speech
Heh	Asiyah	Nefesh	action

These and other correspondences that we will see in this book are not mechanical; they represent very deep connections between us and the higher dimensions. As we saw above, our souls are rooted in the transcendental. As a result, when we think thoughts — for instance when we contemplate some truth, or simply appreciate the fact that we are alive, or realize in an instant that God is really here with us despite all indications to the contrary — these are not mere thoughts that come and go, never to be thought again. No. These are who we really are, and who we really are is eternal. Thoughts such as these are the connection between our souls and God. When we feel something strongly, speak from our heart, act or resist the urge to act, all these are expressions of our souls vibrating and working within and through the medium of our bodies. And, as we shall see, our bodies are sensitive to these higher vibrations, much more sensitive than we are aware...

The ancient masters taught that there are also five levels in the gross material world. Matter is said to be made up of four basic elements and a fifth "source element" that harmonizes and unifies them all. The four elements are fire, air, water and earth. These four elements correspond to four basic types of people, or four basic character traits in each of us (explained below, p.36 and p.40; these elements should not be confused with the chemical elements). The fifth "element" is the tzaddik, the righteous individual who binds all four elements and character traits to each other and to God (see below, Chapters 4–5).

*

The Vacated Space

In *Etz Chaim* (Tree of Life), the ARI describes the way God brought the world into existence:

> Before all things were created...the Supernal Light was simple [i.e., complete and perfect]. It filled all existence. There was no empty space which could be characterized as space, emptiness or void. Everything was filled with that simple *Or Ein Sof* [Light of The Infinite]. There was no category of beginning and no category of end. All was one simple, undifferentiated, Infinite Light.
>
> When it arose in His Simple [i.e. perfect] Will to create worlds and emanate emanations...He constricted [withdrew] His Infinite Essence away from the very centerpoint of His Light. [Of course, since Infinity has no centerpoint, this is only said from the point of view of the Space that is about to be created.] He then withdrew that Light [even further], distancing it to the extremities around this centerpoint, leaving a Vacated Space and Hollow Void.
>
> After this constriction, which resulted in the creation of a Vacated Space and Hollow Void in the very midst of the Infinite Light of *Ein Sof*, there was a *place* for all that was to be emanated [*Atzilut*], created [*Beriyah*], formed [*Yetzirah*], and completed [*Asiyah*]. He then drew a single, straight *Kav* [Ray] down from His Infinite Surrounding Light into the Vacated Space. This *Kav* descended in stages into the Vacated Space. The upper extremity of this *Kav* touched the Infinite Light of *Ein Sof* [that surrounded the Space], and

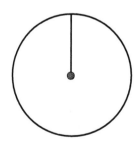

The center dot represents the first *Tzimtzum*, the very first act of Creation. The circle around it is the vacated space, from where God, as it were, withdrew Himself to make room for the Creation. The line represents the *kav*.

extended down [into the Vacated Space towards the center] but not all the way to the bottom extremity [so as not to cause the Vacated Space to collapse and merge back into God's Infinite Light]. It was through this *Kav* [serving as a conduit] that the Light of *Ein Sof* was drawn down and spread out below... Through this *Kav* the outpouring Supernal Light of *Ein Sof* spreads forth and flows down into the universes that are located within that Space and Void (*Etz Chaim, Drush Igulim V'Yosher* 1:2).

Five Olamot and Ten Sefirot

Not only *Ein Sof*, but *Or Ein Sof* (the Light of The Infinite) is so awesome that nothing can withstand it directly. God therefore constricted His Light in order to create a Vacated or Hollow Space, into which He then introduced a measured quantity of that Light via a conduit that the ARI calls the *Kav*. Even this was done in stages so as not to cause the Vacated Space to collapse and merge back into God's Infinite Light.

These stages are the various universes the ARI mentions, in Hebrew, *Olamot* (singular, *olam*) and the *Sefirot* (singular, *sefirah*). As we have seen, the term *OLaM* (עלם) is from the root *ELeM* (עלם), meaning concealment. The *Olamot* serve to conceal God's Light. The ARI continues explaining the place of the *Sefirot* within the *Olamot*:

> The abovementioned *Kav*, which extends...in a straight line from above to below...is made up of ten *Sefirot* in the form of a man who stands upright with 248 limbs distributed along three lines or columns, right, left and center. Each of these ten *Sefirot* is made up of ten, and these ten of ten, *ad infinitum*. This is what the Zohar calls "*tzelem Elohim*" [the Godly image], as in the verse (Genesis 1:27), "Elohim created man in His image; in the image of Elohim He created him; male and female He created them" (*Etz Chaim, ibid.*).

The term *Sefirah* (ספירה) is related to the word *SaPeR* (ספר), meaning to "express" or "communicate." It is also related to the word *SaPiR* (ספיר), "brilliance" or "luminary," and to *SePhaR* (ספר),

"boundary." In essence, these are all related concepts and point to the *Sefirot* as having two basic functions. First, the *Sefirot* are lights or luminaries that serve to reveal and express God's greatness. Second, they are vessels that limit and delineate God's Infinite Light, bringing it into the finite realm of boundaries (see *Innerspace*, p.40).

Five Partzufim and Ten Sefirot

The ARI teaches that the Ten *Sefirot* are divided into five main units known as *Partzufim* (plural of *partzuf*, which means "persona"). The difference between the two is that, whereas a *Sefirah* represents a single Divine Attribute or measured spiritual illumination of God's Light, a *Partzuf* is a complete persona or configuration of *Sefirot*.

Each *Partzuf* corresponds to a particular *Sefirah* or group of *Sefirot*: *Arikh Anpin* (Extended Countenance; Forbearance) parallels *Keter*; *Abba* (Father) parallels *Chokhmah*; *Imma* (Mother) parallels *Binah*; *Zer Anpin* (Diminished Countenance) parallels the six *Sefirot* of *Chesed, Gevurah, Tiferet, Netzach, Hod* and *Yesod*; and *Nukva* of *Zer Anpin* (*Zer Anpin's* Female Counterpart) parallels *Malkhut*.

The Ten *Sefirot* and the Five *Partzufim*:

Sefirah	Partzuf	Translation	Family counterpart
Keter	Arikh Anpin	Extended Countenance	grandfather
Chokhmah	Abba	Father	husband; father
Binah	Imma	Mother	wife; mother
Six *Sefirot*	Zer Anpin	Diminished Countenance	son; groom
Malkhut	Nukva	Female Counterpart	daughter; bride

There is almost a one-to-one correspondence between each *Sefirah* and its parallel *Partzuf*. Yet there are ten *Sefirot* and only five *Partzufim*. The discerning reader will already have noticed that every *Partzuf* parallels one *Sefirah*, except the *Partzuf Zer Anpin*. In addition, the *Partzuf* of *Nukva* of *Zer Anpin* cannot be said to be as complete as the three highest *Partzufim, Arikh Anpin, Abba* and *Imma*. The reason is that whereas *Arikh Anpin, Abba* and *Imma* all begin with complete configurations of Ten *Sefirot*, *Zer Anpin* begins with six *Sefirot*, and *Nukva* begins with only one *Sefirah*. The ARI explains this in great detail and adds that these last two *Partzufim* were intentionally created incomplete. They will receive their final form of Ten *Sefirot* only through man's good deeds (*Etz Chaim* 11:15, 22:1, see *Innerspace*, pp.95–96).

The major ideas in this book show how man's deeds parallel the Ten *Sefirot* and how his deeds, good or otherwise, have an impact upon the upper worlds with their *Partzufim* and the *Sefirot*. The ARI writes that Zer Anpin and Malkhut (corresponding to *Vav* and *Heh* respectively, the two final letters of the Tetragrammaton) are the main interface between God and man. As such, most of man's deeds will relate to these two *Partzufim* and their corresponding *Sefirot*, as will be explained throughout the book, most notably in Parts 8 and 9. However, several deeds do have an effect upon the higher *Partzufim* and *Sefirot*. The implications of these *Partzufim* and their interaction with mankind is discussed below in Parts 4 through 7, and in Chapter 35.

It is very important to point out that the Kabbalistic teachings on the *Partzufim* and the *Sefirot* have no connection whatsoever to any physical images. They are spiritual powers and concepts. Kabbalistic tradition is adamant about the fact that the terminology used is strictly for *our* benefit, so that we may be able to discuss lofty ideas in a way that *we* can understand.

*

The Three Columns

The *Sefirot* are arranged in three columns and are said to resemble a man standing upright. In Hebrew, the word for upright is *yashar*, which refers to man's task of being morally straight and upright in order to resemble God. The *Tikkuney Zohar* explains the concept of the three columns thus:

> The Ten *Sefirot* are arranged in a special order of three columns. The right column is said to be "long" [because it represents God's love and kindness]. The left column is said to be "short" [because it represents judgment and the power of

restraint]. The middle column or trunk is said to be "intermediate" [because it represents mercy, the perfect harmony of love and restraint]... (*Tikkuney Zohar*, Second Introduction, p.17a).

The *Sefirot* are the basic modes of God's creative power and providence with which He guides creation towards its ultimate perfection. As we shall see, in Kabbalistic terms, God is the soul of the "Cosmic Body" of *Olamot*, and the *Sefirot* are its "organs" or "limbs."

The highest of the Ten *Sefirot* is Keter. It parallels the apex of the *Yod*, and corresponds to the crown of the head of the cosmic body. The next *Sefirah*, Chokhmah, parallels the *Yod*, and corresponds to the right brain. Following Chokhmah is Binah. Binah parallels the *Heh*, and corresponds to the left brain. The next six *Sefirot* (Chesed, Gevurah, Tiferet, Netzach, Hod and Yesod) parallel the *Vav*, and correspond to the torso, genitals and legs. Malkhut, the last *sefirah*, parallels the final *Heh*, and corresponds to either the feet or the female counterpart (see Appendix D).

Thus, when the Bible speaks of God creating man as "a Godly image," this actually refers to the spiritual image of man, the powers that are reflected in the *Sefirot*.

*

The Cosmic Body

The *Tikkuney Zohar* goes on to describe the Ten *Sefirot* as a unified system which God fills and directs just as the soul fills and directs the body. The "limbs" of the "cosmic body" are arranged as follows:

Chesed [lovingkindness] is the right arm, Gevurah [restraint] is the left arm, and Tiferet [harmony] is the torso. Netzach [dominance] and Hod [empathy] are the two legs, and Yesod [foundation; channel] is the body's extremity, the sign of the holy covenant. Malkhut [kingship] is the mouth [of the holy covenant]. It is therefore called *Torah She'be'al Peh* ["Torah of the mouth" or "Oral Torah"]. [Above these "limbs" is the "head" in which] Chokhmah [wisdom] is the [right] brain, the seat of thought, and Binah [understanding] is [the left brain and] the heart, the heart's ability to discern. Concerning these, it is written (Deuteronomy 29:28), "The hidden things belong to God [corresponding to the *Sefirah* of Chokhmah] our Lord [corresponding to the *Sefirah* of Binah]." *Keter Elyon* [supernal crown] is the Keter [crown] of Malkhut [kingship], concerning which it is said (Isaiah 46:10), "I [God] declare the end [Malkhut] from the beginning [Keter]."

Together, the entire system of *Olamot* and *Sefirot* was created to filter God's Light in a way that man could interact safely with God without being overwhelmed. Just as the human body disguises the intensity of the soul, the *Sefirot* serve to disguise and conceal the Godly Light.

The anthropomorphic array of the Ten *Sefirot*:

Sefirah	*Depiction*
Keter	cranium
Chokhmah	[right] brain
Binah	[left brain]/heart
Chesed	right arm/hand
Gevurah	left arm/hand
Tiferet	torso
Netzach	right leg/kidney/testicle
Hod	left leg/kidney/testicle
Yesod	sexual organ
Malkhut	feet/crown of sexual organ

We will refer to and clarify the anthropomorphic array of the *Sefirot* in terms of its parallels in the human body throughout this book, as reflected in the entire spectrum of spiritual powers contained within man.

*

Five Levels of Soul

On the verse (Genesis 2:7), "And God breathed into his [man's] nostrils a soul-breath of life," the Zohar adds: "One who exhales, exhales from his innermost being." Once God breathes His "breath" into man, it cannot be severed from Him. Man's soul is an extension of God's "breath" and is directly connected to Him.

This inner connection is seen in the etymology of the five terms defining the levels of man's soul. The word *YeCHiDah* comes from both *eCHaD* and *YiCHuD*, meaning "oneness" and "unity." On the level of *Yechidah* the soul is still one with God, the Source.

The word *ChaYah* derives from both *CHai*, "life," and *CHaYut*, which means "life force." *Chayah* is the very life force of the soul, the level on which it is still bound to all other souls. In the Bible, connection with this level is called being "bound up in the bundle of life" (I Samuel 25:29).

The word *NeSHaMaH* is like *NeSHiMaH*, which means "breath." The reason for this is that God is said to breathe our divine soul into us just as He breathed into Adam. In addition, a person's intellect is reflected in the way he "breathes" — that is, in the way he lives his life (see below, Part 5).

Ruach is often translated as "spirit," but the word is also found to have the connotations of wind, air or direction. It represents a person's character, his ability to choose a direction, make responsible decisions, and be held accountable for those decisions.

The word *NeFeSH* comes from the root *NaFaSH*, meaning "to rest." *Nefesh* is the lowest extremity of the soul almost totally identified with the body, specifically with the bloodstream. The Torah thus states (Deuteronomy 12:23), "The blood is the *nefesh*." The Hebrew *NeFeSh* is also similar to the Aramaic *NaFiSh* which means "to grow or spread." *Nefesh* thus corresponds to the bloodstream in that it spreads throughout the body, bringing life to all the different cells.

The five levels of the soul thus form a chain linking man to the Supernal Universes, and ultimately to God.

*

The Glassblower Analogy

The ancient Kabbalists likened this relationship to a glassblower who wishes to make a beautiful vessel. As Rabbi Aryeh Kaplan wrote (*Innerspace*, pp.17–20):

> The "decision" to make the glass, emanating from the innermost will, is the level of *Yechidah* [Uniqueness]. It corresponds to the universe of *Adam Kadmon* and the apex of the *Yod*.
>
> Next we see the glassblower himself before he begins to blow out. This is the level of *Chayah* [Living Essence], corresponding to the universe of *Atzilut*, where the life force is still within the realm of the Divine. This level parallels the *Yod* of the Tetragrammaton.
>
> Next, the breath [*Neshimah*] emanates from the mouth of the glassblower and flows as a pressurized wind [*Ruach*] through the glassblowing pipe, expanding in all directions and forming a crude vessel. The wind finally comes to rest [*Nafash*] in the completed vessel...

Rabbi Kaplan then uses this analogy as a meditation to rise through five ever-expanding states of consciousness, to greater and greater awareness of the Divine:

> The lowest part of the soul interfaces with the physical body... It is on the level of *Nefesh* that a person gains an awareness of the body as a receptacle for the spiritual. This is only possible, however, when one is able to isolate oneself from the constant stream of internal and external stimuli that occupies one's thoughts. Awareness of the spiritual thus necessarily begins by quieting down the awareness of the physical. It is for this reason that this part of the soul is essentially passive rather than active. Before one is ready to experience the powerful influence of *Ruach*, all static must be tuned out. This is also suggested by the term *Nefesh*, which literally means "resting soul."
>
> The second level of the soul is *Ruach*, the "wind" blowing down to us from God's breath... At this level, a person goes

beyond the quiet spirituality of *Nefesh* and feels a completely different kind of motion. In this state of consciousness, information can be communicated; one can see visions, hear things and become conscious of higher levels of spirituality. Reaching the level of *Ruach*, one feels a moving spirit rather than a quieting one. At the highest levels, this becomes the experience of *Ruach HaKodesh* [Divine Inspiration]. This is the prophetic state in which a person feels himself completely elevated and transformed by God's spirit.

On the level of *Neshamah*, you would experience Divine breath... On this level, you not only become aware of spirituality, but also of its Source. This is exactly the difference between a breath and a wind. Feeling a breeze on a hot summer day is pleasant, but it is very different from having someone you are close to breathe down your neck; this denotes a certain intimacy. Hence, the level of *Neshamah* is when a person reaches a level of a very close intimacy with God...

If you want to go further than *Neshamah*, what would be the next level, beyond breath? Returning to the analogy of the glassblower, you have the breath, the wind, and finally the air settling and forming the vessel. What would come before the breath? The air when it is in the blower's lungs. The very life force of the blower. This is what is called *Chayah* [Living Essence]. It is the fourth level, where it is not yet separated from the blower. It is actually the experience of being within the realm of the Divine.

Finally, what would be the level beyond that? One could think of it as the decision to blow in the first place, getting into the very psyche of the Blower. The unique idea He has of creating would be on the level of *Yechidah* [Unique Essence], the highest of the five levels.

Beyond that, you are in the realm of the unimaginable.

* * *

4

The Body: A Dual-Purpose Garment

We asked: Must the body always obscure the light of the soul? Will the world (*olam*) always conceal (*elem*) the light of the *Ein Sof* that fills it and gives it existence? Can we penetrate the hard outer facade of matter and materiality to feel the living spirit that penetrates every aspect of our lives? (see above, Chapter 2).

We have seen that the five Supernal *Olamot* (Universes) form a system that progressively constricts God's awesome Light as it descends to the lowest level of physicality. Similarly, the *Olamot* are said to act as "garments" for God's Light (cf. Psalms 104:2). A garment serves two purposes: to conceal and to reveal. With respect to God, the universes conceal His true essence, while at the same time attenuating it so that it can be revealed. This is the underlying idea of a body (corresponding to the system of universes) which conceals the true essence of the soul (corresponding to God). Neither God, the Torah, nor the soul can manifest in this "World of Separation" (which corresponds to the Tree of Knowledge of Good and Evil) without some "garment" to conceal the awesome power of their light.

God's purpose in creating the system in this way was to bring a material dimension into existence in which man could function as an independent and free agent. Man could then utilize the system as a ladder upon which to climb back up to God. By the same token, he could penetrate the system and actually find God "clothed" in the very fabric of his life. One way or the other, the purpose of Creation through *Olamot* is to enable man to relate to God. Herein lies the mystery of the relationship between the Holy Temple and the human body. Each is a microcosm of the entire system designed to help man draw down greater and greater revelations of God's Light into the darkness of this world.

Reflecting on the idea that each higher level is concealed within those below it, and that each lower level becomes a "garment" for the levels above it, we can better understand how the body becomes the "garment" of the soul. Just as the lower worlds are garments for the upper worlds, and a garment is made to fit the body it covers, so, too, the body assumes the "shape" of the soul.

This can be seen in the fact that the body is referred to as *chomer* (matter), while the soul is called *tzurah* (form) (see Likutey Moharan I, 170). *Chomer*, the body, is actually pliable "raw material" that assumes the "shape of the soul" as it is molded. Someone who seeks a life of materialism will mold his body according to the chosen requirements of that life, and that body will conceal his soul. One who seeks Godliness, however, will mold and refine his physical nature to be sensitive to the subtlest signals of the soul, so that eventually the soul's own innate spirituality will radiate from his body. Finally, at the highest levels, the physical body of such a person becomes a spiritual body, similar to that of Moses, whose face shone when he descended from Sinai after having received the Torah (Exodus 34:29–30, 35; see above, Chapter 1); similar to Adam before he ate from the Tree of Knowledge of Good and Evil, whose entire body shone brighter than the noonday sun (see Chapter 2); similar to Elijah, who ascended to heaven in a "chariot of fire" (see 2 Kings 2:11).

*

The Four Elements

Above (Chapter 3) we noted that there are four basic elements that make up the material world — fire, air, water and earth. The

ARI explains that these four elements correspond to the four letters of the Tetragrammaton (*Etz Chaim* 42:3).

Tetragrammaton	Element
Yod	Fire
Heh	Air
Vav	Water
Heh	Earth

Ancient tradition also speaks of four levels of physical existence: *domem* (mineral), *tzome'ach* (vegetative), *chai* (animal) and *medaber* (speaking, i.e., man); four main layers of the body: *or* (skin), *basar* (flesh), *gidim* (sinews) and *atzamot* (bones); and four types of body fluids, known as the "four humors." The latter are classified as: white, red, green (greenish-yellow) and black (reddish-brown). They correspond to and are based in the following organs:

Fluids	Organ
white	lymph ducts
red, blood	liver
green, bile	gallbladder
black (foul fluids)	spleen

The four main layers and the four humors will be discussed in their respective chapters below. At this point, we will concentrate on the four elements and their single hidden source (mentioned above, p.22). The following teaching is found in Reb Noson's *Likutey Halakhot* (*Choshen Mishpat, Matzranut* 4:1–3).

*

And a river flows from Eden to water the Garden; from there it divides and becomes four major rivers.

Genesis 2:10

The four elements stem from a single source element. This is alluded to in the verse, "And a *river* flows from Eden to water the Garden; from there it divides and becomes *four* major rivers." That is, there is a single source which divides into four — the four elements. The single source element is the tzaddik, the righteous person in whose merit the world is sustained, as in (Proverbs 10:25) "And the tzaddik is the foundation of the world." He is likened to the "apex of the *Yod*, " the source of the four letters of the Tetragrammaton (see *Likutey Moharan* II, 67). This source element is called the *yesod hapashut*, the "simple element," in that, at the source, everything is united as one, without differentiation.

Everything in the world is composed of four basic elements. Each element contains traces of all the others, even if only in microscopic proportion. Thus, *domem* (mineral) has "earth" as its main component, but one can find traces of "water," "air" and "fire" within. The continued existence of the world is based upon the proper combination and interaction of these elements.

Each element is radically different in makeup from the others, yet God in His infinite wisdom created them in such a way that they could coexist and sustain life in an almost endless array of combinations — as long as that which they are sustaining is alive. When its "life" ends, the elements disperse — creating a situation, conceptually, of the "World of Separation" (see also *Rambam, Hilkhot Yesodey HaTorah* 4:3). Thus, it is the life force that binds the disparate elements together so that man can exist. This life force is the single source element, the tzaddik, who has ascended above the materialism of this world. He acts as a bridge between the spiritual and the physical, and can therefore transmit spiritual life force to the physical world.

In their source (the single source element, the tzaddik), the four elements are actually one — conceptually, the World of Unity — sharing a peaceful coexistence and interaction. Even when they leave their source, the four elements can exist in perfect harmony as long as they continue to receive their life force from the tzaddik. Only when the elements are cut off from this life force for any reason is their harmony upset. At this point, degeneration and dysfunction set in, leading to illness and suffering...

Although every person is made up of all four elements, there are four main roots, corresponding to the four letters of the Tetragrammaton. Each individual is rooted in his particular letter more than all the others. Correspondingly, he is also rooted in the specific element and character trait that derives from that letter. This is what accounts for the tremendous differences we find in people's temperaments. Some temperaments are rooted in fire, some in air, some in earth, some in water. The main thing is to harmonize their differences, for when difference, rather than harmony, is stressed, strife becomes the norm and people resist and oppose each other. This strife reverberates into their root elements, causing disharmony Above. As a result, the world is visited with destruction and sickness.

The main controlling force which can harmonize these differences is found in the single source element, the tzaddik. The tzaddik knows how to establish a proper balance between the various elements in his domain. This brings harmony and peace to each individual and to humanity as a whole. This is the level of the Covenant of Peace that was given to Pinchas. Having achieved this level, Pinchas never died, but rather, as Elijah the Prophet, ascended to heaven in a chariot of fire (*Likutey Halakhot, Matzranut* 4:1–3).

A tzaddik is one who has transcended the "World of Separation" (corresponding to the Tree of Knowledge of Good and Evil) and connected to the "World of Unity" (the Tree of Life). Having harmonized his elements, he becomes the single source element that unites them all.

As we saw above (Chapter 1), the human body reflects the Torah with its 248 positive and 365 negative *mitzvot* (commandments). The tzaddik's synergetic knowledge of the entire Torah ("the whole that is greater than the sum of its parts") binds him to all the mitzvot at once. Connected to unity, he perceives all the mitzvot as a single unified system. He sees how each individual mitzvah of the Torah contains every other mitzvah in unity. In the same way, he binds and harmonizes all 248 limbs and 365 sinews of his body with his soul. He can then act as the single source element for all those below his level.

It is axiomatic throughout Rebbe Nachman's teachings that everyone can become a tzaddik on a level that is suitable for him. To the extent that a person develops himself spiritually, and attains mastery over his body — his four elements — he can merit the title of tzaddik for that level. This applies even to one who is on a relatively low spiritual level. Anyone, at whatever level he may find himself, has it in his power to harmonize the four elements within himself. He can achieve a "Covenant of Peace," total harmony between his body and soul.

* * *

5

Positive and Negative Character Traits

In *Sha'arey Kedushah*, Rabbi Chaim Vital (1542–1620), the ARI's foremost disciple, writes:

> Just as a master craftsman can carve the human figure in stone, so did the Master Craftsman fashion the body in the exact same form as the soul. Since the soul itself parallels the composition of the Torah, with both its positive mitzvot and its prohibitions, so too the limbs of the body, though formed from the four material elements, parallel the "limbs" of the soul and the corresponding mitzvot.
>
> Adam was to have lived eternally. By eating from the Tree of Knowledge of Good and Evil, he sullied both his soul and his body. As a result, illness, suffering and death descended upon humanity, as Adam was warned (Genesis 2:17), "But from the Tree of Knowledge of Good and Evil do not eat, for on the day you eat from it, *mot tamut* [you will surely die]." The double idiom *mot tamut* means literally, "dying, you will die," indicating a double death — both physical and spiritual.
>
> Adam was the paradigm of a spiritual man. However, having eaten from the Tree of Knowledge of Good and Evil, he descended to a material level, dragging down with him all of creation. Furthermore, by partaking of both good and evil, he caused everything in creation to become a mixture of good and evil (*Sha'arey Kedushah* 1:1).

Adam was placed in the Garden of Eden and given a choice. He could have chosen to live a spiritual life, but in partaking of the fruit of the Tree of Knowledge of Good and Evil, he caused good and evil to mingle. Now, everything is an admixture of the two. Man's mission ever since has been to separate the good from the bad, to become purified from the evil that surrounds and is found within him.

*

The Four Servants

The four elements contain all the physical resources that man needs to propel himself in his spiritual growth, but they also contain the very characteristics which can inhibit — and even reverse — that growth. It is for this reason that the four elements are called "servants." They must serve the soul faithfully in order for one to ascend in spirituality (cf. *Likutey Moharan* I, 4:12).

One can infuse one's four material elements with spirit and soul, as in (Ezekiel 37:9), "Prophesy to the *ruach* [spirit, wind or breath]; prophesy, son of man, and say to the *ruach*: This is what the Lord God says, 'Come from the four directions, O *Ruach*, and breathe upon these slain, so that they may live!'" The verse is from Ezekiel's prophecy to the dry bones. First God told him to prophesy to the bones, that they come together. Then he was commanded to prophesy a second time for the *ruach* to enter the still dead bodies and make them come alive.

As Reb Noson explains, the "dead" bodies correspond to the four elements that are "dead" without their connection to the fifth element, the tzaddik. When they are connected, they come alive and can embody all the good qualities that are identified with the concept of tzaddik — love and fear, kindness and restraint, humility, responsibility and zealousness, etc. When they are not connected, the four material elements — in the form of the baser characteristics — will literally control a person's life. He becomes their "servant" and thus susceptible to the "four primary sources of damages," also called "the four types of leprosy" (see *Bava Kama* 1:1;

Nega'im 1:1; the "damages" and "leprosies" are manifest in all types of suffering mankind endures: illness, emotional difficulties, wars, exile, etc.). The four elements then become the source for each of the basic evil characteristics. Rabbi Chaim Vital explains (*Sha'arey Kedushah* 1:2):

> *Fire* is the lightest of the four in its constitution, as its properties cause heat to rise. It is the source of arrogance, of one who regards himself as being "above" others. Fire is also the source of anger. Anger and arrogance also lead to irritability and the desire for power and honor.
>
> *Air* is the source of idle chatter — the tendency to speak about worthless subjects. It also refers to forbidden speech: flattery, falsehood, slander and mockery. Air is also the source of boasting.
>
> *Water* brings pleasure — from the element of water come the cravings for all the various lusts. It also causes jealousy and envy, leading to dishonest behavior and outright theft.
>
> *Earth* is the heaviest of the elements, and denotes laziness and depression. One dominated by the material aspects of earth always bemoans his fate and is never satisfied with his lot.

Character traits and attitudes are not counted among the commandments of the Torah. A perusal of the entire list of 613 mitzvot will confirm this. There is a whole body of commandments revolving around human relations, for example, to love one's fellow man, to give charity to the poor, to help one's enemy in a fix, not to bear a grudge, not to take revenge, not to hate one's brother in one's heart, etc. There are also numerous commandments involving man's relationship to God. Nowhere, however, do we seem to find any command to be moral, humble, loving, kind, benevolent, compassionate, empathetic, giving, etc. Neither are we commanded not to become angry, not to be arrogant, not to be jealous, not to be spiteful. Even a commandment such as (Leviticus 19:17) "Do not hate your brother in your heart" can only be construed as a *behavioral* directive, as opposed to an *attitudinal* directive. If, as we have seen, character traits and attitudes are so essential, why are they not even mentioned in the system of commandments?

The answer is that character traits and attitudes are the goal — and the very basis — of the commandments. Indeed, the refinement and strengthening of our moral characteristics is a pre-condition for the true observance of the commandments. For the basic premise of the commandments is that once we "act" in compliance with the objective morality of the Torah, this morality will become part of the spiritual and emotional makeup of the human personality. Thus, the Torah does not directly command us to "be" but to "do." That is, its commands are clearly designed by God to impact on our basic character traits, but through our actions. Acting lovingly towards somebody, despite the fact that we may dislike them, forces us to overcome the *attitude* we have formed about them which prevents us from seeing them as a fellow human being. Clearly, the goal of the action is an inner transformation. Viewing the commandments as mere behavioral directives misses this crucial point.

We can now see that the system of commandments is designed to help man either express, or develop, or refine an innate character trait. When viewed in this way, the hidden attitudinal directive behind every commandment becomes revealed. The Torah assumes that these attitudes and character traits are the basis of the human personality, and that they are present, in rudimentary form, from infancy. Perfecting the positive character traits on the one hand, and transmuting the energy of the negative traits on the other hand, presents the most serious challenge one faces throughout his life.

Rebbe Nachman taught:

> The main thing is to nullify every one of your personality traits. You should strive to do so until the ego is obliterated, rendered into nothingness before God. Begin with one trait,

transmute it, and then work on a second one. As each trait is thus transmuted, God's glory will begin to shine through and be revealed to you.

The verse states (Ezekiel 43:2), "The earth was alight with His glory." God's glory is like light. A thin rod casts a small shadow, while a more substantial object casts a larger shadow. As more light is obstructed, a larger shadow is cast. The same is true of God's glory. The material obstructs the spiritual and casts shadows over it. The denser the object, the darker the shadow.

When one is bound to a particular emotion or desire, God's glory is obstructed and a shadow is cast. God's light is then hidden. As one transmutes one's negative desires and emotions, the shadow is gradually removed. As the shadow departs, Godliness is revealed. Then, "The earth [one's materialism] is alight with His glory [for the spiritual is no longer concealed]" (*Rabbi Nachman's Wisdom* #136).

As we shall see (below, Part 3), the major characteristics parallel the various organs of the body. The degree that man exercises control over his baser instincts enables him to ascend the spiritual ladder, summoning forth the beauty found within his soul.

Summing up all that we have said about the relationship between the commandments and the basic character traits and attitude, Rabbi Chaim Vital writes (*Sha'arey Kedushah* 1:2):

> Man's basic character traits are not numbered among the actual mitzvot of the Torah... Nevertheless, they are fundamental to being able to fulfill the mitzvot. Perfecting one's character traits enhances one's ability to develop spiritually, whereas allowing negative traits to take root and fester renders one incapable of performing any mitzvot properly. For example, our Sages state (*Sotah* 5a; see also *Zohar* I, 27b), "Arrogance and anger are akin to idolatry." Conversely (*Avodah Zarah* 20b), "Humility can bring a person to the level of prophecy."

* * *

6

The Paradox of Body and Soul

Considering the ethereal composition of the soul vis-à-vis the denseness of the physical body, it is indeed a wonder that the two are able to remain together. The soul is always drawn to its sublime source, God, while the body always seeks material gratification. The miracle of the concordance between body and soul becomes even more apparent and amazing because of their divergent natures.

"The soul of man is God's candle, searching all the innards of the belly" (Proverbs 20:27). Our Sages explain that God implanted within the soul a never-ending quest for perfection. The soul is forever curious: it searches and pursues — always looking for a new experience. One can find satisfaction, whether one seeks it on a spiritual or physical level. The difference between the two is that spiritual satisfaction lingers on, since the soul is eternal, whereas physical satisfaction can be only momentary, and is soon forgotten. One whose soul searches through all his innards and seek the spirituality of life is indeed fortunate (see *Likutey Halakhot, Birkhot HaPeirot* 5:8).

Rebbe Nachman describes the differences between body and soul in terms of a *ko'ach hamoshekh* (force of attraction) and a *ko'ach hamakhriach* (force of repelling). The force of attraction is God, acting like gravity to constantly draw the soul towards Him, its spiritual source. The repellent force is materialism, for it "forces" the soul to remain in the physical world.

Rebbe Nachman taught:

> Everything sits upon the earth. The gravitational pull of the earth attracts everything to it. Only a counterforce allows people and objects to move about freely. According to the strength of the force countering gravity in a given object, that object will distance itself from the earth. But when that force dissipates or is removed, the object returns to the earth.
>
> The tzaddik is the foundation of the earth, as stated in Proverbs (10:25), and everything in the world is built on and rests upon him. By rights, people should be drawn to the tzaddik, since he possesses this spiritual "force of gravity." However, there is a counterforce which separates and distances people from the tzaddik: there are those who do and say things to keep themselves and others away from the tzaddik (*Likutey Moharan* I, 70).

The tzaddik, as we have seen, is the single source element of the four basic elements (above, Chapter 4). By virtue of his purity, he is the symbol of spirituality for everyone. He would draw everyone near to the spiritual source, showing them all the benefits of such a way of life, were it not for the existence of the repellent force. The same is true for each individual. The soul contains within it the properties of Godliness. Left to its own devices, it would soar to the heavens. Commenting on this, Reb Noson writes:

> Every person should be aware that all the obstacles and difficulties he faces in life stem from the "repellent" force, from materialism. The "attracting" force, the tzaddik, is more powerful than the repellent force, since the power of gravity ultimately prevails. Thus, the repellent force is only a temporary force. One who truly desires spirituality can always overcome obstacles and find spirituality.
>
> Indeed, the main mission in life is to overcome the repelling forces and strive for a life of spirituality. The irony of it is that, in this mission, the repelling force becomes a major factor. By

joining the two opposing forces, one can make the most of one's abilities and ascend to the greatest heights.

Observe, for example, a mechanical watch. It has a wire spring, wound tightly against the direction of its natural movement. It then seeks to unwind itself from its forced position. The pressure of the uncoiling spring forces the gears to mesh against one another, with each gear moving another. It is the reaction of one force *against* another opposing force which causes the mechanism to work. Thus, in industrial manufacturing, a productive machine is the result of opposing forces working in unison.

The nature of the soul is to draw itself to its Source, to Godliness, to the true power of "gravity" (*Likutey Halakhot, Yom Tov* 5:1).

Reb Noson concludes by explaining that the interaction between body and soul takes place *because* of their different natures. Despite such diversity, the body and soul together can effect awesome and beautiful wonders in this world, both as receptacles for spirituality, and for developing the necessary material environment in which to grow.

*

"Let Us Make Man..."

The differences between the body and the soul are vast. Yet their combination is what makes "man." They *can* work together in perfect harmony.

Rebbe Nachman taught:

A person must care for his body, so that it shines with each spiritual advancement he achieves. For the soul perceives and understands extremely lofty levels, while the body remains ignorant of them. A person must therefore purify his body, to enable it to share in the soul's perceptions. The soul will also benefit from a body which is finely attuned to spirituality, for if the soul falls from its spiritual level, the body which has experienced Godliness will enable it to regain its previous level of holiness.

This can occur because the body has attained a corresponding level of purity.

For a person to attain this level of harmony and cooperation between body and soul, he must break the brazenness of the body's lusts and desires by countering it with "holy brazenness," the stubborn will to bring himself to spirituality, come what may. In doing so, he allows his soul to blend completely with his body.

The means through which the body blends with the soul is the performance of the mitzvot. The more good deeds a person performs, the greater his body's subjugation to his soul, allowing the body to actually feel the soul's attainments (*Likutey Moharan* I, 22:5, 8).

As for how to achieve "holy brazenness," Rebbe Nachman offers many practical suggestions (such as performing the mitzvot, praying with fervor, dancing, singing, clapping, giving charity, sighing and yearning for spirituality).

*

The following teaching of Rebbe Nachman will clarify various ideas which we have touched upon previously.

The soul corresponds to man, light, life, memory and true wisdom — the wisdom of the Torah. The body corresponds to animal, darkness, death, forgetfulness, alien philosophies and foolishness. Man's mission is to rise above materialism. This is implied in the Hebrew word for man, *ADaM*, spelled *Aleph-Dalet-Mem* (אדם). *Aleph* (א) means to learn wisdom; *dalet* (ד) is equal to the number four, representing the four elements; and the final *mem* is a closed letter (ם), symbolizing the unseen, the World to Come. In order to attain the World to Come [*mem*], one must overcome the evil characteristics that stem from the *dalet* [four] elements. This is done by acquiring true wisdom, Torah wisdom, the *aleph*. This is what is meant by the verse (Genesis 1:26), "Let us make *ADaM*." One who strives for spirituality — for the true essence of life — is called "Adam" (*Likutey Moharan* I, 37:2–3).

*

Good Advice

Reb Noson writes that the true wisdom of the Torah stems from the concept that the 613 mitzvot of the Torah are known as the "613 precepts of advice." These precepts counsel a person and guide him in the choice of which deeds to perform and which to avoid (*Zohar* II, 82b). He explains that advice about how to commit a sin is not considered good advice, for such advice exposes a person to suffering and humiliation. Similarly, if someone comes up with a "brilliant idea" on how to profit financially, but overlooks the fact that such profit may lead him away from spirituality, neither is that good advice, for (Ecclesiastes 5:12), "wealth is sometimes intended for its owner's detriment." If temporal pleasures are pursued and eternal ones neglected, the wealth gained thereby will prove to be detrimental. Therefore, the main advice needed to succeed in this world is advice that leads to eternal life — advice for spirituality. Reb Noson writes:

Had Adam eaten of the Tree of Life, he would have known which advice would lead him to his highest destiny. He would have known the path of spirituality, of true, eternal life. But Adam ate from the Tree of Knowledge of Good and Evil. As a result, the advice a person has available to him now is confused and confusing. Every day requires new decisions, each problem requires a different approach. Worse still, one never knows whether any given choice one makes is correct or not. Some ideas seem very good at the moment, but in the long term their benefits peter out. Other choices might be beneficial were time available, but time always seems to be in short supply, rendering gains from such advice unlikely.

These frustrating circumstances came about because Adam ate from the Tree of Knowledge. He was then banished from the Garden of Eden, and the Revolving Sword was placed at the entrance so that access is limited only to those who merit it (see above, Chapter 2). The Revolving Sword corresponds to the bulk of confusing advice that inundates us. This "Sword," which is referred to as the *Heikhaley HaTemurot* — the Chambers of Exchanges — is what causes ever-changing thoughts and constant doubts in the mind, sabotaging our efforts to concentrate on eternal life. Thus we find that even those seriously focusing on their spiritual lives — though they may already have set out on the proper path — also experience great confusion, with a multitude of choices available to them even within the realm of Torah advice.

Therefore, the only choice a person has is constantly to seek the truth. Whatever is absolutely truthful will assist him in discovering the proper path for himself. This is possible only when coupled with a search for the true tzaddikim, for the Torah consists of two parts — a Written Law and an Oral Law. The Written Law prescribes the 613 mitzvot, but the Oral Law, handed down through the true tzaddikim, explains how we can best fulfill these precepts of advice (*Likutey Halakhot, Sukkah* 7:2–3).

Reb Noson goes on to speak about the importance of placing one's faith in the tzaddikim. Because their spiritual nature is untainted by the Tree of Knowledge of Good and Evil (i.e., they transcend the four elements and correspond to the source element), they are able to lead us on the proper path of spiritual development and eternal benefit. The tzaddikim who transcend materiality are one with the Torah, with good advice. Receiving advice from tzaddikim — for example, accepting the Torah teachings of the tzaddikim — is a rectification for Adam's eating from the Tree of Knowledge and enables one to cling to the Tree of Life. This is the importance of placing one's faith in tzaddikim. Reb Noson continues:

> When Adam was banished from the Garden of Eden, he was also cursed (Genesis 3:19), "By the sweat of your brow you shall eat bread." The necessity for excessive effort to earn a livelihood came about through eating from the Tree of Knowledge. We can see the effects of *excessiveness*, in that it is one of the main causes of confusion. Excessive eating, sleeping or working, for example,

causes confusion and doubts and creates major difficulties in life. Thus, the most reasonable approach is to seek proper advice, and to be able to embark on a life without excesses.

The Tree of Knowledge parallels advice, in that *EtZ* (עץ, Hebrew for "tree") is from the same root as *EitZah* (עצה, "advice"). Advice, which is necessarily blemished in the average person, must now be sought from the tzaddikim, whose level of spirituality binds them to the Tree of Life. The tzaddikim are untainted by the effects of the Tree of Knowledge of Good and Evil and are able to discern proper advice. The sin of eating from the Tree also parallels blemished faith. Seeking advice from the tzaddikim rectifies our partaking of the Tree of Knowledge and directs us to the path of good counsel — for both material and spiritual development.

Reb Noson concludes:

> Death was decreed upon Adam, and through him upon all of mankind, because of the sin of eating from the Tree of Knowledge of Good and Evil. Man can no longer achieve a perfect record, always choosing the correct advice and finding the path on which to reach and enter the Garden of Eden [i.e., total spirituality] during his lifetime. He must pass away from this world. Only after his passing can he embark on the road to the Garden of Eden, the Tree of Life. However, the more a person strengthens his faith in the tzaddikim, the more refined will be the advice he receives from them and can act upon during his lifetime. In this way, he will merit sound advice, which will aid him in rectifying his portion of the sin of Adam, and thus he will find himself inestimably closer to finding his path to the Tree of Life.

> Body and soul correspond to darkness and light. They also correspond to evil and good, for the knowledge of evil derived through the Tree tainted the human body, pushing it into materialism. Had Adam not sinned, evil would automatically have appeared inferior to good, and man would have had clear

direction on how to reach his destiny — the Garden of Eden. In our current state, however, the body must become separated from the soul [in death] before the soul can achieve its ultimate perfection. The body must return to the earth — to the elements whence it was derived.

But this separation is actually a "purification process" (see a detailed explanation of this in Part 3). In death, the body, the part of us closest to succumbing to evil, becomes nullified; in death we shed physicality. Even if a person is truly a tzaddik, he must shed his corporeality, if only because the decree brought about through Adam affects all of mankind (cf. *Shabbat* 55b). Man cannot enter the Garden during this life. Only after the Resurrection, with the revival of the body, will the soul be rejoined with the body, in a state of perfect purity (*Likutey Halakhot, ibid.* 7:9).

*

The soul, having struggled to overcome the trials of materialism, and rectifying itself while still in the material world, is ready for its ultimate reward when the body dies. When the Resurrection takes place, the soul's previous oppressor, the body, will become its beloved servant. The body then willingly submits to this "servitude," as it recognizes the royalty of the soul. But, as in the story of "The Exchanged Children," the soul has even more reason to be satisfied. Specifically *because* of the suffering and purification it endured, it finds a reward awaiting it which is far greater than it had previously imagined.

* * *

Part Three

The Digestive System

The Internal Organs

7

Introduction

Most books on the subject of anatomy begin with an exploration of either the cells or the skeletal system, the main supporting structures of the body. Knowing how the human body is built and how the parts of the body are interconnected can provide the reader with a general picture of where and how each individual organ is placed. However, when exploring the spiritual anatomy, it is more appropriate to begin with a discussion of how one's most basic characteristics develop, for these are the fundamental assets through which man can assume his spiritual form. As such our "picture" will be developed accordingly.

As we have seen, Adam's sin was *eating* from the Tree of Knowledge. Thus, our exploration of the spiritual anatomy will begin with the "digestive system." The organs contained in the digestive system serve as the bases of man's most fundamental characteristics. Only by recognizing the hidden potential in these organs can we move forward in our spiritual growth.

Man's three primary lusts are for wealth, sexual pleasure and food. Rebbe Nachman teaches that the lust for wealth is a bottomless abyss from which return is extremely difficult (see *Likutey Moharan* I, 23); and sexual lust is also a major trial which a person constantly encounters during his lifetime (see *Likutey Moharan* I, 36; *ibid.* 23). Yet it is gluttony which Rebbe Nachman calls "the paramount lust," for food provides man with the strength to pursue all his other desires, and it can never be avoided entirely (*Likutey Moharan* I, 62:5). Furthermore, a person desires to eat immediately upon his entry into the world.

Love, fear, patience and humility, the drive for success or power, jealousy, anger, arrogance and all the other drives become manifest at various stages throughout life. Some characteristics develop during childhood; others, during puberty and adulthood. But the body's need to eat, digest and eliminate wastes begins at birth.

Rebbe Nachman teaches that desires are superfluous. They are compared to the rind of a fruit which one peels and discards. In the same way, one can discard and live without anything extraneous (*Likutey Moharan* I, 62:5), as is obvious from an infant who, amazingly, "knows" how much nourishment he needs and does not eat to excess. For optimal survival, the human body requires a simple balanced diet of carbohydrates, proteins, fats, fruits and vegetables. However, Rebbe Nachman teaches, any food can be elevated to be able to supply that state of complete nourishment which was provided for Adam in the Garden of Eden (see *Likutey Moharan* II, 5:17).

The Talmud states that man should taste everything that is permitted to him in order to be able to appreciate and thank God for His wonderful creations (*Yerushalmi, Kiddushin* 4). Obviously, then, we are expected to experience pleasure from eating. But there is a difference between partaking to a degree that is essential, and lusting for excesses. Although man can live on bread and water, we use butter, margarine, honey or jam to enhance the bread. We flavor our drinks to make them more palatable to the tongue. These are simple examples of permissible extras that can lead to excesses if one is not vigilant.

The proper maintenence of the digestive system is of paramount importance for man's physical growth and well-being. Because the body parallels the soul, the body's well-being indicates a commensurate well-being in the capabilities of the soul. A harmonious relationship between body and soul can be maintained only through eating, for the body must be provided with nourishment in order to exist. The soul alone doesn't require food. Only when the body and soul are joined together is nourishment required (*Likutey Moharan* II, 5:3).

*

For the sake of convenience we treat the organs relating to digesting, processing and excreting food as a unit, under the heading of "The Digestive System," though Western medical science views them as separate systems. (Interestingly, Chinese and other forms of holistic medicine teach that all parts of the body are interdependent.) Thus the stomach, liver, gallbladder, spleen, kidneys and circulatory system, which are all connected in some way to digesting food, processing it for body nutrients and excreting it in the form of waste matter, are discussed in this section.

When a person eats, the food descends to the stomach, where acids and enzymes break it down into smaller particles. The digestive tract processes this food further into nutrients which are then transported to the bloodstream. Enriched with nutrients, the blood flows to the heart, where it is further enriched with oxygen and then pumped throughout the system, bringing nourishment to the body. Whatever is extraneous is rejected and expelled. The body's ability to know exactly what to absorb and what to reject is truly one of God's most awesome wonders.

In the next chapter we will examine the significance of the body's ability to absorb nourishment and eliminate wastes, and how this relates to the spiritual powers which we possess and must employ in order to further our own spiritual growth. However, an integral part of the circulatory system, the blood, which brings oxygen and nutrients to the entire body, plays an important role in the digestive system. We will thus follow our study of the purification process with an exploration of the bloodstream. Since our first contact with material gratification begins with our connection to food, we will then discuss our eating habits and the digestive tract. Afterwards we will examine the other organs involved in the purification process — the liver, the gallbladder, the spleen, the sweat glands and the kidneys.

* * *

8

The Purification Process

Adam was designed with the ability to ascend continually to ever higher levels of spirituality. He was meant to achieve this through the vehicle of his body, by elevating matter to the level of the spiritual. To accommodate his mission, he was placed in the Garden of Eden. But this smoothly run operation was crippled when he submitted to physical lusts (see above, Chapter 2).

The consequences of Adam's fall can be compared to a beautiful and expensive piece of crystal that is dropped from a great height and shatters into thousands of tiny pieces which become scattered over a large area. Adam had contained within himself the souls of all mankind in a state of perfect unity. His fall shattered that holy unity into countless "sparks of holiness" which subsequently became dispersed throughout the entire world. It has since been man's mission, utilizing the spiritual inclinations incorporated within his system, to search for, find, purify and elevate these sparks, that they may return to their source. This will repair, and even improve upon, the vessel from which they originated — Adam.

Wherever a holy spark is found, it must go through a continual process of *birur*, "purification," until it reaches its rectification. These sparks of holiness, which were scattered throughout the world, are found today in all of creation: in minerals and vegetation, in our food and drink. They are found both in animals which can work for man and in those which can become his food. They are found in raw materials used in manufacturing, and are thus found in money and other goods that are traded throughout the world. (See also *Mashiach: Who? What? Why? How? Where? and When?*, Parts 4–5, published by the Breslov Research Institute.) Reb Noson addresses this idea in one of his discourses in *Likutey Halakhot* (*Betziat HaPat* 5:3):

Everything in this world must go through a purification process in order to reach its own perfection. Nowhere is this more evident than in the processing of food. A farmer plows his fields, plants seeds and then waits for them to take root and sprout. He tends his crops until they are ready to be harvested, then separates the wheat from the straw and chaff. Afterwards he grinds the wheat, separating the pure flour from the coarse bran. Even then the flour is inedible. He must mix the flour with water to make dough, form a loaf and then bake. Only then do the seeds which he planted much earlier attain their state of perfection, their intended goal.

The human body was designed to process food in much the same way as the food was originally processed in order to make it edible. When a person eats, he chews and grinds the food with his teeth. The food descends to the stomach, where acids and enzymes continue to break it down into smaller particles. The rest of the digestive tract then takes this food, reducing and purifying it further. The purified food passes into the blood system, bringing nourishment to the body. The waste matter is rejected by the body and expelled.

The purification process that takes place within the body mirrors the purification process of the soul. The body "knows" what to accept and purify, and it "knows" what to eliminate. Just as the body cleanses and purifies the food that enters it, so too, the soul, in its quest for spirituality, cleanses and purifies its nourishing elements, and thereby itself. This process of spiritual purification and growth is an ongoing phenomenon, on both a personal and a universal level.

In keeping with the soul's pursuit of perfection, all the fallen and lost sparks of holiness — shattered and dispersed by Adam's sin — must be retrieved in order to rebuild man's original spiritual *tzurah* (form). Man must now sift through his material surroundings in his search for the spiritual.

Rebbe Nachman teaches that everything in existence, even one's wealth, requires this purification process.

> The same stages required to process food must be employed to refine money. These stages are acceptance, retention, digestion, distribution and expulsion. In eating, one makes use of the powers of acceptance and retention, for the body retains the food for a while. Digestion then causes the food to be absorbed in the body, and the digestive system dispenses the required nutrients throughout the body. The heart and brain receive the choicest nourishment, for they provide the most vital functions. The body then excretes the waste matter.

> The same refinement process is required with money. When you receive money you must be retentive and not spend it right away — not like those who spend their lives pursuing wealth and then, when they acquire it, squander it immediately. You must "digest" this money, holding on to it until it is needed, and only then distributing it. The choicest portion must go to charity and the remainder for your necessities. There is also waste in your expenses (*Rabbi Nachman's Wisdom* #193).

These are some examples of the purification process in the physical realm and, as we have noted, this same process must be applied as well to the spiritual sphere. In all instances, patience is of critical importance. Just as it takes time and concentration to sort out a pile of papers or clothes, it takes endless patience to sort out our lives and spiritual concerns.

*

Patience

One of the main lessons to be learned from the purification process is the virtue of patience. A meal can be eaten in a relatively short amount of time, even in minutes. However, to be digested properly, the food must be processed over a period of several hours — for the nutrients to be separated from the waste matter and for each particle to be sent to its proper destination.

Every one of us must learn patience. For several millennia mankind has been involved in rectifying Adam's sin. From time immemorial, righteous people have been spreading spirituality all over the world, to arouse and unify those dormant sparks which fell and were dispersed through that sin. Though by now we are nearing the end of our wait for a perfected world, the process has been a long and arduous one. The utmost patience is required to achieve this goal on a universal level. The same applies to the spiritual purification of each individual. Though it takes time to realize the benefits of a spiritually oriented life, every effort expended is part of the purification process.

Reb Noson cites a prime example of the critical significance of patience. The Jews reached a very high spiritual level when they received the Torah at Mount Sinai (see *Shabbat* 146a). They were then instructed to wait for a period of forty days until Moses descended from the mountain. Towards the end of their wait they became impatient. This caused them to err in their calculations of Moses' anticipated return. Instead of waiting just a few more hours, as Aaron pleaded with them to do, they rushed ahead and made a golden calf. In their haste, they brought suffering upon themselves and upon all future generations, suffering which will end only with the arrival of the Messiah (*Likutey Halakhot, Birkhot HaShachar* 5:30).

Haste and impulsiveness are associated with the properties of water, as Jacob's observation about his eldest son Reuben attests (Genesis 49:3-4), "Reuben, my firstborn...first in rank and first in power. [But because you were] *unstable as water,* you will no longer be first." As a fluid, water is a factor in nearly all of man's pleasures. We bathe in it, drink it in varieties of fluids, and it is found in most of the foods we eat. Impulsivesness, too, can affect all aspects of a person's life, and it is the trait that allows a person to indulge his pleasures without consideration of the consequences.

Water does not remain stationary. The slightest wind brings

swells and waves along the surface of a body of water, and stronger gusts cause maelstroms even deep below the surface. Impulsiveness has the same effect on a person. Even when things look calm, one slight, uncontrolled urge can cause ripples throughout one's emotional system, ultimately bringing about an inner turbulence that allows no internal peace.

We need abundant patience to wait out the storms which confront us throughout life. Most lusts come to people in a frenzy. Rebbe Nachman teaches that the "storm wind of the wicked" — human lust — is temporary. It rages with evil desires, but only for a short while (*Likutey Moharan* I, 8:3). Patience allows us to wait out the storm and outwit the forces that seek to overcome us.

Reb Noson writes:

> In our daily prayers we praise God: "He mercifully illuminates the earth and its inhabitants, and in His goodness He constantly renews the act of creation each day." The main light is the light of truth, which is the light of God Himself. The main purification is that of truth from falsehood. Each day presents an opportunity to search for truth. Though the truth might often seem to be obscured by falsehood, it is the falsehoods found in each day and in each era that ultimately fall away, while truth endures — as will be revealed one day for all to see. Thus every generation has its evil, which later is rejected and even repudiated by all. Other falsehoods take its place, but these, too, disintegrate and are eventually relegated to the dustbins of history. The patience one maintains while searching for spirituality and Godliness is one's beacon of light and truth, which will ultimately endure (*Likutey Halakhot, Hekhsher Keilim* 4:48).

Patience is thus built into the daily routine of the Jew. He rises in the morning but, instead of immediately eating and tending to his personal business, he sets aside time for daily prayers. Some people rise even earlier to study Torah before praying, or remain after the morning prayers to study or perform good deeds before tending to their mundane affairs. Similarly, before eating a person must exercise restraint by first washing his hands and reciting the appropriate blessings (see *Likutey Halakhot, Birkhot HaShachar* 5:28).

*

The Chariot of God

Through his deeds, man is capable of perfecting himself to such a degree that he can become a "Chariot for God." The Prophet Ezekiel begins his book of prophecy with a description of his vision of God's "Chariot" borne by "four creatures." A person who purifies himself completely, by ridding himself of his negative characteristics and refining his good qualities, becomes worthy of reflecting the essence of those celestial "creatures," capable of "carrying and bearing" the Chariot of God — spirituality.

Each of the four "creatures" of the Chariot has four "faces," reflecting a lion, an ox, an eagle and a man (Ezekiel 1:10). Each of these four "animals" is considered a "king": The lion is king of the beasts, the ox is king of the domesticated animals and the eagle is king of birds. Man was created to be king over all these kings, the sovereign caretaker over *all* life-forms.

Our Sages explain (cf. *Tikkuney Zohar* #21, p.63a) that the lion, ox and eagle correspond to the mind, heart and lungs. They also correspond to the senses of hearing, sight and smell. Man, as the highest order of all living creatures, parallels speech. When he conducts himself in a princely manner, all these major organs and senses act to propel him to ever greater heights.

Nevertheless, our Holy Writings teach that (Ecclesiastes 7:14) "God made one to balance the other." This is the "law of parallelism" — for every spiritual goal there is a corresponding material obstacle. The reason for this is so that at every level, at every moment and juncture in life, we will have free will to choose which path to take.

Therefore, when man falters, he is overwhelmed by three creatures of gross physicality: the dog, the donkey and the hawk, which represent the potential for evil. In his degradation, man also comes under the dominion of three major organs: the liver, the gallbladder and the spleen, the results of which are destruction, anger and wrath. Man, *Adam*, the fourth creature, can regress to the level of "*Adam Bliyaal*," an evil man. This is alluded to in the word *BLiYaaL* (בליעל) which can be read as *BLiY oL* (בלי עול), literally, "one who casts off the heavenly yoke." Since he has distanced himself from God, his speech is said to represent lies, idle chatter and vulgarities. (We will elaborate on these ideas below; see Part 6.)

The food a person eats is digested, absorbed into the bloodstream and then distributed throughout his system. The liver, gallbladder and spleen are among the body's principal organs for processing nutrients, filtering the blood and disposing of excess fluids and waste matter. If they remain subjugated to the higher organs, they will enhance one's spiritual faculties. However, if left unchecked, the negative effects of these organs will bring out a person's worst characteristics — jealousy, lusts and the craving for honor and power — in a most degrading manner (see *Likutey Halakhot, Birkhot HaPeirot* 5:23).

*

Wonder of Wonders

The purification process is so amazing that our Sages instituted a custom of reciting a blessing after relieving oneself. The wording of this blessing is:

> Blessed are You, God, King of the universe, Who formed man with wisdom and created within him many openings, many cavities. It is revealed and known before Your Throne of Glory that if just one of the many openings or cavities were to be ruptured or blocked, it would be impossible to exist or remain standing before You for even a brief moment. Blessed are You, God, Who heals all flesh and Who works wonders.

Reb Noson explains that the purification process is *the* goal of each individual. He points out that the body was created with such incredible powers — it is truly a "wonder of wonders" — as to be the ultimate "purification plant." In fact, it is this unique combination of body *and* soul which brings about ultimate rectification (*Likutey Halakhot, Betziat HaPat* 5).

* * *

9

The Bloodstream

The human body has 248 limbs, corresponding to the 248 positive commandments of the Torah. It also has 365 connecting sinews and vessels (ligaments, arteries, veins, etc.), which correspond to the 365 prohibitions of the Torah (Zohar I, 170b; see above, Chapter 1). A body needs limbs in order to *do* something. Hence the positive commandments correspond to the skeletal and muscular systems (discussed below in Part 8). Conversely, the Torah's prohibitions parallel the cellular tissue and circulatory system of the body — for the blood carries with it all the desires and lusts that must be overcome in order to cultivate the spiritual aspects of one's existence.

Blood is the lifeline of most animal life-forms and is pumped by the heart through an extremely complex network of arteries and veins. The flow of blood has two major purposes: to bring oxygen and nourishment to the muscles and tissues throughout the body, and to extract carbon dioxide and other waste matter so as to rid the body of any poisons it accumulates.

One of the most incredible networks in existence, the circulatory system is as intricate as it is astounding, and it becomes even more astounding when one thinks of its spiritual implications. It contains literally hundreds of millions of cells which transport the body's fuels of food and minerals. The cells receive the processed food from the intestinal tract, transport it to the liver and then on to the heart. The heart sends the blood to the lungs, where it is suffused with oxygen. The blood then returns to the heart and is pumped throughout the body, distributing oxygen and nutrients along the way.

Aside from disseminating these essentials for life, the bloodstream also carries away any impurities found in the body. It is for this reason that bloodletting (phlebotomy) was the primary means of healing in ancient times. Its purpose was to remove one's "used" and "tired" blood, allowing for the elimination of waste products and generating the production of a fresh blood supply. The Talmud thus states (Bava Batra 58b), "I, blood, am the primary cause of illness." Rashbam (Rabbi Shmuel Ben Meir [c.1080–1174], Rashi's grandson) explains (s.v. b'reish), "All illnesses are transported through [the body by] the blood." Some have understood from the Rashbam's teaching that if one were to bloodlet on a regular basis, the impurities which lodge in the bloodstream and overwhelm the system would be purged.

Regarding spiritual impurities, Rebbe Nachman taught, "Bloodletting is beneficial to counter most evil characteristics" (The Aleph-Bet Book, "Evil Thoughts" A:47). Donating blood to a blood bank two or three times a year can duplicate the benefits of bloodletting, both the benefits to oneself, which Rebbe Nachman points out, and the benefits to the recipients, who desperately need the life-giving gift of healthy blood.

*

The Rhythmic Beat

The heart has four main chambers, two atria and two ventricles. The right atrium receives the blood returning from the liver through the veins and pumps it to the right ventricle. While the blood has been cleansed of waste matter, it still carries carbon dioxide. It is thus sent from the right ventricle to the lungs to expel that carbon dioxide and to be replenished with oxygen. The reoxygenated blood then travels to the left atrium, and from there to the left ventricle, from where it is pumped to the rest of the body.

King Solomon writes (Ecclesiastes 10:2), "The wise man's heart is to his right; the fool's is to his left." Throughout Scripture and

Talmud the "right side" represents good, while the "left side" represents foolishness or evil. King Solomon is speaking here about desires. A wise man uses his intellect to seek his proper path in life, while the fool follows the whims of his heart's inclination (*Rashi, loc. cit.*). Thus, the right side corresponds to the good inclination, while the left side corresponds to the evil inclination.

Of the two sides of the heart, the left ventricle needs to work harder at its job because it must pump blood throughout the entire body. The spiritual drawback of this system is that it is on the left side, the side of "the fool." Therefore, whatever blood is pumped into the system flows together with one's evil desires. This does not mean that the evil inclination will automatically gain control over the body. Rather, it indicates the need to maintain control over one's desires. The more control a person exercises over his own inclinations — the more he breathes spirituality — the purer his "bloodstream" will be. Conversely, the stronger a person's desire for materialism, the stronger will be the influence of the evil inclination over his "blood supply."

Rebbe Nachman thus taught:

> The pulse beats rhythmically. Sometimes the beat of the pulse draws a person to serve God; at other times it drives him away. It all depends on the air, or spirit, which enters the body (*Likutey Moharan* I, 160).

Since the blood draws oxygen from the lungs and carries it throughout the body, drawing in unclean air makes the pulse beat in a rhythm that tends towards materialism. Drawing in a breath of clean air — i.e., seeking spirituality — supplies the bloodstream with pure air with which to serve God. (More about breathing and its effects are found below in Parts 5–6.)

*

"Hot" Blood

The red color of blood symbolizes suffering, anger and bloodshed. If someone cuts himself and bleeds, he feels pain and suffering. When he suffers humiliation, his face might turn "bright red." If he becomes angry and "hot under the collar," he may turn "red with anger." These reactions represent the concept of Gevurah (literally, "strength"; "judgment"). When someone is judged for his misdeeds he may suffer humiliation, or when a misfortune befalls him, he may become angry. In this sense, each person has his own self-contained system of justice which can be relied upon to mete out suffering as warranted. Rebbe Nachman explains how this system works:

> The evil inclination of a righteous person is angelic in nature. For most people, however, the evil inclination is actually their own polluted blood. It causes them to act foolishly and to sin (*Likutey Moharan* I, 72).

As we have indicated, suffering implies a spiritual malfunction — it is as if one's bloodstream, polluted by the evil inclination, is demanding justice in order to become purified again. Thus, when someone sees that he is suffering and things are not working out the way he would like, he must realize that this is due to his evil inclination, manifest through his own polluted blood, because the evil inclination is "riding along" with the blood. Rebbe Nachman thus teaches that one can mitigate judgments and suffering by overpowering one's lusts (*Likutey Moharan* I, 72:2, 4). In doing so, one overpowers one's evil inclination, one's "malfunctioning blood system," and purifies it.

Earlier (Chapter 8) we discussed the patience that the human body reflects as it breaks food down into its constituent nutrients. We pointed out how important patience is to one's spiritual development. Taking this a step further, we can understand how important patience is when one is experiencing judgment, such as when one endures suffering or must deal with other unpleasant situations. The exercising of patience is in itself an important factor in mitigating judgments and purifying the bloodstream.

Of course, this does not mean that if a person purifies his bloodstream, the color of his blood will change. Red always implies judgments, and blood will always be red. However, there are judgments which can be beneficial — when they are used to exercise prudence and restraint (e.g., defensive driving or defusing an explosive situation). Spiritually speaking, Gevurah represents the attribute of awe and reverence for God and therefore has a very positive side to it. (These ideas will be discussed below, in Parts 5 and 8, when we view the ten *Sefirot* in terms of their influence on a person's life.) For the moment, however, suffice it to say that blood is synonymous with the evil inclination, which brings judgments and suffering upon a person. The more control a person exercises over his evil inclination, the greater will be his control over the suffering, frustration and humiliation he might have to endure, and the better equipped he will be to handle that suffering. This is because, in this sense, he has established a level of "control" over the judgments themselves.

Considering that the bloodstream serves as a person's internal system of justice, we can understand how it can become the vehicle for his downfall — both physical and spiritual. People get into trouble because of their "hot blood" — their haste, impulsiveness and anger. Through their own actions, they bring judgment upon themselves and dictate that there be consequences to their deeds.

Rebbe Nachman taught elsewhere (*Likutey Moharan* I, 29:5, 9), "A blood system which is polluted through sin causes difficulty in earning a livelihood. One who steals creates putrid blood within himself; the same is true of one who deals dishonestly in business, for the Hebrew word *damim* translates as both 'blood' and 'money.'" The two are interrelated: A pure blood system prevents theft, while stealing pollutes the blood, creating a negative cycle of an ever stronger urge to steal, with the inherent potential for yet more badly tainted blood, which will require a powerful effort to purify.

Furthermore, as Reb Noson points out, the Hebrew word for illusion is *meDaMeh* (מדמה), sharing the same root as *DaM* (דם), "blood" (*Likutey Halakhot, Shluchin* 5:19). Delusory ideas come from an impure blood system — from the same blood that carries all of one's desires and lusts. We also learn that "lusting for sensual pleasure stems from a person's polluted blood" (*Likutey Moharan* I, 36:3). Man is thus his own source of self-deception and the primary cause of his own errors.

*

Victory or Truth

Rebbe Nachman taught:

> Those who possess the evil characteristic of always desiring to outdo others cannot accept the truth. When people have the desire to always be right, even when the truth is plain before their eyes, they will distort it in order to maintain their imagined superiority. This applies in all areas of life (*Likutey Moharan* I, 122).

Elsewhere, the Rebbe teaches that this evil characteristic is akin to strife. He explains that the source of the urge to be victorious, along with the desire to control others, is none other than one's own blood. The verse states (Isaiah 63:3), "*V'yeiz nitzcham* — Their blood was sprinkled." The root of the Hebrew *NiTzCham* (נצחם), "their blood," is *NeTzaCh* (נצח), which also translates as "victory." The desire to be victorious is naturally inherent in the blood. However, someone who serves God with *all* his being succeeds in purifying his blood from evil desires. In this way, he can break down within himself the attribute of strife, and the desire to rule over others, and thus bring about peace (*Likutey Moharan* I, 75:1, 4).

*

Rebbe Nachman taught:

> No one can speak absolute truth until he has cleansed his bloodstream of its impurities, which indicate falsehood. Conversely, no one speaks falsehood without first polluting his bloodstream (*Likutey Moharan* I, 51:1).

In his lesson, Rebbe Nachman introduces several related ideas, beginning with "Falsehood is detrimental to one's eyesight."

Weak vision presents a false picture; a large object might be viewed as a small one, or one object may appear doubled. These are distortions — in effect, untruths.

The Rebbe continues with the idea that teary eyes cause blurred sight. Tears are excess body fluids secreted through the body's lacrimal ducts (part of the body's purification system). Furthermore, the Rebbe explains, based on the verses (Songs 5:6), "*Nafshi* [my *soul*] departed when he *spoke*," and (Deuteronomy 12:23), "The *blood* is the *nefesh* [soul]," that speech, the soul and blood are all connected. By blemishing one's speech — for example, by speaking falsehood — one blemishes one's bloodstream and, by extension, one's very soul. The truth is one; falsehood is many. There can be *only* one truth. Falsehood can be presented in many ways — in literally thousands of ideas, sayings and so on. But it is not truth. Falsehood is thus synonymous with excessiveness. Therefore, falsehood causes an excess of fluids, bringing in its wake tears, which blur and distort one's vision (see *Likutey Moharan* I, 51).

Rebbe Nachman teaches that the converse is also true — speaking truth purifies the blood. Likewise, to attain the level of absolute truth, so that one is free of falsehood, without delusions about life, one needs to purify one's entire system. This is the level reached by the tzaddik. Yet any person, depending on how intensely he strives for truth, can purify his bloodstream. In addition, crying and tears can serve as vehicles for either the purification or the pollution of the bloodstream. Crying to attain superfluous items in life causes putrid blood and unnecessary tears — excess and waste. But crying and praying to eliminate extraneous items and lusts help to purify the bloodstream of unwanted excesses.

*

The Main Path to Repentance

Rebbe Nachman teaches that there are ways to purify the entire bloodstream at once. The cause of sin is the evil inclination, which has taken up residence in the heart, causing putrid blood to flow throughout the body. One way to purify this blood is to remain silent when insulted, to bear embarrassment. By remaining silent, a person controls his desire to return the insult and he refrains from anger, a manifestation of the evil inclination. This is apparent from the reaction one feels when insulted: when a person is shamed, he blushes, and his face becomes flushed with embarrassment. He then turns white, as if his blood were drained. The blood symbolizes his sins, and his reaction of turning "white" symbolizes a cleansing of those sins that have permeated his bloodstream. Even though blood is still rushing through his body, his control over himself and desistance from retort is true repentance, for it constitutes a powerful act of controlling his evil inclination (see *Likutey Moharan* I, 6:2, 5).

Obviously, this method of repentance has its drawbacks. For one, it is extremely difficult to bear embarrassment. In addition, though embarrassment might come by itself, such as when a person makes an error in public, many times embarrassment is caused by others — and we know that it is forbidden to humiliate someone. The Talmud compares embarrassing another to bloodshed and states (*Bava Metzia* 58b), "One who embarrasses another publicly descends to Gehennom, never to ascend!"

Reb Noson addresses this problem and explains that embarrassment might still be caused by others, as it is everyone's choice to act as he sees fit. While one should not seek it, a person who is humiliated should bear in mind the spiritual benefits that accrue through the suffering he undergoes.

But feeling embarrassment need not come about through an external source. Many times people will admit to themselves that they acted foolishly and will experience a sense of shame — even when they are alone. To experience humiliation for one's mistakes and sins is to endure humiliation before God. Although this type of embarrassment does not necessarily require a person to control his anger, the acknowledgement that he has sinned also represents control — a decision to harness his desires and sin no more, thereby avoiding further shame. Thus, someone who truly wishes to repent will feel shame for his sins.

After expounding his lesson on how the best path to repentance is to endure humiliation, Rebbe Nachman asked Reb Noson, "Do you ever feel flushed with embarrassment before God?" (*Siach Sarfei Kodesh* 730).

Once, when Rebbe Nachman was speaking about his early years, he said, "I used to be so timid before God, I could literally feel the shame on my face. I would often stand before God and feel embarrassed, as if I had been humiliated in front of a friend. There were times when I would actually blush, so great was my shame" (*Rabbi Nachman's Wisdom* #168).

Furthermore, Reb Noson explains that every person must endure at least some suffering before attaining spirituality. It might be his personal struggle against his evil inclination, or it might take the form of family opposition, financial difficulties or some other personal problem. Such suffering is also a form of embarrassment, and one can only be patient and wait until the doors of spirituality open up and one finds relief. Thus any suffering, if accepted with patience, is all part of "remaining silent in the face of embarrassment" and can bring about true, complete repentance.

*

"I Will Be"

Rebbe Nachman elaborates on this idea (see *Likutey Moharan* I, 6). As seen throughout the Torah, God is known by several Names. One of these is *EHYeH* (אהיה), which literally means, "I will be." This does not imply that God changes in any way, or that He has to "come into being," God forbid. God is eternal and unchanging. Rather, the concept behind the Name *EHYeH* is "I will be revealed at ever greater levels."

The four letters of the name *EHYeH* (אהיה), *Aleph* (א=1), *Heh* (ה=5), *Yod* (י=10) and *Heh* (ה=5) add up to 21. However, when calculated in retrograde (i.e., by returning each time to the first

letter until the entire word is complete) — א+אה+אהי+אהיה
(1+6+16+21) — they add up to 44. This is also the numerical value
of *DaM* (דם), "blood" (see Appendix D, *gematria* chart). (The ARI explains
that this method of calculation is used when there is a concealment
of holiness. As opposed to *panim* [face to face], this is called
achorayim [backside], indicating a concealment of holiness.) Thus,
hidden within a person's bloodstream is God Himself. Why is He
hidden there? As we have seen, the bloodstream is infused with the
evil inclination. Still, even in such materialistic surroundings, God
Himself is ever present, always patient, waiting for us to turn to
Him. At the very moment of acknowledgement of one's sins, one
can immediately find God!

Sinning lowers a person to a level of "nonexistence." Our
Sages alluded to this level when they taught (*Eruvin* 13b), "It would
have been better had man not been created." Repentance, on the
other hand, is like being born again. It binds a person to God as He
is revealed in the holy Name *EHYeH* (I will be). By enduring
hardship, suffering or embarrassment, a person draws upon
himself the spirituality of *EHYeH* which is concealed within his
bloodstream. This process repeats itself again and again as one
seeks to attain ever higher levels.

Rebbe Nachman points out that this idea is intimated also in
the vowel that is used to pronounce the word *DaM*. The letters of
the Hebrew alphabet are consonants, while the vowels are a series
of dots and dashes (see below, Chapter 24, "The Pulse"). *DaM* is voweled
with a *kamatz* (an "aw" sound). The word *kamatz* means "closed or
concealed," for concealed within the bloodstream are both a holy
presence (*EHYeH*) and the evil inclination (the base
characteristics). The word *DaM* implies that a person must endure
suffering in silence — keeping under control the base
characteristics of anger, jealousy, impatience and so on — in order
to subdue the evil inclination, thereby revealing holiness. The
reason for this is that by remaining silent he changes the *DaM* to
DoM, "silence," replacing the *kamatz* with a *cholam* (an "o" sound), a

vowel point which sits above the consonants. The rushing blood which had previously been used to sin has now been changed to silence for the sake of God, unleashing the Godliness concealed within, which leads to true repentance. This corresponds to the *Sefirah* of Keter (Crown). The *cholam* thus sits above the letter *dalet*, as a crown sits upon the head.

As has been mentioned, Keter, in and of itself, is beyond conception (above, Part 2, and see below, Part 4). However, one can find some aspect of each of the Ten *Sefirot* within one's own spiritual level. Thus, each person has his own "lofty level of Keter" to which he can aspire. By attaining it, he can ascend to the next level of spirituality (see also Appendix C).

*

A Circuit of Joy

Take a deep breath. Hold it. Now exhale. In doing so you are cleansing your blood.

Rebbe Nachman taught:

The blood flows through the body, along with oxygen, cleansing it from waste matter. But sadness can adversely affect this flow. Sadness is expressed through shallow breathing, which is common in morose people. It can induce an inadequate pulse rate, causing one to feel sluggish. Deep, remorseful sighing, brought about through the strong desire to return to the service of God, is a cure for the effects of sadness. Breathing fresh air, bringing oxygen into the system, cleanses it from the impurities brought about through sadness (*Likutey Moharan* I, 56:9).

Rebbe Nachman also taught:

Blood must be able to flow through the veins without impediments. If there is an infection anywhere in the system, it causes large quantities of blood to rush to that location, interrupting the normal blood flow. [The blood vessels dilate in the infected area, allowing for an increased flow of blood.] The *Shalosh Regalim* [Three Festivals] help one to regain one's normal pulse rate. For this reason a Festival is called a *Chag*, the root word also translating as "circle," alluding to the cycle of the blood flow throughout the body (*Likutey Moharan* II, 4:12).

Rebbe Nachman explains that the celebration of each Festival, by virtue of the *reason* for its celebration, reveals a significant amount of Godliness in the world. Pesach enables us to relive the Exodus, together with the miracles of the Ten Plagues and the Crossing of the Red Sea. Shavuot recalls the miracle of the Revelation, outstanding in that God descended upon Mount Sinai and revealed Himself to the Jews while giving them the Torah. Sukkot invokes the memory of the miracle of the Clouds of Glory which protected the Jews during their sojourn in the desert. Thus, celebration of each of the Festivals proclaims the presence of God and allows us to experience the forces of spirituality which transcend the physical.

Regarding the Festivals, it is written (Deuteronomy 16:14), "You shall rejoice in your *Chag* [Festival]." Thus, joy is beneficial for the *chag*, which represents the circuit of the blood. Furthermore, as the Festivals are called *Regalim* (literally, "feet"), being joyous during the Festivals is especially beneficial for the circulation of the blood to the feet (cf. *Likutey Moharan* II, 4:12). Also, in this sense, the feet represent the lower extremities, those places most distant from God. Joy is thus one of the greatest ways of bringing life-giving blood and energy to those who are far from God, filling them with strength and vitality to draw closer to Him than ever before.

*

Recycle and Return

As the blood carries life throughout the body, it is, in a sense, life itself. In addition, we must remember that any given drop of blood does not take the exact same route each time it circulates through the body. One time it will go to the head, the next time to the right arm, and so on. Reb Noson gleans a valuable lesson from this: Since life flows through every part of us, we can "plug in" to any single aspect of Judaism, such as a Torah thought or a kind deed or word, and from there begin anew. Eventually, that renewed vitality will reach every part of us, and our entire relationship with God will be enhanced (*Likutey Halakhot, Matanah* 5, *Roshei Perakim* p.19a).

Expanding on this idea, Reb Noson explains that the Torah mentions the word *admoni* (the red one) in connection with two people: King David and Esau (1 Samuel 16:12; Genesis 25:25). They both represent Gevurah (strength and judgment), one coming from the side of holiness and one from the Other Side. One of the major manifestations of Gevurah, which can be used either for good or evil, is audacity or brazenness. If a person feels that he is distant from God and is ashamed to draw near to Him, notwithstanding his past deeds which caused the distance, he must be audacious and approach God *continually*, until he begins to experience a level of spirituality. This is alluded to in the *continual* flow of blood throughout the body and represents holy brazenness, the quality that King David embodied in fighting battles to reveal God's kingdom.

Conversely, the main source of improper audacity and brazenness is found in one's own "hot blood," representing the aspect of "Esau" that lies within each person, and which one calls forth when seeking material pleasures. This characteristic is an important one and can be controlled and directed towards holiness through the exercising of patience.

This is all alluded to in the *kavanot* (meditations) of the Festival of Chanukah (see *Pri Etz Chaim, Shaar HaChanukah* 4, p.465).

The oppression of the Jews in that period of our history marked a very dark era, with the Greeks sparing neither means nor opportunity to intimidate the Jews into submission to their godless culture. It took extreme brazenness on the part of the Maccabees to fight a war against such superior forces, for the sake of the honor of God. The ARI thus writes that the light of Chanukah is drawn from the Holy Name NaChaL, which is the acrostic of "*Nafsheinu Chiktah La-Adonoy...* — Our souls wait for God; He is our help and our shield" (Psalms 33:20). The Hebrew word NaChaL (נחל) has the numerical equivalent of 88. By adding one to this number to represent the word itself, one gets 89, the numerical equivalent of Chanukah (חנוכה). The Jews suffered severe intimidation and oppression; yet they waited patiently for their salvation, never giving up hope that God would help them. When the opportunity arose, they took advantage of it and overcame the forces of heresy.

In addition, we find that the words *DaM ADaM* (דם אדם, "man's blood") also has the same *gematria* (numerical value) as Chanukah (חנוכה) and *NaChaL* (נחל; 89), again indicating that in one's spiritual search one needs much patience, never slackening in one's desire to serve God. Blood continually courses through the body, and one would do well to take advantage of this lifeline, searching, yearning and waiting patiently for the moment when one can begin one's spiritual ascent. Just as the blood doesn't always follow the same route, but rather it constantly "seeks new direction" within the body, so we can attune ourselves to a course of constantly seeking the proper moment to enhance our relationship with God (*Likutey Halakhot, Matanah* 5:51, 61–63).

*

Alcohol and the Tree of Knowledge

> The Tree of Knowledge from which Adam ate was a grapevine.
>
> *Sanhedrin* 70a

Reb Noson writes:

Wine has two potential powers, one good and one evil. It comes from a very exalted source, as is evident in the Hebrew word for wine, *yayin* (יין), which is numerically equal to 70. Wine thus corresponds to the "Seventy Facets" of Torah and to the "Seventy Elders" ("elders" indicates wisdom; see below, Chapter 34). Partaking of wine in purity and with holy joy can help one ascend to very lofty levels indeed. This is possible with the drinking of the sacramental wine of *Kiddush* on Shabbat and Festivals, on Purim or on the celebration of a mitzvah.

But the power for evil inherent in wine and alcoholic

beverages is also extremely potent. It can arouse a person's lusts, especially the lust for immorality. The verse thus states (Proverbs 23:31), "Do not look upon wine when it is red." Our Sages comment (Sanhedrin 70a), "For its end brings red [i.e., blood, judgments and suffering]." Alcohol abuse befuddles the mind as it enters the bloodstream. One may feel joyous when he is drunk, but this is so only because the wine "heats up" the blood, inciting one to immorality, strife and many other evils (Likutey Halakhot, Yayin Nesekh 4:1–6).

Thus, one who imbibes too much alcohol not only opens himself up to physical ailments, but also harms the spiritual nature of his blood. Conversely, one who is careful with his consumption of wine will merit to drink a very, very old wine, which will bring him true joy — "The wine preserved in its grapes from the Six Days of Creation" (i.e., to taste from the Tree of Life that was prepared for Man in the Garden of Eden) (Berakhot 34b; Likutey Halakhot, Ha'oseh Shliach Ligvot Chov 2:14).

*

A Blood Test

To cleanse the blood and to maintain a pure bloodstream requires much effort, both physical and spiritual. A doctor will almost always order blood tests to detect an imbalance in a person's physical system. How much more necessary is a "blood test" for our spiritual health. Considering the complexities of the bloodstream, a short review of the ideas presented would enable us to test the spiritual state of our blood and rectify any impurities.

Blood represents judgment. It requires much patience to endure suffering (in the form of judgment, humiliation, etc.). Blood also represents repentance and the Sefirah of Keter, the level of EHYeH. When we remain silent in the face of embarrassment and opposition, we purify our blood and achieve our highest potential. A normal flow of blood is facilitated by an attitude of joy which allows us to feel a spirit of renewal.

* * *

10

Eating: The Egyptian Exile

We have discussed how the bloodstream carries nutrients to all parts of the body; now we will explore how the nutrients reach the blood: through eating. This chapter deals with those organs associated with eating — the mouth, the neck and the various organs it contains, and the stomach and its associated organs.

The neck, where the throat is located, is a very narrow part of the body. Thus in Hebrew, the throat is called *MeiTZaR hagaron*, which literally means "the narrow of the neck." Through this narrow passageway pass three life-sustaining organs or vessels: the trachea (windpipe), which is situated on the right side of the throat, carries air; the esophagus, which is situated to the left of and slightly behind the trachea, close to the nape of the neck, carries food; and the jugular veins and carotid arteries carry blood.

Rebbe Nachman teaches that the stories found in the Bible carry messages for contemporary living and he illustrates this through the land of Egypt, *MiTZRayim*, which corresponds to the *MeTZaR hagaron*. The history of the Jews as a nation begins with their descent into exile in Egypt, a result of Joseph having been sold into slavery.

PhaRaOH, the Egyptian ruler, who represents the forces of evil, shares the same root letters as the word *ORePH*, the nape, or back, of the neck, alluding to the esophagus, i.e., eating. To entice the Jews, Pharaoh needed the assistance of his three ministers: the chief butcher, the chief baker and the chief wine steward (Genesis

37:36, 40:2). They represent the main types of nourishment we take into our system: meat (animal), bread (vegetation) and wine (liquids) (see *Likutey Moharan* I, 62:5). Thus, to gain control over the Jews, Pharaoh manipulated them through their most basic need — their need to eat.

Though sold as a slave into Egypt (the *meitzar hagaron*), Joseph, the spiritually inclined person, persevered in his pursuit of Godliness. In the Biblical narration, we find that Joseph faced all three of Pharaoh's ministers under adverse conditions. But Joseph held fast, meriting to become a ruler over his would-be enslavers. This teaches us that one who remains steadfast in his spiritual endeavors can rise above the circumstances of his environment and become master of his own destiny.

However, Joseph's descendants and those of his family — the Jews — succumbed to Pharaoh and his ministers: They befriended their Egyptian neighbors, ate of their bread (i.e., become entrapped in the narrowness of the neck — the *meitzar hagaron*) and eventually became their slaves. Obviously, the road to evil — spiritual slavery — stems from improper eating.

Additionally, we learn that the neck and throat area, *garon*, corresponds to the Holy Name *Elohim*. This is derived thus: *Elohim*, with a numerical value of 86, can be expanded in three ways (for the letter *Heh* can be spelled out with an *aleph*, a *heh* or a *yod*; see Appendix D). Three times the numerical value of *ELoHIM* (אלהים) equals 258. Adding one, to represent the word itself, gives us the sum of 259, the value of *GaRON* (גרון) (*Likutey Moharan* I, 46). This Holy Name of God connotes judgments and constrictions and, by extension, so does *garon*. Thus, being trapped in or by the *garon* — the Egyptian exile or improper eating habits — indicates a concealment of Godliness and bondage to a material way of life.

*

Eating is a basic human need, the primary action which binds body and soul together. Rebbe Nachman teaches that if a person is intent upon spiritual growth when he eats, he can ascend to the highest of levels (*Likutey Moharan* II, 7:10). Conversely, a constant obsession with food, or indulging in gluttony, can lead to spiritual stagnation. Regarding this, Rebbe Nachman taught:

> "The belly of the wicked always feels empty" (Proverbs 13:25). This refers to those who are never satisfied and always crave more (*Likutey Moharan* I, 54:2).

The stomach, having received the ground-up food, stores it as it is being broken down into a pulp. This pulp is then passed into the intestines, where it is broken down further before it passes into the digestive organs. This is the course the nourishment takes as it plays its part through the purification system of the body. Considering that the full stomach takes several hours to void, it is indeed "the belly of the *wicked* [which] always feels empty," for those who constantly crave food never feel satisfied and always hunger for more, even when there is food in their stomach.

Rebbe Nachman also taught:

> Peace and prosperity go hand in hand, while hunger bodes strife and war. Therefore, a craving for food is a sign that one has enemies. By breaking one's craving for food, one can gain peace with one's enemies (*Likutey Moharan* I, 39).

Aside from human enemies — those people who are jealous of or hate others — the "enemies" Rebbe Nachman refers to are actually a person's own internal organs, which can overcome and enslave him. They prey upon his desires, always seeking material gratification, never feeling satisfied. These "enemies" constantly seek to enslave a person more inextricably to his lusts.

*

The Mouth, the Teeth and the Stomach

The mouth is the point of entry for all food into the body. We grind the food with our teeth, then send it down through the esophagus to the stomach. The stomach acts as a storage area, where gastric acids and enzymes dissolve the food so that it can be digested.

The verse states (Exodus 4:11), "*Mi sam peh l'adam* — Who gave a mouth to man?" We can also translate this as: "Who placed man? His mouth!" That is, what qualifies a person to bear the title of man? His mouth. If a person eats out of lust, his mouth classifies him as an animal. However, when a person eats with the intention of nourishing the body so that he can develop spiritually as well as physically, his mouth can bring him to the towering spiritual level of man, for such eating fills his entire body with the awe of God! (*Likutey Moharan* II, 77). The mouth thus serves as a crucial organ in determining how one can become "human" in the fullest sense of the word.

Throughout his teachings Rebbe Nachman expresses in various ways the maxim that an honorable man can be discerned by the way he uses his mouth. Though one can show deference with any of several organs, it is the way one *speaks* to and about others that most notably demonstrates respect. However, honor is not limited only to the way in which one speaks. Rebbe Nachman teaches that "gluttony brings a person to a loss of honor and favor" (*Likutey Moharan* I, 67:2). Thus we see that it is the mouth in both its roles, as spokesman *and* as consumer, that establishes a man's level.

The Baal Shem Tov was once with his followers at an inn. As another patron there was beginning his meal, the Baal Shem Tov told his followers to look closely. They saw that the person's face had a certain bovine quality. The Baal Shem Tov told them that this was because his attitude whenever he ate was that of an ox.

This idea is reinforced when we consider the teeth. Adults have thirty-two teeth which are helpful both for grinding food and for enunciating one's words. Corresponding to the thirty-two teeth is the Hebrew word for honor, *KaVOD* (כבוד), which has a numerical value of 32 (see *Zohar* III, 33a). Thus we see in the teeth yet another indication that it is the mouth which establishes honor — for others as well as for oneself. (The mouth in relationship to speech will be discussed in greater detail below in Part 6.)

Rebbe Nachman taught:

> There are two ways in which one can eat like an animal. Some eat human food but with an animal's appetite. Others eat like humans, but their food is not fit for human consumption. For there are sparks of holiness contained within the food we eat (see Chapter 8), and if these sparks are not properly rectified, both through the observance of the mitzvot related to the food and through eating with all the proper attitudes, that food is fit only for a beast, not for humans. Eating "like an animal" in either of these two ways can result in illness.
>
> The verse states (Psalms 66:12), "You have caused men to ride over our heads; we have gone through fire and water..." When one eats like an animal, one descends to the level of an animal. At that point, "men ride *over* our heads," since one has descended to the lower levels. Then, "we go through fire and water," referring to fevers and chills (i.e., illness). This is true on both the physical and the spiritual planes.
>
> Water and fire correspond to love and awe. One who possesses true knowledge also possesses love and awe of God. However, the person who descends to an animalistic level forfeits his knowledge; he becomes subjugated to inappropriate love and fear: dominated by materialistic forces, his emotions become focused on the mundane rather than on the spiritual essence (*Rabbi Nachman's Wisdom* #143; see also *The Wings of the Sun*, p.428).

*

"The Stomach Sleeps"

Our Sages teach that "the stomach sleeps" (*Berakhot* 61b). The commentaries point out that the efforts required by the stomach for the digestion of food "tire out" a person and bring sleep upon him (*Chidushei HaGeonim, loc. cit.*). Rebbe Nachman presents a similar thought and expands on it in several discourses.

A person's main vitality lies in his intellect. One who is not using his intellect to its full potential is considered asleep. Many people who *seem* to be alive are in fact sleeping their lives away; they are not using their intellect to its fullest capacity. This "sleep" may be brought on by improper eating or by eating the wrong foods (*Likutey Moharan* I, 60:6).

Eating can cause confusion. Immediately after eating, one often feels confused, because the forces of the *kelipot* [the Other Side] also receive their nourishment from the food one eats (*Likutey Moharan* I, 17:3).

The mind develops through the nourishment it receives. When one eats unnecessarily, the superfluous food mars one's sense of judgment. If the body is free of excesses, one is able to experience a clear understanding of how to direct one's life (*Likutey Moharan* I, 61:1).

The functioning of the mind depends on what we eat: The nutrients we ingest are absorbed by the blood and carried to the lungs via the right ventricle of the heart (pulmonary circulation). The oxygenated blood returns from the lungs to the left ventricle of the heart. From there it is pumped into the aorta, traveling via the aortic arch, carotid arteries and other arterial branches, until it finally delivers the oxygen-rich blood to the brain. Thus, the mind is powerfully affected by the food one eats.

Rebbe Nachman further teaches that one's personality traits also depend on diet (*The Aleph-Bet Book, Daat* A:4). This, too, is because food affects the mind through the nourishment, both physical and spiritual, it receives. While healthy foods will help develop the mind, unhealthy foods will have adverse effects. This applies not only to kosher versus non-kosher foods, but to nutritious versus "junk" foods, as well as to foods eaten with a proper or improper attitude.

*

Rebbe Nachman taught:

Overeating can lead to illness. Since everything requires some source of nourishment, even the food one consumes must draw nourishment from somewhere. Eating activates the digestive tract, which processes the food into nutrients. To remain digestible, the nutrients themselves must have a source of life, which is now the body. When one eats in reasonable quantities to supply the body's requirements, the food finds its "life" within the body. However, when one eats in excess of what is required, the food itself finds no source of life support, as it serves no positive purpose for the body. Since it nevertheless persists in seeking its own nourishment for life, it draws sustenance from the body itself and can cause any number of illnesses (*Likutey Moharan* I, 257).

One's lust for food testifies to one's distance from truth [i.e., Godliness], and because of a person's lust for food, God, as it were, hides His face from him, as in (Deuteronomy 31:17), "I will hide My face, and he will be devoured..." That is, his "devouring" causes Me to hide My face. This is why, when troubles beset the Jewish nation, it is customary to fast. Fasting indicates a breaking of one's desire for food, thereby reversing the process and causing Godliness to be revealed (*Likutey Moharan* I, 47).

*

Sweet Dreams

In addition to teaching us about the effects food and eating have on the conscious mind, Rebbe Nachman speaks of their effects on the subconscious mind. The food-turned-nourishment plays a major role in the functioning of one's subconscious, such as in one's dreams. The clearer a person's mind, due to proper nourishment and eating habits, the clearer his subconscious will be, and the more capable he will be of having what the Talmud calls "an angelic dream" (*Berakhot* 55b). This is illustrated by the fact that the Hebrew word for food, *MaAKhaL* (מאכל), has the same letters as *MaLAKh* (מלאך), "angel."

However, if a person's eating is improper, then both his mind and his subconscious are subject to distortions. The dreams he has are "demonic," and they may take the form of nocturnal emissions, nightmares and the like (*Likutey Moharan* II, 5:9, 10). Thus, improper eating enables the subconscious to tilt a person towards materialistic pursuits even if his conscious desire is to find God.

Indeed, Rebbe Nachman teaches in several lessons that negative eating patterns have a consciousness-lowering effect that subsequently prevents one from growing spiritually. The Rebbe brings an analogy of someone sleeping and dreaming. In the dream he lives for seventy years. Upon awakening, he realizes that the seventy years he dreamt took only a quarter of an hour. By comparison, if the mind is not well utilized, one's entire lifetime may amount to only a few minutes of real value — "quality time" — whereas if one uses the mind to its full capacity, one can indeed *live* a full life (*Likutey Moharan* II, 61). Proper eating enables a person to realize his potential and to live a full life — instead of "dreaming" his life away.

*

Eating as a Mitzvah

We now begin to see the debilitating effects of gluttony. Instead of filling the stomach, overeating causes emptiness; a person might feel full, but he is not satisfied. Gluttony creates "enemies" (see above, p.80), and it brings illness. In its clutches, one may never come to live a full, vibrant life. It can affect the mind, and it brings about dishonor. It also distances us from truth, from spirituality, from God. There is no end to the problems — medical, financial, spiritual and emotional — that are caused by gluttony, the "leading lust."

From the above one might conclude that it would be best to become an ascetic, subsisting exclusively on dry bread and water. This is not so. In principle, Rebbe Nachman was against excessive fasting, because we need strength to serve God. It is better to devote one's energies to Torah study and prayer and, Rebbe Nachman tells us, to fast only when required by *Halakhah* (Jewish Law) (see *Likutey Moharan* I, 50).

Furthermore, Rebbe Nachman stressed the importance and

extolled the virtues of eating on Shabbat and Festivals (*Likutey Moharan* I, 57:8; *ibid.*, 277; see *Likutey Halakhot, Birkat HaMazon* 4:7). On those special days a simple meal does not suffice. One must do one's best to prepare and enjoy a sumptuous repast (see *Likutey Moharan* I, 125).

It is clear, then, that eating, per se, is not damaging, only the negative motives which may accompany it. Furthermore, if one eats for the sake of a mitzvah, or in order to have strength to serve God, it can lead one to great spiritual heights.

Reb Yudel, one of Rebbe Nachman's closest followers, married into the poor but saintly family of Reb Leib Trastinetz. Every day he was given a portion of borscht for his meal. After several days, Reb Yudel showed displeasure at his meager and tasteless portions. His father-in-law, Reb Leib, noticed this and offered Reb Yudel a taste of his portion. Reb Yudel had a spoonful and marveled at the incredible taste, as if it were some type of heavenly food. Reb Leib said, "See, my son! It is not the food; it is the eater!" (*oral tradition*).

*

Thought for Food

Rebbe Nachman taught:

Eating with the intention of attaining spirituality is the only way to achieve certain levels of awe of God. Through proper eating one can ascend to a level beyond intellect, beyond any conception [of Godliness] one has yet attained (*Likutey Moharan* II, 7:10).

To better understand this teaching, imagine a king who has the power to allocate his nation's bounty for the welfare of his kingdom. Every human being is considered a "king," and his body, a "kingdom." When he eats he automatically distributes the "bounty" he consumes for the welfare of his "kingdom."

In Kabbalistic terms, God's bounty descends through the upper *Sefirot* to Malkhut (Kingship/Kingdom, the lowest *Sefirah*). From Malkhut it is disbursed throughout all the lower levels of creation. Malkhut must thus draw from the *Sefirot* "above" it, while those *Sefirot* in turn must draw from even higher levels. Providing food for one's body with the understanding that this bounty comes from a Higher Source enables one to attain a higher level of perception. With greater clarity of perception, one can achieve a higher recognition of God's existence, resulting in an overwhelming level of awe of Him (see *Likutey Moharan* II, 7:10). In fact, through eating properly one may be privileged to ascend to a level of absolute humility and actually *feel* the presence of God (*Likutey Moharan* II, 72).

Reb Noson points out that the difficulty of this endeavor is hinted at in the expression "breaking bread." Bread is the "staff of life," and as such is inclusive of all other foodstuffs. This is evidenced by the fact that the blessing recited over bread exempts one from the blessings required for all the other foods which constitute the main part of the meal. The Hebrew word for bread, *LeCHeM* (לחם), is etymologically related to the Hebrew word for waging war, *LoCHeM* (לוחם). Eating bread, and by extension any food, is indeed a battle. For one to attain holiness via eating, one must battle to "break" one's attitudes towards "bread" (*Likutey Halakhot, Netilat Yadayim Li'Seudah* 6:54). That is, one must keep in mind that the eating is for spiritual benefits, not merely for physical gratification.

On Shabbat and Festivals the battle is less intense and the goal easier to attain. On weekdays people are busy with, even consumed by, their work. This situation is liable to upset one's religious-spiritual compass. On Shabbat, however, a person rests and enjoys the time and he has the peace of mind to contemplate his life and consider his deeds. With such tranquility, one is able to eat more peacefully with the right attitude (see *Likutey Moharan* I, 57:5,6).

The Talmud teaches that everything that Shammai ate was for the sake of Shabbat. When he saw a choice piece of meat on a Sunday or a Monday, he would buy it and set it aside for Shabbat.

If he then came upon a tastier piece, he would eat the first piece and keep the better cut for Shabbat (Beitzah 16a).

Shammai drew the spirituality of Shabbat into his weekday meals by keeping his mind focused on Shabbat throughout the entire week. Anyone can do this. Drawing the sanctity and spirituality of Shabbat into the weekday by, for example, making a habit of contemplating one's spiritual progress, allows one to eat during the week not out of gluttony, but out of a genuine desire for spiritual growth.

*

Spiritual Food

One of Rebbe Nachman's best-loved stories is "The Sophisticate and the Simpleton" (Rabbi Nachman's Stories, pp.160–196). At first, despite his great efforts to learn the craft, the Simpleton is at best a shoddy cobbler who barely ekes out a living. Even so, he is extremely happy. Due to his simplicity and joy, the Simpleton becomes the governor of his district and eventually rises to the position of prime minister of his land.

The Simpleton had learned the trade of a shoemaker. Since he was simple, he had to study very hard to master it, and even then he was not very adept at the craft. He married and earned a living from his work. However, as he was simple and not expert in his craft, his livelihood was meager.

Since he had limited skill, he had to work constantly and hardly had time to eat. He would take his first bite of bread while making a hole with his awl. He would then draw the thick sewing thread used by shoemakers in and out, and bite off another piece of bread and eat it. Yet, he was always very happy. He was filled with joy at all times, for he had every type of food, drink and clothing.

He would say to his wife, "My wife, give me something to eat." She would give him a piece of bread, and he would eat it. Then he would say, "Give me some soup with groats," and she would cut him another slice of bread. He would eat it and say, "How nice and delicious this soup is!"

He would then ask her for some meat and other good food, and each time he asked, she would give him another piece of bread. He would enjoy it very much and praise the food highly, saying how well prepared and delicious it was. It was as if he were actually eating the food he had requested (*Rabbi Nachman's Stories*, pp.168–169).

When telling this story, Rebbe Nachman commented that the Simpleton *actually tasted* in the bread whatever type of food he had requested (similar to the manna in the desert, which contained all tastes). This was because of his simplicity and great joy. The story goes on to describe how he tasted in his water every type of beverage and how he felt appropriately attired for any occasion whenever he donned his sheepskin coat. Due to his unpretentiousness, he found happiness and fulfillment in everything he ate, drank and wore. Though he was at first the laughingstock of all who knew him, he eventually became the prime minister of his country.

The battle of eating — be it for physical pleasure, to keep body and soul together or to use as a stepping-stone for greater spirituality — is a lengthy and difficult one. The Simpleton masters his lust through the realization that there is spiritual nourishment contained in every morsel he eats and drinks. Thus, he attains spiritual energy, which propels him to ever greater heights, and he eventually becomes a leader of men.

*

We have discussed the "river that flows from Eden and waters the Garden," which corresponds to the single source element and the four basic elements that make up man (above, Chapter 4). Reb Noson writes that by injecting spirituality into eating, a person can experience the wondrous pleasures of Eden through his food.

There is nourishment for the body [food] and nourishment for the soul [e.g., the sense of smell, prayer, the awe of God].

Partaking of food for the body weakens the soul. How, then, are we permitted to eat? We can nourish the soul by focusing on the spiritual. The more spiritual our motivation when we eat, the more spiritually nourishing our food becomes. The most auspicious time for eating for spirituality is on Shabbat, when we have access to *ONeG*, the special pleasure of Shabbat. *ONeG* (ענג) is an acrostic for *Eden* (עדן, "Paradise"), *Nahar* (נהר, "River") and *Gan* (גן, "Garden"). Thus, the food we enjoy on Shabbat can bring us to those highest of levels represented by *ONeG* (*Likutey Halakhot, Ma'akhalei Akum* 2:1).

*

Gluttony does indeed degrade a person. Nevertheless, even for one who has fallen into the pattern of gluttony, there is hope. Rebbe Nachman taught that one who overeats must regurgitate. Usually, he vomits up more than he has swallowed. In other words, he might even regurgitate what had been ingested previously. In the same way, when the Evil One takes more than he is capable of ingesting, he will be forced to return every bit of good, every precious soul, he has ever swallowed and more. He will even have to "vomit up" his own life force (*Likutey Moharan* II, 8:3). At this point, a person may realize that things have gone too far. The gluttony he indulged may now be the motivation for him to turn his life around. Realizing that he has "gone too far," he learns to reject his former habits and return to a spiritually inclined life.

A person who overeats must go on a diet in order to regain control over his eating habits. Likewise, one who has lost control to the evil inclination can improve one's physical and emotional health. Simply by *deciding* which foods to eat and in what quantities, by eating according to Torah dictates, that is, by refraining from partaking of certain foods and pausing to make a blessing over permitted foods, one can repair any blemish incurred through eating. By understanding the powerful influence eating has upon us, we can utilize the act of eating to rise to the loftiest of spiritual heights.

* * *

11

The Liver, Gallbladder and Spleen

In this chapter we will discuss organs which filter impurities from the body: the liver, the gallbladder and the spleen. The liver and gallbladder are integral parts of the digestive system and the spleen plays an important part in the circulatory and lymphatic systems. Before explaining their spiritual aspects, it is important to understand their functions within the body.

Introduction

The liver is located mostly on the right side of the abdominal cavity. It is the largest organ in the body and has two important roles: producing and regulating chemicals for the body's needs, and neutralizing poisons and waste products. After food has been partially digested it enters the intestinal tract. From there, the nutrients are transferred through the walls of the intestines into the bloodstream. The blood, which has absorbed the nutrients, passes through the liver and its filtering system before returning to the heart and lungs. It is interesting to note that the liver purifies the blood before it is sent to the heart. In this sense, the liver acts as a servant of the heart.

To accommodate the production of new chemicals, the liver takes the raw nutrients and "purifies" them to make them compatible with the body. It manufactures proteins and processes carbohydrates (sugar and starches) by converting them into glucose to supply energy for the body. It also stores some of the sugar for future use. The liver also processes fats and waste products of the blood. Thus, all nutrients absorbed by the liver are refined and then returned to the body, whether to the blood or tissues, or in the form of energy. The enzymes of the liver also cleanse the blood of bacteria and neutralize poisons that have entered the body. As the liver interacts mainly with the blood system, its fluid color is represented as red.

The gallbladder is a small, pear-shaped sac adjacent to the liver. It serves as a storage container for bile, which is a thick, bitter, yellowish-green fluid produced by the liver. Bile, necessary for the digestion of fats, is discharged into the small intestine when the presence of food is indicated. The bile neutralizes acidity and breaks down fats. After the gallbladder has done its job, most of the minerals in the bile return to the liver via the bloodstream and are then reused by the body. This is alluded to in our Sages' statement (*Berakhot* 61b), "The liver becomes angry; the gallbladder emits fluids to pacify that anger." That is, the liver becomes angry when we eat, for it is forced to work hard to purify the system. The gallbladder then emits fluids to pacify that anger — for when the bile returns to the liver, the liver has basically completed its work. The gallbladder also transfers worn-out blood cells to the lymphatic system for their removal from the body.

The spleen is considered by some medical opinions to be part of the lymphatic system, while others see it as an organ of the circulatory and immune systems, for it offers protection against foreign and useless matter within the body and against infection. It is located to the left of the stomach, between the stomach and the diaphragm.

The lymphatic vessels collect the surplus fluids (called "lymph") from the body's tissues. The lymph nodes filter and destroy bacteria and other foreign particles. The color of the lymphocytes, which produce antibodies to fight harmful substances in the body, is milky white. Various other organs which also filter out bacteria from the body, such as the spleen and the tonsils, contain lymphoid tissue similar to the tissue found in the lymphatic system.

The main function of the spleen is to filter the blood system. It removes old, worn-out and abnormal red and white blood cells, and also removes irregular particles and bacteria from the blood. Lymphocytes contained in the spleen also manufacture antibodies to weaken or kill bacteria, viruses and other substances that cause infection. The Talmud teaches that blood which has become tainted is "black" in color (Niddah 19a); hence the spleen is said to be associated with the black fluids of the body.

*

These three organs are all active participants in the purification process of the body and can be relied on to do an excellent job. Yet they are under continual "attack" from impurities which require filtering. In this sense, these organs are man's main connection to his physicality, for they deal exclusively with his material input (food) and its purification.

Oriental medicine ascribes individual characteristics to each organ, which influences the body accordingly. An example is the liver, *kaved* in Hebrew. The nature of the liver is to invade the domain of the other organs (due to its multi-faceted processing abilities, the liver's effect is felt throughout the body). If allowed to do so, it will cause serious problems. If, on the other hand, the liver *serves* the other organs, such as the heart and kidneys, then all goes well. This is reflected in the verse (Exodus 8:28), "*VaYaKhbeiD Paroh et libo* — Pharaoh hardened his heart." The Hebrew for "hardened" is *KaVeD* (similar to liver). That is to say, "Pharaoh 'livered' his heart," allowing his liver, his gross materialism, to master him (Dr. Noach Bittleman). His own self-imposed subservience to his "liver's personality" caused his ultimate downfall. Instead, his heart and kidneys should have reigned. Had he listened to his heart and to good advice (the "kidneys"; see below), he would not have brought destruction upon himself and his country.

Let us now examine the impact these organs have upon man in terms of his basic character and his emotional stability.

*

Egyptian Bondage

The end of the Book of Genesis and the beginning of the Book of Exodus describe the descent of the family of Jacob — the children of Israel — into the land of Egypt. Eventually, as God foretold to Abraham, they found themselves enslaved to "Pharaoh and his ministers." In the Passover Haggadah we say:

> Blessed is the One Who kept His promise to Israel! Blessed is He! The Blessed Holy One calculated the end [of the Egyptian exile] in order to fulfill that which He promised to Abraham at the *Brit Bein HaBetarim* [Covenant between the Halves]. It is thus written (Genesis 15:13-14), "Know with certainty that your descendants will be strangers in a land that is not theirs. For four hundred years, [the people of that land] will enslave them and treat them cruelly. But then I will judge that nation whom they have served, and afterwards they will depart with great wealth."

The first part of this prophecy came true later when (Exodus 1:14) "they [the Egyptians] embittered their [the Jews'] lives with hard labor, with mortar and bricks, and all kinds of work in the field. All the work that they forced them to do was back-breaking."

When speaking of the exiles, the *Tikkuney Zohar* (#69, p.107b) states that man becomes weakened, both physically and spiritually, by the suffering he endures. It then applies the verse quoted above to man's struggle.

Embittered their lives — this alludes to the gallbladder, which stores [yellowish-green] bitter fluids and threatens the body with fever and illness. [In Hebrew, the gallbladder is called *MaRah*, from *MaR*, meaning bitter.]

Hard labor with *chomer* [mortar] and *levainim* [bricks] — *LeVaiNim*, from *LeVaNah* [white], corresponds to the white fluids [lymphocytes] which have been afflicted by excessive eating.

In the field — alludes to the liver [red fluids], as Esau, also known as Edom [Red], was a man of the *field* (Genesis 25:27).

All the work...back-breaking — alludes to the spleen [black fluids].

It is clear from the Zohar that a person can become subject to illness and suffering as a result of "strenuous labor" on the part of his digestive system. The Rambam (Maimonides, 1135–1204), well known for his medical proficiency, also teaches (*Hilkhot Deot* 4:15), "Most illnesses are due to excessive eating." Overeating stimulates extensive activity by the body fluids which can overtax the body's organs and can thus lead to serious illness. As we now explore the spiritual aspects of these organs, we will see how closely these principles are mirrored in the spiritual realm.

*

The Liver

Rebbe Nachman taught:

The liver is called *kaved*, which also translates as "heavy" or "weighty." This is because the liver purifies blood that is "weighted" with unnecessary substances (*Likutey Moharan* I, 29:9).

The liver's task, as well as that of the other filtering systems of the body, is a weighty one indeed. If it is provided with the proper nourishment, the liver functions as the body's primary filter to purify the system. If not, it processes but returns the impurities into the blood. These non-essential products begin to accumulate in the body and eventually act counter to the body's well-being. This system has repercussions in the spiritual realm; for the food the body digests can either nourish and purify the system or it can be detrimental to the functioning of the body, depending on the manner it is ingested and the nature of the food. Thus it can either add strength to a person and assist him in his spiritual quest or debilitate him and inhibit his ability to rise spiritually.

In our discussion of the liver, bear in mind that the *Nefesh*, the part of the soul that interfaces with the body, resides in the blood (above, Chapter 3) and is therefore fundamentally connected to the liver, an organ whose primary function involves the blood. The word *NeFeSh* is associated with desire, as in the verse (Genesis 23:8), "*Im yeish et NaFSh'khem* — If it is your desire." Thus the bloodstream carries our basic desires and lusts. The degree to which we "filter our bloodstream" — that is, how we develop our spirituality and master our baser instincts — will determine the path of our ascent up the spiritual ladder.

*

The Talmud teaches (*Chullin* 109b, Rashi s.v. *hakaved*), "The liver is full of blood." As we have seen, the liver is a major stopover for all the blood which is the human lifeline flowing through the body (see above, Chapter 9). Thus, as the organ which purifies our lifeline, the importance of the liver to the body cannot be overestimated.

Situated at the "crossroads" of the blood system, the liver can serve either as an effective purifier of the polluted blood that surges through our systems, or it can pollute that blood further. As noted (Chapter 9), the bloodstream is a major element in our spiritual makeup. If someone desires (i.e., *nefesh*) a materialistic life, his blood will reflect his choice. The liver will absorb the "nutrients of lust" and will process gluttony back into his system. If he desires spirituality, his liver will process "spiritual nutrients" and will discharge pure blood into his system.

Blood, which is red, symbolizes heat, anger and bloodshed. This corresponds to Esau, who was "red" (Genesis 25:25). Esau thus represents both the forces of evil and the liver, a focal point of the blood's activity within the body. Anger and accusations are his power, so that one who falls victim to these attributes places himself under the influence and control of Esau (*Likutey Moharan* I, 57:6).

But blood and red should not be seen only as entities inimical to spiritual existence. In the Kabbalah, red represents the *Gevurot*, judgments or strengths, and is associated with the attribute of Fear. When a person desires Godliness, his blood (i.e., strength) will be channeled to a corresponding degree into the Fear of God to serve

Him properly. Such a person comes under the dominion of God alone and is free of the influence of Esau.

*

Rebbe Nachman taught:

> Each Jewish soul is rooted in one of the seventy souls of the Children of Israel who first descended into Egypt (Genesis 46:27). These seventy souls are rooted in the seventy facets of the Torah. When someone fulfills the Torah, he draws spirituality — God — towards himself. If, however, he distances himself from Torah, it is as if he has involved himself in idol worship. He draws the forces of the Other Side — which are manifest through the seventy nations — towards himself (see *Tikkuney Zohar* #32, p.76b). These "forces" are then actualized in the seventy aspects of one's character (*Likutey Moharan* I, 36:1).

The Children of Israel are rooted in the Torah, which has "seventy facets" — thoughts and teachings which guide a person on the spiritual path and transmute his or her evil characteristics. These evil characteristics are called "the seventy aspects of one's character" and refer to those characteristics embodied in the makeup of the seventy nations. (The term "seventy nations" comes from the number of nations enumerated in Genesis 10.) One who distances himself from the spiritual light of Torah allows the negative characteristics of the nations to take root in himself and manifest themselves in wicked or immoral behavior.

Furthermore, just as the seventy souls of Israel are rooted in Jacob, the seventy nations are rooted in Esau and Ishmael. The liver, as the organ that represents gross materialism, has a total of seventy major blood vessels, which correspond to the negative influences of the "seventy nations." The liver itself corresponds to Esau, while its lobes correspond to Ishmael (*Tikkuney Zohar* #21, p.52a). Thus, a person can choose Torah and connect himself to the source of Jacob, or he can seek materialism and connect himself to the evil sources of Esau and Ishmael.

*

Anger and Pride: The Element of Fire

Throughout our Holy Writings, it would be impossible to find an organ so disparaged as the liver. The Zohar compares the liver to "Esau, the Red One" (Genesis 25:30; *Tikkuney Zohar* #21, p.52a) who, until he purifies himself and returns to God, embodies the power of evil itself. The liver also corresponds to idolatry, which is akin to haughtiness and arrogance (*ibid.*, p.49a; see also *Sotah* 4b), and corresponds to the fire of Gehennom (*Tikkuney Zohar, ibid.*, p.69b) — anger and rage.

Of the four elements, fire is hot and dry, and is the lightest in its physical makeup [the properties of heat cause it to rise]. In the personality, the element of fire is thus the source of pride, of one who thinks of himself as being "above" others. A by-product of the fire of pride is anger. Because of haughtiness, a person is quick to anger when his desires are not satisfied as he wishes. A humble person is more capable of exercising restraint. Therefore haughtiness and anger stand together as two of man's worst characteristics. They also lead to irritability and to the desire for power and honor. Thus, arrogance and anger lead to hatred for those whose status is higher than one's own (*Sha'arey Kedushah* 1:2).

Anger, pride, irritability and hatred need no commentary. Everyone acknowledges that these traits are despicable. Nevertheless, they are disproportionately prevalent throughout society. It is thus appropriate at this point to cite some of Rebbe Nachman's teachings on the gravity of these characteristics, and on how to control and influence the liver and gallbladder in a positive manner, in order to overcome their negative effects.

*

Pride and Humility

- Pride brings about poverty (*Advice*, p.55, #3).
- Eating and drinking produce haughtiness (*The Aleph-Bet Book, Haughtiness* A:16).
- Haughtiness is tantamount to idolatry. Through a close association with the tzaddik, one can overcome haughtiness (*Likutey Moharan* I, 10:5).

- Many individuals pose as humble people, for they realize that arrogance is a despicable trait. Therefore, they put on airs as if they were modest and unwilling to accept honor, though they actually crave respect from others and chase after honor. This false humility, which is in fact arrogance, is idolatry. This chasing after honor is the reason the exile has not ended (*Likutey Moharan* I, 11:8).

- Arrogance and sexual immorality are linked (*Advice*, p.56, #10).

- Haughtiness leads to homosexuality and anger (*The Aleph-Bet Book, Haughtiness* A:2).

- Intelligence, power and material possessions are the three main factors over which one becomes haughty (*Advice*, p.57, #13).

- A haughty man is a deformed person (*The Aleph-Bet Book, Haughtiness* A:23).

- Arrogance begets troubles (*Advice* p.58, #25). When things seem to go counter to one's will, it is a sign of arrogance (*Likutey Moharan* II, 82).

- The Torah (i.e., spirituality) can find a place only within a humble person (*Likutey Moharan* I, 14:5).

- Faith engenders humility (*The Aleph-Bet Book, Humility* A:3).

- Humility leads to repentance (*Advice* p.55, #4).

- Experiencing Shabbat and celebrating the Festivals with joy cultivates humility (*Advice*, p.58, #18, 22).

- True humility does not mean to be slovenly or to act as if one is worthless. One should be aware of one's full worth, yet still act in a humble manner (*Likutey Moharan* II, 72).

- Humility eliminates dispute and suffering and brings one life (*The Aleph-Bet Book, Humility* A:7, 12).

- The indescribable bliss of the eternal life of the World to Come can be experienced only to the extent that one has attained humility in this world (*Likutey Moharan* II, 72).

*

Anger and Irritability

- Anger is rooted in the liver, which is full of blood. This corresponds to Esau, who was born with a ruddy complexion. Since Esau represents anger, his power extends over all those who allow themselves to become enraged (*Likutey Moharan* I, 57:6).

- When a person gives in to anger, it provokes the great accuser, Esau (i.e., the Evil One). The "accusations" of Esau are the obstacles, hindrances and enemies that one faces during one's lifetime. They literally take charge of the furious man. His rage puts his wisdom to flight, and the image of God disappears from his face (*Likutey Moharan* I, 57:6).

- Anger causes one to tear his soul apart! (*Likutey Moharan* I, 68).

- Anger causes one to have foolish children and shortens one's life (*The Aleph-Bet Book, Anger* A:24,25).

- Anger brings disgrace; the angry person humiliates himself (*The Aleph-Bet Book, Anger* A:3,16).

- Anger [in Hebrew, *ChaiMaH*, חמה] causes a person to lose his money. Wealth is called a protective wall, *ChoMaH* in Hebrew [חומה]. When one becomes angry, he turns the *chomah* into *chaimah*, and so loses his wealth (*Likutey Moharan* I, 68).

- Anger leads to depression (*The Aleph-Bet Book, Anger* A:34).

- Anger causes a person to lose his wisdom and foresight (*The Aleph-Bet Book, Anger* A:5).

- Patience and restraining one's anger brings one wealth (*Likutey Moharan* I, 68).

- Break the force of anger with love by restraining yourself and by acting with kindness. Then you can understand the true goals to which you should aspire (*Likutey Moharan* I, 18:2).

- Anger and unkindness arise when people's understanding is limited. The deeper their understanding, the more their anger disappears and kindness, love and peace spread. Torah study gives one the ability to attain a deep understanding (*Advice*, p.128).

- The sanctity of the Land of Israel is beneficial to help a person break his anger (*Likutey Moharan* I, 155).

- By breaking and overcoming your anger, you draw the spirit of the Messiah into the world. You also become worthy of rich blessings and of gaining people's respect and admiration. When you overcome your anger, you will succeed in reaching your goals (*Likutey Moharan* I, 66:3).

*

Love and Hate

- Unwarranted hatred causes a person to eat nonkosher food (*The Aleph-Bet Book, Love* B:4). [This "feeds" the liver, the source of anger and hatred, causing further hatred.]

- Turmoil is a sign of hatred (*Likutey Moharan* I, 17:5).

- Dialogue comes with peace. Strife causes open relationships to be curtailed (*Likutey Moharan* I, 239).

- A person's lust for food causes him to favor one of his children over the others (*The Aleph-Bet Book, Love* B:5).

- Eating on Shabbat brings love and peace (*The Aleph-Bet Book, Love* A:6).

- Love and kindness are synonymous (*Likutey Moharan* I, 31:6).

- Love leads to encouragement (*The Aleph-Bet Book, Love* A:6).

- Love brings joy (*Likutey Moharan* I, 61:8).

*

Rebbe Nachman taught:

When a person eats, the liver is nourished first. It then transfers nutrients into the body, which eventually reach the brain. When one fasts, the liver is bypassed, for the brain must draw on nutrients already present in the body, and the liver is left without fresh nutrients. Thus, through fasting, the liver is made subordinate to the brain.

There are two types of peace. One is a cease-fire; the other a peaceful dialogue. Fasting represents a cease-fire [the temporary subduing of one's enemies, of the powers of "Esau," found in the liver; it is not a permanent peace]. Conversely, Shabbat, when we are required to eat, stands for a more permanent peace — a peaceful dialogue between conflicting forces, wherein one *can* eat without being subjected to Esau's influence. On Shabbat, the mind reigns supreme (*Likutey Moharan* I, 57:7–8).

As discussed above (Chapter 11), eating in the "spirit of Shabbat" can elevate a person's spiritual perspectives. Through the very physical act of eating, one can ascend above the physical of which one partakes! This is because *ShaBbaT* (שבת) is like *SheVeT*

(שבת), "sitting calmly and peacefully." Eating, which can lead to calmness, such as when one eats a leisurely Shabbat meal with one's family, can subdue one's enemies and bring peace.

*

The Gallbladder

Most people will (or should) admit that their suffering is brought about by their own actions. If a person is not careful with his health, he will bring illness upon himself. If he acts irresponsibly with money, he will bring financial ruin upon himself. Family strife is usually the result of a "minor" slip of the tongue. The list is endless.

Rebbe Nachman once said, "If you are not willing to suffer a little, you will suffer a lot!" (oral tradition). It is indeed painful to realize and come to terms with one's errors, but this is the first step towards rectifying them. By ignoring one's mistakes, not only is the pain not avoided, but one inevitably ends up making more of the same, causing even greater suffering.

A Little Bitter(ness)...

Rebbe Nachman taught:

> The soul always seeks to perform the will of its Maker. However, when it sees that the body that houses it does not serve God, it seeks to leave that body and return to its Maker, bringing illness to the body. Medicines can lead a person back to health. Illness comes about because the person has become accustomed to indulging his lusts. When he is sick, he loses his appetite for food in general and is forced to swallow all kinds of medications and bitter pills in order to get better. In this way [quite unintentionally, to be sure], he shows that he is perfectly capable of controlling his desires for the sake of a purpose he understands. As a result, his soul returns to him in the hope that he will accept the "bitterness" necessary to return to a spiritual path as well (Likutey Moharan I, 268).

The bile stored in the gallbladder is extremely bitter, yet

this very bitterness is one of the most significant "sweeteners" found in the body. Produced in the liver, bile neutralizes acidity and breaks down fats. After performing its task, some of its fluid returns to its source, "pacifying and cooling down" the liver from its intense work of cleansing the blood. This is alluded to in our Sages' statement cited above (*Berakhot* 61b): "The liver becomes angry; the gallbladder emits fluids to pacify that anger." Thus, from the very stuff of which our anger is made, a pacifier is created to placate that anger. Likewise, from within our suffering, our acknowledgment of our error brings about rectification.

...And Peace

Rebbe Nachman taught:

> Peace is the universal healer, as it is written (Isaiah 57:19), "'Peace to the one who is far and peace to the one who is near,' says God, 'and I will heal him.'" When a person is ill, it is usually because his body's systems are not functioning in harmony — his four humors or elements are somehow in conflict. He requires medicines which will restore balance and allow healing to take place. Interestingly, medicines are generally very bitter. Yet people are willing to endure a little bitterness in order to be healed — in order to attain inner peace.
>
> The same is true of spiritual healing. A person might have to endure a certain amount of suffering — and it might be bitter indeed — but then he realizes that this suffering stems from his own spiritual inadequacies; he himself is the source of his own bitterness. Recognizing his faults, he is led to improve himself. The bitterness itself thus turns into the healing power, bringing him ever closer to spiritual peace (*Likutey Moharan* I, 27:7).

*

The Spleen

The functions of the spleen include maintaining blood volume, production of some types of blood cells and the recovery of material from worn-out blood cells (filtering impurities from the blood). As such, its energy is focused on the impurities found in the body, and it wages a constant battle to weed out excesses from the system. The more excesses there are in the body, the harder the spleen must work.

The spleen has traditionally been associated with melancholy. The connection is clear: the spleen represents the "black bile," and melancholy depression is attributed to an excess of "black bile." Thus the spleen, working on a steady basis with superfluous matter, has a very "depressing" job indeed.

*

The Seat of Depression

Rebbe Nachman taught:

> Melancholy is associated with the spleen. The spleen can filter only a limited quantity of blood at any given time, and this activity is very beneficial to one's health. However, when an unreasonable amount of excesses exist within one's system, the spleen cannot filter them properly. These excesses induce sadness and depression [which themselves pollute the blood further, leading to illness] (*Likutey Moharan* II, 6).

The spleen, called *t'chol* in Hebrew, is considered "cold and dry," as is the element of earth (*chol* in Hebrew means sand), the lowest and densest of the four elements. As the lowest and heaviest of the four elements, earth corresponds to depression. The sadder one is, the more one's personality is dominated by the inner inertia which is rooted in the element of earth. This leads to laziness and indifference, which brings with it greater depression and lethargy. The polluted blood which the spleen purifies is likewise sluggish in nature (see *Tikkuney Zohar* #70, p.134). Furthermore, Rebbe Nachman taught that the main "bite of the Serpent" is sadness and sluggishness. This is because the Serpent was cursed with (Isaiah 65:25), "Dust shall be the Serpent's food." The element of dust represents sluggishness and sadness, both of which stem from the element of earth (*Likutey Moharan* I, 189).

For the same reason, Rebbe Nachman cautioned against spiritual excesses (i.e., stringencies) in one's search for spirituality. The verse states (Leviticus 18:5), "You shall live by them." "You shall *live* — and not die — by them" (see *Yoma* 85b). People who are always seeking stringencies because they are never confident about their accomplishments in their spiritual devotions are generally very depressed. Overstringency in lifestyle, in devotion, and indeed in all areas of life, leads to depression (*Rabbi Nachman's Wisdom* #235). This is seen in the word *ChuMRot* (stringencies) which is similar to *ChoMeR* (matter, as opposed to spirituality). Thus these stringencies will have the opposite effect than intended, for depression is an obstacle to achieving spiritual greatness.

*

Avarice: Obsession and Jealousy

Nowhere does depression manifest itself so powerfully as in the pursuit of wealth. In one of his major lessons, Rebbe Nachman speaks about the connection between avarice and depression. Rebbe Nachman taught:

The face of sanctity is the shining face, representing life and joy. The face of unholiness is the darkened face, representing melancholy and idolatry.

There are those who are overcome with a desire for wealth but refuse to believe that God can provide for them with a minimum of effort on their part. These people invest all their efforts in the chase after fortune, but, having accumulated vast wealth, it gives them no pleasure, as in (Genesis 3:17), "With sadness shall you eat." They are afflicted by the forces of evil, of idolatry and death (*Likutey Moharan* I, 23:1).

On the other hand, Reb Noson writes that faith corresponds to the earth, as the verse states (Psalms 37:3), "Dwell in the land [i.e., earth] and cultivate faith." This can be understood in light of the fact that just as man stands upon and is dependent upon the earth, so too, his spirituality is dependent on his faith. Thus, just as the pursuit of wealth corresponds to a lack of faith in God's ability to provide, having faith in God that He *can* provide will elevate one from "material earth" to a spiritual plane (see *Likutey Tefilot* I, #128).

*

The Spleen Laughs

Rebbe Nachman devotes the greater part of the lesson cited above to bring additional supports for this teaching, pointing out several actions that can lead one to avarice, such as the blemishing of one's Covenant, speaking falsehood and so on. Afterwards, he introduces the spleen as playing a major role in this lust for wealth.

The spleen represents Lilith, the "wife" of Satan, the Angel of Death. She is the "mother" of the mixed multitude (cf. Exodus 12:38), the levity of the fool. She teases people with wealth and then kills them (*Tikkuney Zohar*, p.140a).

When Adam ate from the Tree of Knowledge of Good and Evil, he was cursed, "With sadness shall you eat." The Serpent, too, was cursed (Genesis 3:14): "Dust you shall eat all the days of your life." "Dust" corresponds to money, as in (Job 28:6), "Its dust is gold." Rebbe Nachman explains: When someone becomes obsessed with wealth and spends "all the days of his life" seeking it, his curse is identical to that of the Serpent; that is, the pursuit of wealth actually "eats up" the days of his life! He spends his life seeking wealth (i.e., dust). Such a person truly eats with sadness and melancholy (see *Likutey Moharan* I, 23:6).

As we have pointed out, the spleen corresponds to melancholy. Melancholy is an abnormal state attributed to an excess of "black bile." It is characterized by depression, grouchiness and delusions — perhaps man's greatest enemies. People who make the pursuit of wealth their sole enterprise in life often have grandiose aspirations. As they are never content with their possessions, they experience constant depression and sadness, and they tend to be irascible.

Rebbe Nachman continues by explaining what the Zohar means by representing the spleen as "Lilith, the 'mother' of the mixed multitude, the levity of the fool, who teases people with wealth and then kills them." The mixed multitude did not seek spirituality. Rather, they were impressed by the Jews' newfound greatness, but were still too steeped in materialism to appreciate the significance of that greatness. They left Egypt with the Children of Israel but elected to worship (money and) the Golden Calf while in the desert. This was idolatry, "the levity of the fool," for "she teased them," offering them wealth as a replacement for true spirituality. This is what is meant by, "She teases people with wealth and then kills them." The spleen, which corresponds to avarice and depression, represents "Lilith." She teases people throughout their lives, for they are always thinking that "now" they will profit, and "now" they will make money, but in fact they "eat dust all the days of their lives." Their avarice leaves them empty, characterized by melancholy.

Interestingly, she is called "LiYLith" (לילית), because in Hebrew the word for wailing is *YeLaLah* (יללה) (*Likutey Moharan* I, 205). Those who are plagued by the trait of avarice are constantly wailing and complaining about how hard they work and what they are lacking.

A natural consequence of avarice is envy — coveting the possessions of others. "The truth is," says Rebbe Nachman, "a man is sometimes given great wealth. Everyone else envies him, and they spend their lives pursuing wealth because of this envy. This is all the work of the Evil One; he works hard to make one man rich so that many others will waste their lives envying him. May God save us from this misleading notion" (*Rabbi Nachman's Wisdom* #284).

Furthermore, "levity is associated with the spleen" (*Likutey Moharan* II, 83:6). This is the meaning of, "She is the levity of the fool." Avarice makes fools of people who hope to strike it rich. Instead of becoming wealthy, they spend their lives pursuing wealth. More often than not, they end up barely solvent and often deeply in debt. Where, then, is the wealth that was sought "all the days of their lives?" (*Likutey Moharan* I, 23:5). This is what our Sages meant when they said, "The spleen laughs" (*Berakhot* 61b).

*

When used correctly, wealth is a powerful medium for attaining spirituality. Rebbe Nachman teaches that there are certain paths of Torah that are unattainable except through great wealth, which is why Moses, and many of the prophets and tzaddikim who followed after him, were extremely wealthy. That wealth was necessary for them to achieve the great spiritual revelations they experienced, and afterwards to communicate those revelations to others (see *Likutey Moharan* I, 60:1).

Yet Rebbe Nachman also said that the *desire* to amass wealth and gain power is the major lust of our times. Even low-level administrators exult in their authority (*Tzaddik* #470). All this is the work of Lilith, the spleen. "She teases people with wealth [i.e., power]," but then, having developed within them an obsession with wealth and power, "she kills them." An entire lifetime may be spent pursuing wealth and never finding it, and, far from a pleasurable exercise, this search may cause one's entire lifetime to be dominated by feelings of moroseness and deep depression. But the Rebbe also teaches that joy generates the vitality of life, so that one who falls into depression can counter its negative effects by bringing himself — and even forcing himself — to joy (*Likutey Moharan* I, 56:9).

* * *

12

Purifying Body and Soul

One of the most essential steps in the purification process is the removal of waste matter from the body. There are five basic systems which accomplish this task: sweat exits through the skin; the lungs filter out carbon dioxide; the liver, gallbladder and spleen process nutrients and filter the blood; the kidneys filter and excrete fluids; and the large intestine excretes solid waste matter.

Obviously, just as physical waste products must be removed from the body, so must spiritual excess. While physical waste is eliminated automatically through the bodily functions, a great deal of effort is required to remove spiritual waste. Just as our bodies were endowed with the means for purifying themselves, so are we provided by God with all the tools necessary to cleanse ourselves spiritually. The difference is that the desire to use these tools must be present in order for our efforts to be successful.

Blood, Sweat...
Rebbe Nachman taught:

> Sweating is extremely beneficial, because it rids the body of polluted fluids. These pollutants result from the spleen's inability to filter all the fluids which pass through it. Polluted fluids in the body cause depression; therefore sweating — i.e., removing the pollution which leads to depression — brings joy
> (*Likutey Moharan* II, 6).

Rebbe Nachman belonged to the school of thought which extolled hard work. He repeatedly told his followers that nothing of value can be attained except through the efforts one puts into one's devotions (see *Rabbi Nachman's Wisdom* #165–170).

A person can break out in sweat through hard work; or he can sweat by "breaking out in joy." One's efforts can bring about a physical purification by removing the excesses from the body. Spiritual efforts expended to arouse joy can be beneficial to the body as well. Thus Rebbe Nachman concludes the above lesson:

> "Good sweat," which results from expending effort in the search for spirituality [through performing mitzvot, for example] brings joy. A day on which one sweats for good reasons is a day to rejoice; it is like a Festival. The Hebrew word for sweat is *ZeYAH*, which is the acrostic of (Psalms 118:24), *"Zeh Hayom Asah YHVH...* — This is the day that God has made [i.e., a Festival]; let us be glad and rejoice in it" (*Likutey Moharan* II, 6).

Breaking out in a sweat for the sake of spirituality warrants a festival!

To illustrate the benefits of hard work and sweat as a means to cleanse the body, Dr. Riphael (Robert) Rosen, who was director of the Midwest Dialysis Center in Duncan, Oklahoma, related the following story: One patient, a cowboy, informed the Center that he was going away for ten days to round up wild horses. He was advised not to take the trip, as he required dialysis three times a week, for his kidneys did not work at all. He went anyway. Upon his return, he looked good, felt good, had not gained any fluid weight and his blood tests were only slightly worse than usual. In Dr. Rosen's words, "We then saw the benefit of hard work and sweating — to the extent that it replaced his dialysis treatment!"

(We do not suggest that any person who requires dialysis opt for this method of ridding the body of waste matter. We merely point out the benefits of hard work and sweat for one's good health.)

Rebbe Nachman also teaches that regular bathing and immersing in the mikveh (ritual bath) are beneficial for opening the pores (*Likutey Moharan* II, 123). Opening the pores allows for cleansing one's body of excess fluids and poisons.

*

...And Tears

Rebbe Nachman taught:

> Tears come from melancholy, which results from one's excesses (*Likutey Moharan* I, 51:1).

It is human nature to cry when one is depressed and suffering. As we have seen (previous chapter), depression is associated with excesses in the body. Tears, then, are also "excess" and serve as filters to rid the body of superfluous fluids and poisons.

Rebbe Nachman also taught:

> The spleen corresponds to depression, which is one of the major causes of immorality. Lilith is the "mother of the mixed multitude." She corresponds to a harlot, one who is promiscuous and begets "mixed children." She is also compared to the "maidservant" who should be subjugated to her matron. So too, the forces of materialism should remain under the dominion of the Kingdom of Heaven, the force of spirituality. It is for this reason that reciting the *Shema* — accepting the yoke of Heaven upon oneself — helps a person to take control of his materialistic tendencies and to overcome his lustful desires.
>
> However, if one is subjected to many lustful thoughts, merely *reciting* the *Shema* is insufficient. One must also shed tears while accepting the yoke of Heaven, because tears are excess fluids in the body. In shedding tears, one in effect removes the waste matter that exudes from the spleen — one's melancholy. Thus, shedding tears for the sake of spirituality counters the effects of moroseness (*Likutey Moharan* I, 36:3–4).

*

Esau vs. Leah

On a spiritual level, there are two types of tears. One is like the tears of Esau, who cried bitterly in his desire to experience all the lusts of this world (Genesis 27:38). The second is like the tears of Leah, who cried in her pleadings that she not fall to Esau's lot and be forced to marry him (Genesis 29:17; Rashi, *loc. cit.*; *Likutey Halakhot, Shluchin* 3, p.201b).

Reb Noson writes:

A person must see to it that he rids himself of his lusts, the excesses of his system. If he does not, these excesses remain in his body, poisoning it. Superfluous fluids, which represent depression and give rise to bad character traits, correspond to Esau and Ishmael, the forces of evil (see previous chapter, "The Liver"). When these impurities are not filtered, they can continue coursing through the body and will eventually affect the mind, convincing one of the "necessity" of lusts, God forbid.

Esau and Ishmael represent the alien philosophies that steer a person away from the path of righteousness. This is compared to the Tree of Knowledge of Good and Evil. Adam and Eve were commanded not to eat from that Tree. The Serpent, knowing this, began to rationalize with them: "If you eat you will be God-like...," and so on. In the end, they succumbed to the Serpent's rationalization and ate from the Tree. Thus, it was excessive thinking and rationalization that brought Adam to sin. Similar rationalizations cause extensive damage to one's ability to distinguish between what is proper and what is improper.

Crying, the shedding of tears for spirituality, removes excesses from the body. Crying, begging and pleading to God in prayer to help one grow spiritually help to filter the impure excesses, the "Esau and Ishmael," from one's system (*Likutey Halakhot, Yom Kippur* 2:4).

*

The Kidneys

The kidneys contain thousands of tiny filtering units which process fluids and waste matter and pass them on to their intended destinations, either recycling them back into the body or excreting them to be eliminated from the body. The kidneys also control the level of salt and other essential minerals in the body. It is significant that each person has a right and a left kidney. Medical science does not explain why there is a need for a *pair* of kidneys, since a person can live with only one. But spiritually, it makes all the sense in the world.

The Talmud teaches (*Berakhot* 61a), "The kidneys advise." Rashi explains that this idea stems from the verse (Psalms 16:7), "I will bless God Who counsels me; even at night my kidneys admonish me." The Maharsha comments that the pair of kidneys indicates man's free will, his ability to choose right from wrong. It is also noted (*Chidushei HaGeonim, loc. cit.*) that the main physical activity of the kidneys, the processing and purifying of poisons and waste materials in the body, occurs at night, when a person rests. (When a person lies down with his legs up, there is an increase in the flow of blood to the kidneys, hence an increase in the amount of purification of that blood by the kidneys.) This is alluded to in the words "even at *night* my kidneys admonish me." The verse also indicates that the spiritual activity of the kidneys follows the pattern of the physical.

Both good and evil can at times *seem* to be the proper choice. Conceptually, the kidneys show us that there is a right and left side, representing right and wrong; and they admonish us "at night" (when it is dark and we are most prone to sin), so that at the most crucial times we can best choose that which is right. Just as the kidneys recycle the usable and excrete the waste, so too must we choose what is good and make use of it, while rejecting evil. Thus (*Berakhot* 61a), "The kidneys advise and the heart understands." A prime example of this is the teaching of our Sages (*Bereishit Rabbah* 61:1): "Abraham had no teacher. How, then, did he study Torah? God caused his kidneys to act as two fountains of wisdom, and they taught him Torah and wisdom." They acted as *two* fountains: one to teach Abraham the positive commandments and how to perform them, and the other to steer him clear of transgressing the prohibitive commandments. Our Sages thus teach (*Kiddushin* 82a), "Abraham fulfilled the entire Torah even before it was given!"

*

The Tree of Knowledge

We have seen (Chapter 6) that the Tree of Knowledge of Good and Evil corresponds to advice. Through our study of the kidneys we now see that the human body contains its own "Tree of Knowledge of Good and Evil," with the ability to distinguish good from evil, right from wrong. The clarity of the choices one is able to make depends upon what one feeds these filters. Will one allow oneself to be fed the fruits of the Tree of Knowledge of Good and Evil by the Serpent, or will one seek the path of spirituality and gain nourishment from a true tzaddik?

Rebbe Nachman taught:

> The kidneys advise. The kidneys also participate in the reproductive system [through the adrenal glands, which are intimately associated with the kidneys]. Receiving advice from someone else is like receiving "seed" from him. This advice can then "give birth" to choices and actions. It is thus crucial to receive only good, valid advice from those capable of giving advice — from the true tzaddikim. The mind of the tzaddik is pure, so his advice is correct (*Likutey Moharan* I, 7:3).

The reproductive organs (i.e., the "advice" of the kidneys) can be seen as the "parts of the body that give birth to new ideas." It is important to understand that if a person's mind is in some way blemished, he will be unable to determine whether the advice he receives or chooses is proper and worthy. Rebbe Nachman therefore suggests that one seek advice only from a tzaddik. In this way he won't need to rely solely on his own "filtering system," which may or may not be functioning properly.

The Rebbe's equating of reproduction with the giving of advice has even greater implications. A child is not born a polished diamond. Many, many years of intense effort must go into raising and teaching a child, and only after the child reaches maturity do we begin to see the real fruits of our labors. Even then, we can only hope and pray that the child will continue to develop along the proper path. Giving or receiving advice works in much the same way. If you seek advice, you cannot know what the results of following that advice will be. You can only hope that you have chosen a good advisor, one whose advice will bring satisfaction and stability in the future.

Many people consider themselves capable of advising others — and even themselves — but can they really see "beyond the horizon?" Just as a tree requires many years of nurturing for it to bear fruit, so following the advice of the tzaddikim on how to attain a spiritual life requires years of effort before one will see truly satisfactory results. Just as childbirth doesn't produce a mature individual immediately, the advice of tzaddikim must be absorbed, contemplated and acted upon judiciously over time, according to each individual's ability. It requires much patience, filtering through the system time and time again, until one has purified oneself. Only then can one begin to truly experience a spiritual life.

*

The "End" Result

> This is their *kesel* — their foolish way; they speak soothingly about their end.
>
> Psalms 49:14

This chapter in Psalms speaks about how people do not acknowledge death as being applicable to them. They think of themselves as immortal, even while acknowledging that no man lives forever. Instead of preparing themselves with spiritual provisions to accompany them on their long path, people too often occupy themselves with purely material pursuits. Concerning this, Reb Noson writes:

> Although the Red Heifer was made to purify those who were impure, interestingly, it was not a devotion that was performed within the confines of the Holy Temple. In fact, everything done in connection with the Red Heifer had to be performed only outside the Temple walls! (see Numbers 19).
>
> One might think that exactly the opposite should be true: If the

service performed with the Red Heifer achieves purification for even the most impure person, shouldn't it be a requirement that each of the steps of its preparation be performed in a holy place? Yet this is precisely why it must be done *outside* the holiest confines: conceptually, the Red Heifer stands for extremely deep advice — how to reach out to those who seem utterly estranged from spirituality and extend to them a helping hand. Even in those places most distant from holiness, one can still grasp the vain hollowness of a materialistic life and begin to search for spirituality.

The truth is that this materialistic world is all vanity — a passing shadow — and life is so fleeting, because materialism seems so attractive that people tend to overlook its more dangerous implications. They may lose track of the good advice available to them and instead pursue the material. "What can we do?" they say. "We are already so entrenched in physicality."

This is the meaning of the verse, "This is their *kesel* — their foolish way; they speak soothingly about their end." Rashi explains (*loc. cit.*), "You might think that they forget their mortality. Yet the verse states, 'They speak soothingly about their *end.*' But it is their *kesel*, their foolishness, which causes them to disregard their end."

The Hebrew word for *kesel* translates as both "folly" and "flanks" (the fats covering the kidneys). If misguided individuals would but heed the advice of their kidneys regarding how to purify their systems, they would certainly grow spiritually. But there are "fats" that cover and conceal the kidneys. These are the lures of the materialistic world that camouflage man's true objective.

Thus, the purpose of the service performed with the Red Heifer is to demonstrate that even "outside" — in the most remote places, farthest from spirituality — Moses, embodied within the true tzaddik, is ready with advice to assist those who desire to overcome their material surroundings. Even there, he illuminates the darkest surroundings with true advice, enabling a person to draw near to God (*Likutey Halakhot, Shechitah* 5:19).

*

Trust

> You desire truth in my kidneys [*batuchot*], and teach me wisdom in my heart.
>
> Psalms 51:8
>
> For me to gain truth so that my kidneys advise me properly, You must place wisdom within me.
>
> Metzudat David, ad. loc.

Bitachon in Hebrew means trust. Having *bitachon* in God, trusting that He supplies man with his needs, is a very high level indeed. The kidneys in Hebrew are called *BaTuChot*, which is similar to *BiTaChon*, "trust."

Rebbe Nachman taught:

All bounty comes when one trusts in God. Hearing stories and teachings from the true tzaddikim arouses a person from his spiritual slumber. That person can then express himself fervently before God. His words help strengthen his faith and trust in God, which brings greater bounty to the world. But there exist false and misplaced trusts, of which one must beware. Building trust in God helps to eliminate the false trusts, bringing about prosperity (*Likutey Moharan* I, 60:8).

When a person works diligently to attain a spiritual lifestyle, then his kidneys, i.e., the advice he chooses, will direct him to continually place more of his trust in God. God, in turn, will place His wisdom within that person, so that he will find himself directed even more towards spirituality. Since turning to God is the main reason for the creation of man, when man does turn to God He provides bounty so that man can continue his spiritual ascent.

* * *

13

In Review

In this section, we have seen the negative influences that man's baser instincts can have upon his soul, along with several ways to counter them. We have also examined the four humors, three of the four basic elements — fire, water and earth — and some of their effects upon the emotions. (The element of air will be explored below in our discussion of speech, in Part 6.)

The internal system of a human being seems to be designed to nurture his negative characteristics. The digestive system *seems* to be designed to steer a person towards materialism. The very veins through which impure blood and excess desires flow spearhead man's immoral drives and emotional instability. This explains why man's physical and emotional attraction to materialism begins very early in life, in fact from birth. As our Sages teach (*Sanhedrin* 91b), "The evil inclination begins its work as soon as the infant is born!"

But this does not imply that man is without resources, nor that he cannot wage battle against these evil characteristics. For (Ecclesiastes 7:14) "God made one against the other." Thus, the "law of parallelism" dictates that man has free will to choose the path he wishes to follow (as shown by the kidneys). Hence, if God designed man to have evil inclinations, He also provided the tools with which man can overcome that evil, for, as we have seen, those very internal systems which tend to lead us away from spirituality contain the necessary elements which can guide us towards a spiritual existence.

In the next section, we will begin to examine the vast array of powerful forces that God provided to help man counter — and ascend above — his negative desires.

* * *

Part Four

The Central Nervous System

The Head and the Brain

14

Introduction

The brain is by far the most complex organ in the human body. Together with the spinal cord, the thick cord of nervous tissue which extends from the brain, it makes up the central nervous system. It is made up of a mass of soft tissue, referred to colloquially as "gray matter" (though it contains both gray and white matter), and as the director of the nervous system, it is the organ which accommodates thought and neural coordination. With its tens of billions of cells, the brain receives and delivers millions of messages per minute from the entire body and from its surrounding environment; for instance, it controls the heart and respiration rate and maintains the body's chemical balance, while it also responds to the various stimuli around us. (The peripheral nervous system, which includes the organs of sight, sound, smell, taste and touch, will be discussed below in Part 7.)

The brain functions much like the central processing unit of a super-computer. It constantly receives information from, and coordinates activity between, all the various organs and receptors, and it stores this information in its memory bank. The brain also acts as a command post, ensuring the overall synergy of the organism. In short, everything that happens in the body has at some point been processed through this gray matter called the brain. Rebbe Nachman thus taught, "The mind is the commander-in-chief of the body" (*Likutey Moharan* I, 29:7).

The brain has three major sections — the cerebrum, the cerebellum and the brain stem (midbrain/medulla oblongata).

Each of these sections has different yet closely coordinated functions. The cerebrum is the seat of the intellect, the cerebellum coordinates the body's movements, and the brain stem (consisting of the medulla, pons, midbrain and hypothalamus) transmits impulses throughout the entire nervous system. These three fundamental areas of the brain act as the vehicles of their corresponding *mochin*, the spiritual powers of intellect: the cerebrum is the seat of Chokhmah (Wisdom); the cerebellum is the seat of Binah (Understanding); and the brain stem is the seat of Daat (Knowledge). The cranium, which houses the *mochin*, corresponds to Keter (Crown).

*

The Central Nervous System

The cerebrum is the largest part of the brain, taking up most of the area inside the cranium or skull, which encases and surrounds the brain. The cerebrum acts as the center of intellect, memory, language and consciousness. It receives and interprets the information transmitted from the senses and controls the motor functions of the body. The cerebrum is divided into two parts, known as the right and left hemispheres. The right hemisphere is associated with the nonverbal, nontemporal, relational, intuitive and holistic abilities of the brain. The left hemisphere is associated with the verbal, temporal, analytical, rational, logical and linear abilities of the brain.

The cerebellum is the second largest part of the brain. It lies just beneath the cerebrum towards the back of the cranium, adjacent to the brain stem. The cerebellum is responsible for posture, muscle coordination and tone, and equilibrium.

The brain stem sits near the center of the brain and extends downward to the pons and medulla oblongata where it connects to the spinal cord. It consists mainly of the nerve tracts passing through the spinal cord to the brain, thus serving as the conduit for transmitting messages between the brain and the body through the nervous system. It also controls and regulates many automatic and involuntary functions of the body.

The spinal cord is made up of nerve tissue which passes through the spinal column or backbone. Thirty-one pairs of spinal nerves link the brain to the spinal cord and the spinal cord to the muscles, sensory system and other parts of the body. They, together with twelve pairs of cranial nerves (so called because they link directly with the brain), control voluntary movements and sensations in the body. The nerves of the autonomic nervous system, which controls and regulates involuntary motor functions, such as those of the heart, lungs, intestines and blood vessels, also originate here.

*

The *Mochin*: A Kabbalistic Overview

Throughout the Bible and Talmudic and Kabbalistic writings, we find references made to Chokhmah (Wisdom), Binah (or *Tevunah*; Understanding and/or Logic) and Daat (Knowledge). These three form the "Head" of the "*Sefirotic* Tree of Life" and are generally referred to as the *mochin* (intellectual powers). The seven lower *Sefirot* correspond to the "Body" and are referred to as the *midot* (character attributes) through which the *mochin* manifest themselves. (A diagram is provided in Appendix D to help visualize the array of the *Sefirotic* Tree of Life.)

When meditating on the *Sefirot* it is advisable to alternate between visualizing them as a single unified system and considering them as individual powers or groups of powers. As a unified system, the *Sefirot* represent stages of development from an initial impulse or will (Keter) to a final act that accomplishes that will (Malkhut). Keter can be seen as Cause and Malkhut as Effect. All the other *Sefirot* — everything that happens along the way — are stages in the process of bringing the first impulse to its final fulfillment.

The *Sefirotic* Tree of Life is traditionally depicted in three columns: right, left and center (as mentioned above, Chapter 3). On the right, corresponding to the right brain, right arm and right leg respectively, are Chokhmah, Chesed and Netzach. On the left, corresponding to the left brain, left arm and left leg, are Binah, Gevurah and Hod. In the middle, corresponding to the brain stem, spinal column and sexual organs, are Keter, Tiferet, Yesod and Malkhut. (As we shall discuss, the quasi-sefirah of Daat is included among the *Sefirot* only when Keter is not, and vice versa.)

In the Kabbalah, "right" represents the concept of unrestrained and unconditional Mercy, Love and Enlightenment. "Left" represents the concept of restrained or conditional giving (dependent upon the recipient's worthiness or capacity to receive). "Center" represents the optimal synergy of the two polarities. As we have seen above (Chapter 3), the concept of right, left and center is alluded to in the Introduction of the *Tikkuney Zohar* (p.17a), called *Petichat Eliyahu* (Elijah's Discourse), which appears in many Siddurim:

> These Ten *Sefirot* are arranged in a special order of three columns. The right column is said to be "long" [because it represents love and kindness]. The left column is said to be "short" [because it represents judgment and the power of restraint]. The central column or trunk is said to be "intermediate" [because it represents mercy, the perfect harmony of love and restraint]. [In this way, the Ten *Sefirot* serve as conduits through which God regulates His interaction with human beings according to their deeds.] Above all, it is He alone Who directs them. No power directs Him — neither above nor below, nor from any side.

Another way of viewing the *Sefirot* is in groups of triads. Keter, Chokhmah and Binah form the uppermost triad; Chesed, Gevurah and Tiferet form the second, middle triad; Netzach, Hod and Yesod form the third, bottom triad (see Appendix D). With each triad comprising a full complement of right, left and center, each expresses a complete action. The highest triad represents the greatest bestowal of Mercy, irrespective of how much we may deserve it. The central and lower triads reflect progressively stronger consideration of our worthiness, to the point where God may withhold His Mercy if we are not deserving of it.

Of course, withholding is also an expression of love. This principle can be compared to the relationship between parents and their children. A loving parent will not yield to a child's every whim. True love involves the setting of limits, which shows a child that what he does has repercussions. Without clear-cut boundaries, a child cannot be held responsible for his actions; without responsibility, he can never fully mature.

God is the ultimate Parent. He desires nothing more than to bestow His kindnesses on us. He restrains Himself, however, for our own good, until we "grow up." All of this and much more is alluded to in the various combinations and configurations inherent in the *Sefirotic* Tree of Life.

*

(The following material on the *mochin* is based on *Innerspace* [Chapters 4–6], by Rabbi Aryeh Kaplan. With the permission of Moznaim Publishers, we have adapted the ideas found there to accommodate the purposes of this book.)

Keter: The Crown

The word *keter* means "crown." Just as a crown rests atop the head, so too Keter is above all the other *Sefirot*. Thus Keter is often referred to in the Zohar as "*gulgolta*" (cranium). It also corresponds to the spiritual light, or aura, that surrounds our bodies and connects us to our soul's root in the spiritual dimension.

Keter is a code word for God's Will, the ultimate reason and cause for which He brought everything into existence, as well as the final purpose and goal towards which creation is headed. The sole purpose of this world is for man to pursue a spiritual life, to search for Godliness. As we ascend the spiritual ladder, we draw ever closer to God's ultimate Will (see *Likutey Moharan* I, 24).

This is precisely why Keter is associated with the most basic, and the strongest, level of our free will. On the level of Keter, we are compelled neither by internal predisposition nor by external circumstances; our decisions are completely independent of all other considerations. This is because our "will power" emanates from our essence, that part of us which resembles God. When we connect to this deep level of inner volition, we can move mountains, and we have the ability to propel ourselves to the highest spiritual levels. Rebbe Nachman thus taught:

> Who can say, "I am truly serving God!" God is so great and awesome that even the angels cannot comprehend Him. This being the case, to what avail are our devotions? The answer is that one must *desire* to serve God. This desire, this will, is so powerful that it defines the very purpose of creation: that a human being should *want* to serve God (*Rabbi Nachman's Wisdom* #51).

Reb Noson adds: "Even if someone cannot fulfill the mitzvah he seeks to perform, even if his very ability to perform the good deed is taken away from him, no one can control his mind; no one can take away his will. He who takes full advantage of the energy of his own will becomes included in the 'Will of Wills,' the highest of levels, Keter!" (*Likutey Halakhot, Birkhot HaShachar* 5:28).

*

Chokhmah (Wisdom) and Binah (Understanding)

As Keter parallels the skull, Chokhmah and Binah are likened to the two hemispheres of the brain. Together, Chokhmah and Binah are called "the hidden things," because just as a person's thoughts are apparent only through his deeds, so too, the effects of Chokhmah and Binah are visible only when actualized by the lower *Sefirot.*

One of the Biblical sources for Chokhmah and Binah is the verse in Proverbs (3:19), "God founded the earth with *Chokhmah*; He established the heavens with *Binah.*" The Bible here is stating that Chokhmah and Binah are the basic forces which God employed in creating the world. In a divine sense, Chokhmah constitutes the axioms which define the world, while Binah comprises the logical system which connects these axioms. All the laws of nature are essentially axioms, and the simplest axiom contains several levels. For example, the axiom that the shortest distance between two points is a straight line implies that a point exists, straight lines exist, space exists, and so on. These categories all exist in Chokhmah. In Binah, they interplay logically and emerge as a coherent system of laws.

On a human level, Chokhmah is manifest as divine wisdom communicated through prophetic revelation. It denotes the ability to penetrate the superficial layers of reality and perceive the essence of things. This can be seen through the construction of the word "Chokhmah" itself. If we transpose the first two letters, we obtain *Ko'aCH MaH* — literally, "the potential of 'what?'," or the power to question. In this sense, Chokhmah, *Ko'aCH MaH*, refers to the question of what something really is, its essence.

Chokhmah is called "beginning," as in (Psalms 111:10), *"Reishit chokhmah* — The beginning is wisdom."* Paralleling the nonverbal, right hemisphere of the brain, Chokhmah corresponds to the fundamental axioms of cognition that lie behind all our thought processes. These axioms are both built into our minds at birth and integrated into our minds through our life experiences. They form the basis of our capacity to structure and categorize information, and thereby to gain wisdom.

Binah is the ability to deduce additional information from data which has already been received. The Talmud (*Sanhedrin* 93b) defines *BiNah* as "the ability to understand or distinguish one thing from another." It is related to the Hebrew word *BeiN*, meaning "between." In this sense, Binah implies the ability to grasp underlying relationships. Thus, whereas Chokhmah allows us to arrive at the essence of something, Binah enables us to perceive that thing in relation to others. On the level of Chokhmah, all that exists is undifferentiated potential or essence. It is through Binah that the mind differentiates things.

Chokhmah thus represents undifferentiated knowledge, whereas Binah is the source of the ability to analyze this knowledge and to break it down into its component parts. We may draw an analogy to water (Chokhmah) flowing through a system of pipes (Binah). Water itself is an "undifferentiated" fluid, having no essential macroscopic structure. Structure is imposed on it when it flows through the system of pipes.

It should be pointed out that, in general, people tend to oscillate in their applications of Chokhmah and Binah. They do this unconsciously. The Kabbalah's system of thought, however, emphasizes becoming aware of these subtle shifts of consciousness and integrating them so that they function together. This is the meaning of the statement in the *Sefer Yetzirah* ("Book of Formation" 1:4), "Understand with wisdom and be wise with understanding," a meditative directive.

The relationship between Chokhmah and Binah is also expressed in the Kabbalah in terms of male and female. In the formation of a human being, the male supplies the sperm, and the female holds it in her womb for nine months until a fully developed child emerges. In the same way, Chokhmah takes the form of a series of facts which we can put into the "womb" of Binah in order to develop from it an entire logical structure. Thus we see that the creative force of the male can be brought to fruition only when received, channeled and processed within the female "womb." (This is consistent with the relationship we have defined between a *Sefirah* and a *Partzuf* [above, Chapter 3]. We pointed out that the *Sefirah* of Chokhmah corresponds to the *Partzuf* of *Abba* [Father], while that of Binah corresponds to *Imma* [Mother].)

In another sense, Chokhmah alludes to the past, while Binah refers to the future. This is seen in the Hebrew words for "male" and "female." The Hebrew word for "male" is *ZaKHar*, which is composed of the same consonants as *ZoKHeR* (to remember). "Female" in Hebrew is *NeKeVah*, which contains the same consonants as *NiKeV* (pierce; penetrate). Thus the male "remembers" the past, while the female "penetrates" into the future. Both Chokhmah and the past can be explained in terms of "the information we possess." The future, on the other hand, exists only in our imaginative projections, which are a product of Binah. We must therefore employ our Binah in order to "see" it.

*

Daat (Knowledge)

As we have seen, Chokhmah "impregnates" Binah, the "womb," which "stores" the past and "gives birth" to the future. Yet, while we might remember the past and perhaps anticipate the future, it is only the present that we *know*. Daat (Knowledge) is the product of the confluence of Chokhmah and Binah. The present moment, lying at the interchange of the past and the future, corresponds to Daat.

Daat thus represents the idea of the perfect union of opposites. It is for this reason that the Torah uses the term in reference to marital relations, as in the verse (Genesis 4:1), "And Adam *knew* his wife Eve." There is no more intimate relationship than that of a husband and wife — two opposites — *knowing* one another. Through marital relations, a husband and wife become "one flesh" (ibid. 2:24) and can conceive a child who will constitute a tangible unification of their own characteristics. Thus, both the union of husband and wife, and the child born of that union, embody the concept of Daat.

Daat is also a special manifestation of Keter. This is seen in the interesting fact that we almost never find both Keter and Daat together in a representation of the *Sefirotic* array. Whenever Keter is counted among the Ten *Sefirot*, Daat is excluded, and vice versa.

The ARI discusses the mutually exclusive relationship of Keter and Daat in a number of places. Keter and Daat are respectively the internal and external manifestations of the same concept. Keter, as we have seen, is equivalent to our most basic will and inviolable inner volition. Daat, on the other hand, is the level of intellect that we employ to connect with the world.

In relation to Chokhmah and Binah, Daat represents an external manifestation. Chokhmah and Binah are completely internal processes, called the "hidden things," while Daat is the ability to express that inner activity to others. Thus, Chokhmah and Binah, and to a higher degree Keter, are the forces which lie behind the internal thought processes, whereas Daat lies behind one's ability to communicate one's thoughts effectively.

Expressed in terms of human consciousness, we have seen that Chokhmah represents what could be called pure, undifferentiated thought, which has not yet been broken down into differentiated concepts or ideas. At the level of Chokhmah we find the most basic axioms of existence in a kind of pristine unity. Binah is the level which immediately follows Chokhmah. It represents the power of differentiation, the ability to scrutinize and make logical distinctions. In this sense, Binah is the system of logic by which the basic axioms of Chokhmah are delineated and defined. Daat could be called "applied logic," the manifestation of that inner mind.

Thus, Daat is the ability to communicate that which we know. This is seen in the Talmudic definition of one who is deaf and dumb. The Talmud (*Chagigah* 2b) states that "a deaf-mute has no Daat." He may possess the powers of intellect but, as long as he lacks the ability to communicate his knowledge to the world, he is considered to have no Daat. On the other hand, the moment he can communicate, whether through writing or sign language, he is no longer considered a "mute" according to Jewish law. We thus see that the basic ability to communicate and develop an intelligent relationship with the external world is a function of Daat (see *Likutey Moharan* I, 25:1).

Together, Chokhmah, Binah and Daat constitute the basic mental processes that underlie all creative expression. Yet, although they may represent the most abstract levels of mind, they are in fact derivatives of the primal impulse of Will (Keter), which is far more subtle and abstract, and which transcends the axioms and logic of creation. Keter thus contains Chokhmah, Binah and Daat within itself in a transcendent unity. This is expressed in a very powerful *gematria* (numerical equivalent): the total numerical value of *Chokhmah* (חכמה, 73) plus *Binah* (בינה, 67) plus *v'Daat* (ודעת, 480) is 620, which is the exact value of *Keter* (כתר).

*

Creation: The Nerve Center

> God founded the earth with Chokhmah; He established the heavens with Binah; and with Daat He divided the depths.

> Proverbs 3:19–20

In the story of Creation (Genesis 1), we find the Divine Name *Elohim* mentioned thirty-two times. This parallels the Thirty-Two Paths of Wisdom with which God created the world (*Sefer Yetzirah* 1:1). If we were to seek a parallel in the human body, these Thirty-Two Paths of Wisdom would correspond to the nervous system. Thirty-one pairs of spinal nerves link the spinal cord with the muscles, sensory system and other parts of the body. The thirty-second path corresponds to the entire complex of cranial nerves, the highest level of the thirty-two paths.

> [And Esau said:] "How fitting that he was named Jacob! For he has 'outsmarted' me twice. First he took my birthright, and now he has taken my blessing!"

> Genesis 27:36

Based on this verse, Rebbe Nachman teaches that the Patriarch Jacob (*YaAKoV*) parallels the intellect. This is verified in the Aramaic *Targum* (translation) of our verse, in which "He has outsmarted me" — "*vaYaAKVeiny*" — is translated as "*v'ChaKhMeini*" (derived from *ChoKhMah*). As is known, Jacob had twelve sons. Jacob and his sons correspond to the highest path of wisdom: Jacob corresponds to the brain and his twelve sons correspond to the twelve cranial nerves which connect to four of the five senses: sight, sound, smell and taste.

The thirty-one pairs of spinal nerves that extend throughout the body from the spinal cord correspond to the remaining thirty-one paths of wisdom. These nerves accommodate most of the remaining fifth sense, that of touch, which connects the brain to the remainder of the body. The thirty-one spinal nerves thus correspond to Daat, which resides in the brain stem and spreads forth through the spinal cord and nervous system to connect the entire body with the mind. This approach is in harmony with the general principle that whatever is formulated in Chokhmah and Binah is channeled to the lower *Sefirot* through the medium of Daat. Through Daat we integrate the higher levels of consciousness, Chokhmah and Binah, into our every action.

We can thus explain the verse cited above in terms of our understanding of the upper *Sefirot*: "God founded the earth [man] with Chokhmah; He established the heavens with Binah [the integration of Chokhmah]; and with Daat He divided the depths [created a system by which man can gain access to the depths of all of creation and integrate it within his every action]." If we develop our intellect by focusing upon spirituality, we invoke the very powers of Creation!

* * *

15

Faithful Intellect

Chokhmah and Binah are said to correspond to intellect, that which we know and understand. Keter, on the other hand, corresponds to faith — not to a "mindless" faith, but a faith that both includes and transcends intellect.

God's Intellect is Infinite; ours is not. No matter how high we climb on the spiritual ladder, there remain higher levels that we have not even begun to approach. The human intellect can be compared to the mind of a child who is constantly learning — whether through teachers, books or life experiences. As he grows, he comprehends more; at the same time he is empowered by the knowledge he has gained, and impelled to learn even more. Each new discovery opens up vast new horizons. He realizes how much more there is to know than he had thought initially. There will always remain entire fields of knowledge as yet unknown to him, ever higher levels of wisdom he has yet to master. This is a humbling realization.

We are this child. Before charging ahead like the proverbial "bull in a china shop," we must first be humbled by an awareness of our current limitations. While our desire is to attain the highest levels of spiritual understanding, we cannot rely solely upon our own budding intellects to get us there. We must develop a healthy respect for our teachers, placing our faith in those who are wiser than ourselves. Above all, we must have faith in the fact that there *is* a God Whose Intellect infinitely transcends ours. This faith will itself propel us towards the loftiest heights of intellect. It will also create within us the humility to avoid progressing in our quest too far, too fast.

Rebbe Nachman taught:

> A Jew must always focus on the higher wisdom and inner intellect that is found in everything. He must bind himself to this intellect so that it may illuminate his own intellect. In this way, he will be able to draw closer to God through any given object. For the inner intellect is a great light that constantly shines for a person. It is thus written (Ecclesiastes 8:1), "A person's wisdom causes his countenance to shine" (*Likutey Moharan* I, 1:2).

The above quote is from the opening discourse of Rebbe Nachman's *magnum opus*, *Likutey Moharan*. This lesson speaks about the importance of developing one's intellect to the fullest. By seeking wisdom, one can ascend to the soul level of *Chayah*, the highest and innermost level of Chokhmah (see above, Chapter 3; Appendix D), drawing Living Essence into one's daily life.

Rebbe Nachman explains this phenomenon by comparing the mind to sunlight, that bright source of light which allows us to see clearly what is before us, and thus to know which path to take in life. But, he points out, the light of the sun is extremely bright, so intense that we cannot gaze directly at it, lest we be blinded. We may gaze at the sun only through a filter or screen, or see its light reflected by the moon. In the same way, man's intellect is a bright light that can "blind" the person who uses it without "filters," that is, someone who tries to become "too smart" and begins to think that he knows all there is to know. In order to protect ourselves from this attitude, we require the filter of faith. Just as the moon reflects the light of the sun, faith reflects the light of the intellect. This filter of faith is, in effect, our knowledge that there is a higher intellect. Knowing this, no one will be so arrogant as to think he knows it all. Yet, because he cannot actually comprehend this intellect, as one cannot see the sun, he relies on that same faith to give him confidence to continue gaining knowledge.

Everyone, no matter how confident he may seem, faces

doubts. People are confronted by all manner of questions and confusions throughout life. One's intellect cannot always "see" beyond the turmoil of life. On the contrary, there are many instances when the "sun," i.e., the ability to make a decision, is hidden and darkness prevails. One simply cannot "see" one's way out of problems. It is one's faith (reflected light) in the existence of a solution that carries the day. This is alluded to in the verse (Isaiah 30:26), "The light of the moon shall be like the light of the sun." When one's faith is strong, the "light of the moon" will eventually increase and shine as brightly as that of the sun. Faith will guide a person through difficult moments until he attains genuine clarity — true intellect.

But not everything that presents itself as intellect is *true* intellect. There are philosophies and ideas that seem very impressive, yet they can distance a person from God. Such intellect is also called "sunlight," but the light it reflects is that of false beliefs. As is frequently evident, people's lives can be ruined by erroneous beliefs. Regarding this brand of intellect it is written (Isaiah 24:23), "The moon shall be embarrassed and the sun ashamed..."

Jacob and Esau

The Bible relates that Jacob was "a wholesome man" who studied Torah and sought spirituality, while Esau was "a skilled trapper, a man of the field." One of the key episodes in the story of Jacob and Esau is their battle over the birthright of the firstborn. One day, Esau returned from the field tired and hungry after having committed murder, adultery and idolatry. He demanded that Jacob feed him, which Jacob happily did — on condition that Esau renounce his claim to the birthright. Esau did so in exchange for a portion of lentils (Genesis 25; *Rashi* on Genesis 25:29; *Bava Batra* 16b).

Rebbe Nachman interprets their struggle in the following manner: Jacob sought a spiritual life. Esau, on the other hand, was interested only in a material existence. We saw above (Chapter 14) that Chokhmah is associated with the concept of "beginning," of being "first," as in the verse (Psalms 111:10), "The beginning is wisdom." Jacob, who sought true wisdom, understood the importance of the right of the firstborn (i.e., Chokhmah, which is called *reishit*, the "beginning"). Thus, one who seeks spirituality is associated conceptually with the Patriarch Jacob, who parallels the intellect. By virtue of his quest for spirituality, Jacob gained the opportunity to receive the birthright, prominence and blessing.

Esau, on the other hand, chose to pursue his physical desires, seeking only a material life. He was willing to discard true intellect for temporal, material pleasure. Those who choose the path of Esau spend their entire lives obstructing the light of true intellect. They distance themselves from God and may even find themselves committing the ultimate transgressions of adultery, idolatry and murder (often manifest in their habit of embarrassing and ridiculing others, which our Sages equate with murder and which the world recognizes as "character assassination").

Reb Noson explains that this pursuit of the material life is tantamount to the punishment of *karet*, being spiritually cut off. When a person seeks true Chokhmah, he is led ever closer to Keter, the highest level of communion with God. However, one who breaks his connection with *KeTeR*, God forbid, experiences *KaReT*, a cutting off from his Source. His very pursuit of the material life becomes his punishment, for such a pursuit can never bring genuine satisfaction (*Likutey Halakhot, Hekhsher Keilim* 4:7). This approach is found in the personage of Esau, who despised the spiritual, and it finds expression in a person's feelings of alienation from God, from family, and even from his own self.

*

True Intellect

Reb Noson writes:

> No matter how intelligent a person is, if his words are not words of truth, they are worthless and can even prove harmful. For example, a doctor may prescribe a certain medical treatment. With his specialized knowledge, he explains carefully how this

will benefit the patient and brings proofs to support his view. If the patient then suffers as a result of his treatment, of what worth is that doctor's wisdom? This principle applies to everything in this world. If one does not attain the *truth* of a matter, then one has not attained wisdom at all. The only genuine intellect is truth.

True intellect can be obtained only through faith. Though, on the face of it, faith seems to apply only at the point where intellect is incapable of grasping something, at their source faith and intellect (truth) are one. This is because through faith one is able to discern and accept from others [the true tzaddikim] what one "knows" to be true (*Likutey Halakhot, Giluach* 4:12).

In summation, "Knowledge is called knowledge only when it brings one to the recognition of God" (*Likutey Moharan* II, 7:4).

*

Transcendent and Immanent Intellect

We have seen (Chapter 3) that the soul comprises five interlocking levels (*Nefesh, Ruach, Neshamah, Chayah* and *Yechidah*). The first three, *Nefesh, Ruach* and *Neshamah*, are referred to as the "immanent levels of the soul." They correspond respectively to our unconscious urges, conscious identity (self), and higher consciousness. The last two levels, *Chayah* and *Yechidah*, correspond to Chokhmah and Keter respectively. They are currently beyond our ability to internalize. As such they are called *makifim* (surrounding levels of consciousness), for they "hover beyond" our current level of Binah (understanding).

How can we go about attaining these higher levels? The answer is that we must relive all the stages of our own physical development (embryo, infancy, childhood, adolescence, adult maturity). In the Kabbalah, this development is said to unfold in three principle stages: *ibur* (gestation), *yenikah* (suckling), and *mochin* (mature intellect). In essence they represent the human progression from a state of embryonic, potential consciousness to one of the internalization and actualization of the higher levels of our souls. They involve phases of spiritual growth and transformation rather than mental and emotional development. That is, more than marking the birth of new levels of intellect, they represent the main stages involved in "giving birth" to oneself.

Great effort must be invested in the attainment of these higher levels. The struggle and difficulties involved correspond to the stages of gestation and suckling. Yet this struggle leads to the gratification of seeing a "child" grow to full maturity, through the internalization of an expanded awareness of God in every facet of one's life.

Rebbe Nachman illustrates this concept with the analogy of a woman in labor. Every childbirth is accompanied by some degree of pain. As the moment of birth approaches, the pain can become almost unbearable, and at that stage, many women cry out as if they were dying. Then a new life comes into existence. So too, to "give birth" to a higher level of consciousness, we must endure the "birth pains," crying out to God for help (see *Likutey Moharan* I, 21:7).

Rebbe Nachman also explains that whenever we internalize that level of transcendent intellect which had been just beyond our grasp and make it immanent, the next higher level beyond that — the transcendent intellect that was hitherto impossible for us to reach — becomes attainable. It is like moving toward a point on the distant horizon, beyond which we cannot currently see. When we arrive at this point, a new horizon opens up before our eyes. In exactly the same way, our spiritual/intellectual growth and maturation process is destined to continue into eternity, literally, *ad infinitum*. Even after one's physical death, the eternal soul continues to seek the Infinite. This is God's gift to His creatures: the ability to attain eternal life, to achieve ever greater levels of Godliness, to come ever closer to Him, continually ascending the cosmic ladder, internalizing one level after another, forever.

*

"Na'aseh v'Nishma"

> Whatever God says, *Na'aseh v'Nishma* [we will do and we will hear]!
>
> Exodus 24:7

> When Israel received the Torah at Sinai and declared, *"Na'aseh v'Nishma!"* angels descended and placed two crowns upon the head of each and every Jew. One crown paralleled *"Na'aseh,"* and the other paralleled *"Nishma."* These crowns were removed later after Israel worshiped the Golden Calf, but will be restored in the Future. It is thus written (Isaiah 35:10), "God's redeemed will return and enter Zion with joyous song and everlasting joy upon their heads."
>
> *Shabbat* 88a; *Rashi, loc. cit.*

The commentaries all ask the obvious question: How can *Na'aseh* precede *Nishma*? How can a person *do* something before he *hears* what he has to do? How could Israel have rushed to accept the Torah even before they knew what they were accepting?

The general consensus is that *doing* refers to fulfilling the mitzvot, while *hearing* refers to *understanding* what the mitzvot mean. This can be compared to an adult who knows what is best for a child and tells him to fulfill his obligations, hoping that, as the child matures, the understanding of the importance and necessity of those obligations will become clear to him. But the Bible and the teachings of our Sages always contain a great deal more depth than is readily apparent, and Rebbe Nachman explains the seeming paradox of *Na'aseh v'Nishma* in a unique approach. Rebbe Nachman taught:

> The words *"Na'aseh v'Nishma"* correspond to the hidden and revealed aspects of Torah. *"Na'aseh* — We will do" is synonymous with the revealed Torah, meaning the precepts that each and every person can fulfill commensurate with his level. *"Nishma* — We will hear" is synonymous with the hidden Torah, that which is beyond a person's current level of understanding.
>
> This same relationship exists between Torah and prayer. "We will do" is synonymous with Torah — that which is revealed to us, that which we know how to fulfill. "We will hear"

is synonymous with that which is hidden, corresponding to that which he have to pray for (*Likutey Moharan* I, 22:9).

Torah is the revealed aspect of knowledge. Prayer parallels the aspect of the hidden Torah — what is beyond our ability to grasp and internalize at the moment. It corresponds to the *makif* (the surrounding light) which we pray to attain and make our own.

By defining this dynamic relationship, Rebbe Nachman is teaching us that our goal should be to understand what is currently concealed and transform it into the revealed. This is attained by learning Torah with the intention of fulfilling its precepts, and then praying to God that we merit to understand the depths of what we have just learned. This was King David's intent when he prayed (Psalms 119:18), "Uncover my eyes so that I may behold hidden wonders from Your Torah!" This is what all our great prophets and sages did, and this is what King David did throughout the Five Books of Psalms which, significantly, correspond to the Five Books of the Torah. Through the Psalms, King David effectively turned Torah into prayer.

We can do the same. The Torah is God's Will, and after we study it, we can transform the very Torah we learn into the form of a prayer. By "praying God's Torah back to Him" (i.e., praying that we fulfill our studies and merit to understand the depths of the Torah), we are telling God that we want what He wants. We complete the circuit, transforming our will into His. In doing so, we merit to have our prayers rendered into more and deeper Torah — that which was hidden is transformed into that which is revealed; that which had been completely beyond our grasp becomes internalized in every aspect of our lives. We can then merit the two crowns of "*Na'aseh v'Nishma*" which adorned the Jewish people at Sinai!

Rebbe Nachman concludes that these crowns are the essence of the great joy we will experience in the World to Come — they are "the Keter" which we strive to reach, the highest level of communion with God. This is why the verse states (Isaiah 35:10),

"God's redeemed will return and enter Zion with joyous song and everlasting joy upon their heads." "Everlasting joy" is the joy of the World to Come which is at present beyond our ability to comprehend. When we "pray God's Torah," which aligns our will with His desire to bring us to the level of meriting eternal life, we can attain the joy and contentment of the World to Come even now, in this world.

* * *

16

Keter: The Skull

Intellect is man's "crowning" achievement in life. Nevertheless, as we saw in the previous chapter, intellect must have a control, a filter. This filter is faith. On the one hand, faith corresponds to the *Sefirah* of Keter. On the other hand, it corresponds to the *Sefirah* of Malkhut. This presents us with a paradox.

Consider: Keter, the highest *Sefirah*, corresponds to the skull or cranium. The skull is generally considered to have reached its maximum size in a person's late twenties. As a result, the brain's physical expansion and growth, which has been taking place during this time, reaches its extreme limit. Its physical expansion is brought to a standstill. This is the relationship of faith (Keter; the cranium) to intellect (Chokhmah and Binah; the right and left hemispheres of the brain). Faith prevents intellect from going beyond a certain boundary.

At the same time, however, faith corresponds to Malkhut, the lowest *Sefirah*. As such, Malkhut serves as the gateway to all the higher *Sefirot*. Its very essence bespeaks the desire to grow beyond one's present limitations.

How can faith be both Keter and Malkhut? How can it simultaneously limit expansion and allow for it?

The Spiritual Ladder

To explain this paradox, we must understand another of the ARI's teachings. Recall that, based on God's Ineffable Name, *YHVH*, the Kabbalah speaks of a megasystem of Five Supernal

Universes. Each of these Supernal Universes is a microcosm of the whole, a miniature replica made up of countless levels within levels which are in turn miniature replicas of the Universe (and of the entire megasystem of Universes) of which they are a part. (See Chapter 3, above.)

An analogy to this system can be found in our physical world, in the cell of a living organism. Encoded within each cell is the basic information necessary to recreate the entire organism (referred to as its DNA). In the same way, within each Universe, and within each level or *Sefirah* within each Universe, there exist countless myriads of levels, each a miniature replica of the entire system.

Similarly, as we have seen, the human soul can be compared to a ladder consisting of five major rungs (*Nefesh, Ruach, Neshamah, Chayah* and *Yechidah*) that reaches the highest levels of the spiritual dimension. Each of these rungs in turn is made up of five sub-rungs. For instance, there are *Nefesh, Ruach, Neshamah, Chayah, Yechidah* of *Nefesh; Nefesh, Ruach, Neshamah, Chayah, Yechidah* of *Ruach; Nefesh, Ruach, Neshamah, Chayah, Yechidah* of *Neshamah,* and so on, yielding twenty-five sub-rungs in all. The system does not stop there, for it is subdivided over and over again. Every sub-rung has five more sub-rungs, bringing the total to one hundred and twenty-five sub-rungs. While the system is even more complex than this, with many more subdivisions, we will stop here to consider the meaning of this profusion of levels within levels within levels. This begs the question: Why so many levels?

Think about it for a moment. Even the *Nefesh* of *Nefesh* has five sub-rungs; that is, even the lowest level of *Nefesh* contains an illumination of the highest level of *Yechidah*. Where does this "*Yechidah* of *Nefesh* of *Nefesh*" come from? The answer is that it is based in the "*Nefesh* of *Nefesh* of *Yechidah*." This means that an illumination of *Yechidah* shines down all the way into the lowest level of our *Nefesh*. The implications of this are astounding.

It means that the entire system is interconnected. In terms of *Yechidah* of *Nefesh*, for instance, the highest level of *Nefesh* is never disconnected from its source in *Yechidah*. *Yechidah* of *Nefesh* is literally an extension of *Nefesh* of *Yechidah*. This means that the highest spiritual level that we can attain (*Yechidah*) is present in our lives right now (*Nefesh*). We can break through to eternity right here and now, and draw down its life-giving light into our most mundane experiences. It is our job to actualize the *Yechidah* of our *Nefesh*, to bring it from a state of potential and give it a dominant place in our lives.

One benefit we gain from the phenomenon of multiple sub-levels is proximity. "Traveling distance" between each major rung of our individual spiritual ladders is lessened. Thus, the highest soul level of *Nefesh* (*Yechidah* of *Nefesh* of *Nefesh*) is now much closer to the lowest extremity of *Ruach* (*Nefesh* of *Nefesh* of *Ruach*), which is immediately above it.

This is exactly analogous to the experience of climbing up and down a physical ladder. It is impossible to climb from one rung to the next if the rungs are spread too far apart. The same is true with regard to ascending the spiritual ladder of our soul. Since each sub-level is much closer to the sub-level immediately above it, there is no need for us to climb the ladder by leaps and bounds. We can approach spiritual growth one small step at a time, maintaining a consistency in our devotions and ascending a little more each day, without becoming discouraged over what lies ahead. Likewise, small steps are an advantage if there is a spiritual descent. If our level of devotion wanes, God forbid, we won't lose everything all at once. We are given a great deal of support along the way and ample opportunity to pick ourselves up, return to our former level, and continue ever higher in our ascent.

The ARI teaches that the highest level of *Nefesh* (*Yechidah* of *Nefesh*) is a temple for the lowest extremity of *Ruach* (*Nefesh* of *Ruach*). Indeed, it is here that the levels overlap and become one. Thus, as we grow, we internalize and integrate the level which previously, perhaps, had been beyond our reach. For example, whereas until now we had been unable to go beyond *Yechidah* of

Nefesh, we now attain *Nefesh* of *Ruach*. In addition, the light of *Ruach* now permeates our *Nefesh*, to the point that *Ruach* itself elevates *Nefesh* into itself. This principle holds true at every level of ascent. The higher level always elevates and transforms the level below it.

This explains our original paradox: Each Universe has Ten *Sefirot*, and Ten *Sefirot* within Ten *Sefirot*. Within each universe, Malkhut (corresponding to *Nefesh*) is the lowest *Sefirah*, while Keter (corresponding to *Yechidah*) is the highest. As one ascends the spiritual ladder, the Keter of a lower Universe *becomes* the Malkhut of a higher Universe.

The human skull, which encompasses and limits the intellect, corresponds to Keter, which reflects our faith in a higher intellect that transcends what we can presently understand. This very limitation is a gateway to ever higher levels of intellect and faith. Our current Keter is really the Malkhut of our next, higher level.

The Talmud thus teaches (Berakhot 17a), "In the future, the righteous will sit with their crowns *in* their heads, delighting in the radiance of the *Shekhinah* [Divine Presence]." Rebbe Nachman asks, "Shouldn't it say, 'crowns *on* their heads'? That is, shouldn't the transcendent intellect which corresponds to Keter rest *upon* their heads?" The answer is that "in" alludes to the transcendent intellect (Keter), which at present encircles the heads of the righteous, but which in the future will become internalized and immanent. When this internalization takes place, a greater transcendental intellect will open up, which is the Malkhut of the next highest level (Likutey Moharan I, 21:4).

*

Keter and Patience

In one way or another, all Rebbe Nachman's teachings provide deep insights into the dynamics of true spiritual ascent. In one of his major teachings (which we will cite below) he explains that, up to a certain point, all growth and advancement take place within the limitations of one's current level. For example, when a person is at the level of *Nefesh*, all his spiritual efforts up to that point have been to rectify the five levels of his soul within the level of *Nefesh*. Only after he has completely accomplished this rectification is he ready to advance to the next level of *Ruach*.

At this point, however, a problem arises. How does anyone know when he has reached his personal zenith in the lower level so that he is ready to advance to the next level? How can he understand the implications of rising to the next level?

In addition, restraint is necessary to hold the mind in check, so that he does not become exposed to overly powerful levels which are beyond the capabilities he has thus far developed. How does he safely rise above his current level without going beyond the constraints of his rational mind?

This is the function of Keter. The word *KeTeR* means *crown*, but it also connotes *waiting*, as in (Job 36:2), "Wait [*KaTaR*] for me a while." The "crown" indicates that there is "something above," something that compels a person to ascend to the higher level. Yet one must realize that it is impossible to reach that level directly. There is a "barrier" which surrounds a person and which holds him back from advancing *beyond* his reach. This barrier, Keter, is manifest in the characteristic of patience, which imposes a waiting period between absorption of the knowledge at the level already attained and advancement to a higher level. One who "uses his head" will know the difference. With his intellect under control, he will be able to recognize his limitations and shortcomings. At the same time, he will always seek to strive for higher levels and be ready to take advantage of an opportunity for growth.

Thus, Keter acts as an automatic barrier that holds a person back from going "too far, too fast." To be able to continually ascend the spiritual ladder, each person must work on cultivating the virtue of patience, an absolute necessity for attaining Keter — the higher intellect.

Let us see how Rebbe Nachman translates these teachings into practical advice for anyone seeking a spiritual way of life.

*

The Nine Chambers

> From inside this curtain, through the chasing of the [upper] thought that reaches and yet does not reach, Nine Chambers are created. They are neither [from the level of] lights, nor spirits, nor supernal souls. No one can comprehend them... They do not make themselves attainable or known.
>
> *Zohar I, 65a*

The brain never rests. Even while a person is sleeping, his mind is active, albeit on a subconscious level. In the spiritual dimension, the highest level of the brain is Keter, where one strives to attain intellect of a transcendent nature. But how high can one rise intellectually? How far can the mind actually reach? Considering that there are so many levels, even in the lowest world of *Asiyah*, let alone in the higher Universes, is it possible for man to "reach the sky?" Can man ever hope to attain absolute Knowledge of God? In one of his deepest lessons, Rebbe Nachman explains:

> Know! There is a light which is higher than *Nefesh, Ruach* and *Neshamah*. This is the Light of the Infinite One. And though the intellect cannot grasp this Light, the racing of the mind nevertheless constantly pursues it. By virtue of this "racing," it is possible for the intellect to grasp the Light in the sense of "reaching and not reaching." For the truth is that it is not possible actually to grasp it, because this Light is on a level above *Nefesh, Ruach* and *Neshamah*. And know that it is impossible to grasp this Light even in the sense of "reaching and not reaching" except by performing the mitzvot with joy *(Likutey Moharan I, 24:12)*.

Rebbe Nachman goes on to explain that by performing the mitzvot with joy, one redeems and elevates the *Shekhinah* (the Divine Presence of God, corresponding to the *Sefirah* of Malkhut) from its exile. The concept of the *Shekhinah* in exile can be understood on a simple level as God being hidden — man is unable to be cognizant of God at all times because His Divine Presence is not readily felt. This is also why the *Shekhinah* corresponds to

Malkhut: Malkhut translates as Kingship, and it is the *Sefirah* where interaction between God and man takes place. By fully accepting God as King, man displays his awareness and acceptance of His Divine Presence. Thus the term "*Shekhinah* in exile" implies that man has not yet fully recognized God's Malkhut and does not *feel* His Presence. In order to become fully aware of the *Shekhinah*, one must perform the mitzvot with joy.

The Zohar teaches (III, 278b) that all the mitzvot of the Torah correspond to the level of *Nefesh*, and thus, by extension, they also correspond to the level of Malkhut. We see this from the verse (Leviticus 4:2), "If a soul [*nefesh*] commits an inadvertent sin by violating a prohibitive mitzvah..." Scripture's usage of the word "mitzvah" in connection with "*nefesh*" indicates that the mitzvot of the Torah correspond to the level of *Nefesh*. A sin blemishes *Nefesh* and its corresponding levels — Malkhut and the *Shekhinah*. Conversely, performing the mitzvot rectifies Malkhut, and performing them with joy elevates Malkhut. This can actually be felt, for when a person is joyous, he feels uplifted and becomes exhilarated.

In the anthropomorphic array of the *Sefirot*, Malkhut parallels the feet. Joy is a means of elevating "the feet" and beginning one's ascent to higher levels. Starting to climb from the bottom rung of the spiritual ladder, one progresses from Malkhut (the "feet") through the next six *Sefirot* and on upwards until one reaches the level of the *mochin*: Chokhmah, Binah and Daat. This pattern can be compared to a child who first learns to build with a simple set of building blocks. Once he has mastered the use of basic blocks, he is ready for a different set of building blocks which fit together to achieve a more intricate level of designing and building. He can then graduate to an erector set, which requires additional tools, and so on.

In one's spiritual ascent, as we saw above, up to a certain point, all growth and advancement take place within the limitations of one's current level. *KeTeR*, which, as mentioned above, is related to the word *KaTaR* (to wait), acts to hold the mind back from advancing *beyond* its reach to the next level before the person is ready. This explains why Keter is manifest in a person's patience. He *recognizes* (i.e., he is aware of) his shortcomings, but at the same time continues to strive for higher levels.

Thus, Rebbe Nachman calls Keter the *mesader u'meyashev* of the *mochin*. *Mesader* means "that which puts in order," while *meyashev* means "that which settles." Keter "makes order" when the mind runs senselessly amok, beyond its current abilities. It settles a person in his place, allowing for the proper balance of spiritual growth. In essence it supplies the rudiments of patience, while, at the same time, teaching a more focused patience to those willing to strive for it.

This aspect of Keter becomes even more critical at the highest spiritual level that a human being can reach. At this loftiest of levels, the three *mochin* interact with one another, causing their spiritual force to triple (that is, Chokhmah, Binah and Daat of Chokhmah interact with Chokhmah, Binah and Daat of Binah and of Daat). Thus, by climbing the ladder through joy, a force "times nine" (three *mochin* times three) of spiritual powers is created. Now, if Keter is required on the lower levels, where one is dealing with one force, how much more is Keter needed when a person is faced with three forces tripled. The intellect may now be "exploding," potentially growing out of all proportion. The restraining force of Keter is necessary to hold the mind in check.

Rebbe Nachman explains that this is the mystery of the Nine Chambers mentioned in the Zohar. The three *mochin* of Chokhmah, Binah and Daat interact with one another. The interaction transforms the three *mochin* and expands them into Nine Chambers of spiritual energy and knowledge. The Zohar teaches that these Chambers are beyond description: they refer to the loftiest of levels, to a level that "reaches, yet does not reach" direct contact with the Infinite. That is, although this level is beyond human conception, still the mind races towards it. Every soul seeks its source, and every mind seeks the

Ultimate Knowledge, the knowledge of God. One who learns proper restraint, utilizing both intellect and faith, and blends them so that they act in unison, can succeed in attaining the Keter of his current level. Then he can progress onward and upwards — through joy — until he enters spiritual levels that are very awesome indeed. He can then continually ascend to ever higher levels — to approach the Nine Chambers.

*

Ratzon (Will)

(In our discussion of the respiratory system, we will speak more about the concept of desire. Will and desire are closely related, but could also be perfect opposites: will is usually based in a rational choice, while desire usually stems from deep emotion. We make a distinction between Keter, the primal will [or instinct], and Daat, the development of that instinct, which is manifest as desire. Keter, as the first *Sefirah* or emanation, is looked upon as "the primal will" because at the time Keter was formed there was nothing except the Light of the Infinite. Keter is therefore an "Original Will," while Daat, which follows Chokhmah and Binah, is a developed manifestation of that Will and is thus more closely associated with desire. This aspect of Daat will be explained in more detail later, in Chapter 19.)

Keter is the source of man's free will — his ability to choose how he acts and reacts to life's situations. When it is directed towards good, this will can bring a person to the level of Keter. Yet it can also become a detrimental force in one's life.

When asked by a follower to define free will, Rebbe Nachman replied: "It is really very simple: If you wish, you do. If you do not wish, you don't do."

Reb Noson comments that this seemingly simple statement is actually a very important teaching. People generally act as if they are trapped by their desires or impulses. Sometimes people justify a negative action or reaction by claiming that that is the way they are; they can't change. The Rebbe teaches here that every person, at any time during his life, *can* change, simply by choosing differently (*Likutey Moharan* II, 110).

Reb Noson attributes to this teaching very broad ramifications. From the moment God created man, Reb Noson explains, He placed this power of free will into his hands. If a person decides to seek spirituality, that decision "coerces" God, as it were, to activate the powers found in creation to support his desire. Conversely, if a person chooses to follow his heart's basest desires — even outright evil — that decision in effect "coerces" God to support and assist him in the path of his choice (*Likutey Halakhot, Birkhot HaShachar* 5:76–79).

By applying his will, a person can either break away from his past, by ascending to the Keter of his current level and from there to points beyond, or he can break away from any good he might have achieved and descend to levels far beneath those of his current standing. Will controls both behavioral and spiritual movements. As man's primal instinct, will becomes the first step in the quest for spirituality.

*

The "Will of Wills"

Reb Noson, in one of his classic discourses on this subject, defines will in the following manner: The main force in life is will. Man must accustom himself to long, to want, to crave, to desire and to yearn at every moment for Godliness — to study His Torah, to perform His mitzvot and in every other way to serve Him in a fitting manner (*Likutey Halakhot, Arev* 3).

Rebbe Nachman taught that *will* is the principle service of God. Even angels cannot claim truly to serve God as befits Him, due to His greatness and exaltedness, which is beyond description. If so, how can man ever hope to serve God? Through his *desire* to serve God. In this area, every person can be equal. Although everyone is different, and no two people have the same desires, each person's own will and desire act as his greatest power in his struggle to reach the highest of levels (see *Rabbi Nachman's Wisdom* #51).

One who directs his will towards God will ultimately rise to a level of true spirituality. Even if such a person is prevented by outside forces from accomplishing what he wants in the service of God, this is not held against him. As long as he does not despair of *wanting* to do good and to serve God, he will be rewarded, for his desire has been in the right direction.

The main reward that awaits the soul is the attainment of the Ultimate Will which, in the language of the Zohar, is called *Ra'ava d'Ra'avin* (literally, "Will of Wills"). The soul was sent down from the highest realm into this gross material universe. While his soul is encased in an earthly body, a person must learn to direct his will towards the Will of his Creator. We can compare this to the experiences of two people who feel very close to one another. The greater the distance that separates them, the greater is their will to come together again. Similarly, the soul has journeyed from the highest of levels — Keter — to this lowly world. Here it must learn to direct its will to return to its Source and to merit closeness to God in the World to Come. On the other hand, an evil will directs one away from God; just as good desires will ultimately bring a person to good deeds, evil desires will lower a person and distance him from God.

Reb Noson goes on to explain that since Keter is the first manifestation of God's Will to create the world, everything in creation reflects an aspect of God's Will (see also *Likutey Moharan* I, 17:1). For this reason, man can find God everywhere, for His Will is present in everything. Thus, despair does not exist for one who seeks spirituality, because no matter where he is, no matter on what level he finds himself, man can always find God. This is man's main occupation in life, to long and yearn for Godliness (*Likutey Halakhot, Arev* 3:1–5).

Reb Noson further explains that the reward for one who seeks spirituality is the ability to advance spiritually, with constant growing awareness and knowledge of God, to align his will with God's Will and to be included within His Unity. In directing one's will to serve God to the best of one's abilities, one connects with Keter, the Ultimate Will. As we have seen, since Keter is defined as both the Ultimate Purpose of creation and the reward of the World to Come, a person can actually experience and taste his eternal reward even in this world (*Likutey Halakhot, Netilat Yadayim LiSeudah* 6:57).

Interestingly, Rebbe Nachman teaches that through eating one can attain a heightened awareness of this will (*Likutey Moharan* II, 7:10). This is surprising in light of the fact that will represents Keter, the highest spiritual level, while eating seems to be a grossly mundane function. Nevertheless, Reb Noson explains, eating facilitates the attainment of man's spiritual objective in this world: it sustains life, keeping the soul connected to the body. This is especially true of eating with the intention of gaining the strength necessary for the attainment of spirituality, for this type of eating elevates the holy sparks found in the food. Eating with this attitude can bring one to an intense will and desire for the spiritual (to the point that one can almost merge with Keter) (*Likutey Halakhot, Netilat Yadayim LiSeudah* 6:45).

* * *

17

Thought and Imagination

Keter, the primal will, is called *Ayin* (Nothingness), because it transcends the level of thought that begins in Chokhmah. Chokhmah, on the other hand, is *reishit*, beginning, the ability to create. As such, it is the interface between nothingness and creation. Rebbe Nachman thus taught (*Likutey Moharan* II, 53), "Thought is extremely precious. One can actually *create* things with one's mind."

Guard your thoughts carefully, for thought can literally create a living thing. The higher a faculty, the further it can reach. You can kick something with your foot, but throw it higher with your hand. You can reach still farther with your voice, calling to a person very far away. Hearing reaches yet further, for you can hear sounds like gunfire from a very great distance. Your sight reaches even further, seeing things in the sky. Highest of all is the mind, which can penetrate the loftiest heights. You must therefore safeguard your mind above all else (*Rabbi Nachman's Wisdom* #46).

*

The Amalek Within

> Man's thoughts are *rak ra kol hayom* [only evil all the day].
> Genesis 6:5

Knowing that thought can reach the loftiest heights, we must realize that thoughts are never mere thoughts. We must never allow ourselves to entertain the notion that it doesn't matter what we think. Good thoughts are extremely beneficial both to those who think them and to the world at large, while evil thoughts are most detrimental.

Rebbe Nachman taught:

> In ancient amphitheaters, monarchs used to stage battles between wild beasts and their prey. The same type of battle is waged daily in one's mind: battles between good thoughts and evil thoughts. When the good thoughts emerge victorious from the battle, it causes great pleasure Above (*Likutey Moharan* I, 233).

Rebbe Nachman also explains a related passage from the Zohar (III, 123a): "Every day contains hidden good. But accompanying each day is an angel that prevents people [who are unworthy] from partaking of this good. This angel can take many forms — darkness, thorns, snakes, scorpions — all of which act as guardians to protect the good of that day and to prevent anyone who is unworthy from benefiting. Indeed, were it not for these guardians, the wicked would be able to freely enter into the mysteries of the Torah [and partake of the hidden good of that day]. It is for this reason that when someone who is not worthy attempts to gain entrance into the Torah's mysteries, troops of destroying angels, which manifest as darkness, concealment, confusion, etc., immediately surround him and confuse his thoughts, preventing him from trespassing. However, when one who is worthy wishes to enter, these guardians assist him... They bring him to the hidden good and speak in his favor to the Master of the Universe..."

The "snakes and scorpions" are the thoughts that confuse a person when he wants to learn the mysteries of the Torah. Yet if he persists in his desire to find God, these very thoughts will assist him; then he will find great good every day... For a person has the ability to incline his thoughts in any direction he wants. Even when his thoughts stray, it is within his power to harness them and return them to the straight path (see *Likutey Moharan* I, 84:1; *ibid.* II, 50).

Rebbe Nachman teaches that the harmful thoughts that assail people serve as a reminder of the ongoing battle with Amalek, the archenemy of the Jewish nation. This is the meaning of the verse cited above, "Man's thoughts are *raK rA koL hayoM* [only evil all the day]." In Hebrew, the final letters of these words spell AMaLeK. Lustful and evil thoughts represent the Amalek within (*Likutey Halakhot, Minchah* 7:19).

Amalek also alludes to doubts and confusion. This is seen in the numerical value of the word *Safek* (ספק, doubt), which is 240, the same as the numerical equivalent of the word Amalek (עמלק). Like Amalek, doubts attack a person stealthily. Even before we realize we are under siege, we find ourselves overwhelmed by conflicting thoughts and emotions. It is therefore a Biblical commandment to remember Amalek, that is, to be aware of him and his stealthy manner and to wage a constant battle against him (see *Esther: A Breslov Commentary on the Megillah*, Appendix A).

*

The Power of Thought
Rebbe Nachman taught:

- Whatever a person thinks, that is where he is (*Likutey Moharan* I, 21:12).

- Thought has incredible power. Concentrating all your energy on accomplishing something is the key. This is true even when concentrating on something mundane. The only condition is that your concentration be absolute, even to the point of being prepared literally to give up your life in order to attain your goal (*Likutey Moharan* I, 192).

- Melancholy and depression prevent you from collecting your thoughts. With joy, you can direct your mind properly (*Likutey Moharan* II, 10:2).

- Stealing causes one to have illicit thoughts. Even coveting another's possessions is a very serious offense. Since the power of one's mind is so strong, even thinking covetously about another's possessions is considered a form of stealing (*Likutey Moharan* I, 69:6).

- Thought is a very exalted level, transcending that of speech. If you wish to ascend to the level of Thought, you must remain silent: for even good, worthy speech can cause you to lose this level of Thought (*Likutey Moharan* I, 234:2).

- The thoughts of the mind are truly among God's wonders. Thoughts exist in the mind in groups, like bundles [of information], one on top of the other. When a person needs a fact, he remembers it by "drawing" it from its place in his mind. This in itself is a great wonder, for where had this thought been located until then? There are many associations and symbols, all located within these bundles in the mind. One remembers something because one encounters some idea that stimulates the association and symbolism identified with a particular thought. That thought is then brought forth out of all the "bundles" arranged in one's mind. When a particular thought is withdrawn, then all the other thoughts in one's mind are turned over and rearranged in a different pattern [as with physical bundles, where removing any one item from a pile causes its entire order to be upset] (*Rabbi Nachman's Wisdom* #25).

- Evil thoughts are compared to *chametz* [leavened bread, which expands as it ferments]. One must take care that these thoughts do not "expand" their influence over one's mind. When these thoughts "expand," they "fill" the entire cranium, leaving no room for the fear of Heaven to enter. One whose mind is blemished with foreign thoughts will always become aware of strife and arguments [which will occupy his mind and so direct him away from spirituality] (*Likutey Moharan* I, 5:4).

- Torah study at night is beneficial for protecting one's thoughts (*Likutey Moharan* I, 3:1).

- One should guard oneself constantly and absolutely against any immoral thoughts. Such thoughts can tear a person away from God, the Source of all life (*Likutey Moharan* II, 114).

- A person's evil thoughts might at times seem to overwhelm him. He may try to overcome them by fighting them directly — shaking his head, confronting the issue, etc. However, this doesn't really help, for thoughts seem to grow stronger in proportion to the vigor with which one fights them. It is far more beneficial to digress altogether in one's mind to other subjects. Concentrating on a chosen topic will ease one's efforts to overcome evil thoughts (*Likutey Moharan* I, 72:4).

*

A Humbling Thought

The best way to attain wisdom is to acquire the trait of humility. The verse states (Job 28:12), "Chokhmah comes from *Ayin* [naught]." As we have seen, *Ayin* corresponds to Keter, and Chokhmah is drawn from Keter. Since *Ayin* refers to naught, nothingness, one who acquires the attribute of humility (i.e., negating oneself) can attain true Chokhmah.

However, a person who disengages his wisdom from humility separates himself from Keter, the source of true wisdom. His wisdom becomes his own, but it is a flawed wisdom, both in thought and in the creative ability that follows thought. He no longer accepts his own shortcomings, and, as Rebbe Nachman taught (*Likutey Moharan* II, 12:1), "Someone who relies solely on his own mind can seriously err and come to terrible evil." The Rebbe thus said (*Likutey Moharan* I, 10:4), "One's intellect constantly warns one not to become haughty." One should rather understand that "the main service of God is in total simplicity, devoid of any sophistication" (*Likutey Moharan* II, 19:1). By setting aside sophistication and self-importance, one can become "whole" and serve God with total simplicity.

Today, in an era when cults, especially "religious" cults, are widespread, there may be those who would challenge Rebbe Nachman's statement, "Someone who relies solely on his own mind can seriously err and come to terrible evil." Cult members are taught that independent thinking is dangerous, and they are drawn into mindlessness. However, the difference between the guided thought process of Chokhmah and inane mindlessness is that Chokhmah is an expression of *Ko'aCH MaH*, "the power of 'what'?" — which indicates the power to wonder and question. Time and again, in his conversations and lessons, Rebbe Nachman encouraged students to ask questions and exhorted his followers to use their mental faculties to their fullest potential. The Rebbe's warning about the dangers of relying on one's own intellect refers to intellect devoid of Torah. It was directed to the leading members of the Enlightenment of his day. These were learned men who had cast off their observance of Torah, following the dictates of their minds rather than those of our Sages. The result was *KaReT* (being cut off) from KeTeR, a complete alienation from Judaism and assimilation with their material surroundings. It can be said that by employing their *own* Chokhmah, they disconnected themselves from Keter, thereby losing those safeguards that would have protected them and kept them within the realm of spirituality.

*

Imagination or Illusion

As we shall see, Daat corresponds to both the Sanctuary and the Holy Temple (Chapter 19). Building the inner sanctum of the mind is no easy task. To build any physical structure, plans must be drawn up and approved; workers must be hired for the job and building materials assembled. Even when all seems ready, numerous obstacles may crop up, causing all sorts of delays. So too, when engaged in the spiritual building of the mind, plans, workers and supplies are required, and the obstacles that inevitably arise must be dealt with.

God in His kindness gave us all the necessary plans for developing ourselves spiritually when He gave us the Torah. The Torah contains a general set of rules which have the capacity to open up the heart and mind to realms far beyond those of the material world. Even the most simple-minded person can experience spirituality, the joys of Shabbat and the Festivals, the touching, heartfelt prayers that liberate one's emotions, the lasting satisfaction of giving charity to help others and so on. This is possible because the structure of Torah parallels the human form. Man in this world, no matter what his status, is thus always able to connect with the Torah — and thereby to God (see Chapters 1–2).

The "workers and supplies" are the senses, the limbs and organs of the body. Obstacles and barriers are also built into the system. But the major opposition we encounter in trying to build our own inner sanctum is found in the mind itself. As Rebbe

Nachman taught (*Likutey Moharan* II, 46:2), "The greatest obstacles one faces are those of the mind." This refers to the powers of imagination and illusion.

*

"God formed Adam from the dust of the *adamah* [earth]." ADaM was so called because he was formed from the *ADaMah*.

Genesis 2:7; *Bereishit Rabbah* 17:4

Rebbe Nachman taught:

A person must rise above his imagination in order to attain intellect. No one can enter the gates of holiness until he has learned to subdue his illusions (*Likutey Moharan* I, 25:1, 4).

Imagination: an incredible "fuel" for thought. Imagination stimulates the mind to search for the unknown, to seek new ideas, new inventions and new perceptions. It allows the intellect to surpass its current constraints. Yet it also facilitates the mind's wandering into forbidden areas.

We have seen how man's uniqueness is found in his intellect, and how he was provided with the necessary tools to help him use that intellect wisely. We have also seen that man was given the freedom to choose whether he wishes to use or abuse his intellect. As the Biblical narrative teaches us, Adam was formed from the *adamah* (earth). The Hebrew word *aDaMaH* is similar to the word *meDaMeH*, which means "imagination." Man is formed not only from *adamah*, but also from his power of *medameh* (imagination). If man chooses to abuse his intellect, his imagination will aid him in his path, serving as an obstacle to attaining true intellect. However, if he truly wishes to do God's Will, imagination is necessary, for it is only through a person's imagination that he can even begin to grasp spirituality. This is seen in Scripture's use of *meDaMeH*, as in (Isaiah 14:14), *"EDaMeh l'Elyon* — I will resemble the Supernal."

This was Rebbe Nachman's intent in his statement that one must subjugate one's imagination to one's power of intellect. Imagination is a powerful force. It is the source of man's creative ability and can launch him to the noblest heights when used properly, but if not guided by true intellect it can also mislead him.

*

Imagination: The Bridge between the Physical and the Spiritual

Reb Noson writes:

> The imagination acts as an intermediary. It serves as a bridge between the physical and the spiritual, between body and soul. The ability to visualize something in the mind comes from the power of imagination. That which we visualize might in fact be a physical object, but the visualization of that object in the mind is actually a "spiritual" experience. Imagination can thus be thought of as both the highest point of the physical realm and the lowest point of the spiritual realm. It is the bridge between the material and the ethereal.
>
> The power of the intellect extends far beyond the limitations of the physical. One with pure intellect is very distant from sin and even from error. However, since Adam's sin, the physical body has become so coarse that we can hardly "imagine" being completely free from imperfection. What is needed is a bridge of some kind, to accommodate the interaction of the intellect with the material, so that one can master one's physical desires. Herein lies the power of the imagination: it joins the forces of body and soul. If a person utilizes his imagination wisely, he can truly raise himself from the level of the physical to that of the spiritual.
>
> For this reason, man was called ADaM. He is formed of ADaMah, the dust, the physical; but he can ascend above the material world through the use of his imagination and can reach a level of prophecy. The Hebrew word for "I will imagine" is ADaMeh. In this sense, we can understand the meaning of the verse (Hosea 12:11), "Through the prophets ADaMeh, [I will be imagined]" (Likutey Halakhot, Birkhat HaReiach 4:14–16).

One who remains steeped in physicality can relate to spirituality only through conjecture; it is all abstract to him.

However, if he uses his imagination to search for spirituality, he can ascend to very high levels of Godliness.

*

Angelic or Demonic

Rebbe Nachman teaches (*Likutey Moharan* II, 8:7), "Faith exists only in one's imagination. In that sphere which the mind is able to comprehend, the concept of faith cannot exist." Because faith is required where understanding is lacking, faith strengthens man, encouraging him to seek that which is currently beyond him, and it keeps him focused on the spiritual. Thus, imagination can be the catalyst for attaining spirituality.

On the other hand, the Talmud teaches (*Sotah* 2a), "A man does not sin unless a spirit of folly overcomes him." If a person lets his guard down, thinking that a sin will not harm him, he has erred. With such an attitude he falls from intellect into folly, blemishing his mind in the process. His imagination, where his faith is rooted, also becomes flawed, manifesting in illusory thoughts. Rebbe Nachman thus taught (*Likutey Moharan* I, 54:7), "Blemishing the intellect increases the power of illusion." Succumbing to the negative power of illusion, he loses something of his Godliness and descends from a human to an animal level; although animals possess a modicum of intellect, they lack clear, distinct knowledge. One whose thoughts so degenerate necessarily descends from spirituality (see *Likutey Moharan* I, 54:5).

Rebbe Nachman compares this type of illusory, blemished intellect to demons. Our Sages teach that "demons were created on the first Friday afternoon, just before sundown. As the sun set, only their spirits were created, for there was no time to form bodies for them. Because of this, demons have a spirit but no physical body" (*Zohar* I, 47b). Demons are therefore always seeking someone's body to inhabit.

Imagination can be likened to a spirit without a body — a "disembodied" spirit or thought. Thus, when a person acts too hastily upon his imagined thoughts or objectives without exercising restraint (Keter), it is tantamount to providing a demon with a body — his own — easily falling into "demonic" behavior. In such a state, one is vulnerable to the forces of evil and is never quite sure where one will end up. Rebbe Nachman therefore taught that no one can enter the gates of holiness until he subdues the illusory powers within him. He emphasized further that the negative aspects of imagination — the "demon" in each person — is even more potent in a spiritually oriented person. The "demon" of illusion that seeks a body in which to rest is more likely to choose that of one who studies Torah and, more specifically, one well versed in *halakhah* (the Codes of Jewish Law).

The reason for this is connected with the necessity of maintaining the balance of good and evil in the world. The study of, and meticulous adherence to, *halakhah* helps to define clearly the spiritual path of a person, giving form and shape to his lifestyle. Thus such a person's knowledge is a clear knowledge — he knows what is permissible and what is forbidden. Without some force to counteract this knowledge he would find it easy to choose the correct path; it is crystal clear to him which way to go. Therefore, to maintain free choice, the power of illusion seeks to overwhelm this decisive, clear knowledge (*Likutey Moharan* I, 54:6).

This is even clearer in Rebbe Nachman's teaching that, as one begins to attain a clear intellect, these "demons" which stem from one's imagination become even stronger. There are always higher levels of intellect to be attained, and we must never think that since we have entered certain gates of holiness we have finally subdued our illusions. In this life, the balance between good and evil is maintained at all levels, in order to ensure free choice at *every* stage along the way. Thus, at every level one encounters obstacles and illusions. One must continually confront these obstacles and overcome them (*Likutey Moharan* I, 25:3).

Rebbe Nachman also taught that the originating of Torah ideas serves as a rectification for improper thoughts. This is because a person must work at developing his imagination until he is able to form a "body" for these new ideas. Virtually all human thoughts are products of the imagination, and originating a Torah concept certainly requires imagination. Yet one must always examine the relationship between one's existing knowledge and the novel ideas one is originating to be certain that the new ideas are in keeping with a valid Torah outlook. This serves to rectify one's improper thoughts and blemished imagination (*Likutey Moharan* II, 105:1,3). However, basing one's original teachings upon ideas distant from Torah only heightens one's illusory powers, as we shall now see.

*

The Chambers of Exchanges

> **The woman saw that the tree was good to eat and desirable to the eyes... She took some of its fruit and ate it. She also gave some to her husband, and he ate it.**
>
> Genesis 3:6

When the Serpent approached Eve to entice her to eat from the Tree of Knowledge, he said, "You will be God-like, knowing good and evil," and immediately, "she saw that the tree was good to eat and desirable to the eyes... She took some of its fruit and ate it. She also gave some to her husband, and he ate it."

Reb Noson writes that their mistake was that they tried to reach beyond the limits of their Keter, their upper barrier. In this way, they thought, they could be God-like. Instead, they descended into the Chambers of Exchanges, where good becomes evil and evil, good.

The Chambers of Exchanges are, in fact, blemished imagination wherein one *thinks* one knows or understands, but actually does not. The verse states (Isaiah 5:20), "Woe to those who call evil good and good evil. They exchange darkness for light and light for darkness; they exchange bitter for sweet and sweet for bitter." All bitterness in life, including hatred and anger, sadness and jealousy, strife, conquest, the pursuit of honor, arises from the imagination (*Likutey Halakhot, Hoda'ah* 6:46–50).

*

Rebbe Nachman once said:

> The Talmud states that the Evil Inclination has seven names: evil one, uncircumcised one, impure one, enemy, stumbling block, stone, and sneak (*Sukkah* 52a). In our days, the evil one should be given an additional name: the power of illusion (*Likutey Moharan* I, 25:8).

* * *

18

Chokhmah and Binah

The ARI teaches that Chokhmah and Binah are inseparable. They are called "two friends who never part" (*Zohar* III, 4a). They parallel the cerebrum, which is divided into the right and left hemispheres. Although each has its own identity, they never separate. As we have discussed, Chokhmah represents an undifferentiated wisdom, the "nonverbal" right hemisphere, while Binah is the manifestation of that wisdom, the "verbal" left hemisphere. The *Sefer Yetzirah* (1:4) states, "Understand with Wisdom and be Wise with Understanding," meaning that in order to attain the highest levels of God-awareness, Chokhmah and Binah must be utilized in tandem.

Alternatively, Chokhmah and Binah correspond respectively to the cerebrum, which controls the brain's thought process, and the cerebellum, which is responsible for muscle coordination and the body's equilibrium. In this sense, Chokhmah represents man's overall intellect, the ability to master a subject and to integrate its fundamental principles into his mental processes. Binah indicates man's ability to direct the body based on the mind's commands. This is achieved through the mind's ability to derive additional information from data already received. In order to strive for spirituality, a person needs both.

To illustrate this, on the level of Chokhmah, every human being knows that there is a God. Even those who do not seek God possess a latent recognition of Him. Even a self-claimed atheist possesses a deep sense of God, albeit concealed. Binah directs the struggle to understand and develop this latent knowledge. Without Binah, innate Chokhmah serves no purpose.

Rebbe Nachman thus taught:

> Know! There are wicked people who spend their entire lives trying to uproot themselves from God and His Torah. Nevertheless, a tiny spark of spirituality remains, always seeking to rekindle the spiritual flame within them. Yet because they have become so deeply entrenched in their wickedness, they redouble their efforts to uproot themselves so that they eventually toss off even the minutest connection to God. Unfortunately, in most cases, when people reach this level of atheism, they die. Then they immediately see the truth of what they tried so hard to deny, but it is too late. May God save us!
> (*Likutey Moharan* I, 274).

*

The Metropolis of Rome

> **When King Solomon married Pharaoh's daughter, [the archangel] Gavriel [Gabriel] descended and planted a *KaNeH* [reed] in the sea. A sandbank developed [around this reed], upon which was later built the metropolis of Rome.**
> *Shabbat* 56b

Rebbe Nachman taught:

> There are two types of *KaNeH*. One is *K'NeH* [acquire], as in (Proverbs 4:5) "*K'NeH Chokhmah, K'NeH Binah* — Acquire wisdom, acquire understanding." The other is that which is associated with (Psalms 68:31), "Rebuke the wild beast of the *KaNeH* [reed]." Chokhmah represents pure wisdom, which is the knowledge of God, while false beliefs and undesirable lifestyles are compared to wild beasts. Planting false beliefs in one's mind allows the "beast" to take root and fester, replacing true wisdom (*Likutey Moharan* I, 35:1).

True wisdom is spirituality. A person begins his sojourn on this earth with an open mind, ready to imbibe all types of knowledge and information. As time goes on, accumulated information is stored in the mind, taking root and expanding. If he then directs his mind towards spiritual pursuits, it can expand ever further, for the spiritual is beyond time and space, and hence never-ending. However, if he opts for material pursuits, with their accompanying false beliefs and undesirable lifestyles, his mind becomes polluted with unnatural lusts. First a small quantity of evil takes root, then a little more; finally, evil desires dominate the entire mind. The brain, having absorbed and stored vast amounts of materialism, is left with little room for anything else to enter or develop. The spiritual is all but banished.

In this lesson, Rebbe Nachman explains the meaning of the Talmudic passage cited above. "King Solomon represents spiritual wisdom. Pharaoh's daughter represents false beliefs and an undesirable lifestyle. *GaVRiel* corresponds to *GeVuRot*, or judgments. The sea represents the 'sea of wisdom,' which is found in a person's mind. Rome represents atheism" (Likutey Moharan I, 35:1).

King Solomon's marriage to Pharaoh's daughter parallels a person using his mind to accumulate false beliefs. The angel Gavriel represents the judgments, constrictions and restraints he now faces in life, resulting from his material pursuits. The material desires are likened to a reed planted in the sea. The mind, originally open to spaceless spirituality, now has a tiny material object planted within it, taking up space. As Rashi explains (Shabbat, loc. cit.), a sea without obstructions flows freely, whereas a single reed attracts whatever dirt is floating by. As the dirt accumulates, the reed becomes a sandbank and eventually forms into a large body of land. In this way, false beliefs, which may have begun as something very tiny, become an attraction to which other unethical ideas will be drawn. These "seemingly minute" infractions eventually add up and acquire the size and strength of "the city of Rome," the capital city of the empire that destroyed the Temple and tormented and murdered millions of people: the archetypal atheist.

*

An Open or Narrow Mind?

In light of Rebbe Nachman's teaching above we can see that people who define themselves as scientific, secular-liberal and open-minded are actually very narrow-minded in their scope. Instead of seeing an Infinite Intelligence manifest in the chemistry of life, and in the miracle of human consciousness that that chemistry supports, they choose to perceive chance and random processes. Having closed their minds to Godliness, they simply cannot fathom what spiritual and religious people are all about. Furthermore, because they think only in materialistic terms, they close themselves off from seeing that which lies beyond matter — or within it.

Let anyone who is skeptical about the existence of God look through an electron microscope into a piece of wood. Let him see how it is made of fibers, which are made of cellulose, which is made of molecules, which are made of atoms, which are made up of sub-atomic particles such as protons, electrons, and neutrons, which are made up of sub-sub-particles called quarks and leptons. Let him understand that these are not physical entities, but rather bundles of vibrating energies; and these vibrating energies are frequencies of a single basic force of vibrating energy that is continually creating and recreating all the atoms and molecules in the universe at every moment. Let him understand that what was once prophetic or Kabbalistic knowledge of the "inside" of matter is now accepted scientific theory. Anyone who fails to see the wonder of this is truly narrow-minded, as his mind is clogged with his own limited preconceptions.

Let us examine the attitude of broad-mindedness as opposed to narrow-mindedness in the context of the events experienced by the Jews at the Red Sea. They were faced with the sea in front of them, a desert full of wild beasts on one side, sheer, impassable cliffs on the other, and the Egyptians pursuing them from the rear. As they saw it, they were faced with very few, very painful choices: jump into the sea, return to Egyptian bondage, battle the

Egyptians, or flee into the desert (*Shemot Rabbah* 21:5). But God's powers are not limited to the confines of time and space. His choice was "Split the Red Sea!"

Of course we don't face these situations daily. Nor do we really expect to see a revealed miracle in our day and age...or do we?

Actually, in the spiritual realm, anything can happen. When faced with difficulties, someone living an exclusively materialistic existence can sort out his options only according to the way he sees things. Thus, he will opt for a "natural" solution, based on the way he understands his problems. Such a person is narrow-minded; by seeking only those solutions which can be conceived by his finite mind, he automatically rules out an entire array of possible solutions that do not conform to his ideas. However, he who seeks spirituality knows that he can always rely on God. Since God is Infinite, He can make available any number of solutions. This person will certainly seek solutions that he can figure out by himself, but he will also be alert to other possibilities that might crop up, because he knows that God in His Infinite Wisdom can help him in countless ways. Many times during the course of one's life it may appear as though there is no viable solution, or that the available choices are not feasible. Yet somehow an unexpected solution materializes.

There is no limit to what God can do. Accordingly, the spiritual realm is defined as being beyond the limitations of space or time. It does not conform to any picture that the finite, human mind can imagine. For this reason, believing in God and seeking a spiritual life is a sure indication of true open-mindedness. Since God is above time and space, one who relates to God can expect anything to happen. Conversely, the narrow-mindedness of one who seeks materialism alone limits his potential to nothing more than that which the material world can provide him. He can never really appreciate the wonders that are inherent in creation.

*

Memory: Remembering the Future...

Who is wise? He who sees the *nolad* [future].

Tamid 32a

Rabbi Moshe Sofer (*Chatam Sofer*, 1763–1839) comments that the word *nolad* (literally, "born") indicates a profound connection between that which has already been "born" in the past and that which is yet to be "born" in the future. It teaches us that the future can be viewed and understood only by studying the past (*Rabbi Eliyahu Chaim Rosen*).

As we noted above, Chokhmah and Binah represent "remembrance" of the past and "penetration" of the future (Chapter 14). We have seen how imagination can bridge the gap between the spiritual and the material. Memory can likewise be understood as a bridge between the past and the future.

Rebbe Nachman thus taught:

> The image of one's goals should always be kept in mind (*Likutey Moharan* I, 18:1).

The Rebbe explains that if you intend to build a house, you must first envision what you want it to look like. With this picture in mind, you can design its every detail, draw up the necessary plans, acquire materials, and then work to complete the structure. The mental image not only guides your steps along the way, it also acts as a powerful impetus to spur you to bring the entire plan to fruition. The main incentive comes from keeping the final structure foremost in your mind at every stage.

This approach is crucial to success in life in general. The ultimate goal of life, which we must always bear in mind, is the World to Come. Rebbe Nachman speaks of "constantly *remembering* the World to Come and keeping this goal uppermost in one's mind" (*ibid.*). How can we remember something that lies in the future?

One answer is that the World to Come represents a dimension which lies outside of our current dimension, one in which time is not yet segmented, and past, present and future are one. From the vantage point of our current state of consciousness, the World to Come lies in the future; but from the point of view of our transcendent souls, this dimension is *now* (because the transcendent soul also transcends the dimension of time). Furthermore, since our souls originate in that dimension, and return to it every night while we sleep, its memory is indeed embedded deeply in our psyche. Therefore, we can "remember" the future.

In Rebbe Nachman's story of "The Exchanged Children," the true prince, though raised as a servant, was still drawn to the ways of royalty. What was naturally embedded in his psyche had never been completely erased. In the end, the true prince became master of the former king (who was in reality his servant) and eventually ruled the "Foolish Land" as its "Wise King." As Reb Noson explains, the struggle between the true prince and the servant symbolizes the ongoing battle between body (servant) and soul (prince). Though it finds itself in this material world, the soul never completely forgets its origin and ultimately will seek it out. In the World to Come, man's soul will transcend this material life to enter a dimension in which the soul reigns supreme.

*

Rebbe Nachman taught:

> The Torah is vast. How can anyone expect to study the entire Torah and retain it in his mind? Consider a barrel full of water: If one wishes to add water, even a small amount, some of the existing contents of the barrel must be spilled out to make room for the fresh water. However, unlike the barrel and its contents, the spiritual nature of Torah transcends the concept of space. Thus, one who seeks the spirituality of Torah can always increase his Torah knowledge without losing any of his previously acquired wisdom (*Likutey Moharan* I, 110).

The more spirituality one has cultivated within one's intellect, the greater becomes one's capacity to store more such information in the mind. Still, it is very easy to forget the true goal.

Considering the many physical needs of life, the effort involved in earning a living and tending to a family can easily cause an individual to forget his spiritual nature and potential. As Rebbe Nachman teaches (*Likutey Moharan* I, 67:8), "Forgetfulness is compared to 'clouds that cover the eyes.'" One's vision may become impaired, and the future (the World to Come) may easily be forgotten. The Rebbe therefore teaches (*Likutey Moharan* I, 54:1), "A person must guard his memory, that he not fall into forgetfulness. Forgetfulness parallels the concept of a 'dying heart' [the heart is an aspect of Binah, referring to the future] and is prevalent among those who consider this corporeal world to be the only world. The main effort of one's memory should be employed to *remember the memory* of the future."

Rebbe Nachman teaches that prayer, song and joy aid memory and combat forgetfulness. Through prayer one can guard one's memory and harbor a constant awareness of the World to Come (*Likutey Moharan* I, 7:7; *ibid.* I, 54:12).

*

...And Forgetting the Past

Rebbe Nachman also teaches that the human tendency towards forgetfulness is, in certain ways, greatly beneficial:

> If you did not forget, it would be utterly impossible to serve God. You would remember your entire past, and the [unpleasant] memories would drag you down and would not allow you to raise yourself towards God. Whatever you attempted would constantly be overshadowed by your memories of the past.

> But God has given you the power to forget and to disregard the past. The past is gone forever and need never be called to mind. Because you can forget, you do not have to be dominated by the past.

> This is very important to understand when serving God. Most people become distressed by past events, especially during their prayers. When a person recites his prayers, his devotions

are often distracted by memories. He may think about his business or household affairs, worrying whether he did something wrong or neglected something important. While attempting to serve God through prayer or study, he might be troubled thinking of his many sins and shortcomings. This is a universal problem, and each person recognizes his own difficulties.

The best advice for this is simply to forget. As soon as a [painful] event is behind you, forget it completely and never think about it again. Understand this well, for it is a most fundamental concept (*Rabbi Nachman's Wisdom* #26).

Rebbe Nachman continues:

In our sacred literature, we find that God gave us the power to forget, so that we could always appreciate the Torah as if it were the first time we learned it. Because you forget, you can relearn a lesson or review it, and it is like learning it anew; therefore you can appreciate it as much as you did the first time you learned it.

The Midrash likens this to workers who have been hired to fill leaky barrels at per-diem wages. The more they pour into the barrels, the more leaks out. The fools complain, "Why are we working in vain? What good is it to fill the barrels if it all leaks out?" But the wise ones reply, "What difference does it make? Don't we get paid for every day we work? If the barrels leak, our wages are not reduced" (*Vayikra Rabbah* 19:2).

The same attitude should be applied to your sacred studies. You might forget them, but your reward is not reduced. In the future, God will make everyone remember everything he ever learned, even if it was forgotten during his lifetime (*Rabbi Nachman's Wisdom* #26).

*

Pharaoh's Dream

Pharaoh said: "In my dream, I was standing on the bank of the Nile.

Suddenly, seven fat, handsome cows emerged...Then, just as
suddenly, seven other cows [emerged], lean and badly formed...The
emaciated and bad-looking cows proceeded to eat the first seven fat
cows. They completely swallowed them, but there was no way of
telling that they were inside. They looked just as bad as they had at
first."

Genesis 41:17–21

When speaking of forgetting, Reb Noson warns that one must
beware of "Pharaoh's dream." The Bible relates that Pharaoh
dreamed about seven fat cows and seven lean cows. After
swallowing the fat cows, the lean cows didn't show a trace of ever
having consumed a "fat cow." The dream alludes to people's
tendency to "swallow up every bit of good" that exists in their lives
— that is, forgetting the good so entirely that not even a trace of its
memory remains. True, one must forget one's evil deeds and past
errors, which could inhibit spiritual growth, while at the same time
remembering past mistakes in order to work on correcting them.
Still, one *must* remember the good one has done. Keeping the
positive in mind enables one to draw upon one's inner strengths
in order to grow continually. This can bring a person to joy, which
in turn guards his memory (*Likutey Halakhot, Netilat Yadayim Shacharit* 4:7).

Elsewhere, Reb Noson explains that PHaRaoH is related to
HaPHRa'aH, "interference," implying the disturbing thoughts and
delusions that infiltrate one's mind. One must always battle
Pharaoh's dream and can do so with the aid of the tzaddik's
strength. It was Joseph who provided Pharaoh with the solution
whereby he could save himself and his land (in fact, all the affected
lands) from famine, indicating that the advice of the tzaddikim can
counter the evil effects of bad dreams and evil delusions.

We saw (Chapter 6) that Adam's sin was that he partook of the
Tree of Knowledge of Good and Evil, which separated him from
proper advice. This advice can be rediscovered in the teachings of
the tzaddikim. One who truly wishes to overcome his evil
inclination — with its delusions, evil thoughts and bad memories

— will benefit tremendously by studying the advice offered by the true tzaddikim (*Likutey Halakhot, Rosh Chodesh* 7:54).

*

Creation Ex Nihilo

In His goodness He constantly renews the act of creation each day. How innumerable are Your deeds, O God; You made everything with Chokhmah!

Morning prayers

Rebbe Nachman taught:

One must be careful to entertain only good and productive thoughts, thereby renewing and invigorating one's intellect daily. This is akin to the Creation, when (Psalms 104:24) "You made everything with Chokhmah." God repeats the act of creating the world anew, *ex nihilo* [from nothingness] each day. In the same way, one must renew one's mind and intellect daily (*Likutey Moharan* I, 35:2).

The first step is to begin each day without any preconceptions. Just as Creation took place *ex nihilo*, so must you approach each new day with an *ex nihilo* attitude. Say, "This is not the same old thing. This day is entirely new!" Leave yourself open to new and fresh ideas without locking yourself into routines. Meet even your routine daily schedule with a fresh new attitude (*Likutey Halakhot, Basar v'Chalav* 4:12).

Most inventions have been made by people who rejected preconceived notions and ideas, who were willing to test fresh approaches to their intended goals. The same can be said of the quest for spirituality. Using a fresh approach each day opens new spiritual vistas.

Reb Noson adds that God injects this power of renewal into each day. "Imagine," he writes, "an artist who creates the most beautiful works. Can one envision such a creative person making the same thing every single time? God, the Master Artist, recreates the entire world every single day. Can one think for a moment that God — Who created such an incredible world and everything in it

— would do the same thing day in and day out for so many millennia without creating anything new each day? Absolutely not! Each day is a brand-new creation. Just as God renews the world, bringing something novel to it daily, you too can draw from this freshness on a daily basis. The secret is to approach each new day as an absolutely new creation, a creation *ex nihilo"* (*Likutey Halakhot, Birkhot HaShachar* 5:28).

*

Twenty-four Hour News Update

Daat [Intellect] is life itself!

Likutey Moharan I, 1:2

Who doesn't get up in the morning to the newspaper or radio informing him of all the "important events of the day?" Who manages to sit down at the dinner table without having his fill of the seven o'clock news? How can anyone get a decent night's rest without first checking out what's going on in the world? If we accept the media's advice, we can't live without the news. The question is, Which news? Why, in fact, is the world so obsessed with news?

We have pointed out that God injects the power of renewal into every single day. Thus, every day has its own "news of the day," in which one can find and taste the freshness of God's Creation. Furthermore, we have seen that the reward of the World to Come is an ever-increasing level of knowledge of Godliness. Thus, our appetite for news is in fact an instinctive desire for Daat, that is, for Godliness, the source of life. Since the concept of Creation — the innumerable novelties that God brings into existence each day — corresponds to Chokhmah and Binah, it is an inborn tendency of the mind to always seek what is new. Which news you seek is an individual choice. You can be spoon-fed the local journalists' choice of fodder, or you can seek the truly novel and refreshing renewal found in each day, which can invigorate you with a fresh zest for life.

* * *

19

Daat: The Holy Temple

Moses was commanded to build the Sanctuary in which God's Divine Presence would be revealed on earth. "Behold!" God told him: "I have called upon Bezalel... I have filled him with a Godly spirit, with Chokhmah (Wisdom), Tevunah (Understanding) and Daat (Knowledge)..." (Exodus 31:2–3). Rashi defines Daat as *ruach hakodesh*, divine inspiration. When the powers of Chokhmah and Binah are combined, Daat (Knowledge) is attained and a Sanctuary is built. This can be achieved on an individual level, too. Every person is capable of making himself a Holy Temple in which *ruach hakodesh* can be manifest!

Rebbe Nachman thus taught (cf. *Likutey Moharan I, 13:1*), "Acquiring Daat is comparable to the building of the Holy Temple, while an absence of Daat corresponds to its destruction." Man's goal must therefore be the pursuit of Daat, to build his own personal sanctuary of spirituality, wherein Godliness can be revealed.

As we have seen (Chapter 14), Daat is the external manifestation of Keter. It is a quasi-*sefirah* that must be formed by the confluence of Chokhmah and Binah. Indeed, the main rectification of everything blemished in this world comes about through the building of the intellect of Daat. Reb Noson explains that the main reason for this is Adam's sin of eating from the *Etz HaDaat*, the Tree of Knowledge of Good and Evil. Since the blemish that he created with this sin was in the realm of Daat, its rectification must also come about through Daat (*Likutey Halakhot, K'riat HaTorah 6:11*).

*

Daat: The Brain Stem and Spinal Column

Rebbe Nachman taught:

> Chokhmah is potential intellect; Binah is the logical intellect; Daat is the actual wisdom acquired (cf. *Likutey Moharan* I, 25:1).

Chokhmah is the very first revelation of intellect. It is potential intellect, for it is as yet undifferentiated. Binah is the logical thought process through which Chokhmah becomes manifest. Finally, when that which has been absorbed and understood can be applied on a *practical* level, one has reached Daat.

This can be better understood by remembering that Daat parallels the brain stem and the spinal column. Whatever is processed in the brain is manifest in the body's response to the brain's direction. The spinal column, being the extension of the brain stem, reflects Daat's ability to receive from Chokhmah and Binah. As we have seen, Chokhmah represents the past while Binah represents the future. Daat is the force of the present, the here and now, where we interact with the forces around us. As such, it is only through Daat that we can truly become aware of the Godliness that surrounds and permeates us.

To learn how to become aware of spirituality through Daat, recall that in the array of the *Sefirot*, Chokhmah is on the right side and Binah is on the left side (see Appendix D). The right and left sides correspond respectively to *Chassadim* (Lovingkindness) and *Gevurot* (Judgment). Earlier (Chapter 14), we explained that Chokhmah is the male aspect that unites with Binah, the female aspect, to create Daat. It is the *combination* of Chokhmah and Binah that is so crucial to the functioning of Daat.

On a practical level, if we attempted to structure our lives with only kindness, we would be overwhelmed and unable to function. If we tried to live a purely judgmental life we could never exist, for every slight deviation from one's responsibilities would demand severe punishment. A proper balance of kindness and judgment is crucial for a healthy existence.

In the same way, achieving a perfect blend of love (Chesed) of, and respect (Gevurah) for, God is tantamount to attaining knowledge of Him. Love allows you to give of yourself unreservedly, while respect helps you maintain the proper distance necessary to serve One so exalted as God.

Daat also creates a healthy balance in human relationships. Daat represents compassion, a state in which both kindness and restraint are exercised simultaneously. An example of this combination can be clearly found in the wise disciplining of a child. A parent may punish a child harshly, to appease his own anger, or he may avoid discipline altogether, for fear of further antagonizing the child. Either approach is detrimental to the child. Properly administered, discipline can be employed in such a way that the child is left with an understanding of what behavior is unacceptable, and how he is to behave properly in the future. Restraint is used in the form of punishment but is combined with love for the child. This is true compassion, a compassion created through Daat.

*

Ayeh? and Melo: Hope, Not Despair

The knowledge that a blend between opposite forces (Chesed and Gevurah) is necessary to sustain creation can help us to understand how Godliness is present on this gross, earthly planet. The most basic principle of existence is that God permeates all of Creation, from the highest of levels down to the very lowest. On the one hand, the higher the level to which a person ascends, the greater the revelation of Godliness he will experience, and the more he will be drawn to spirituality. On lower existential levels, on the other hand, the presence of God becomes progressively more concealed. On the lowest of levels, it may appear that He is, God forbid, nonexistent. The question thus faces us: considering the gross material world in which we live, how can mere humans ever hope to experience God?

Rebbe Nachman taught:

> There exists a level on which the revelation of God's greatness is so lofty that we cannot begin to fathom it. This is the level of "*Ayeh mekom Kevodo?* — Where is the Place of His Glory?" Even the tzaddikim cannot fathom *mekom Kevodo* (Place of His Glory) because the higher they ascend, the more they realize God's greatness as opposed to their own insignificance. They are left with the question, "*Ayeh?*"
>
> On the opposite end of the scale there are the worst sinners, those who are so distant from spirituality that they seem to have no connection whatsoever with God. How can they even begin to seek Him? In order to progress, they must realize that God's awesomeness and great mercy extend all the way down from the very highest of levels, into this material world. In this way God sustains the world, and "*Melo kol ha'aretz kevodo* — The whole world is filled with His Glory*" (Isaiah 6:3). It follows that, despite God's awesome greatness, we can always find Him, for He is everywhere.
>
> In every generation there is a tzaddik who is so great that he grasps both of these concepts of *Ayeh?* and *Melo*. He shows the spiritually inclined that, no matter how much they've attained, they haven't even begun to understand the essence of God. At the same time, he can show the person most distant from spirituality that God is right next to him, accessible at all times (*Likutey Moharan* II, 7:7).

We see that the concepts of *Ayeh?* and *Melo* represent two opposite extremes of the spectrum. One indicates a constant state of yearning and questioning: "When will I arrive at my intended goal?" The other is typified by a feeling of being unable to find God and unworthy of approaching holiness, so that one must be "shown" that "the whole world is filled with His Glory." It would seem that logically the two could never coexist. Ostensibly, one who is spiritually inclined is removed from materialism; one who is materialistic never seeks the spiritual.

Yet it is interesting to note that everyone experiences these extremes in his daily life. We often fluctuate between hope and despair; we are also aware of the consequences of either thinking that we have "arrived," or despairing altogether of ever being able to begin anew.

Daat is the "bridge" between these two extremes. With Daat we can *always* find God — wherever we are. Even in the lowest abyss, we can take heart in the awareness of His closeness to us while, at the same time, we are aware of our distance from Him. A tzaddik is one who has perfected his Daat and is therefore able to grasp both these concepts and weave them together, understanding them as one. His shuttling between the upper and lower worlds is as natural as walking back and forth between two rooms. Because he has united the two seeming opposites within himself, he can illumine everyone else's Daat, so that anyone who accepts his guidance will be able to perceive God on his own level.

*

The Three Partitions

A person does not come to sin unless a spirit of folly overcomes him.

Sotah 2a

Rebbe Nachman taught:

> Daat indicates a binding and a union, as it is written (Genesis 4:1), "Adam *knew* his wife Eve." Union can take two forms. Holy union is binding oneself to the tzaddikim, to the Torah, to God. Such union comes from holy Daat. Sinful unions, on the other hand, come from blemished Daat (*Likutey Moharan* I, 43).

We have seen that the brain is divided into three major sections: the cerebrum, the cerebellum and the brain stem. This division parallels the mind's ability to compartmentalize information and to analyze it prior to arriving at logical conclusions. According to Rebbe Nachman, this three-step process (compartmentalization, analysis and conclusive decision-making) demonstrates the mind's ability to "set up partitions" in order to protect a person against sin, especially against sins of immorality.

The partitions of the brain correspond to Chokhmah, Binah and Daat, as we have explained. When you focus your mind on attaining greater spirituality, you direct yourself towards holiness. Your internal union, your blend of wisdom and understanding, then creates a Daat of holiness, a sanctuary where Godliness can be revealed. If, however, you stray from holiness by entertaining false beliefs, or by squandering your mental energy on immoral or sinful thoughts, you blemish your ability to attain holy Daat. The partitions in your mind become fragmented; your wisdom (Chokhmah) dissipates, and your logic (Binah) leaves you. Indeed, the ARI teaches that only the forces of holiness possess Daat, whereas the forces of evil exist without Daat. The Zohar teaches (II, 95a), "They [the forces of evil] commence in unity but conclude in separation." Unity cannot endure in the realm of evil, for there is no possibility of a merging of love and fear, of kindness and restraint. You cannot then achieve Daat, that beneficial blend which results in compassion.

When Daat is blemished, compassion is diminished, and kindness is replaced by cruelty. People in this state become insensitive to the feelings of others and negligent towards property. Damage and abuse become commonplace. Worse still, compassion is totally misplaced, so that one's compassion is often spent — and wasted — on those who are unworthy (Likutey Moharan II, 8:2).

When immorality reigns, Daat becomes blemished. People's sense of compassion becomes tainted: compassion is shown towards criminals — terrorists, murderers, rapists and so on — while law-abiding citizens fear for their lives, and individuals who don't deserve judgment experience unjustified restrictions. Some show the utmost concern for wildlife, while humanity languishes in poverty. It is for this reason that God created man with a "triumvirate" planted firmly within his mind: Chokhmah, Binah and Daat. By striving to blend the kindnesses of Chokhmah with the restraints of Binah, a person can develop a well-formed Daat and know how to build and create with moderation, for his own benefit and for the benefit of mankind as a whole.

God gave man the opportunity to build solid "partitions" in his mind, thereby cultivating his Daat. As one's Daat grows, these partitions act as barriers against evil thoughts, so that a person can banish any immoral thought or deed before it has a chance to establish a stronghold in his mind. Should he fall prey to an immoral thought, he may reinforce himself with the assistance of these partitions, to battle immorality even before it becomes a spoken word or an actual deed. He has a chance to analyze and categorize the thought and then decide what to do with it: to banish it or let it manifest itself as a deed or a word. Through overcoming immoral thoughts in this way, one rectifies one's Daat and attains greater Daat. Someone who has achieved this can radiate love and kindness in the proper manner, to benefit mankind.

As an aid to overcoming immoral tendencies, Rebbe Nachman suggests Torah study. "Torah is called Daat. With Daat one can subdue all evil characteristics, especially immorality" (*Likutey Moharan* I, 36:2).

*

The Tree of Knowledge: Good and Evil

We have glimpsed the importance of the intellect, especially in its aspect of Daat as it relates to our ability to function as a holy people in this world. Let us now look at the influence it exerts, both positive and negative.

Rebbe Nachman taught:

- Daat is so called when, through it, one comes to recognize God (*Likutey Moharan* II, 7:4).

- Daat corresponds to peace, while strife indicates a constricted form of Daat (*Likutey Moharan* I, 56:8).

- The way to achieve the status of "man" is through Torah study (Numbers 19:14; cf. *Berakhot* 43b). This is because the Torah is acquired in three stages: learning Torah, which corresponds to Chokhmah; understanding the study, which parallels Binah; and mastering the subject matter, which is equivalent to Daat. The principal aspects of the intellect, Chokhmah and Binah (for Daat results from their confluence), correspond to the first two letters of the Tetragrammaton, *Yod* and *Heh*. *Yod* and *Heh* together have the numerical value of 15, and [since *Yod* and *Heh* can be expanded in three different ways; see Appendix D] three times 15 equals 45, which is the numerical equivalent of *ADaM*, man (*Likutey Moharan* I, 101).

- Daat comprises the true joy of the World to Come. You can experience a taste of that Daat while still in this world, through the study of *halakhah*, the Codes. Every single law that is learned from the Codes gives you a *new* piece of Daat (*Likutey Moharan* II, 2:2).

- When your Daat is complete, your soul can develop. Conversely, if your Daat is blemished, you are said to be "barren," unable to develop and produce offspring. Barren in Hebrew is *LiMLaiCHah*, related to the word *MeLaCH* [salt, i.e., bitterness]. Just as salt makes a person thirsty, so does the soul thirst for spirituality, and this thirst corresponds to suffering. You can quench this thirst with original Torah insights (*Likutey Moharan* I, 65:5).

- Attaining Daat for oneself alone is insufficient. A person must transmit Daat to others, so that even after death he can "live on" through the Daat that he left behind in this world. This can be accomplished through one's children, who are created from the seed that originates in the *mochin* (see below, Part 9). It can also be accomplished by teaching Torah to others (*Likutey Moharan* II, 7:4).

- Daat is compared to the light of day. Someone who achieves complete faith in God attains Daat. Then even his "nights" are as bright as day (*Likutey Halakhot, Birkhot HaShachar* 5:28).

- Man is distinguished by his Daat, by his ability to discern good from evil (*Likutey Moharan* II, 7:2).

- One who studies Torah without Daat [without applying this knowledge] is compared to Laban, who resorted only to deceit. Such a person uses his Daat to outdo others and to create strife (*Likutey Moharan* I, 12:1).

- He who lacks Daat must work harder for his livelihood. The more

Daat one lacks, the more one must work. The manna, which was the food of the Israelites in the desert, alludes to great Daat. So it is that one who possesses Daat has an easier livelihood (*Likutey Moharan* I, 56:6).

- Life is experienced through the intellect. A person who fails to make proper use of his intellect is considered to be sleeping his life away. This "sleep" is brought on by improper eating (*Likutey Moharan* I, 60:6).

- True poverty is that of the mind (*Likutey Moharan* II, 7:3).

- When one's Daat exceeds one's ability to manage that Daat, then that intellect creates heresies. A person's ability to control his intellect is commensurate with his good deeds (*Likutey Moharan* I, 55:6).

- All pain, suffering and even exile result from a lack of Daat (*Likutey Moharan* I, 21:12).

*

Rebbe Nachman also offers suggestions to help rectify and develop our Daat:

- Intellect is imperfect without a corresponding attachment to the tzaddikim. In order for the intellect to reach a degree of completeness, it must be pure. The tzaddikim, who are pure, help one to attain purity of mind (*Likutey Moharan* I, 211).

- The Holy Land has the power to purify one's mind (*Likutey Moharan* I, 44).

- Joy elevates one's mind (*Likutey Moharan* I, 89).

- Dealing honestly in business enables one to pray with a pure mind (*Likutey Moharan* I, 93:2).

- The three *mochin* correspond to the three Festivals. Observing the three Festivals can rectify the *mochin* (*Likutey Moharan* II, 1:5).

*

Mental Illness...

Psychiatrists and psychologists are hard-pressed to keep up with new developments in the field of mental health today. New types of neuroses seem to be appearing at an alarming rate, and new disorders are continually being discovered. The medical profession is unable to rationalize this phenomenon. Concrete solutions have yet to be formulated, and in the meantime, drugs are being dispensed freely to compensate for our lack of understanding of the root of the problem. A vicious cycle may be initiated when, for example, a slight disorder calls for medication. The *Physician's Drug Reference Manual* clearly outlines how each type of medication has its own side effects, which lead to other problems, calling for different drugs. Unfortunately, a fair share of mankind suffers from mental and emotional disorders, some of which are considered hereditary, while others are known to result from life circumstances; may God send a complete cure to them all.

Just as the physiology of man parallels his spiritual makeup, so too, mental health mirrors spiritual health. We have seen that Keter indicates waiting and patience (Chapter 16). The mind must have a monitor that tells it, "Now is not the time. Wait, be patient. You can't have everything you want right away; you might fulfill your desires at some point in the future, but not at present. You must learn patience; now you must work hard and strive to better yourself. Live your life to the fullest in the *present*. As your life unfolds, you should be able to attain your goals."

Herein lies the key to virtually all mental disorders. When a person's Keter is blemished, his ability to create a framework within which his mental and emotional state can grow and flourish is damaged. The outcome: abnormalties abound. We find therefore that many disorders are associated with compulsive tendencies such as bipolar (manic-depressive) or obsessive-compulsive disorders. Furthermore, all lusts — obsession with immoral thoughts, workaholism, compulsive eating, etc. — while commonly recognized as disorders, are actually associated with unrestrained impulses. As the Talmud teaches (Pesachim 66b), "Anger causes a loss of intellect"; anger denotes a lack of patience. The reason for this loss of intellect is that a lack of patience reflects a blemish on the level of Keter, and when the Keter is blemished, the mind suffers. In addition, we have seen that a blemishing of Keter leads to *karet* (being cut off), and accounts for one's "alienation disorders," such as various psychoses.

We have seen (Chapter 16) that Keter (Will) relates to man's power of free choice. Man has the ability to choose and act without the slightest compulsion. His decisions can be made completely independent of all external considerations. Man can be a truly responsible being, employing patience, meaning the wisdom to know what one should or should not do, as the key to living a normal life.

Yet modern man is subjected to pressures, both from within and from without, the likes of which were unheard of several decades ago. Instead of accepting and dealing with the modern moral challenge and facing the harsh realities, many have lost patience and chosen the easy way out: they have opted out of spiritual responsibility. Rather than wait for the proper moment, people often feel "compelled" to act in a certain way, to "push" a particular idea or "force" a given issue. "He who hesitates is lost," the saying goes, so one generally feels one "must" do something: buy...run...play... get...have, etc. Compulsion — not patience — is the rule of the day.

Furthermore, instead of simply admitting their mistakes when they have erred, people get caught up in rationalizing their deeds. With this approach, in effect, they shirk responsibility for themselves, their actions and their environment. Not so very long ago, it became the style for analysts to try to make people feel good about themselves — a most noble idea, one that Rebbe Nachman taught two hundred years ago! However, the manner in which this advice was handed out too often came at the expense of a basic sense of responsibility. The prevalent motto was, "As long as I feel good, it doesn't matter what I do or what happens around me." Thank God, this school of thought is on the decline, for very often the result has clearly been not mental health but rather a severe form of mental illness, while those closest to the one who sought such misguided self-fulfillment were hurt the most.

...And Suggested Remedies

Responsibility is the key to mature living, and this implies responsibility not only for one's deeds but for one's thoughts as well. Just as each person's deeds have a visible effect upon his environment, so too his thoughts have an effect — though not necessarily immediately apparent — upon himself and his character. A responsible individual is one whose sense of responsibility is strongly rooted within his character. As the Talmud states (*Sanhedrin* 37a), "Each person must say, 'The world was created for me.'" Rebbe Nachman explains this to mean (*Likutey Moharan* I, 1:5), "I am responsible for making the world a better place."

The Talmud teaches (*Sotah* 2a), "A person does not come to sin unless a spirit of folly overcomes him." This "spirit of folly" is an inner compulsion that pushes us off balance and causes us to do things we might not have done had our minds been focused properly. To overcome this compulsion we must observe our actions calmly and objectively. If we become aware of having done something wrong, our first response must be to overcome the natural instinct to deny or rationalize the action. In this sense, mental health can be defined as the ability to distinguish between "myself" and "my actions."

It is only when we shirk our responsibility, allowing our own actions to go unnoticed, as it were, that the spirit of folly begins to take up residence within us. The further we allow ourselves to fall, the more it becomes part of us. Of course, God created us with the abilities and opportunities for us to choose life, and thereby to free ourselves of all inner compulsions. Until we realize how precious these opportunities are, however, each sin we commit allows that much more foolishness to enter and reside within us. This is especially true of sins involving immorality. Since man's seed originates in his mind, any act involving wasted seed is actually a wanton waste of one's mind.

Reb Noson writes that most people indulge in eccentricities which are obviously foolish. This is due to their not having taken responsibility and repented for their transgressions of the past, as can be understood from the Talmudic passage cited above. Eventually, a person may bring himself to a state in which his identity is one of mostly foolishness and only a minute amount of intellect. Reb Noson points out that, this being the case, most people might be classified as lunatics! However, we must realize that the intellect is so powerful that even a tiny portion of it is sufficient to counter all the nonsense that one has brought upon oneself. Even those people who are left with only the smallest vestige of intellect still possess free will, and they can immediately, at any point, alter their lifestyles and live normal, sin-free and guiltless lives (*Likutey Halakhot, Netilat Yadayim LiSeudah* 6:37).

*

Rebbe Nachman taught:

When a person's inherent sense of good is aroused, this allows him to elevate himself from the foolishness in which he has become entrenched, enabling him to rectify his mind (*Likutey Moharan* I, 17:8).

Rebbe Nachman teaches that "charity is judgment" (*Likutey Moharan* I, 2:4). Someone who is approached to give charity is faced with the need to make decisions. He must decide: Is the cause worthy? What and how much should I give? And so on. Thus, giving charity is likened to passing judgment. In this way, giving charity helps a person to attain Daat and to rectify his mind.

The Talmud teaches (*Berakhot* 33a), "It is forbidden to show pity to one who lacks Daat." But elsewhere it states (*Shabbat* 151b), "Whoever shows compassion to others will be shown compassion from Heaven" — if one lacks Daat, how can Heaven pity him [it is forbidden]? The answer is that someone who has given charity has shown compassion for others. In this way, he has become worthy of attaining Daat and is deserving of compassion from Heaven. By attaining Daat, he is protected from sin, since "a person does not come to sin unless a spirit of folly overcomes him" (*Sotah* 2a; see *Likutey*

Moharan I, 116). Thus, charity protects one's Daat, and with Daat intact, one is protected from sin.

*

Depression or Joy

Rebbe Nachman taught:

> The only reason people are distant from God and are not interested in spirituality is that they do not have *yishuv haDaat* [mental calm; serenity of mind]. When a person is depressed, he cannot control his mind enough to attain that serenity; therefore, one must always seek joy (*Likutey Moharan* II, 10).

When a person has *yishuv haDaat*, his mind can remain focused upon the spiritual. He is able to sift through the mounds of information to which he is exposed, and so becomes attuned to the knowledge which will help him to attain his goal. We have seen that Keter is the *mesader u'meyashev* of the intellect. *Mesader* means "that which puts in order," while *meyashev* means "that which settles" (Chapter 16). In this sense, *yishuv haDaat* means "to settle one's Daat." Motivating oneself to settle one's mind enables one to connect one's Daat to Keter, i.e., to the spiritual.

In the above-mentioned lesson, Rebbe Nachman is teaching us that life's day-to-day routine automatically tends to steer people away from spirituality. Material needs, even the barest necessities, tend to distract us from concentrating on our goals — especially when our goals are spiritual! Were we to examine our spiritual progress daily and reflect upon the viability of our goals, we would be more certain of their worthiness and could truly seek Daat more effectively.

The problem is that, in general, people's ability to concentrate on the larger issues in life is intermittent at best. People become overwhelmed by what they perceive to be the magnitude of their difficulties. Instead of feeling serene contentment, they are likely to become depressed. Depression is one of the evil inclination's most effective means of preventing us from concentrating on our goals, and so the cycle reinforces itself.

Rebbe Nachman associates this state of mind with the exile. Regarding the redemption it is written (Isaiah 55:12), "You shall leave [exile] with joy." Joy indicates freedom. Mental calm brings us to joy, which in turn frees our mind. Joy restores to us the ability to direct our lives towards our highest goal, the goal of Redemption. Depression, on the other hand, is associated with exile and subjugation.

The Mishnah states (*Avot* 4:1), "Who is wealthy? He who rejoices in his portion." The path to true fulfillment in life is to rejoice in our portion. This "portion" is not necessarily the tangible objects that we have at any particular moment. It has more to do with what is really important to us, what really matters, beginning with an appreciation of being alive. It is the discovery of who we are and the joy of knowing why we were born; it is the ability to uncover and to develop our potential — what Rebbe Nachman calls "the good points" within ourselves. Who is wealthy? He who can see and appreciate the good; he who can maintain a positive outlook on life. Of course, this is easier said than done, but if one strives for it, then one can attain joy, and a life of happiness and contentment. (See *The Treasury of Unearned Gifts*, published by the Breslov Research Institute, which discusses Rebbe Nachman's path to happiness and contentment in life.)

*

Splitting the Sea

> During the Exodus, Moses used his *staff* to split open the sea. During the final Redemption, the *quill* will open the "Sea of Wisdom."
>
> *Tikkuney Zohar* #21, p.43a

As we have discussed, Adam was created to attain a state of perfection. He lost his chance when he ate from the *Etz HaDaat* (Tree of Knowledge) and descended into the domain of evil. This descent itself was for the sake of an ultimate ascent. Only by first descending is it possible not only to regain what was lost but to achieve a higher level. In this sense, it is not by chance that the descent was caused by a blemish in Daat and that, as a result, "Daat itself went into exile" (that is, true Daat is now very difficult to attain). Only when the Mashiach comes will Daat be redeemed, for then (Isaiah 11:9) "the earth will be filled with the Daat [Knowledge] of God, as the waters cover the sea."

As part of their cosmic role of rectifying the sin of Adam, the Jewish people's mission is to redeem Daat from its exile, to repair the blemished Daat. The paradigm for this mission is the Jews' redemption from the Egyptian exile. This exile was the necessary descent that served the purpose of preparing Israel to ascend to Sinai, and ultimately to enter the Holy Land and build the Temple (all of which are aspects of holy, rectified Daat). Only through the strength and merit of Moses were the Jews able to leave the Egyptian exile, for, as the ARI writes, Moses corresponds to Daat (Etz Chaim 32:1; see Appendix D). As such, it was his mission to bring Israel into the Holy Land to effect the final rectification of Daat.

Unfortunately, although Moses did succeed in rectifying a great deal, he was not able to complete his mission. The reason for this is one of the most profound mysteries of the Torah. Ostensibly, Israel's sins disqualified them from entering the Holy Land with Moses. This is certainly true, but the deeper reasons are not written for all to see. Suffice it to say that during those crucial forty years in the desert Moses and the Children of Israel planted the seeds of the future Redemption. There they were lifted to the highest levels of prophetic vision; there they saw miracles and came to understand God's plan for Israel and for all of mankind. Although they strove with all their being to usher in the final Redemption, they understood that the time had not yet come. Their job was to plow the ground and plant the seeds for later generations to harvest. In their merit, God has planned even greater miracles and wonders than those witnessed and experienced by the Jewish people when they crossed the Red Sea.

When Israel left Egypt, the Red Sea stood in their way and prevented them from directly entering the Promised Land. In our days, too, a "sea" obstructs our ability to return to the spirituality of the Holy Land. This "sea" is the sea of improper wisdom and false beliefs (blemished, impure Daat) that bombard us daily and prevent us from seeing Godliness everywhere. To help us overcome this obstacle, God is in the process of splitting the "Sea of Wisdom," uncovering the mysteries of Torah found in the Kabbalah so that His Presence will be revealed in the world. The Zohar, the ARI's writings, and the teachings of the true tzaddikim, who represent Moses, all contain the most awesome mysteries found in Torah literature. These teachings are part of the hidden aspects of the Torah which will be revealed in the days of the Mashiach. Their source is the level of Keter, the most exalted level of knowledge of God that can be attained in the world (*Zohar* III, 152a).

Reb Noson explains that this is alluded to in the concept of the quill (mentioned above in the quote from the *Tikkuney Zohar*). The quill represents the writing and recording of the Torah teachings which reveal Godliness. Just as the staff of Moses was used to split the Red Sea, this quill is used to split the "Sea of Wisdom." The tzaddikim who reveal these Torah teachings are constantly engaged in the "splitting of the Sea of Wisdom" in order to reveal God's Presence in this world. As these teachings are disseminated, more people turn to spirituality, and the "split" in the sea of false beliefs widens. More and more people pass through, until, eventually, true Daat and good will gain a complete triumph; the Mashiach will come and reveal the greater spiritual dimension that exists beyond that which is apparent and from which all mankind may partake (cf. *Likutey Halakhot, Pikadon* 5:41).

Rebbe Nachman thus taught:

> The main suffering of the current exile is a result of Israel's having fallen from supernal Daat [faith in God's miraculous providence], and subsequently having arrived at the mistaken belief that everything depends on nature, on chance or on fate. In fact, this belief is the very cause of people's suffering. Living among the gentile nations and learning from their ways has led people to think that everything depends on [the laws of] nature and fate. When they again attain Daat [Knowledge] of Divine

Providence, people will suffer no longer; for the truth is that Israel is above natural law. Only when they sin, God forbid, do they fall under nature's dominion. It is then that they suffer exile and humiliation (*Likutey Moharan* I, 250:2).

*

Daat: The Holy Temple

Whoever has *Daat* — it is as if the Holy Temple was built in his days.
Berakhot 33a

When God sees fit, He will send the Mashiach, whose responsibility it will be to build the Holy Temple, which will be used for prayer and for sacrifices. Yet we may well ask, is the building of the Third Temple, for which we long with all our hearts, intended just to accommodate the offering of some sacrifices? There must be more to this than meets the eye. What, in fact, *is* the Temple, and what do the sacrifices represent?

The Messianic era will herald the dawning of an age of great Daat, Knowledge of God. The technological advances of recent years are very great revelations of knowledge, but they lack the endurance of Daat. The fact that science and technology cannot create anything eternal indicates that there must be something beyond them, that there *is* a knowledge greater than all the advances which can be made by researchers and scientists. And there is: that greater knowledge is spirituality — Godliness.

We have seen (above, Chapter 14) that the world was established with a system of "three columns." These are manifest in the three attributes of Chokhmah, Binah and Daat. Chokhmah parallels the wisdom that one possesses, that which a person has studied and knows. Binah corresponds to the incorporating of that wisdom in building one's life. Daat is the final application of one's learning — the forming of a complete structure that is functional. Daat is the "center column" — the blend of the wisdom that one has acquired and the ability to use it logically, in order to arrive at responsible and rewarding conclusions.

Closer analysis of our Sages' statement that Daat is synonymous with the Holy Temple will better enable us to understand what the Holy Temple means on several levels. As a physical structure, it will contain an altar upon which to offer the various sacrifices. But this Holy Temple also represents the building of one's *mind* — the attainment of a level of Daat and purity. This is the level at which one is capable of absorbing spirituality — of making oneself a temple for the Godly soul. This, then, leads to developing an expanded awareness of God. Developing this awareness is not an easy task. Sacrifices must be made.

For on that day...a fountain shall flow from the House of God...

Joel 4:18

What does it mean to offer a sacrifice in the Holy Temple, and how is it relevant to us? The Hebrew word for sacrifice is *korban*. Its purpose is to bring an offering to God — whether a thanksgiving offering, a sin offering or a burnt offering. The ARI explains that a human being is the highest form of life, but when he sins he loses his human advantage and descends to the level of an animal. When he repents, he brings an animal for a sacrifice, indicating that he wishes to "sacrifice" his base, animalistic tendencies and return to his former level of a human being. The sinner thus comes to the House of God and offers his animal upon the altar, taking a lower form of life and offering it to God, elevating himself from the lower levels to which he has fallen and bringing himself back to the highest levels.

At the same time, through his sacrifice, he draws God, as it were, down from His lofty residence, and reveals His presence even on the lowest of levels. His sacrifice effectively draws to him, in this lowly world, God's presence. It is thus the "sacrifice" which binds all the worlds together — the lowly material world with the spiritual Universes — bringing forth a revelation of Godliness that was hitherto unrecognized (see *Pri Etz Chaim, Shaar HaTefillah* 5).

We can carry this idea further. The word *KoRBan* (קרבן) stems from the word *KaReV* (קרב), "to draw near." (The *b* and *v* are represented by the same letter in Hebrew: ב, *bet or vet*.) Thus, when a person brings a sacrifice for the sake of God, it literally draws him near to God. When a sacrifice is offered, neither the *kohen* (priest) who performs the sacrificial rites nor the animal are allowed to have a blemish (Leviticus 21:18, 22:20). In a broader sense, the act of bringing a sacrifice indicates that, in serving God, a person should strive to attain *temimut* (wholeness; integrity). The Torah speaks of the thanksgiving offering as *zevach haShLaMim* (peace offering) (Leviticus 7:11). The root *ShaLeM* means whole, complete or perfect, as well as peace. Thus, bringing the thanksgiving offering is akin to drawing near to God through attaining wholeness, for the *korban* brings all the worlds to their perfect, complete state. This in turn brings peace, the peace that will reign in the days of the Mashiach (*Likutey Moharan* I, 14:8).

The reason the Temple is the only location permitted for the offering of the sacrifices, which draw a person near to God, is that it corresponds to Daat, Knowledge of God. This knowledge, which will be revealed to all in the future, is a "fountain of wisdom" that will continuously flow from the Holy Temple, which is symbolic of the expanded intellect. The Prophet Joel (4:18) foresaw an era in which this knowledge will be available to everyone, when people will have risen above their animalistic instincts which currently bar their way to understanding the Divine.

The truth is that a person's mind is the Holy Temple; or at least, it could be. With Daat, man can master and refine his baser instincts, through elevating his animalistic nature, in order to draw near to God. One who accomplishes this with joy merits a revelation of Godliness, even in these times, similar to the global revelation that will be experienced when the Mashiach comes.

*

In the end, Daat will certainly be revealed. The attainment of true Daat will herald the end of all suffering. It will lead to the ingathering of the exiles, the coming of the Mashiach and the rebuilding of the Holy Temple, in the spiritual as well as in the physical sense. Such is the power of Daat.

May it come to pass, speedily in our days. Amen.

* * *

Part Five

The Circulatory System

20

The Thoracic Cavity

O xygen is essential for survival — an absolute necessity for the blood, for the tissues, in fact for every cell in our bodies. We draw oxygen into our lungs which use this vital substance to purify our blood. This newly vitalized and "oxygenated" blood then flows into the heart, which pumps it to the rest of the body.

If the heart and lungs perform critical life functions on a physical level, their task is no less crucial on a spiritual level. And just as they are physically structured to work together, they are also spiritually interdependent, as we shall see. Our study of the circulatory system will begin with a brief description of how these organs are built and how they function. (The bloodstream, an integral part of the circulatory system, has been discussed above, in Chapter 9.)

*

The lungs are two distinct organs made up of masses of spongy tissues housed in the thorax, or chest cavity. The left lung is smaller than the right lung (to allow room for the heart, which lies to the left, between the two lungs). Each lung is divided into lobes (sections); the right lung has three lobes, and the left has two. The lungs draw in fresh air to bring oxygen to the entire system while removing carbon dioxide, a waste product. The air passages are connected to the pharynx, which extends into the trachea, branching off into bronchi. Through these, oxygen passes into the lungs. There the blood picks up the oxygen and brings it to the heart, where it is pumped to the rest of the body.

Situated off-center in the thorax, the greater portion of the heart is on the left side of the body. About the size of a person's fist, the heart is a muscle made up of four chambers with a system of vessels and valves that coordinate to pump the blood throughout the body. The four chambers of the heart consist of two atria and two ventricles. The atria act as accumulation sacs for the blood before it is allowed to flow into the ventricles, where it is pumped out of the heart. The left atrium receives the blood which has been enriched with oxygen in the lungs through the pulmonary veins. The blood is emptied from the left atrium into the left ventricle, which then pumps this oxygenated blood throughout the entire body. After completing its job of bringing oxygen to all parts of the body, the blood, now full of carbon dioxide, returns through the veins to the right atrium, which passes it on to the right ventricle. The right ventricle pumps the blood into the pulmonary artery, which transports it through the lungs to remove the waste matter. The blood then returns to the heart (via the left atrium) enriched with oxygen from the lungs, and the cycle repeats itself.

It is interesting to note, in a general sense, the interaction between the heart and lungs. The Zohar describes the heart as being "hot" — a constantly moving muscle that receives "hot" and worn-out blood and returns it, purified and refreshed, to all parts of the body. The lungs draw in the fresh, cool air which "cools down the heat" of the heart. This is accomplished through the "fluttering" of the lobes of the lungs, which act as "fans," "cooling" the heart. In the course of our study, we shall see a similar spiritual pattern emerge.

*

The Chariot of God

The Zohar speaks of the four faces of the creatures in Ezekiel's vision of the Holy Chariot: a lion, an ox, an eagle and a man (see above, Chapter 8). These faces correspond to the mind, the heart, the lungs and the power of thought, respectively. The mind, heart and lungs also correspond to Chokhmah, Binah and Daat, the three upper *Sefirot* in the array of the Ten *Sefirot*, which represent the mentalities (*mochin*).

The following chart shows the relationship between the faces of the Chariot, the organs and their corresponding *Sefirot*.

Face of Chariot	Function	Sefirah/Position
Lion	Mind	Chokhmah/right
Ox	Heart	Binah/left
Eagle	Lungs	Daat/center
Man	Thought	

The lion/mind corresponds to Chokhmah, which is on the right side of the array. The ox/heart corresponds to Binah, on the left side of the array, as we find in the verse (Ezekiel 1:10), "The face of the ox on the left"; note that the heart is situated off-center to the left side of the body. The eagle represents the lungs, which correspond to Daat, the merging of Chokhmah and Binah; comparable to the eagle's wings, the lobes of the lungs "flutter" (see *Tikkuney Zohar* #21, p.63a). Daat is the "middle path" that blends the opposite forces of Chokhmah and Binah — right and left (see above, Part 4); so too, the lungs are situated on both the right and left sides of the body.

When a person devotes himself to living a spiritual life, all of these diverse forces unite to transform him into a "Chariot of Godliness." As we have seen throughout our study, there is a level of spirituality which corresponds to every aspect of physicality. At every moment in life, each person has free will to choose the path upon which he wishes to embark (or at the very least, the manner in which he will walk upon a given path). As dynamic as they are, the inherent life-sustaining faculties of the heart and lungs also hold potential for sin. Man's mission is to take charge of his own direction and destiny — to become a Chariot of Godliness — and propel himself ever closer to God.

* * *

21

Tzimtzum: The Vacated Space

A lthough God created man as well as the world in which he lives, man is responsible for what he does with the world. To man was given the job of perfecting the world, and he must fulfill this job, with or without God's overt intervention. The work of perfection, or rectification, takes place on two planes simultaneously: in thought and in deed. "Deed" corresponds to the seven lower *Sefirot*, and "thought" corresponds to the three upper *Sefirot*, the *mochin*. Quite literally, it is the thought behind every deed that determines the power of that deed to effect rectification.

The Hebrew expression *hirhurei lev*, literally, "thoughts of the heart," refers specifically to the kind of thoughts that involve a conflict, or a vacillation between two opposing ways of processing reality. Such conflict is associated with the heart because its right and left ventricles are said to be the "seats" of the good and evil inclinations, respectively. This accounts for the conflicting emotions that people continually face.

The "wisdom of the heart" — the internalization of Chokhmah into the Binah of the heart — consists of recognizing and choosing the advice of the right ventricle, associated with the good inclination, over the advice of the left, which is associated with the evil inclination. This wisdom must be creative enough to counter any direct or flank attack of the evil inclination. In this respect, the heart is truly a wonder, for its creative action mirrors the original act of Creation. To understand this thought, let us glance at one of Rebbe Nachman's most famous teachings — the Torah of the Vacated Space. Although the concepts we are about to discuss are quite difficult, and the effort required to understand them very great, the rewards are commensurate with the effort.

The Paradox of Creation

Above (Chapter 3) we touched upon the ARI's teaching about the Vacated Space, known in Hebrew as the *Challal HaPanuy*. Prior to the Creation, there was only God. God is known as the *Ein Sof*, the Eternal, the Infinite — He has no beginning, no middle and no end. He is confined neither in time nor by space; He is omnipresent. Since God is everywhere, there was no "room" for the Creation to come into being, no *place* which could accommodate His Infinite Light. God thus constricted His Light away from a "center point," as it were, to create the Vacated Space. In this space would be created all the supernal Universes, and also the material world — the galaxies, our solar system, the planet earth and man (see diagram on p.23).

At first, God's Light surrounded this Vacated Space from without. He then reintroduced His Light, in the form of a *Kav* (Ray), into the Vacated Space, in a highly measured form, to prevent the Vacated Space from becoming filled too quickly with too much Light, which would cause it to collapse back into the *Ein Sof*. In this way, God proceeded to create the supernal Universes within the Vacated Space, beginning with the Ten *Sefirot* of the Universe of *Adam Kadmon* (Primordial Man), and continuing with the *Sefirot* of the Universes of *Atzilut* (Nearness or Emanation), *Beriyah* (Creation), *Yetzirah* (Formation), and finally the Universe of *Asiyah* (Action or Completion), in which our physical world became manifest.

Of course, the image of God's withdrawing His Light and then reintroducing it should not be taken literally. God exists equally everywhere, at all times. "Withdrawing His Light" from the "Vacated Space" to "make room" for Creation in no way implies that He was or is no longer there. God was "there" equally, both before and after He created the Vacated Space, and before and after He introduced the *Kav*. The difference between "before" and "after" exists only from our vantage point — because the whole world was created only for the sake of mankind. As the ARI explains, the reason God constricted His Light and created the Vacated Space was so that man could have independent existence and free will. God certainly exists within all of Creation, for without Godliness nothing can exist. Yet if God's existence were clear and obvious in this world, man would not have free will. For this reason God contracted His Light, as it were, concealing Himself from man, making it *seem* to man's limited vision as if there is a vacuum, a place devoid of Godliness.

This is the mystery of the *Tzimtzum* (Self-constriction). On the one hand, the Vacated Space must be thought of as devoid of Godliness — if this were not the case it would not be a "vacated" space. On the other hand, God must necessarily be present in the Vacated Space — for nothing, not even so-called "empty space," can exist without the presence of Godliness.

Regarding this paradox of the Vacated Space, Rebbe Nachman taught:

The Blessed Name created the world out of His deep compassion. He wished to reveal His compassion, but without a world, to whom could He show it? He therefore brought the entire Creation into existence, from the highest emanation down to the lowest point within the center of the physical world, all in order to demonstrate His compassion.

When the Blessed Name wished to create the worlds, however, there was no place in which to do so. This was due to the fact that all that existed was His Infinite Essence [which precluded the existence of anything finite]. He therefore constricted His Light. By virtue of this *Tzimtzum* [Self-constriction], a Vacated Space was brought into existence. It was within this Vacated Space that all the Divine Persona [*Partzufim*] and Attributes [*Sefirot*] were brought into being.

The Vacated Space was absolutely necessary for Creation. Without it, there would have been no place in which to create the universe. This *Tzimtzum*, which resulted in the Vacated Space, is at the moment incomprehensible to us. The only time we will be able to grasp its concept is in the Ultimate Future. This is because we can attribute [to the Vacated Space] only two mutually exclusive states, namely, existence and nonexistence.

The Vacated Space came into being as a result of the *Tzimtzum*, from which [to the extent that we can express it] God constricted [withdrew] His Essence. Therefore, God's Essence does not exist [in this Space]. If His Essence were there, this Space would not be vacated, and there would be nothing besides the Infinite Essence. If this were true, there would be no place whatsoever for the creation of the universe.

The actual truth, however, is that God's Essence must nevertheless be in this Space, for it is beyond any doubt that nothing can exist without His Life Force. [Therefore, if God's Essence did not exist in the Vacated Space, nothing else could exist there either.] It is impossible for any human being to understand the concept of the Vacated Space; only in the Ultimate Future will it be understood (*Likutey Moharan* I, 64).

Let us now apply this approach to Creation to each individual, on a daily, hourly, even momentary basis.

*

Rebbe Nachman taught:

Prior to Creation, the Light of the Holy One was *Ein Sof* [Infinite]. The Holy One wanted to reveal [the Attribute of] His *Malkhut* [Kingship]. However, since there can be no king without a nation, He "needed," as it were, to create human beings who would accept the yoke of His Kingship.

It is impossible to perceive His *Malkhut* except through His Attributes [i.e., *Sefirot*], for through the Attributes we perceive His Godliness, and then we can know that there is a Lord, a Ruler and a Sovereign Authority. He thus contracted the Light of *Ein*

Sof to the extremities, leaving the *Challal HaPanuy* [Vacated Space], and within this *Challal HaPanuy* He created the Universes, which are themselves the Attributes (*Likutey Moharan* I, 49:1).

We can better understand the necessity of the Creation and the Vacated Space through the verse (Psalms 104:24), "How manifold are Your works, God; You made them all with Chokhmah [Wisdom]." As we have seen, Chokhmah represents an undifferentiated wisdom, while Binah is the manifestation of that wisdom. On the level of Chokhmah, all that exists is undifferentiated potential or essence, whereas Binah is the source of the ability to analyze this knowledge and to break it down into its component parts (see above, Chapters 14 and 18). When applied to the Act of Creation and to the Vacated Space, the Creation represents Chokhmah while the Vacated Space represents Binah. With Chokhmah alone, there would be no diversification within Creation. It is through the Vacated Space, corresponding to Binah, that the design of all the Universes comes into being.

Rebbe Nachman continues:

The *tzayar* [designer] of the Attributes is the heart [which represents Binah]. It is thus written (Exodus 31:6), "In the hearts of the wise, I have placed wisdom." The thought of Creation originated in Chokhmah, as it is written (Psalms 104:24), "How manifold are Your works, God; You made them all with Chokhmah," and takes form in the heart. The heart, however, is the *tZayaR* [יצר, the one that gives form to this thought], as it is written (*ibid.* 73:26), "*tZuR* [צור, rock] of my heart."

But there is a *YetZiRah* [formation] for good and a *YetZiRah* for evil. On the verse (Genesis 2:7), "*VaYeetZeR YHVH Elohim —* And the Lord God formed [the man from the dust of the earth]," the Sages taught (*Berakhot* 61a), "*VaYeetZeR* [וייצר] has two *yods* [when one could have sufficed]. Why? They stand for the two *YetZaRin* [inclinations], the good inclination and the evil inclination." Good thoughts are [an expression of] the good inclination; evil thoughts are [an expression of] the evil inclination..."

[Thus when a person thinks good thoughts, he purifies the Space of Creation.] But when a person thinks evil thoughts, he clogs up Creation's Space, that is, the space where the Attributes are revealed. For the heart is the "*tZuR* of the worlds" (cf. Isaiah 26:4), meaning, *tZayaR*, the one that gives form to the Attributes.

On an individual level, as long as the heart of a Jew burns with a flaming passion, revelation of the [finite] Attributes is impossible. This is because the passion of the heart is really an infinite desire for the *Ein Sof*. The heart must therefore contract its burning desire and create an "empty space," as King David wrote (Psalms 109:22), "My heart is a *challal* [hollow space] within me." Only by contracting the desire of the heart can one experience a revelation of the *MiDot* [finite Attributes], that is, the ability to serve the Blessed Name in stages, in the proper *MiDah* [measure]...

We see, then, that when a person entertains in his heart good thoughts of how to serve the Blessed Name, his heart becomes an aspect of "*tzur* [i.e., *tzayar*] of my heart," and of "my heart is a *challal* [hollow space] within me." Within the *challal* of his heart his deeds can be revealed, and through his good deeds and attributes it is revealed that he wholly accepts the yoke of the Kingship of Heaven (Likutey Moharan I, 49:1).

As has been explained, if it were patently obvious that Godly wisdom penetrates all levels of Creation, man would have no choice but to serve God. He would literally see God's greatness and be consumed with an irresistible desire to unite with His Infinite Light. To prevent this, the heart must make of itself a hollow space wherein Godliness can be revealed in stages. The verse thus states (Psalms 109:22), "My heart is hollow within me." Thus the heart (Binah) corresponds to the hollow of Creation, the Vacated Space. Within the Vacated Space is placed Godliness, but gradually, in stages. This is the meaning of (Exodus 31:6), "In the hearts of the wise, I have placed wisdom." For Godly Chokhmah is concealed within Binah, which corresponds to the heart. Thus, even in the Vacated Space, Godliness exists in concealed form. Binah, then, is conceptually the Vacated Space wherein the formation of all the Universes takes place.

In order to find the concealed Godliness, we must think good and positive thoughts. These good thoughts lead us to perform good deeds, for our thoughts result in a "good creation." If, however, we think evil thoughts, our "creation" is evil [it obstructs Godliness]. Our hollow, our "vacated space," becomes the source of evil characteristics and bad attributes and we are, in a sense, destroying Creation, filling the Vacated Space with evil, God forbid.

Herein lies the secret of the Vacated Space. God's Light was everywhere, yet He carved out a "Vacated Space" to make "room" for Creation. So too must we "make room" for a "good creation" in our heart, into which Godliness can enter and dwell. This we accomplish through thinking good thoughts, bringing about a good creation — a higher and better level of conciousness. Then we can merit an even greater revelation of Godliness. In fact, when we turn our hearts into a Vacated Space to receive Godliness, then simply by thinking good thoughts we have formed a new creation. We can then rise to the level of performing miracles — in emulation of the original miracle of Creation (see *Likutey Moharan* I, 49:4, 13).

If the mystery of the Vacated Space has proven difficult to comprehend, we can take comfort with a different teaching of Rebbe Nachman: "When a person truly has a 'heart,' his location [or his space] is of no consequence. God is called *HaMakom* [The Place] of the Universe, and when someone *feels* God in his heart, that is the only *place* that matters!" (*Likutey Moharan* II, 56).

*

Cardiac Arrest

A heart attack can have various causes. It may result from insufficient blood reaching the heart, caused by a clogging of the arteries that feed it. Heart failure may also occur when the heart cannot pump blood adequately, because the heart itself is weak. These same risk factors are present in the spiritual dimension.

The heart has a deeply rooted yearning to serve God, but the vessels through which the "blood" of this yearning must be pumped sometimes become clogged or worn out. As long as a person has not divested himself of the excessive buildup of "fats and cholesterol" — material desires — within his spiritual system, his vessels cannot bear up to the pressure of the heart's pumping activity. His "blood flow" becomes polluted by the impurities of his evil thoughts. When his deeds are good, as a result of good thoughts, the heart remains healthy. Impure thoughts, on the other hand, clog up his system with evil deeds, causing a spiritual "heart attack."

Spiritual "cardiac arrest" can occur when the heart diminishes its resolve to serve God; this results from improper thoughts. These thoughts clog the heart, preventing it from doing its job properly. This invariably leads to a weakening — sometimes even a cessation — of one's resolve to seek spirituality.

How can one prevent spiritual cardiac arrest? Understanding the nature of the "illness" will lead to finding the "cure."

As we have seen, Creation has two opposite aspects: good and evil. The heart gives form and body to one's thoughts, enabling ideas to manifest. In this sense, man's thoughts parallel the Act of Creation. Every time we think, we should realize that we are engaging in an act of creation (see *Likutey Moharan* I, 49:1). In view of this, Rebbe Nachman cautions against letting things get out of hand. Based on the principle that everything in creation tends to seek its source, he teaches that one's heart (Binah), too, instinctively seeks its source (Chokhmah), so that the heart naturally burns with an all-consuming desire to serve God. The inherent danger is that one might try to ascend the spiritual ladder faster than one can actually climb. This gives rise to spiritual exhaustion or "burnout" — when someone who is as yet incapable of absorbing the spiritual levels he strives for lapses in his devotions; or when his level of mitzvah observance is inadequate for the spiritual awareness he is seeking. In the latter case, his yearning heart is not supplied with enough practical nourishment to keep it pumping properly.

The cure for such an individual can be found in the Act of Creation. God formed the Universes within the Vacated Space. In order to fulfill the purpose of Creation it was necessary to form lower worlds, each on its own appropriate level, as a framework into which the soul could descend to serve God, even when He is hidden. Man in his own realm also functions on varying levels. His heart "thinks," and accordingly the lower levels of his body translate those thoughts into physical deeds. If the thoughts coming from the heart are good, the physical deeds will be good; while evil thoughts generate evil deeds. Once the good deeds manifest, they keep the heart going, "supplying" the heart with a sense of accomplishment, strengthening its desire to perform more good deeds.

We can see that we must guard our thoughts very carefully, for every thought carries with it awesome potential. Good thoughts keep the heart spiritually healthy, so that it can keep "pumping" in a controlled manner, yearning for spirituality, while at the same time being held in check to prevent it from "burning" beyond its capabilities (see *Likutey Moharan* I, 49).

*

Heart Medication: Faith

The steps which must be taken to forestall a "cardiac arrest" are daunting. If a physical heart attack is difficult to prevent, how much more so a spiritual one!

As we have seen, Rebbe Nachman taught that the heart corresponds to the Vacated Space. In this Vacated Space there are many questions which demand answers; however, answers are not always forthcoming. This is due to the paradox of the Vacated Space: "God is there..." "He isn't..." "He must be...." Confusion reigns, which may give a person a "heavy heart," since all questions which stem from the paradox of the Vacated Space must necessarily preclude answers. It is extremely difficult to find God in these questions; in this matter one must rely on faith to "lighten" the overburdened heart, for God exists even (and especially) where there are unanswerable questions. Even someone who is plagued by a "heavy heart" can find God, if he strengthens himself with faith (*Likutey Moharan* I, 64:6).

Questions of faith, along with other burdens, such as financial problems or difficulties in the home, all weigh heavily upon the "understanding heart." Such unrelenting pressures all too often can contribute to an unstable heart condition. Sometimes a "change of diet," such as a switch to reading materials which are more conducive to faith than to heresy, can suffice to alleviate the pressure. Other remedies may call for "medication" — a daily dosage of prayer, for instance. Unfortunately, there are times when "bypass" or "open-heart" surgery is required, necessitating one to change one's lifestyle radically in order to attain spirituality.

In the next chapter, we will see how questions can lead to a divided heart. Rebbe Nachman taught that we must strengthen our faith so that we can attain a level of inner peace. This inner peace becomes the answer to any heretical questions that may arise in one's heart (see *Likutey Moharan* I, 62:2).

*

It is customary to lift up one's hands after washing for bread, before drying them. When one does so, one draws down holiness.

Orach Chaim 162:1; *Sha'ar HaMitzvot, Ekev*

The verse states (Psalms 134:2), "Lift up your hands in holiness and bless God." This indicates that when we lift our hands up to our eyes or forehead (i.e., the mind), indicating Chokhmah, we are able to draw down blessing into the heart (Binah) (see *Shaar HaMitzvot, Ekev* p.91).

Rebbe Nachman teaches that the main source of faith is in one's heart, but that faith becomes *true* conviction when it spreads throughout one's entire body (*Likutey Moharan* I, 91). The Rebbe explains that we are able to draw holiness into ourselves through lifting up our hands by *believing* that raising the hands accomplishes this. This is what is meant by the verse (Psalms 119:86), "All Your mitzvot are faith" — we must have faith that by observing the mitzvot, we draw holiness down from the heavens into ourselves. In this sense, we extend our faith outwards from our heart to our hands (which are the "vehicles" through which we draw down influences from Above). Thus a person can spread his faith so that his entire body can experience it and transform his faith into *true faith*. Someone who attains true faith effectively raises his intellect to a higher level, so that he can truly *understand* what he previously knew only through faith. This is what is meant by being able to draw down holiness (Chokhmah) into the heart (Binah).

Faith goes a long way in strengthening one's ability to stand up to the tribulations of life, but one must be willing to exert oneself to achieve such a level. Working on faith is no easy task. It involves the entire body.

*

Prayer and Hitbodedut: *Meditations of the Heart*

> **Serve God with all your heart.**
>> Deuteronomy 11:13

> **Which devotion is performed in the heart? Prayer!**
>> Ta'anit 2a

In the array of the Ten *Sefirot*, Chesed (Lovingkindness) on the right and Gevurah (Judgment) on the left follow immediately after Binah (see Appendix D). Binah, directly above Gevurah, is actually the source of all judgments, as in (Proverbs 8:14), "I am Binah; strength [Gevurah] is mine." Furthermore, we know that Binah is rooted in the heart, which is situated slightly to the left in the body (Zohar I, 10b; Likutey Moharan I, 41). We can understand from this that Binah, as the source of Gevurah (strength), indicates that the heart has tremendous *power* which, when properly channeled, can direct a person towards God. Rebbe Nachman thus teaches that when someone arouses his heart to serve God, both the strength and the judgments (found in the heart) inspire him with warm words.

Conceptually, the judgments one faces are the sufferings one endures (e.g. family problems, confusion, doubts, adversity; see also above, Chapter 9, "The Bloodstream"). These judgments inspire a person to examine his thoughts and deeds to see if they are rooted in good or, God forbid, in evil. Once he has seen the truth of his actions, whether he is spurred on to change his ways or his good deeds inspire him to do even more good deeds, he can then cry out to God with warm words of prayer with absolute truth (*Likutey Moharan* I, 38:5; see also *ibid.* 15:2). This arousal of one's heart in prayer thus mitigates judgments, since serving God with truth in one's heart reveals the choice (i.e., the better judgment and sincerity) of that person's desires. His truthful prayers act as a guide to direct the person on a path that will eventually alleviate his sufferings. Thus the act of praying gives one the power to bring abundant lovingkindness and bounty, the opposite of judgment, into the world (*Likutey Moharan* I, 45, 46).

Rebbe Nachman teaches that prayer is the most effective means by which to achieve a revelation of Godliness within the heart. This explains why the *Amidah* (Eighteen Benedictions) prayer is recited silently, for it expresses the deepest yearning of the heart, which is concealed (*Likutey Moharan* I, 49:2, 4).

One of Rebbe Nachman's strongest recommendations is for everyone to seclude himself in *hitbodedut* every single day without fail. *Hitbodedut* is the expression of one's own private prayers and communications with God, said in a secluded spot. Each person should choose a period of time daily to reflect upon his past deeds; he should then meditate upon his current situation and pray for the future. An hour's time to be set aside for this purpose every day is the Rebbe's suggestion, but one can (and should) start with shorter periods of time, even five or ten minutes, and later, as one advances, extend the time. The prayers he recites during *hitbodedut* should be said in one's mother tongue, because (*Likutey Moharan* II, 120) "when praying in one's mother tongue, the prayers flow more readily from the heart."

In a sense, practicing *hitbodedut* is also a way of mitigating the judgments of the heart. There is no one who does not feel confusion, frustration, anger and guilt, and rarely do people find a way of expressing these feelings without hurting themselves or others, most often those closest to themselves. Rebbe Nachman's prescription of *hitbodedut*, judging oneself, one's thoughts and one's deeds, allows for a venting of these feelings in a safe and positive manner.

Rebbe Nachman thus taught:

> The heart is the source of judgment. The practice of *hitbodedut* rectifies the heart; it establishes a proper sense of judgment within a person, while at the same time lessening his potential for evil (see *Likutey Moharan* I, 59:2).

This form of prayer is a powerful instrument to help one attain spirituality. It allows an individual to express to God everything that weighs heavily upon his heart, to express his innermost feelings: his pain, his joy, his thanks, his grief — anything that accumulates in his heart. Through *hitbodedut*, he can gather his thoughts, confront himself directly and analyze his daily routine. He can judge his past deeds, assess his current situation and envision his future. Most importantly, through *hitbodedut* he can articulate these thoughts in prayer before God.

Hitbodedut is a powerful form of self-expression, yet without the feeling of shame one experiences when confessing one's shortcomings to another person. It helps to eliminate the frustrations that stem from having pent-up emotions and nowhere to turn with them. God is always extremely near, for God resides within one's heart — within one's "vacated space." And God *always* listens.

* * *

22

The Understanding Heart

Kings, presidents and prime ministers are regarded by all as the commanders-in-chief of their respective armed forces. However, actual command of an army is assigned to the chief of staff, who directs all the troops in carrying out the general orders of the commander-in-chief. In the body, the mind might be considered the commander-in-chief, while the heart is the chief of staff; and in order to respond properly to every situation, the heart must be able to understand the needs of its troops, i.e., the body.

As the chief of staff, the heart's job is quite difficult. It must constantly exhort its troops to do their best, keep up their morale, and pump life and energy into them. It has to be creative, always coming up with "fresh ideas" to hold the body and soul together. Rebbe Nachman taught:

Hearing depends on the heart, as it is written (I Kings 3:9), "Grant Your servant a hearing [understanding] heart to judge Your people and to distinguish between right and wrong." If spoken words do not penetrate the listener's heart, it is as if they were never heard. In Hebrew, the concept of "paying attention" is called *tesumat lev* [literally, "attentiveness of the heart"]. In order to truly hear what someone is saying to us — not just their words, but their intention — the heart must be attentive. [This idea can be applied to] prayer, the "service of the heart (*Ta'anit* 2a; see *Likutey Moharan* I, 22:9). When we pray, we must concentrate our heart's attention and hear the words we are saying so that they will penetrate our hearts. Only then will God Himself actually "hear" and hearken to our prayers (see *Likutey Moharan* I, 29:1).

Rebbe Nachman thus taught:

> The heart "hears." The hearing process commences with the ears, but must end up with the heart's understanding what is said. A teacher must speak to his student's heart, while the student must take heed and engrave those words upon his own heart (*Likutey Moharan* II, 91:1).

Thus understanding is rooted in the heart, and it is an important tool in its role as "chief of staff" of the body.

*

Binah (Understanding)

As we have seen (above, Chapter 16), Chokhmah is the wisdom we learn from others, through study, by observation and so on. It represents the ability to master a subject and to integrate its fundamental axioms into our mental processes. Binah is the ability to extract additional data from information which has been already integrated, and to understand or distinguish one thing from another. It is related to the Hebrew word *bein*, meaning "between." In this sense, Binah implies distance and separation: in order to view something objectively, you must place yourself at a distance from it. Thus, Binah is the ability to examine everything that has already been learned through Chokhmah, to distance yourself, emotionally and intellectually, from that information, and to research and investigate it.

Every human being has both a mind and a heart, which correspond respectively to the *Sefirot* of Chokhmah and Binah. Each of us possesses his own basic cache of knowledge upon which the mind acts and accordingly directs the body. However, the directives of the mind are essentially neural impulses, which are automatic responses. It is in the heart, Binah, which focuses differently from the mind, where we come fully to appreciate and understand a given situation. The way in which our hearts "hear" and "understand" a predicament will determine the manner in which we respond to it.

Man is instinctively aware of this: figures of speech depict people as having "a heart of stone," "a heart of gold," "a cold heart" or "an understanding heart." The heart is susceptible to all the various aches and pains experienced throughout the body. It also feels one's joys and apprehensions, and responds to love and fear. Regarding the heart's understanding, Rebbe Nachman taught:

> The heart is Binah, which refers to understanding. When a person suffers, the heart "understands" the suffering, and feels it most sharply. This is because when the entire body faces danger, the blood rushes to the heart — its commanding officer — seeking advice. The heart attempts to "push away" this extra "invading blood" that has rushed to it, which is why the heart pounds more rapidly when faced with danger (*Likutey Moharan* II, 2:2).

> The verse states, "Deep waters are the counsel in a man's heart, but a man of understanding will draw them forth" (Proverbs 20:5). The "deep waters" in one's heart are the ideas [i.e., new teachings and perceptions], logically thought through, that counsel a person as to how to attain his goal in life (see *Likutey Moharan* I, 61:5).

*

Maintaining command over the body, with all its complexities, is not an easy task. As we have seen, many opposing forces which cause suffering are found in the body, each one pulling the individual in a different direction. The heart must therefore be a very unique organ to be able to command its "troops." It must play a fully active role, directing all bodily activities to meet and overcome every challenge to the body's well-being.

Yet there may at times arise circumstances in which the heart as chief of staff does not function as an effective leader. It becomes a pawn of those over whom it ostensibly rules. In such instances the heart surrenders its commanding position. It becomes (Ecclesiastes 10:2) "a foolish heart" — a lustful heart — craving the body's self-induced passions (produced by the various internal organs, which return polluted blood to the heart). (See above, Chapter 10, where we discussed the "liverization" of the heart.)

All this is manifest within the physical structure of the heart. Its right and left chambers house the good and evil inclinations; thus it is the heart that contains the potential for choosing between right and wrong. The right side of the heart expels evil (carbon dioxide) and generates good (by pumping blood to the lungs, bringing fresh, life-giving oxygen from the lungs to enrich the blood). Spiritually speaking, the task of dispensing the good then falls to the left side of the heart, the residence of the evil inclination, whose task it is to obscure the good and to tempt people to do evil. If the "understanding heart" is to perform its function well, as it was intended to do, it must maintain control over its soldiers, pumping its blood in such a way that it will produce spiritually beneficial results.

Rebbe Nachman taught:

> Man's main strength is in his heart. One who has a "strong heart" will fear nothing. Such a person can achieve many victories. This is what is meant by our Sages' teaching (Avot 4:1), "Who is mighty? One who conquers his inclination" (Likutey Moharan I, 249).

With a strong heart, we can maintain control in any situation and overcome all obstacles. When we overcome our evil inclination, we achieve a powerful victory. Rebbe Nachman thus taught (Likutey Moharan II, 43), "One who is strong-hearted [strong-willed and determined] will not fear to enter into battle [against the evil one]."

Let us explore some of the effects the evil inclination has on the heart, and the "weapons" that are available to us to combat it.

*

Treatment for a Congested Heart

Congestive heart failure can be fatal. Sometimes such a

condition requires surgery. The same applies to a spiritually congested heart condition.

Rebbe Nachman taught:

Evil thoughts congest the heart (*Likutey Moharan* I, 49:1).

Desires originate in the heart; the wicked are controlled by their hearts' desires (*Likutey Moharan* I, 33:7–8). The three major lusts that prevent one's heart from feeling awe and love for God are: avarice, sexual lust and gluttony. Burning desires for material pleasures are felt primarily in the heart; they effectively block out feelings of spirituality (*Likutey Moharan* II, 1:4).

Yet even if these obstacles appear insurmountable, treatment is available; there is a recommended "surgery." Rebbe Nachman teaches that "a 'heart of stone' refers to those distant from charity, while a 'merciful heart' applies to charitable people" (*Likutey Moharan* II, 15:1). Acts of charity can alleviate the effects of a spiritually congested heart.

The Rebbe thus promotes charity as a cure-all for the heart's spiritual maladies. But, many ask, what if one cannot afford to give charity? The Talmud teaches (cf. *Sukkah* 49b) that charity has many levels which can be divided into two main categories: *tzedakah* (charity) and *gemilut chasadim* (acts of kindness). While charity is generally assumed to involve a monetary gift, this is not always true. It can take the form of assistance in other ways, such as raising funds, volunteering time and so on.

Furthermore, the Talmud explains (*ibid.*) that *gemilut chasadim* (acts of kindness) are considered even greater than monetary gifts in three ways:

1. Charity involves only financial assistance. An act of kindness can be performed with one's body, with one's money, or with anything else one owns.

2. Charity is given only to the poor. An act of kindness can be performed for the wealthy and the poor alike.

3. Charity is given only to the living. An act of kindness can be performed for both the living and the deceased.

We can understand from the Talmud that Rebbe Nachman's use of the term "charity" is not limited to financial contributions for worthy causes (though these are very important when possible). Any charitable deed or appropriate act of kindness serves to "open up" a person's heart and to "make room" in it for another person's needs. This is because charity is an act of love, a compassionate deed. This is what helps to relieve the heart of its spiritual "congestion."

The benefits of giving charity are indeed far-reaching. Rebbe Nachman taught that there is a *no'am elyon*, a great, exalted pleasure, emanating from the Divine Source, which is constantly descending to this world for man's benefit. In order to become a recipient of this great pleasure, each person must first arouse his own heart with genuine love for God. This love is aroused by the giving of charity. Charity in general, and that which benefits the Holy Land in particular, grants the giver a greater portion of this Divine pleasure (*Likutey Moharan* II, 71:7).

*

Division and Strife
Rebbe Nachman taught:

A person's heart contains two inclinations, one towards good and one towards evil. This causes division within the heart. [An example of this division is] when a person feels he "knows" that God is always present, yet is lax in using his prayer time to really speak to God. If he truly felt God's presence, he would certainly pray with all his might. The fact that he is lax and does not exert himself to pray with full concentration shows that part of him "does not acknowledge" God's presence. This is the result of a "divided" heart (*Likutey Moharan* I, 62:2).

Strife, simply defined, is a lack of accord between two parties. Two countries might argue between themselves; so might two families or two individuals. The strife that exists within one's own heart is the result of a schism between one's right side, which strives for spirituality, and one's left side, which pulls towards materialism. Someone who has not yet succeeded in fully purifying his heart will always feel this "inner strife." Questions of faith, and confusion concerning both one's immediate and long-term goals, are all symptomatic of a divided heart. Rebbe Nachman explained it this way:

> The world is full of strife. There are wars between the great world powers; there are conflicts within different localities; there are feuds among families; there is discord between neighbors and friction within a household: between man and wife, between parents and children... Life is short; people die a little each day. The day that just passed will never return, but people still fight, and never once do they remember their ultimate goal in life.
>
> The characteristic traits of each nation are reflected in individuals. Some nations are known for their anger, for example, and others for bloodthirstiness. Each nation has its own particular trait. In the same way, these traits are to be found in each household. Even someone who wishes to live in peace can be dragged into conflict by virtue of his living among conflicting parties.
>
> Man is a microcosm, holding within himself the world and everything in it. A man living alone can become insane, because his personality is forced to focus upon the "warring nations" within him, and he finds no peace. When Mashiach comes, *all* these wars will be abolished (*Rabbi Nachman's Wisdom #77*).

If someone's heart is divided, what can he do to "pull himself together"?

Rebbe Nachman placed much emphasis on the study of the Codes of Law. The Codes abound with discussions, sometimes quite heated, between the various Sages regarding what is permitted and what is forbidden, what is pure and what is impure, and so on. One's goal during one's studies should be to clarify the opinions of the Sages, bringing "peace" to the opposing views and coming to a clear conclusion. This method of study — examining opposing views and arriving at a peaceful solution — can have a deep and lasting effect upon a person's character. Employing one's Binah (Understanding) to resolve a conflict of Torah law can bring "peace" to one's divided heart, the heart divided between two inclinations (see *Likutey Moharan* I, 62:2). Though this method of study is an advanced one and will certainly pose difficulties for those who are unfamiliar with the system of Talmudic research, Rebbe Nachman's directive to study the Codes in order to achieve lasting benefit is a universal one. In several lessons, he speaks about the importance of studying and knowing the Codes in order to proceed on the proper path in life.

Rebbe Nachman taught further:

> The good inclination is known as (Ecclesiastes 4:13) "a poor but wise child" [poor, because few listen to him; wise, because he leads one on the path of life]. The evil inclination is compared to (*ibid.*) "an old, foolish king" [people tend to listen because he is king, but his advice is foolish]. These two inclinations represent the kingdom of holiness and the kingdom of impurity. One who studies Torah with effort strengthens the kingdom of holiness (*Likutey Moharan* I, 1:2).

> The ARI used to expend tremendous effort in his studies of the Codes. He exerted himself so much that it caused him to break out in a sweat (*Shaar HaMitzvot, Va'etchanan* p.79).

Rebbe Nachman teaches that advice which comes from improper sources overwhelms the heart and putrefies it. The heart is then compared to an outhouse; the advice of that heart is malodorous (*Likutey Moharan* I, 61:4). Rabbi Chaim Vital thus writes (*Shaar HaMitzvot, loc. cit.*) that the reason the ARI worked himself into a sweat when he studied was in order to break the illusory powers of the evil inclination that envelop the heart. We have seen (Chapter 12) how excess waste products pollute one's system and how sweating is one way of purifying the body of this waste. We have pointed out (Chapter 6) that the 613 commandments of the Torah are called the "613 precepts of advice." This type of advice also brings harmony to the heart, clearing it of division.

* * *

23

The Seat of Emotion

The heart is the seat of the emotions, and love and fear (awe) encompass all one's emotions. Love of God is the ultimate level to strive for in the service of God, but it is unattainable until one first achieves the level of awe of God.

One of the 613 mitzvot of the Torah is to honor and respect the elderly and the wise, as it is written (Leviticus 19:32), "Honor the elderly...and fear your God." Our Sages, with their penetrating insight into human behavior, ask: "What about one who closes his eyes and pretends not to see the elderly and so does not rise to honor them? [They answer:] For this very reason, concerning every thought concealed within one's heart it is written, 'Fear your God'" (*Kiddushin* 32b; see *Likutey Moharan* I, 14:7).

Rashi explains that every individual knows deep in his heart whether he has acknowledged a person deserving of honor or whether he has chosen to ignore him. He might be able to fool others by pretending that he hasn't noticed the person; he might even fool others into thinking he is righteous, for he does "rise to the occasion" whenever he can't escape their scrutiny. In truth, however, this individual is unscrupulous. For this reason it is written, "Fear your God": since God knows all thoughts, if man fears Him he could never sidestep the mitzvot (*ibid., s.v. davar*). He may be able to fool other people into thinking he is fulfilling a mitzvah, but he cannot fool God.

Love and fear (or awe) are the two aspects of serving God most often referred to in Torah literature. Most sources point out that these two are inclusive of virtually all other teachings in the Torah. Love corresponds to the 248 positive commandments, for a person will be zealous in performing a mitzvah when he performs it as a labor of love. On the other hand, fear and awe correspond to the 365 prohibitions, for it is often only fear that restrains a person from transgressing (see *Tikkuney Zohar* #21, p.51a).

This fear can be the fear of God, or it might be the fear of being discovered while engaged in an illegal or immoral act, or fear of a monetary loss or illness. Whatever the reason, it is usually fear that prevents one from crossing the line when confronted by sin. Our Sages thus recommend that when it is one's thoughts that must be controlled, when one's deep inner convictions are being challenged by mixed emotions, one should focus upon the fear of God in the heart.

*

Jerusalem: Perfected Fear

> Abraham called the place [where he went to sacrifice Isaac] *YiRah* [fear]. Shem called it *SHaLeM* [perfection]. Therefore, declared the Holy One, in order not to slight either one of these tzaddikim, its name shall be *YeRuSHaLayiM* [Jerusalem].
>
> *Bereishit Rabbah* 56:10

What could be more thrilling than to witness the rebuilding of Jerusalem? After two millennia of war and desolation, Jerusalem is today being built up more rapidly than any other city in the world. These events were foreseen by our Prophets and foretold by our Sages, so it should not come as a total surprise. But the most exciting aspect of the rebuilding of Jerusalem is the knowledge that every person can make his own personal contribution to it every single moment of his life! How is this possible?

Rebbe Nachman taught:

> The source of fear is in the heart. Everyone must strive to develop his fear of God. The perfection of one's awe of God in effect causes Jerusalem to be rebuilt, for Jerusalem is *YeruShalem* [literally, "perfected fear"] (*Likutey Moharan* II, 1:4).

This teaching encapsulates some of Rebbe Nachman's most important lessons. One of the basic mitzvot that we are required to perform on a continual basis is that of *Yirat HaShem* (fear, reverence, awe of God), maintaining a constant awareness and awe of God at all times. This mitzvah applies at all times, irrespective of what we are doing, whether we are involved in spiritual pursuits or in the more mundane.

How can we manage to be constantly aware of God's presence? Throughout Rebbe Nachman's discourses, we find teachings about building up the level of one's awe of God through working on controlling the impulses of one's heart.

*

In the same lesson, Rebbe Nachman taught:

The rebuilding of Jerusalem is not the only benefit of developing one's fear of God. "Prophecy was lost after the destruction of the Holy Temple" (cf. *Bava Batra* 12b) and will return only with the rebuilding of Jerusalem. As the source of prophecy is fear of God, when fear of God is perfected, it becomes elevated and revealed in the world. This chain of events creates an angel which can effect prophecy (*Likutey Moharan* II, 1:6).

There are three major factors which dull the sense of awe in one's heart. They are the three lusts: avarice, immorality and gluttony. The heart's burning desire for these lusts displaces the potential for the awe of God. To rectify these lusts, one must draw Chokhmah, Binah and Daat into one's heart. These three *mochin* correspond respectively to the three lusts in the heart. [This teaches us that] the power of intellect can be used to overcome the negative aspects of the emotions (*Likutey Moharan* II, 1:4–5).

In this lesson, Rebbe Nachman goes on to explain that each of the major lusts can be rectified through one of the Three Festivals. At the time of the Exodus, the Jews were given great wealth, whence we derive that the festival of Pesach can rectify avarice. Prior to the Revelation on Mount Sinai, the Jews were commanded to abstain from marital relations; thus Shavuot rectifies sexual sin and misconduct. Sukkot is the time of year when the crops are gathered in; thus inherent within Sukkot is the potential to rectify gluttony. It is no coincidence that on each of these Festivals we are commanded to ascend to Jerusalem: on a deeper level, this indicates that by rectifying these lusts, we can ascend to the level of fear of God. Since each Festival has its own unique characteristics, we can conclude that on each one of them a new level of intellect, or a new revelation of Godliness, is revealed. In this way, the three *mochin* can counteract the effects of the three lusts.

Here again we see how important it is for the heart to maintain its command over the body. It is the major lusts that impede the heart from achieving perfected fear, and so from rebuilding Jerusalem. These lusts, which emanate from uncontrolled emotions, directly affect the heart. However, controlling one's desires leads to a pure heart and perfected awe, through which one can experience Godliness. This accomplishes a level of the rebuilding of Jerusalem, for when Jerusalem is rebuilt, God's presence will be revealed for all to see. As Rebbe Nachman went on to teach, by "rebuilding Jerusalem" — by rectifying the awe of God in one's heart — an angel is created (*Likutey Moharan* II, 1:6), which in turn bestows spiritual powers and angelic qualities upon a person!

*

The Key to the Treasury

> He [God] shall be the stability of time, a store of salvation, wisdom and knowledge; [yet it is] the fear of God [which] is His treasure.
> Isaiah 33:6

When speaking of the trials and tribulations that the Jewish people will face prior to the Ultimate Redemption, Isaiah prophesied that the ability to maintain faith in God at this time would depend on the extent of a person's fear of God. Fear is therefore called "God's treasure," for it is an inexhaustible source of strength in times of need. Our Sages point out that the above verse contains six key terms followed by a seventh. The six correspond to the six orders of the Mishnah (and the six *Sefirot* from Chesed to Yesod). The seventh, again, is the "fear of God," His treasure (corresponding to Malkhut). The verse thus teaches us that, without fear of God, one cannot hope to plumb the depths of the Torah. Without fear and awe of God, one cannot enter the inner precincts of the Torah. The gates remain locked. Thus, "One who studies Torah without awe of Heaven is compared to one who has been given the keys to the inner storehouse, but does not possess the keys to the outer gate. How can this person enter?" (*Shabbat* 31a).

*

Joy

The main place of joy is in the heart.

Likutey Moharan I, 24:2

Of all man's emotions, joy is the most exhilarating, as well as the most elusive. One who feels joy in one's marriage, job and environment will be eager to continue productively on his or her chosen path. On the other hand, depression, the opposite of joy, is man's worst enemy and the greatest stumbling block to his achievements.

Rebbe Nachman teaches that joy and happiness can free a person from the restraints that bind him to the material world. "One cannot attain *yishuv haDaat* [mental calm, serenity of mind, careful consideration, sober judgment] unless one first attains a joyous state of mind" (*Likutey Moharan* II, 10). The joy Rebbe Nachman refers to here cannot be a "surface laugh" or a general light-heartedness. It must be a powerful joy that penetrates the barricades which have been established by the many problems and confusions of life, and that can find its way into the heart. The verse tells us (Isaiah 55:12), "You shall depart [the exile] with joy..." With joy we can leave behind our frustrations and anticipate God's help and salvation.

The power of joy is so intense that it can bring one to a

revelation of Godliness within one's heart. Rebbe Nachman further teaches that, in a sense, the Divine Presence corresponds to the joy of the heart. One who performs the mitzvot with joy elevates the Divine Presence from its exile (*Likutey Moharan* I, 24:2; see above, Chapter 16). In this way, one is able to "see" God, for His Presence becomes revealed!

However, depression, mankind's most common affliction, stands in the way. We have already seen how depression stems from within — from the desire for excess as well as from unrealistic expectations of perfection (Chapter 19). When a person experiences a "bad day," his emotions become frazzled; anger sets in, and nerves become frayed. He automatically closes his mind and heart to any potential feelings of joy. Even if a person actively seeks happiness at this point, it tends to allude him.

Rebbe Nachman teaches that of all the devotions necessary to serve God, joy is the most difficult to attain, and once attained, the most difficult to maintain (see *Rabbi Nachman's Wisdom* #20). When one is beset by difficulties, surrounded by financial, family and/or health problems, there may seem to be no alternative to descending into depression. Yet it is especially then that the heart must be the seat of joy. As "chief of staff" of the human body, the heart has the ability to overcome grief and depression; it can reawaken our spirit and inspire us to reassume our responsibilities in life.

This phenomenon can be seen in countless situations, Rebbe Nachman teaches. When a person is intensely joyous, he can become enlivened to the point that he will dance and clap his hands. He draws this spirit from a joyous heart (*Likutey Moharan* I, 10:1,6), for when joy abounds, his spirit is uplifted. The hands and feet receive positive messages from the heart and act accordingly. Furthermore, the Rebbe tells us, "A heavy heart [filled with sadness, jealousy, etc.] causes a sad face," whereas "a happy heart improves one's appearance!" (*Likutey Moharan* I, 60:6; see *ibid.* II, 5:11).

*

Yearning

Rebbe Nachman taught:

> One's heart always yearns and burns. Sometimes that yearning is for holiness; at other times, for physical desires, for example, for avarice. There is a *ruach* which can descend and "cool off" that burning heart. This *ruach* is compared to the Divine Presence and is drawn into the heart through the giving of charity (*Likutey Moharan* I, 13:1).

Craving and longing are embedded in human nature. Everyone feels pangs of want, but it is the nature of a person's deep desires that will determine whether he yearns for spirituality or for material gratification. Furthermore, a person's desires might grow and become more than he can handle. We have seen (above, Chapter 21, "Cardiac Arrest") that even spiritual urges can be dangerous, when a person seeks more spirituality than he is intellectually or emotionally prepared for. Thus Rebbe Nachman taught (*Likutey Moharan* II, 9:2), "A person's spirit [*ruach*] must be regulated in order for the heart to burn properly [for God]."

The Rebbe teaches that a person's heart will sometimes burn for spirituality, while at other times it will burn with desires for the mundane; Torah study has the power to regulate both these types of burning desires (*Likutey Moharan* I, 78:4). Furthermore, when someone has a burning desire for God in his heart, if he *wants* to study Torah or pray, but is, for some reason, unable to (for example, he finds himself in the desert or without books), then this burning desire alone inscribes a [new] Torah teaching on High. One's burning desire for Torah and spirituality enables one to draw from the spirituality of the Supernal Heart (Binah) (*Likutey Moharan* I, 142). As we shall see (in Chapters, 24–25), the Torah consists of Five Books, which correspond to the five lobes of the lung. Since the lungs have a "cooling effect" upon the heart, it follows that the study of Torah can help "cool down" and control one's burning desires, whether they be for materialism, or for a degree of spirituality which is as yet beyond one's grasp.

The Rebbe also teaches that charity has the same power as the Torah in helping to overcome one's lusts. He illustrates this with the case of a person who is filled with avarice, the burning desire for wealth and material possessions. If this person gives charity, he displays his faith in God, that it is He Who provides. By giving charity, he temporarily overcomes his material lusts and merits assistance in achieving true spirituality.

*

Love

Perhaps the most powerful emotion of all is love. Love can be so all-consuming that nothing can stand in its path. King Solomon understood this well when he said (Songs 8:7), "Many waters cannot extinguish love." This is because human love is rooted in the Divine Attribute of Chesed (Lovingkindness). Since God is constantly bestowing His kindness upon Creation, feelings of kindness and love always abound in the world. They can drive man to incredible heights — or to the lowest depths.

Love of money can drive a person to risk his own life — or the lives of others who stand in his way. Sexual immorality is a perversion of love; too often it leads to broken homes and illegitimate or unwanted children. The love of power has all too often in the annals of history led to open warfare and large-scale bloodshed. Conversely, that same attribute of love, when properly applied, can build a healthy marriage and a warm, understanding home. It can propel a person to creative heights for the benefit of all mankind.

Thus, the awesome power of love — both its constructive and its destructive aspects — is best explained by Chesed's approximation to Binah (it immediately follows Binah; see Appendix D). The higher *Sefirot* (Keter, Chokhmah and Binah, the "mentalities") are concealed. The very first manifestation of those awesome powers in the lower Sefirot is through the Sefirah of Chesed, which indicates reaching out towards others and extending oneself on behalf of others. Seen in another light, Chesed is higher than Gevurah, indicating that it is "above and beyond" restraint, which is evidence to the great power of love. As we have seen throughout this book, a parallel exists between good and evil — whatever power exists for good can contain the very same potential for evil. Thus, if love is not harnessed properly — through Gevurah, i.e., awe and fear of God — it can be most destructive. If love is properly controlled, it is the most effective tool for the building of humanity and peace. Thus the verse states (Psalms 89:3), "The world is built through Chesed."

*

In our discussion of the respiratory system (Part 6), we will further examine the power of the attribute of love. We conclude this section with one of the Rebbe's teachings about love:

One who spreads love and brings peace between people effects great rectifications Above (*Likutey Moharan* I, 75:4).

* * *

24

The Pulse

The blood transports everything that circulates through the body along with it. Should an illness be present in the body, God forbid, it can often be detected through the pulse, which responds to and varies with every illness. Thus, variations in the pulse can be used to diagnose the specific illness that needs to be treated. Though this approach is not dealt with or even acknowledged in modern Western medical science, it is actively practiced in oriental and alternative forms of medicine and has proven quite effective.

As we have seen, the flow of blood is affected by the way in which we introduce oxygen into our bloodstream. The pulse, which has ten modes, corresponds to the Ten Commandments. The lungs, which have five lobes, corresponds to the Five Books of Moses (Torah) and the Five Books of Psalms (Prayer). Thus, Torah and prayer are beneficial for the pulse *(Likutey Moharan I, 8:9)*.

The source for the ten modes of pulse is found in the *Tikkuney Zohar* (#69, p.108).

> The Ten *Sefirot* are represented by the ten vowels of the Hebrew alphabet. According to the pulse, one can diagnose the illness....

In the Zohar, the ten modes are seen to parallel the Ten Sefirot which in turn correspond to the ten types of vowel points that are used in the Hebrew language (actually, there are nine, with the tenth being the complete absence of any vowels, just as Malkhut is said to have no light of its own, and only reflects the various different energies of the higher *Sefirot* as they flow through it). These vowel points serve as a kind of Morse Code. The code here is very simple: a vowel point is made up either of one, two or three dots (in various formations), a dash with a dot beneath it, or a dash. By comparing the pulse rhythm at particular spots on the body with the various vowel points, one can identify the spiritual source of sickness that lies behind any physical symptom. The Zohar thus states:

> At times, a pulse is made up of a short single beat. If its beat is low, it is a *Chirik* (a single point that is placed below a letter). If it is above, it corresponds to *Cholam* (a single point above a letter). If it is in the center, it corresponds to *Shuruk* (a single point in the middle of a letter)... At times, a pulse is made up of two equal beats, one immediately following the other. This corresponds to *Tzeiri* (two points placed below a letter side by side). If one beat beats high and the other low, this is *Shva* (two dots below a letter, one atop the other)... At times one beat goes up and one goes down... At times, one beat is long (like a dash) and one short...

For the purpose of our study of the pulse, let's review some basic Kabbalistic correspondences before we go on. Recall that the Ten *Sefirot* correspond to the four letters of the Tetragrammaton, *YHVH*, together with the apex of the *Yod*. From the top down, Keter corresponds to this apex, Chokhmah corresponds to the *Yod* itself, Binah to the first *Heh*, the Six *Sefirot* from Chesed to Yesod correspond to the *Vav*; and Malkhut corresponds to the final Heh.

By extension, these five levels correspond with the five levels of the soul — *Yechidah*, *Chayah*, *Neshamah*, *Ruach* and *Nefesh* — and with the five universes — *Adam Kadmon*, *Atzilut*, *Beriyah*, *Yetzirah* and *Asiyah*. Finally, these correspond with the Five *Partzufim* — *Arikh Anpin*, *Abba*, *Imma*, *Zer Anpin* and *Nukva* of *Zer Anpin* (Malkhut) (see above, Chapter 3).

Now, let us focus on the *Partzuf* of *Abba*, which, as we have seen, corresponds to the *Sefirah* of Chokhmah, the Universe of *Atzilut*, and the soul level of *Chayah*. A beautiful allusion to the connection between Chokhmah (Wisdom) and *Chayah* (Life Essence) is seen in the verse (Ecclesiastes 7:12), "*Chokhmah t'chayeh ba'aleha* — Wisdom enlivens its owner." Based on this connection, the ARI explains that concealed within the *Sefirah* of Chokhmah is the Life Essence of God which enlivens all the levels below it.

The expansion of the Tetragrammaton associated with *Chokhmah-Abba-Chayah* (when written by the method of *achorayim* — יוד הי ויו הי, יוד הי ויו, יוד הי, יוד) adds up to 184 (see Appendix D). This is the numerical value of the word *DoPheK* (דפק), Hebrew for pulse: *dalet* (ד=4), *peh* (פ=80), *kuf* (ק=100). Thus, the Life Essence, which provides the human lifeline, can be found and felt in the pulse. Rabbi Chaim Vital records that his master, the ARI, was in fact able to determine a person's spiritual deficiency or illness by feeling his pulse (*Shaar Ruach HaKodesh*, p.14).

We have seen that the body is comprised of four basic elements: fire, air, water and earth. There is natural body heat (fire), the blood carries oxygen through the system (air), a large proportion of the body is fluid (water), and the body itself is made of the element of earth. When every part of the body is working properly, harmony prevails and one enjoys good health. Should any of these elements begin to behave erratically, illness ensues. This illness, being present in the body, finds its way into the bloodstream; hence it can readily be detected in the pulse. The Zohar continues:

> A single low-key beat corresponds to the vowel point *chirik*, indicating that the element of water [body fluids and their sources] is not stable. If the pulse beats in single high-key beats [i.e., *cholam*], the element of fire [body heat and its sources] is too strong. A triple beat, corresponding to the *kubutz*, denotes that the element of air is blowing ill, either by agitating the body fluids or by wreaking havoc with the body temperature. Other double-rhythm beats correspond to *tseireh* and *sh'va*. Each signifies that a certain element

is in some way running amok, causing illness. However, a steady pulse corresponds to *patach* or *kamatz*, which signify healing and health (*Tikkuney Zohar* #69, p.108a).

The Zohar continues with further examples explaining the significance of the pauses between the pulse beats. These allow for the drawing (i.e., growing awareness) of the spiritual life force in stages, to accommodate man's ability to absorb it. The ARI also explains how, with each vowel point — each pulse beat — one can detect which of the *Sefirot* is dominant at any given time, thereby recognizing the specific sin which is the prevailing influence within the person and enabling its rectification (*Shaar Ruach HaKodesh*, p.15; see Appendix C).

A doctor once boasted to the Baal Shem Tov that he could diagnose any illness by feeling the pulse. The Baal Shem Tov said that he, too, could diagnose illnesses in a similar manner. The Baal Shem Tov took the doctor's wrist, felt his pulse, and correctly diagnosed his illness. The doctor then took the Baal Shem Tov's wrist, felt his pulse, but was stymied. He could not read the pulse beat properly. After he had gone, the Baal Shem Tov said, "I suffer from an illness that he does not understand: 'I am sick with love [for God]' (Songs 2:5). This illness the doctor is unfamiliar with; therefore he could not diagnose it!"

*

The Princess and the Water Castle

Perhaps the most famous of all Rebbe Nachman's stories is "The Seven Beggars" (*Rabbi Nachman's Stories*, pp.354–437). We present here excerpts from the story, along with some of Reb Noson's commentary, which offers some profound insights into the spiritual dimension of the pulse.

Rebbe Nachman said, "I will tell you how people once rejoiced."

He goes on to tell of a young boy and girl who became lost in a forest. Each day for seven days, a Beggar with a different "deformity" appeared and gave them bread and water. In order of their appearance in the story, the Beggars were blind, deaf, speech-impaired, of deformed neck, hunchbacked, handless and footless. Each Beggar left the children with some extra bread and blessed them that they should "be like him." Afterwards, the children began to seek their fortunes. They finally left the forest and reentered civilization, joining the ranks of the homeless and ultimately marrying one another.

At their wedding celebration and during the seven following days, they recalled God's kindnesses when He provided them with food in their early days in the forest, through the Beggars. They yearned deeply for those Beggars, and on each of the days following their marriage, one of the Beggars came to rejoice with them. Each Beggar had a story of his own to tell, through which he explained that his deformity was not really a handicap, but was indeed his greatest asset, which explained why each had blessed the children that they "be like him."

On the Sixth Day, they were rejoicing and yearned very much [saying], "How could the one without hands be brought here?" Suddenly he appeared and said, "Here I am! I have come to your wedding!" He spoke to them in the same manner as the other [Beggars], and kissed them.

Then he said: "[You think there is something wrong with my hands.] Actually, there is nothing wrong with my hands. I have great power in my hands. But I do not use my hands for the physical world, since I need this power for something else entirely. Regarding this, I have the affirmation of the Water Castle."

The Handless Beggar relates how he was once sitting with a group of men who boasted about what they could accomplish with their hands. Assuring them that he had more power in his hands than they had in theirs, the Handless Beggar relates the incredible story of the Princess and the Water Castle.

Once there was a king who desired a certain Princess. He devised all kinds of plots to capture her, until he was finally successful and took her captive. The king then had a dream in which the Princess was standing over him, and then killed him. When he awoke, he took this dream to heart. He summoned all the dream interpreters, and they all said that the dream would come true in its literal sense, and that the Princess would indeed kill him.

The king could not decide what to do with her. If he killed her, it would grieve him. If he sent her away, this would anger him since another man would then have her. This would frustrate him terribly, since he had worked so hard to get her. Furthermore, if he exiled her and she ended up with another man, there would be an even stronger chance of the dream coming true. With an ally, it would be easier for her to kill him. Still, he was afraid because of the dream and did not want to keep her near him. The king did not know what to do with her.

As a result of the dream, his love for her gradually began to wane. As time passed, his desire for her grew less and less, which affected her feelings for him — her love for him declined more and more until she hated him. Eventually, she fled. The king sent his men to search for her. When they returned, they reported that she was near the Water Castle. This castle was made entirely of water. It had ten walls, one inside the other, all made of water. The floors inside this castle were also made of water. [This castle] also had trees and fruit, all made of water. It goes without saying how beautiful this castle was and how unusual. A castle of water is certainly something wonderful and unusual.

It is impossible for anyone to enter the Water Castle. It is made entirely of water and anyone entering it would drown.

Meanwhile, the Princess who had fled was going around the Water Castle. The king was informed that she was circling the castle. The king took his army and set out to capture her. When the Princess saw them coming, she decided that she would have to flee into the castle. She would rather drown than be captured by the king and have to remain with him. There was also the possibility that she would survive and would actually be able to enter the

Water Castle. When the king saw her fleeing into the water, he said, "If this is how it is..." and he gave orders to shoot her [saying], "If she dies, she dies."

[The soldiers] shot her with all ten types of arrows, rubbed with all ten types of poisons. She ran into the castle and went through the gates into the walls of water. She passed through all ten walls of the Water Castle, until she came to its interior. When she got there, she fell unconscious.

Before relating the story of the Princess, in describing his meeting with the men who boasted about the great power of their hands, the Beggar told of one who claimed he could retrieve an arrow even after it had been shot and had hit its target. The Handless Beggar asked him if he could retrieve all ten types of arrows, that is, ten arrows rubbed with ten types of poisons, each more toxic than the previous one. He admitted that he could retrieve only one type of arrow. "If this is true," the Handless Beggar concluded, "then you cannot heal the Princess."

Another boasted of his power of charity, for whenever he received something from someone, he was actually *giving* to that person. The Handless Beggar informed him that there are ten types of charity and asked which one he could give. He replied that he gave tithes. "If so," the Handless Beggar concluded, "you cannot heal the Princess. You cannot even approach the place where she is; you can go through only one wall." Water is likened to charity as in (Isaiah 48:18), "Your charity is like the waves of the sea." Thus, he could not enter all ten walls of the Water Castle to save the Princess.

A third boasted of his power to confer wisdom upon others through his hands. The Handless Beggar asked him, "What type of wisdom can you confer with your hands? There are ten types of wisdom." When he replied that he could confer just one type, the Beggar replied, "If this is the case, you cannot heal the Princess. You cannot understand her pulse, since there are ten modes of pulse." He could confer only one type of wisdom, and therefore understood only one mode of pulse.

A fourth boasted of his ability to hold back storm winds with his hands. He could then turn the wind and make it blow properly, so that it would be beneficial. The Handless Beggar told him that there are ten types of wind, corresponding to ten types of melody (see *Pesachim* 117a). Since he could control only one type of wind, he too would be unable to save or heal the Princess.

Finally, all present asked the Handless Beggar what his ability was. He replied, "I can do what you cannot do. [In each of the cases that you discussed] there are nine portions that you cannot accomplish. I can accomplish them all." He then proceeded to tell the story of the Princess. We resume the story now as she lies unconscious in the Water Castle, having been struck by ten poisoned arrows.

I heal her. Someone who does not possess all ten types of charity cannot enter all ten walls; he will drown in the water. The king and his army tried to pursue her, but they all drowned in the water. I, on the other hand, was able to go through all ten walls of water.

These ten walls of water are like the waves of the sea which stand like a wall. The winds support the waves and lift them up... I was able to enter through all ten walls. I was also able to draw all ten types of arrows out of the Princess. I also know all ten modes of pulse and could detect them with my ten fingers. Each one of the ten fingers has the power to detect one of the ten modes of pulse. I could then heal her through the ten types of melody. I thus heal her, for I have this great power in my hands. I am now giving you [the new couple] this power as a gift. [When he finished his speech] there was great joy and tremendous celebration.

*

The Handless Beggar represents the great tzaddik. He can enter the Water Castle and will not drown because he possesses the ten types of charity. He is able to draw out the ten types of arrows (which inflict illness) and detect the ailment through the ten modes of pulse. The Handless Beggar can then effect remedy through the ten types of song, because joy represents health and healing.

The Princess is the soul captured by the king, the evil inclination. At first she feels comfortable, but gradually she begins to realize that there is more to life than material gratification, and so she flees. But the evil inclination is relentless. He is constantly in pursuit. The Princess realizes that she must choose between a life of materialism and a life of spirituality. Just as the Jews chose to enter the Red Sea when chased by the Egyptians, so too the Princess chooses to enter the Water Castle, rather than be taken by the evil inclination. The Water Castle represents true knowledge, as in (Isaiah 11:9), "The world will be filled with knowledge of God as the waters cover the sea." But to be able to enter these walls, to gain knowledge of the Torah, one needs to give charity; otherwise one is liable to fall and drown in heretical wisdoms.

Only the true tzaddik possesses the necessary knowledge, and so only he can safely enter the castle walls. He can feel the soul's pulse, accurately determine its spiritual illnesses and heal it with the ten types of song. Rebbe Nachman teaches that these ten types of song are found in Psalms, praising God and recounting His kindness, His charity to us. Ultimately, only the "Handless Beggar," the true tzaddik, is capable of reading the Princess' pulse correctly and healing her.

(The story of the Sixth Beggar, the ten modes of pulse and its connection to joy is discussed in detail in *The Wings of the Sun: Traditional Jewish Healing in Theory and Practice*, section 4, Chapter 13, by Avraham Greenbaum, published by the Breslov Research Institute. The Ten Types of Song are discussed below in Part 6, "The Respiratory System.")

*

The pulse is a dominant factor in determining the state of one's health, spiritual as well as physical. How can a proper flow of blood be established? Through joy! And joy is attained through the ten types of melody. These ten types of melody regulate the ten types of pulse, unclogging the bloodstream so that the blood flows smoothly through the arteries and veins. A healthy pulse — both physical and spiritual — indicates good health.

* * *

Part Six

The Respiratory System

25

The Lungs

When fresh air is drawn in through the nose or mouth, it descends to the lungs, where its life-sustaining oxygen is absorbed into the circulatory system, channeled through the heart and distributed by the blood. The oxygen is used up, resulting in the waste product carbon dioxide, which is brought back to the lungs via the blood to be exhaled. The general functioning of the lungs in conjunction with the heart has already been discussed (above, Chapter 20). In this section, we shall explore more deeply the spiritual side of the heart-lungs partnership, as well as the lungs' relationship to the mouth and nose (the organs of breathing), the trachea, the larynx and the neck. We will also discuss the power of speech.

In our discussion of the respiratory system, the Hebrew word *ruach* will crop up repeatedly. *Ruach* is a word with many meanings. In the physical world, *ruach* can refer to a wind that blows, or to the air which becomes wind when we breathe it. In the metaphysical world, *ruach* can be a spirit, or it can be spirituality itself; man's *ruach* is the basic spiritual essence of his personality. A person can also be possessed by a disembodied *ruach* (spirit), by a *ruach* of despair or a *ruach* of joy. A Godly *ruach* may rest upon a prophet. *Ruach HaKodesh* (Divine inspiration) may enlighten his mind, or a *ruach se'arah* (a stormwind, i.e., mental or emotional upheaval) may threaten to uproot his faith.

The Mashiach (Messiah) will be blessed with six qualities of *ruach*: "God's *ruach* will rest upon him — a *ruach* of wisdom and understanding, a *ruach* of counsel and might, a *ruach* of knowledge and fear of God" (Isaiah 11:2). It is no wonder that (belief in) the Mashiach is literally the *ruach apeinu* ("the breath of our nostrils") (Lamentations 4:20). Before the Mashiach appears, a *ruach* of Godlessness will sweep through the world. When he finally arrives, a contrasting *ruach* of Godliness will cleanse our hearts, ridding the world of the *ruach* of impurity that prevents us from seeing and experiencing God (cf. Zekhariah 13:2).

As we begin our study of Rebbe Nachman's teachings about the heart and lungs, all these meanings should be borne in mind. At times, the Rebbe will seem to mix meanings, speaking about physical *ruach* and a spiritual *ruach* in one breath. This is intentional: for Rebbe Nachman, the two were inseparable. Physical and spiritual realities are always intertwined with one another.

*

Rebbe Nachman taught:

The *Tikkuney Zohar* (#13, p.27) states, "The blood vessels in the heart are regulated by the *ruach* [that issues forth from the lungs]. This is the meaning of (Ezekiel 1:12) 'They [the living angels] moved wherever the *ruach* went.' [The living angels correspond to the blood vessels in the heart; the *ruach* corresponds to the oxygen that enters the heart through the lungs.] For without the *ruach* that is created by the *kanfei rei'ah* ["wings," i.e., lobes of the lungs] constantly fanning and cooling the heart, its heat would consume the entire body" (*Likutey Moharan* II, 9:1).

Rebbe Nachman notes in this lesson how a powerful *ruach* (wind) will sometimes extinguish a flame, while at other times it may rekindle a dying ember. He explains in detail what happens when a wind fans a flame that is about to go out for lack of oxygen, how suddenly the flame is rekindled and comes to life again.

Throughout this lesson, the Rebbe wants us to remember that man's soul is likened to a candle. Just as a candle whose flame is about to go out can be rekindled, so the slightest touch of God's *ruach* on a man's soul can revive him and rekindle his love and awe for God instantaneously.

Returning to the metaphor of the heart and lungs, Rebbe Nachman likens the spiritual leaders of the Jewish people to the *ruach* created by the wing-like fluttering of the lobes of the lungs, and the Jews themselves to the heart. It is the task of the leaders, he says, to blow life-giving *ruach* into the heart of each and every Jew.

It is the task of the lungs to regulate the heart's activity, to keep it running smoothly, allowing it neither to overheat nor to become stone cold. In a spiritual sense, it is likewise necessary to fan the Godly flame in our hearts, lest our devotions become dry and lifeless. At the same time, we must be careful to maintain our equilibrium, lest our spiritual yearning itself become so powerful that it threatens to "consume the entire body." As Rebbe Nachman said (*Likutey Moharan II*, 9:2), "The *ruach* must be regulated in order for the heart to burn properly [for God]." The flow of *ruach* must be regulated according to the level of one's enthusiasm, lest the yearning flame of one's heart become either extinguished or overheated.

*

But how is the air brought into the lungs — and the spirit — regulated? When the heart is in danger, the lungs must act quickly. They will draw in fresh, moist air, cool the heart and thus help it maintain an even body temperature. Rebbe Nachman teaches that man benefits from the same system in his spiritual life. We should make an effort to breathe in moist air — not just physical air, but the moist spiritual air of Torah, for the Torah is compared to water (see *Sukkah* 52b). Indeed, we are to inhale Torah and then exhale that same Torah in the form of prayer. Breathing Torah and prayer gives our lungs their ability to regulate the heart's "burning desire" to serve God, without experiencing spiritual "burnout." Rebbe Nachman taught:

> Man draws his life force from God's attribute of Malkhut [Kingship], which is the very root of existence. For Malkhut is the aspect of *Ruach HaKodesh*, the level of (Esther 5:1) "And Esther dressed in Malkhut," concerning which our Sages noted (*Megillah* 14b), it is not written "'dressed in *clothes* of Malkhut' but 'dressed

in Malkhut,' alluding to the fact that *Ruach HaKodesh* had descended upon Esther."

Life depends on breath. And what is breath? It is the inhaling and exhaling of life-giving oxygen, which can be compared to the verse (Ezekiel 1:14), "The living angels ran and returned like the appearance of lightning." [Again, the living angels refer to the heart, which pumps life to the body.] When one binds oneself to God's holy Malkhut, by speaking words of Torah and prayer, one inhales and exhales *Ruach HaKodesh* — Godly spirit. This is the meaning of (Ezekiel 36:26), "I will place a holy *ruach* within you." This *ruach* is none other than the Godly spirit that one inhales when one breathes words of holiness. [This spirit enters the heart, which keeps it burning incessantly for God.]

This is implied in the verse (Genesis 1:2), "The *ruach* of God hovered over the waters." When a person learns Torah, which itself is likened to water, then the *ruach* of God, which is *Ruach HaKodesh*, hovers over him and breathes life into him. For [just as it is impossible to live without air] it is impossible to live without Torah, as we have learned (*Tikkuney Zohar* #13), "Without the *ruach* of the lobes of the lungs constantly fanning and cooling the heart, its heat would consume the entire body." And we have also learned (*Zohar* III, 218a), "The lungs represent the quality of water, the water of Torah." Without this "water" [or moist air, as mentioned above] a Jew's burning desire to come close to God would consume him. When his desire is clothed in words of Torah and prayer, however, he is protected... (*Likutey Moharan* I, 78:1).

This lesson emphasizes the importance of holy speech, which is an act of drawing in and expelling *ruach*. When you breathe "holy *ruach*" such as when praying or studying Torah, or when speaking kind and comforting words, you are breathing spirituality. The air you breathe is then considered "holy *ruach*." This is the kind of *ruach* that "cools off" the burning desires of the heart.

*

A Healthy Lung

Bearing in mind that words of Torah are beneficial for the lungs and heart, we can understand Rebbe Nachman's teaching in which he connects the festival of Shavuot to the lungs. Rebbe Nachman taught:

> The festival of Shavuot is a cure for the lungs. The five lobes of the lungs correspond to the Five Books of the Torah. Annually, on Shavuot, we receive the Torah anew. Hence Shavuot is an especially beneficial time for one's lungs; at this time, we can receive "new life" (*Likutey Moharan* I, 267).

Yet the study of Torah alone is not sufficient. We must also cultivate a high level of faith. When Moses first descended to Egypt and spoke to the Jews about their forthcoming redemption, they refused to listen to him. The verse explains (Exodus 6:9), "They were unable to listen to Moses because of *kotzer ruach* and heavy labor." The words *kotzer ruach* mean literally, "shortness of breath." Rebbe Nachman explains that the Jews at that time lacked *faith* in Moses' promise. From this he teaches that a lack of faith indicates a blemished lung — "shortness of breath." Thus, strengthening one's faith serves to rectify the lungs (see *Likutey Moharan* II, 5:16; *ibid.* II, 86).

A healthy lung ensures far more than one's physical well-being. Sufficient oxygen is necessary to keep the brain functioning well. Rebbe Nachman taught that "a healthy lung improves vision and helps a person attain great Daat [Intellect]" (*Likutey Moharan* II, 7:12). This is as the Talmud states (*Chullin* 49a), "Why is the lung called *ReI'AH*? Because it *meIRAH* [brightens] the eyes!" When a person is confused, his intellect cannot "see" well, and his ability to deduce is impaired. In the same way that a physically healthy lung supports the brain with sufficient oxygen, a spiritually healthy lung can open one's mind.

* * *

26

Breathing

Breathing is the body's way of intaking and expelling air. We breathe through the nose and mouth. The air passages are connected to the pharynx, which extends into the trachea, branching off into bronchi. Through these, oxygen passes into the lungs. The larynx, where the vocal cords are located, is adjacent to the pharynx. Just as all these organs are connected physically, they are likewise interrelated on the spiritual plane.

Breathing, though quite a natural activity, is actually a very complex process. It involves three basic functions: exhaling, the pause between breaths and inhaling. The inhalation process alone has three phases: diaphragmatic, intercostal and clavicular. These three phases represent the movements of the lungs at the abdomen, the center of the rib cage and near the top of the lungs, to facilitate the intake of fresh air.

Physical exertion leads to rapid breathing, while nervousness and tension restrict the breathing process, leading to short, shallow breaths. Composure and tranquility are associated with smoother, deeper breathing. Since we know that an adequate supply of oxygen is necessary to sustain the brain, it follows that if your breathing is correct, your brain will receive the proper measure of oxygen necessary for it to function optimally. Many studies have been conducted on effective breathing exercises, and there are several guides to proper breathing available (see also *Under the Table*, pp.83–95). The spiritual implications of proper breathing, however, are even more specific and far-reaching.

*

The Sigh

> It came to pass in those days that the ruler of Egypt died; the Children of Israel *sighed* due to their bondage and they *cried*; and their *screams* rose up from their hard labor. God heard their *groaning*, and He remembered His covenant with Abraham, Isaac and Jacob. God looked upon the Children of Israel, and He knew [that the time for salvation had come].
>
> Exodus 2:23-25

Notice that these verses do not mention prayer or speech. They speak only of sighing, crying, screaming and groaning (*Zohar* II, 19b). When Pharaoh died, the Jews were given a short respite: instead of working, they were forced to attend their "benevolent" ruler's funeral. They could not speak — they were too deeply entrenched in their enslavement. But they never lost their capacity to sigh and groan before God. Pharaoh's funeral provided the perfect opportunity for them to vent their intense feelings. The Egyptians thought that the Jews were saddened by Pharaoh's death, but in truth they were crying out for Divine assistance. In this way they were able to arouse God's mercy. Immediately after this, the Torah relates the story of Moses at the burning bush, when God heralded the redemption. This juxtaposition of events in the Torah is not arbitrary. In fact, the Jews' spiritual journey from slavery to the Revelation at Sinai began with their sighing.

The Talmud teaches (*Berakhot* 58b), "Sighing breaks a person's body." Rebbe Nachman explains that sighing in one's desire to attain spirituality breaks the gross physical barriers of the body and strengthens the soul, allowing one to embark on a spiritual ascent.

When Rebbe Nachman was young, he engaged in many devotions aimed at breaking his physicality, in order to attain higher levels of spirituality. Among these was the act of sighing. The Talmud teaches that "sighing breaks a person's body."

Rebbe Nachman therefore engaged often in sighing before God. He would then note his physical reactions. Many times he found himself unable to move his arms immediately after a session of sighing (*Rabbi Nachman's Wisdom* #167).

Rebbe Nachman later taught, "Sighing for the sake of holiness benefits a person more than self-mortification" (*Likutey Moharan* I, 109:2). "Sighing deeply is akin to circumcising oneself. Just as the removal of the foreskin is a rectification, so too, deep sighing for the sake of spirituality removes the foreskin of the heart" (*Likutey Moharan* I, 22:5). Earlier (Chapter 23) we saw that the heart is the seat of many of man's deepest emotions. Rebbe Nachman teaches us that sighing is helpful not merely in transcending these emotions, but also in transmuting them and directing them towards spirituality.

*

With the word of God the heavens were made; with the breath of His mouth, all their hosts.

Psalms 33:6

Rebbe Nachman taught:

The entire world was created with breath — the breath of God. Divine breath is the great sustainer of life. If breath is lacking, life is lacking. Hence, if one feels something lacking in one's life, this indicates a shortage of "breath," that breath which is the spirit of God, which created and sustains everything (*Likutey Moharan* I, 8:1).

Rebbe Nachman goes on to explain that drawing in a deep breath offsets this feeling of "lack" in one's life and produces a sense of fulfillment. Since a shortage of breath indicates a lack, the act of breathing deeply can fill that lack. Since whatever one has — or lacks — is generally felt in the heart, that which is lacking can be made complete through the act of sighing. With a sigh, one draws spirit, life and vitality into one's heart, filling the void. Take a deep breath and sigh. Say to yourself, "I want to draw greater life force into my heart. I want to draw God's breath into my life."

Proper breathing is an art. With proper breathing you can fill a void in your life. Without it, a void can become amplified and potentially devastating to your emotional and/or spiritual equilibrium. When sighing, you take a long, deep breath, drawing from the spirit of God that He breathed into you when you were created. Furthermore, throughout the course of our lives we all make mistakes and become disconnected to some degree — both from ourselves and from God's spirit. Sighing with regret over our past misdeeds reconnects us.

If, however, we have cultivated within ourselves a desire for material fulfillment, and groan and sigh over our inability to attain it, those sighs defile our breath and spirit. We then become distressed and depressed over not having achieved our material goals. In this way we only distance ourselves further from God, and so from perfection. Like the businessman who has achieved financial success, yet constantly craves and desires additional wealth, it is easy for us to concentrate on how much we lack rather than on how much we have.

Rebbe Nachman therefore teaches that the art of concentrated, deep breathing is the formula for a full and fulfilling life. One can practice deep breathing for its own sake, or for the sake of the "spirit." The physical benefit will be the same in either case; but sighing and deep breathing with the intention of attaining spirituality actually bonds one to one's Source, which is none other than God Himself.

*

The Lifeline

Rebbe Nachman taught:

> In order to breathe, one must draw in air. There are two "lifelines" from which people can draw this sustenance: one is the lifeline of holiness; the other is of impurity. The righteous draw in pure air, while the evil draw in impure air. One cannot survive without drawing in air through one of these two channels. Should a person regret his evil deeds and desire to repent, he severs his

link with the impure source of air. He can then begin to breathe in a fresh, new supply of air from the Source of holiness. Conversely, one who desires evil, and sighs when unable to attain it, cuts himself off from the source of pure air and automatically attaches himself to impurity (Likutey Moharan I, 109:1).

Rebbe Nachman thus taught, "For a single [evil] desire that will keep a person content for a quarter of an hour, he can lose his entire share, both in this world and in the World to Come" (Likutey Moharan II, 108).

Reb Shmuel Isaac (d.1827) was one of Rebbe Nachman's closest followers. Once Rebbe Nachman clutched Reb Shmuel Isaac's clothes next to his heart and said, "Just because of a little blood in your heart [evil desires] you will lose this world and the next? Krekhtz es ois! [Sigh it away!]" (Tzaddik #441).

*

The Nose and Mouth

The nose is the main passageway for air. It contains various filters composed of mucous membranes and microscopic hairlike projections, called cilia, to purify the air as it enters the system. As we have seen (Chapter 8), the human body has many systems for filtering and eliminating waste matter. The nose also acts as a filter, weeding out impurities from the air, and redirecting waste matter to eventually be expelled.

Af, one of the Hebrew words for "nose," also means "anger," as in (Deuteronomy 9:19) "I feared the af [anger]." In another sense, the nose represents patience, as in (Exodus 34:6) "Erekh Apayim" — literally "of extended nose," i.e., long of breath, slow to anger, patient. Rebbe Nachman speaks at length of the value of patience and the benefits of "waiting out" one's anger. He compares anger to a violent storm wind which is stirred up, but which eventually will die down. Patience helps us to wait out such storms and to reconnect ourselves to God's "long-winded breath," the Source of all life! (Likutey Moharan I, 8:3).

(The importance of patience in our spiritual struggles has been explained above [Chapter 8] in connection with the purification process. The additional function of the nose, the sense of smell, will be discussed below in Part 7. The chapters in this section will concentrate on the mouth as an essential part of the respiratory system. The neck, throat and trachea will be discussed in Chapter 28, and the mouth as it relates to the power of speech in Chapter 29.)

*

Malkhut is the mouth — the Torah of the mouth [Oral Torah].

Tikkuney Zohar, p.17a

Malkhut is the principal Attribute through which man can interact with God. Malkhut is also sometimes referred to as the *Shekhinah*, God's Divine Presence. Our acceptance of God's Malkhut (Kingship) is the first and foremost requirement in recognizing His sovereignty and in serving Him. The reason that Malkhut is associated with the mouth is that a *melekh* (king) rules principally through speech. His edicts, which stem from the thoughts of his mind, must be expressed in order for his subjects to obey them; these thoughts of the *melekh* are made known only through words, which serve to disclose the king's intentions.

The same correlation applies to the Written Torah and the body of oral teachings from Sinai that accompany it. The Oral Torah, which is associated with Malkhut, allows us to understand God's Will as it is expressed in the Written Torah. The Written Law contains a great many mitzvot that are not clearly spelled out. It is only through the Oral Torah that we understand what God wants of us, enabling us to serve Him properly. This is why Malkhut refers both to "the mouth" and to the Oral Law, for it is the revelation of God's Will (see *Likutey Moharan* I, 18:6). Rebbe Nachman thus taught:

> The mouth corresponds to the Oral Law. One who studies Torah for God's sake and for God's honor rectifies his mouth. He merits intimate closeness with God's *Shekhinah* [which corresponds to His mouth]. Conversely, one who studies Torah in order to

further his own goals of honor, wealth, etc., causes the Divine Presence to be exiled [i.e., concealed from him] (*Likutey Moharan* I, 12:1; *ibid.*, 101:1).

Such is the power of the mouth in our quest for spirituality. With pure motives, the words we speak can be used to create the most intimate connection to God. On the other hand, words spoken with an ulterior motive, spoken not for God's sake but for our own personal gain or for someone else's loss, cause the Divine Presence to shun us. The reason for this is clear: words that counter the purpose of Creation are equivalent to shunning God and casting off the yoke of His sovereignty. When we sense ourselves distant from God, it is a clear sign that we have shunned Him through our speech. When we send the Divine Presence into exile (explained above, Chapter 16), our own spiritual and physical exile is bound to follow.

*

The Trachea and Larynx: Constriction...

Wisdom is expressed through speech; yet not every thought can or should be articulated at length. One must gather one's thoughts before expressing them, either to release them or to contain them. This principle is represented in the construction of the trachea and the larynx. Because they are narrow there is suction pressure during breathing, and it is necessary for them to be supported by rings of cartilage to prevent them from collapsing. Rebbe Nachman taught:

> The trachea, through which air passes, is called *kaneh* in Hebrew. The Hebrew word *kaneh* has other meanings as well: it can be translated as "acquire" or "reed." One such usage is (Proverbs 4:5), "*K'NeH* [acquire] wisdom." Another is (Psalms 68:31), "Rebuke the wild beast of the *KaNaH* [reeds]." Thus *KaNeH*, in one sense, represents pure wisdom which, when acquired, leads to spirituality; in another sense, alien philosophies which lead away from spirituality are represented by wild beasts of the reeds.

The trachea can be used to acquire wisdom, to speak words of spirituality, or it can be used for sin, by expounding "alien philosophies" and immoral ideals. One must know when it is appropriate to *express* one's thoughts and speak, i.e., to learn Torah and to use speech in order to serve God. Conversely, a person must know when to *contain* his speech — when he has the urge to use inappropriate speech or expound philosophies which do not represent God's truth.

Rebbe Nachman teaches further that the study of Talmud corresponds to the larynx. The Talmud, which is comprised of the six sections of the Mishnah, corresponds to the six rings of cartilage found in the trachea (*Likutey Moharan* I, 3:1). (There are actually nine sections of cartilage in the trachea. The "six rings" the Rebbe refers to here are the three *pairs* of cartilage: the arytenoid, the cornicula and the cuneiform.) This parallel serves to show us how we should be using the larynx: for Torah study and serving God.

*

...and Creation

> For with *YaH*, YHVH formed worlds.
>
> Isaiah 26:4
>
> For with the letters *Yod* and *Heh* of the Tetragrammaton, YHVH formed worlds — this world and the World to Come.
>
> *Menachot* 29b

God formed the world with the first two letters of the Tetragrammaton (YHVH). With the tiny letter *Yod*, which corresponds to Chokhmah (Wisdom), He formed the World to Come. With the letter *Heh*, which corresponds to Binah (Understanding), He formed this world.

Yod and Chokhmah corresponds to the level of pure thought, the soul of the Torah which will be revealed in the World to Come. *Heh* and Binah corresponds to the level of Torah that God used to "speak" this world into existence. The numerical value of the letter *Heh* is 5, which corresponds to the five phonetic families of the Hebrew alphabet: gutturals, labials, palatals, linguals and dentals. When we articulate our Torah thoughts, we arouse the very powers of Creation.

* * *

27

Clean Air

Imagine awakening in the morning to clean, fresh air; no worrisome pollution to fret about, no acid rain, no carbon monoxide or dozens of other waste emissions that contaminate the air about us — just clean, healthy air to breath safely.

Unfortunately, modern technology has made this experience a virtual impossibility, for even the most basic conveniences use energy sources which foul the air around us. Pollutants are spread by automobiles, factories, conventional energy plants and countless other technological phenomena of modern life. One would have to travel far from metropolitan centers in order to experience a breath of fresh air, but neither will that air be absolutely pure, as pollution has affected even the most remote locations. Paradoxically, in the name of progress we've made clean air almost as extinct as the dodo bird!

Everyone is in an uproar today over clean air. Environmentalists are clamoring for policies which would force industry to clean up our air and water supplies. Federal, state and local governments are enacting tough legislation against pollutants. Spiritually, though, the "legislation" for clean air has long been in effect. Whether it has been adhered to, and how spiritually based pollution can be rectified and even made beneficial, is the issue we now take up for discussion.
Rebbe Nachman taught:

A person's breath carries [with it] his innermost desires and affects all those around him. Good feelings and desires radiate good thoughts to others. Evil desires influence others in harmful ways (*Likutey Moharan* I, 31:8).

We know that when we exhale we expel carbon dioxide, a waste product; but it is important to realize that at the same time, we also "exhale" our innermost thoughts and feelings. These feelings, once they're out, remain in the air and can be carried to others. We may likewise be on the receiving end of these "airborne emotions." Depending on the *force* behind the feelings, we can sometimes even "read" another's thoughts, because we have already absorbed their feelings.

We may experience this by observing the ways in which people react to one another — both in the way they radiate their own feelings and in the way they respond to the feelings of others. On a "good day," people radiate warmth. On a "bad day," they might be contentious: "Watch out for his mood..."

As the heart is the seat of emotions (see Chapter 23), the feelings people radiate come from there. The heart's constant activity arouses desires, which define themselves as thoughts. These thoughts are constantly "exhaled" while at the same time, foreign ideas and emotions are "inhaled," in the same way that the heart receives oxygen from the lungs and through them expels carbon dioxide. Thus, along with sound waves, radio waves, bacteria and other minuscule particles, the air "carries" thoughts. Spiritually "clean" air is dependent upon the desires and emotions of the individuals in the vicinity. Where people seek good, everyone can breathe fresh, clean air.

*

Creating Souls

Nafshi [my soul] departed from me when He spoke.

Songs 5:6

The Hebrew word *nefesh* translates as either "soul" or "desire." We have already seen (Chapter 3) that *Nefesh* is that part of the soul that interfaces with the body. Through the *Nefesh*, the soul can attain an awareness of the physical body as a receptacle for the spiritual. In several lessons, Rebbe Nachman discusses the etymological connection between the concepts of "desire" and "soul," as found in the term *Nefesh*, showing how a person's desires can actually create souls.

The crux of this phenomenon comes from the idea expressed above: that a person "exhales" the desires of his heart. The important thing, the Rebbe points out, is *how* a person's desires are expressed. "My soul [*nafshi*] departed from me when He spoke." "*Nafshi*" denotes "my desire"; "spoke" refers to the verbal articulation of those desires. The manner in which a person expresses his innermost desires — whether they be for spiritual or material objectives — will determine the outcome of those desires. The individual's real objective, which is always some form of a new creation, is equivalent to the "creating of new souls." How does Rebbe Nachman arrive at this parallel?

Rebbe Nachman explains that the fact that desires or thoughts can be "carried" through the air, thus creating souls, can be either a potent catalyst for good or a deadly evil force. He relates this concept to the linguistic structure of the Hebrew language, which is called *Lashon HaKodesh*, the "Holy Tongue" (see *Likutey Moharan* I, 31:6-8). Unlike the alphabets of many languages, which have both vowels and consonants, the Hebrew alphabet contains only consonants. Like inanimate matter, those consonants are unable to "move," that is, they cannot direct the reader as to how to pronounce the words they form. In this way, they correspond to the body, which needs a soul to direct its movements. Correct pronunciation can be known only with the aid of the vowel points, the dots and dashes that form the "souls" of the letters. They determine not only the pronunciation of the words, but also their meanings and usage. Consider, for example, the letters of the word ישב, *y-sh-v*. Depending on how the vowels are arranged, the word they form can be pronounced *yashav*, *yoshev* or *yeishev*, all different tenses of "sitting," or *yashuv, yashiv, yashov* or *yushav*, various aspects of "returning."

> ...necklaces of gold with *nekudot hakesef* [points of silver].
>
> Songs 1:11

A body is lifeless without its soul. So too are the Hebrew letters lifeless without their vowels. To create the "life" of the Hebrew language, one must create the vowel points as well. This is accomplished through *nekudot hakesef. Nekudot* translates as points (or vowels), while *kesef* comes from the root *likhsof*, "to yearn" or "to desire." It is the desire of the individual that creates the dots, the vowel points, which are the souls of the letters, bringing them to life. Depending on what he desires those letters to say, he will choose the vowels that will *create* those words. In the same way, Rebbe Nachman teaches, a person's breathing, which carries his desires, creates a *life force* which has the power either to elevate or to deplete him spiritually. As we have explained, this very breath travels to others, influencing them as well.

A visit to the Western Wall in Jerusalem, for example, can evoke thoughts of Godliness even in those lacking any spiritual background. Somehow, people can find themselves aroused to cry out to God or to utter even a simple thought in communication with their Creator when at the Wall. The stones themselves are steeped in the tears, prayers and devotions of the millions of people who have come there throughout the ages. Conversely, if a person finds himself in an immoral environment, he will be hard-pressed to avoid being tainted by his surroundings.

Rebbe Nachman thus taught:

> When one desires good, he creates a good feeling which can be shared and expressed in many ways for good purposes. Evil desires create the opposite effect. One should articulate one's good desires in order to compound their influences (*Likutey Moharan* I, 31:6–7).

Rebbe Nachman pointed out that many times one has unfulfilled desires. This fact is in itself perplexing, because God's bounty is descending constantly to the world. He explains that the reason people experience unfulfilled desires is that they do not possess the "vessels" necessary to *receive* the bounty. By consciously focusing on one's deepest feelings and directing them "outward," through articulated speech, one can create the vessels necessary to receive blessings.

What steps can be taken when someone tries to create the proper vessels, but still does not see his "dreams" come true? Rebbe Nachman taught:

> When someone truly desires something [of spiritual value], but fails to achieve it, he should never console himself with the fact that it seems unattainable. He should desire and yearn incessantly until he merits to fulfill his desires and attain his objective. Articulating one's desires brings one's goals closer to reality (*Likutey Moharan* I, 66:8).

> Just as a person can be aroused and inspired spiritually by observing the devotions of others, he can also become inspired by *his own* cries and desires to serve God (*Likutey Moharan* I, 270).

In another lesson, Rebbe Nachman adds:

> The desire to travel to the tzaddik creates a vessel in which to receive blessing (*Likutey Moharan* I, 185:2).

*

Air Pollution

A person's thoughts (formed within the realm of Daat, which also corresponds to the lungs) are manifestations of his will, which is based in Keter. When a person is possessed of good desires, it is a sign that his will, which is the reflection of his Keter, is attuned to spirituality. We have just seen that good thoughts and desires purify the air of the spiritual environment which surrounds us, while evil thoughts and desires contaminate the environment. Rebbe Nachman taught that "a person's Torah study, which is a manifestation of his good desires, can benefit the world" (see *Likutey Moharan* I, 159). Conversely, as we have pointed out, evil desires putrefy the air.

Mockery, profane language and slander are considered blemished speech which putrefies the environment. Many obvious examples of blemished speech are found in the media which thrive on sensationalizing the news, compounding society's ills under the veneer of "objective reporting." This is not to say that all news is tainted but that great discrimination is needed to separate the "gold" from the "dross." In the meantime, the media exert a powerful influence on the way people think and feel, leading them from one "newsworthy" topic to the next, involving them in one heated discussion after another, all in the name of "free speech." From a spiritual vantage point, the media divert people's attention from what is really important and foul the air with words and more words which obscure the truth and prevent people from understanding the Godly drama that is unfolding before their very eyes. This is a dangerous form of air pollution which should be eradicated.

What if you are unable to think of the appropriate words or to utter even a short prayer? You may have a strong desire for spirituality, but cannot articulate it. For this situation, Reb Noson offers the following advice: "Desire is so potent that even when you cannot utter a word, even if you find yourself prevented from expressing yourself in any kind of speech, your desire alone remains a most powerful weapon; even if you are unable to say what is on your mind, no one can ever take away from you your *desire* for good" (*Likutey Halakhot, Hekhsher Keilim* 4:18).

* * *

28

The Neck: Exile and Exodus

A ir passages connect to the pharynx, which extends into the trachea, then on through the bronchioles into the lungs. Clearly, the neck and throat play a crucial role in the respiratory system. And as the throat area houses the vocal cords and thus man's ability to speak, it has many spiritual implications.

Rebbe Nachman taught:

> For a thought to be actualized, one must express it. Every deed follows a three-step process: thought, speech and the actual deed. Thoughts originate in the mind, are articulated in speech, and are then brought into action. The Zohar teaches that "all thoughts are expressed" (see *Zohar* III, 294a). Thus, even if a person is unaware of this process, his thoughts are articulated, often in subtle ways. He must therefore take extreme care to guard his thoughts, since they will eventually become spoken words. Thoughts become contracted and constricted in speech. Speech exits through the "narrow passageway of the throat" and eventually is expressed in deeds (*Likutey Moharan* I, 66:4).

> One's inability to actualize good desires is often due to "incomplete speech." One should therefore clearly enunciate one's desires, expressing them before God. One's thoughts will then emerge from their constrictions, the "narrowness of the neck," and become complete in their expression. Complete, perfected speech will enable a person to fulfill his desires and to realize his goals (*Likutey Moharan* I, 66:9).

In Hebrew, the neck is called *meitzar hagaron*, the narrow passageway of the throat. It represents the concept of *tzimtzum*, contraction — specifically the contraction that must occur before thought and speech can be manifest (see above, Chapter 21, about the concept of *tzimtzum* relative to the *Challal HaPanuy*). This *tzimtzum* is preceded by an earlier act of *tzimtzum* which takes place between a thought and its verbal expression, since thought must be channeled through speech. The words must then pass through the throat before they become actualized. Articulating ideas, expressing them in words, crystallizes the thoughts, bringing them closer to realization.

*

Descent to Egypt

The Torah relates that Abraham traveled from Mesopotamia to the Land of Canaan. Shortly after his arrival there, a famine set in, and he headed further south toward Egypt. As he was approaching Egypt, he decided to conceal his wife Sarah in a large chest. The Egyptian border guards discovered her, however, and were stricken by her beauty, which surpassed that of any woman they had ever seen. They decided to commandeer her for Pharaoh's pleasure. Realizing what this meant in terms of the danger to his own life, Abraham told them that Sarah was his sister.

That night, Pharaoh tried to approach Sarah, but was prevented from doing so by a supernatural force. Every time he came near her, he was struck another powerful blow. Understanding the significance of the situation, he summoned Abraham to him in the morning. "How could you do this to me?" he complained. "Why didn't you tell me that she was your wife? Why did you say she was your sister, allowing me to think that I could take her for myself as a wife?" Restoring Sarah to Abraham, Pharaoh sent them off laden with gifts (Genesis, Chapter 12).

Rebbe Nachman interprets this story with a lesson applicable to Jews in all generations. Abraham represents every individual who seeks holiness. Wherever he goes, he searches for Godliness.

As a result, he is drawn to the Land of Canaan, with its tremendous potential for the revelation of Godliness. His "wife" and lifetime partner is his power of speech, represented by Sarah, whose name derives from the Hebrew *SaR* (officer or ruler), and is therefore related conceptually to "*Malkhut peh*" (Kingship which belongs to the mouth). However, when a "famine" sets in, indicative of a some laxity in his spirituality, "Abraham" descends to "Egypt."

Egypt, *MiTZRayim* in Hebrew, represents the neck and throat area, as indicated by *MeiTZaR hagaron*. In Egypt, the quality of refined speech was in exile. PHaRAoh (פרעה), the generic term used to designate all Egyptian rulers, shares the letters of *ORePH* (עורף), the nape of the neck, as well as *PeH RA* (פה רע), evil speech. The main exile in Egypt was the entrapment of the power of speech by Pharaoh and his nation. (In a sense, Pharaoh can be considered the ancient "media mogul" who intercepted free speech and enslaved it to his ideology; see previous Chapter.)

There are times when one wishes to speak words of spirituality — represented by Sarah — yet one's words are somehow intercepted and cannot manifest themselves in virtuous speech. Rather, Pharaoh's officers "deliver" the speech to Pharaoh who, upon seeing the beauty of the potential held by speech, takes "Sarah" for himself. His officers and ministers represent the *kelipot* (forces of evil) that try to trap holy speech.

When someone regrets his misdirected involvement in the material world and seeks to repent, "Pharaoh" (materialistic desire), who thought he had assumed control over spirituality, becomes afflicted. Not only must Pharaoh return "Sarah" (holy speech) to Abraham (the seeker of spirituality), but he must also present him with "gifts," i.e., additional sparks of holiness which had previously fallen prey to Pharaoh and his officers as a result of our misusing our power of speech (see *Likutey Moharan* I, 62:5; *ibid.* 163). As long as one's desires and speech are good in their intent, even if one has fallen prey to "Pharaoh and his advisors," one can elevate one's speech to a level of holiness. The search for spirituality then becomes a true purification process, cleansing the soul and even bringing merit and purification to others who may have been trapped in exile.

That is why PeSaCh — the festival which commemorates the Exodus from the constriction that is Egypt — is referred to in the Kabbalah as *Peh SaCh*, "the mouth that speaks," indicating "free speech." Pure speech leads to freedom; blemished speech corresponds to exile. If we rectify our speech, we merit the "Exodus"; we become a free people, an exalted creation. Such is the great value and power of speech.

Of course, the concept of "free speech" can be misleading. One needn't look far to see the havoc wrought under the banner of "freedom of speech." These three words have ravaged society to its very core, allowing anyone to say anything, regardless of who may be hurt, offended or otherwise adversely affected.

The Talmud gives another definition of "free speech." Free speech is that which may be uttered without insulting, causing discomfort to others or arousing negative passions. Thus we learn (*Erakhin* 15b), "Rabbi Yosi said, 'I never spoke in a manner that necessitated my having to excuse myself.'" Rashi offers two explanations of Rabbi Yosi's words (*s.v. v'chazarti*): "I never had to watch who was around me" (as he never spoke against another), or "I never had reason to deny having said anything." This is free speech, of which one never needs to be ashamed.

Our Sages state (*Bereishit Rabbah* 14:11), "With each breath, one should praise God." Rebbe Nachman comments (*Likutey Moharan* I, 55:7), "With every breath one takes, with every word uttered, one *can* invoke God's honor. Speaking properly, even when speaking of mundane matters — and avoiding blemished speech — brings man continually closer to God. This is the meaning of "free speech": words that a person can speak wherever he is and in whatever situation he finds himself. These are words through which we merit the "Exodus." Through them, we become free men.

* * *

29

Therapeutic Sound

Not everything we express with our mouths is worthy of being called "speech." Rebbe Nachman points out that only words that are accepted are considered speech. This is understood from the verse (Psalms 19:4), "It is considered neither speech nor words when [what is said is] not listened to." When our words contain "good," people will accept them, for people naturally tend to seek good. Words that lack good are generally rejected. In order to know what good is, we need Daat. Only when we draw Daat into our speech will our words be accepted (Likutey Moharan I, 29:1).

Here Rebbe Nachman extolls the importance of good speech. "Good" is a relative term. One can span the entire spectrum of life and find that "good" has countless levels. Evil can masquerade as good, which accounts for the many lies that are accepted along with true, good speech, while everyone will agree that slander and other kinds of blemished speech are not "good." These types of speech have a strong, detrimental effect upon the person who speaks them — aside from the damage they cause to the listener and to the person who is slandered. Yet the "good" that one should draw into one's speech must be defined.

When Rebbe Nachman speaks about "drawing Daat into speech," he is referring to the knowledge and recognition of God. There are many ways by which to arrive at a recognition of God, even in mundane matters. One can come to recognize Him through joy, awe, prayer, love or any of the many other emotions — or even frustrations — that every person experiences. It is necessary to consciously stimulate our intellects in order to recognize God. Armed with an awareness of God, when we speak we will automatically draw Daat into our words.

*

Voice

A person's voice also has great power, as Rebbe Nachman taught:

- The voice of one who prays with vigor and deep concentration is likened to thunder. This "thunder" arouses the fear of Heaven in his heart. With fear of Heaven, one's voice can arouse others to serve God as well (*Likutey Moharan* I, 5:3).

- When a person learns a Torah teaching, and mentions the name of the tzaddik who first revealed this teaching, that tzaddik, although he is in Gan Eden [Paradise], listens to the person's voice (*Likutey Moharan* I, 12:3).

- When a person attains purity, then God will help him, even without speech [that is, even if he only calls out to God with cries and sighs, without giving words to his prayers] (*Likutey Moharan* I, 27:5).

Rebbe Nachman also taught that studying Torah with love and awe for God corresponds to the first two letters of the Tetragrammaton, *Yod* and *Heh*. (Love and awe are contained in Chokhmah and Binah which correspond to the letters *Yod* and *Heh*; see *Tikkuney Zohar* #10, p.25b.) The drawing out of the words from within oneself is compared to the letter Vav (ו), which is shaped like a "pipe" or conduit. The air that is expelled with one's words corresponds to the final Heh of the Tetragrammaton. Thus, articulated Torah study corresponds to the complete Tetragrammaton (*Likutey Moharan* I, 77).

*

Song

Song is in some ways a more powerful form of expressing our inner thoughts than speech. We therefore find songs that reflect every emotional state, such as joyous music, serene tunes and melancholy melodies. As such, song can play an important role in our emotional and physical well-being, as an expression of our innermost feelings.

Rebbe Nachman taught:

> There are Ten Types of Song (see *Pesachim* 117a). These ten types of song bring vitality to the ten modes of pulse (see above, Chapter 24). When joy [expressed through song] is blemished, the pulse is negatively affected. Illness can thus result from sadness and melancholy (*Likutey Moharan* 24:1; see above, Chapter 24; see also *Wings of the Sun*, Part 3; *Rabbi Nachman's Tikkun*, published by the Breslov Research Institute, discusses the Ten Types of Song and the Ten Psalms revealed by the Rebbe).

Rebbe Nachman encouraged his followers to sing many *zemirot* (tunes customarily sung at the Shabbat table) on Shabbat. Rebbe Nachman, until he took ill with tuberculosis a few years before his death, himself sang the *zemirot* (*Likutey Moharan* II, 104).

Rebbe Nachman taught:

- Singing mitigates decrees (*Likutey Moharan* I, 42).
- Through song and joy, one can guard and preserve one's memory, and will come to bear in mind the World to Come (*Likutey Moharan* I, 54:12).
- Each type of wisdom has its own song and its own melody. Torah wisdom has its own melodies, as do heretical wisdoms. There is a special song which corresponds to faith (*Likutey Moharan* I, 64:5).

Rebbe Nachman often spoke of the power of song to move a person to serve God:

> It is good to make a habit of inspiring yourself with a melody. Great concepts are contained in each holy melody, and they can arouse your heart and draw it towards God. Even if you cannot sing well, you can still inspire yourself with a melody sung to the best of your ability when you are alone. The loftiness of melody is beyond measure (*Rabbi Nachman's Wisdom* #273).

*

Speech Therapy

Many people have speech defects. Some defects are barely noticeable, while others are unfortunately very pronounced. Even Moses, the greatest tzaddik of all time, had difficulty speaking. Just as therapy may remedy physical speech impediments, so too can the proper therapeutic approach eliminate spiritual speech blockages, for speech impediments certainly exist on a spiritual plane. Following are several of Rebbe Nachman's suggestions for overcoming the spiritual impediments to "free speech."

- The reason people's requests are not always granted is that their words lack eloquence, and so those words do not enter the heart of the one who is being petitioned. The Torah is called (Proverbs 5:19) "a graceful gazelle," for its eloquence brings grace and charm to those who study it diligently (see *Eruvin* 54a). Concentrating on Torah study enhances one's intellect and brings eloquence to one's ability to express oneself. Then one's requests, be they prayers and supplications to God or requests to friends and family, will be accepted (*Likutey Moharan* I, 1:3). For this reason one should accustom oneself to articulate the words of Torah. Reading them silently is not sufficient (*Likutey Moharan* I, 56:3).

- There are times when a person wishes to pray, but finds his mind clouded with dark and foreign thoughts. To "see" his way out of the darkness, he should express his words of prayer with absolute sincerity and truth. God's existence is truth, and He is the main light by which one can see a path through the darkness. The more one speaks truth, the closer one comes to the Absolute Truth. Thus, speaking the truth brings one to a state of rectified speech (*Likutey Moharan* I, 9:3).

- Charity rectifies one's speech (*Likutey Moharan* I, 2:4).

- Charity elevates a person to the true level of a human being. The most important difference between man and animal lies in the power of speech. Even animals have a "language," comprised of their own sounds, but enunciating words, pronouncing letters properly and coherently, is unique to the human race. Our Sages teach (Deuteronomy 23:24), "'Which you pledged with your *mouth*' — this refers to charity" (*Rosh HaShanah* 6a). Thus charity rectifies the mouth, and through it the power of speech — which is the standard that establishes one's level as a human being (*Likutey Moharan* I, 225).

• Giving charity creates a tranquil atmosphere. Helping and being helped encourages feelings of closeness between people. This tranquility enhances the power of speech by causing sound waves to move more efficiently and to travel greater distances. With charity, one who has perfected his own speech can reach a wider range of people and arouse them to serve God (*Likutey Moharan* I, 17:5).

*

Lashon HaKodesh: The Holy Tongue

The Hebrew language is generally referred to as "the holy language," but *lashon* in Hebrew means tongue, so the term indicates that one's tongue itself should be kept holy. In the context of Rebbe Nachman's lessons, it is clear that when he speaks of a holy tongue, he refers to the use of speech for holy purposes, for example, Torah, prayer and kind, encouraging and sympathetic words. Conversely, one must refrain from profanity, slander, mockery and the like, which are the opposite of, and leave no room for, holiness. While it is true that people must use mundane speech in the course of daily living, everything mundane can be done with the intention of furthering spirituality. This attitude enhances speech and elevates it to a level of holiness (see *Likutey Moharan* I, 19:3–5).

Many awesome levels of purity can be attained through developing a "holy tongue," as Rebbe Nachman teaches:

> The value of a "holy tongue" is very great indeed. It is the essence of the language God used in the Creation of the world (Rashi, Genesis 2:23). Everyone should therefore strive to attain a holy tongue. Commensurate with the level of the holy tongue that one achieves, one can arouse the specific power that God used to create the world (*Likutey Moharan* I, 19:3,6-8).

Rebbe Nachman taught that the Jewish exile is a reflection of blemished speech.

> The seventy original souls of the Jewish nation (Genesis,

Chapter 46) are rooted in the seventy facets of Torah. In contrast, the seventy languages are the source of the seventy nations of the world, who are steeped in the seventy evil character traits. These seventy languages are very distant from the seventy facets of Torah. Falling into the particular evil character trait that corresponds to one of the seventy languages is akin to falling into exile under the yoke of the nation that is rooted in that language (*Likutey Moharan* I, 36:1).

Rebbe Nachman thus offers us an antidote to having fallen into blemished speech:

In Hebrew, the name Chavah [Eve] can refer to speech, as in (Psalms 19:3), "Night to night *yeChaVeH* [will express] Daat." Therefore Eve, who was created by God through the holy tongue, represents pure speech. Since Eve was (Genesis 3:20) "the *mother* of all life," we understand that a person's speech accompanies him everywhere throughout his life, just like a mother who accompanies her young child even in the most sordid of places. Therefore, if someone strives to attain holiness of speech, even if he descends to the lowest of levels, his holy speech [i.e., Eve] will accompany him and will constantly remind him of God's presence (*Likutey Moharan* I, 78:3).

*

Mashiach

Everyone yearns for the days after Mashiach's arrival. It will be a time of unadulterated happiness and joy, good health, wealth, contentment and increased awareness of spirituality. It will be a perennial Shabbat, a time of peace and meaningful dialogue between man and wife, between man and his neighbors, between man and his community, between all of mankind — indeed, between man and all of Creation. Rebbe Nachman teaches that one can experience a taste of this grand future even nowadays, for each of us has a little bit of the Mashiach within him!

Rebbe Nachman taught:

> *MaShIaCH* is an aspect of speech, as in "*MeSIaCH ilmim* [God
> causes the mute to speak]" (*Likutey Moharan* II, 83:1).

The era of the Mashiach will be one in which people will be
able to speak their minds freely without causing pain to others, for
everyone will be dedicated to the pursuit of peace and spirituality.
The meaningful dialogue that will take place then will be the
expression of each individual's longing for truth, the sincere wish
to be able to "see" and "feel" Godliness. The means for attaining
this level of speech is found in the Torah, the manifestation of
God's wisdom. Thus, Rebbe Nachman taught:

> "The spirit of God hovered over the waters" (Genesis 1:2) —
> this refers to the spirit of Mashiach (*Zohar* I, 192b); "waters" refers
> to the Torah (see Chapter 28). The verse tells us that the spirit of
> Mashiach is to be found in the Torah. One who articulates his
> Torah study, especially his original Torah thoughts, causes the
> spirit of Mashiach to rest upon himself (*Likutey Moharan* I, 118).

When Mashiach comes, the ingathering of the exiles will be
completed. All Jews who have not yet found their way to the Land
of Israel by then will gather from around the globe and will head
for the Holy Land, where the greatest revelation of Godliness will
occur.

And even in our current era, one can "taste" the spirituality
of the Land.

The Holy Land

Rebbe Nachman taught:

> Speech is an aspect of Malkhut, the lowest of the *Sefirot*,
> which corresponds to the earth [as opposed to the heavens,
> which correspond to thought]. When one engages in holy
> speech, one's speech corresponds to the Holy Land; when one
> speaks of mundane matters, that speech corresponds to the other
> lands. Of course, even righteous people must at times engage in
> mundane conversation; however, when the tzaddik speaks of

worldly affairs, his intention is to elevate those residing in "other lands" to the status of the Holy Land (*Likutey Moharan* I, 81:1).

By the same token, speaking with holiness has the power to draw the spirituality of the Holy Land to the speaker.

Furthermore, when Mashiach comes, he will openly proclaim God's absolute dominion. People will then discard their many forms of idolatry and pursue only Godliness. Regarding the times of the Mashiach, Rebbe Nachman taught (*Likutey Moharan* I, 62:4), "When speech is purified, it will become the speech of faith. This speech will spread faith among the nations." Thus, every person, to the degree that he desires to bring Mashiach, must continually express his faith in God. It is this expression of faith that calls forth the aspect of Mashiach within each of us.

Rebbe Nachman taught:

> Faith is dependent upon one's mouth. To strengthen one's faith, one should constantly speak words of faith, over and over again (*Likutey Moharan* II, 44:1).

We have seen that "Malkhut is the mouth." Thus, speaking words of faith, which is equivalent to accepting God's Malkhut, can perfect one's tongue. Words of faith can bring all people to communicate through a common "language" — that of serving God (*Likutey Moharan* I, 18:6).

Rebbe Nachman thus taught:

> Currently, man's speech is imperfect. When all mankind turns to God, then speech will be perfected, as in (Zephaniah 3:9) "Then I will convert all the nations to a clear tongue, that they may all call out to God to serve Him of one accord" (*Likutey Moharan* I, 66:3).

* * *

Part Seven

The Peripheral Nervous System

The Head, Face and Senses

30

Introduction

In any army, the competence of a commanding officer is measured by how well he handles his subordinate officers and by the way his troops perform in battle. Likewise in the body, the level of competence of the brain (commander-in-chief) and heart (chief of staff) can be judged only by the performance of their "officers" and "troops." The "officers" are the five senses — sight, sound, smell, taste and touch — which comprise the peripheral nervous system. The "troops" are the other systems of the body.

It is significant that four of our sense organs — eyes, ears, nose and mouth — are located in our head and face. King Solomon taught (Ecclesiastes 2:14), "The wise man's eyes are in his head, but the fool walks in darkness." The Talmud asks (Yerushalmi, Sotah 8:10), "Are the fool's eyes then in his feet? Rather, the meaning is that while still in the process of planning his moves, the wise man is already *thinking ahead* to the end result."

Our sense organs were not placed in our heads by chance. The head represents purposeful design and willful action, the concept of "final actions" having been conceived "first in thought" (Lekhah Dodi Prayer). Since the sense organs are essential in deciding which actions are required in different circumstances, it is appropriate that they be located in the head, where all planning and thought takes place. And, of course, the ultimate goal that must be in one's thoughts and guide one's actions throughout one's life is the World to Come. If our eyes, ears, nose and mouth are to perform their roles effectively and faithfully as officers of the intellect, they must direct us and guide us to this final goal.

We shall begin this section with a short discussion of the physical qualities of the four senses which are based in the head and face. A study of the spiritual qualities of these senses is presented in the following chapters. The sense of touch, though it functions in the head as well, is associated more with other parts of the body and will be discussed in Part 8, "The Skeletal and Muscular System."

*

The Head, Face and Forehead

The brain sits in the cranium just behind the forehead. For someone with penetrating spiritual vision, the forehead of another person is like a window to his soul. The ARI, for instance, could see the record of a person's previous incarnations imprinted in his forehead. In the Zohar's treatment of physiognomy, the science of the face, a lengthy section is devoted to the *metzach* (forehead) (Zohar II, 71b–72b). Character traits, thoughts and actions are outlined in the size, shape, complexion, type, number of creases and other qualities of a person's forehead. Even an untrained eye can see how a forehead reflects the state of one's mind. Try paying attention to the foreheads of people with whom you come in contact. You will soon learn to discern far more about them than their words convey.

In a similar fashion, a person's state of mind can be easily detected in his countenance: joy shines upon the face, as does clarity of thought; a gloomy state of mind is reflected in a "darkened countenance," which is readily perceived by others. Thus, both the forehead and the face mirror thoughts.

*

The Sense Organs

The eyeball is covered by protective tissues known as the sclera (the white of the eye) and cornea. Surrounding the sclera are the exterior or extrinsic muscles. These muscles coordinate the movement of the two eyes, enabling them to function and focus in tandem. Though not normally visible, the extrinsic muscles are red. The pupil is the black circular opening in the middle of the eye through which light passes. The iris, the colored membrane which surrounds the pupil, is composed of muscle tissue and regulates the amount of light entering the eye. Like a camera with an adjustable lens, the muscles of the iris dilate or contract the pupil, depending upon light conditions and focus.

The ear is composed of three sections: an outer ear, a middle ear and an inner ear through which sound waves are transmitted to the brain via the auditory nerve. The sound waves enter through the outer ear and are amplified in the middle ear. They then pass on to the inner ear, where sensory receptors convert them to nerve impulses. There are air spaces in the middle ear that help equalize pressure in the ear. Air pressure is maintained by the air entering from outside the ear and by the eustachean tube, which connects the middle ear to the throat. Fluids found in the inner ear help to maintain equilibrium in the body.

The nose is our organ of smell, as well as an integral part of the breathing process. It has sensory cells that transmit odors to the brain via the olfactory nerve. The breathing process and its spiritual implications have been discussed above in Part 6 (The Respiratory System). In this section we will deal primarily with the nose's ability to discern varying odors.

The tongue is the major organ of the sense of taste, though other parts of the mouth are also involved in tasting. There are four main taste categories — sweet, sour, salty and bitter — detected by the approximately ten thousand taste buds in the mouth. Various nerves are involved in transmitting tastes to the brain. The process begins when we begin to chew and the taste buds demand assistance from the salivary glands. Thus, several parts of the body are called upon to create the experience of tasting food.

Touch receptors are located all over the body. Though we generally associate touch with the hands and feet, sensory receptors which respond to touch, pressure, pain, temperature and vibration are found throughout our skin and hair. The sense of touch will be discussed briefly in this section as part of the five senses, but the "power of touch" will be explained later, in Part 8.

* * *

31

The Menorah of Seven Lamps

> When you [Aaron] light the Menorah, its seven lamps shall shine toward the center [literally, "face"] of the Menorah.
>
> Numbers 8:2

The Zohar compares the human head to the *Menorah* (Candelabrum) of the Sanctuary. The Menorah had seven lamps in which oil was placed. The oil that was used in the Menorah corresponds to the *mochin* (intellect powers), while the seven lamps represent the seven apertures of the head: two eyes, two ears, two nostrils and the mouth (*Tikkuney Zohar*, Introduction, p.13b)

Rebbe Nachman taught (*Likutey Moharan* I, 21:12) that the seven "lamps" (apertures) of the head can radiate the Godly light only if they themselves are sanctified. Sanctification of these lamps can be attained through adherence to the following guidelines:

- *The eyes:* Avoid looking at evil and temptation; pay attention to and "see" the good in everything.
- *The ears:* Listen to the wise and avoid listening to slander and evil speech; have faith in the tzaddikim and banish heretical thoughts.
- *The nose:* Strive for the fear of Heaven (as in, "He will breathe with the fear of God" — Isaiah 11:3); rise above the "shallow breathing" of material desires.
- *The mouth:* Speak the truth and stay far away from falsehood; use words to build instead of to hurt or undermine others; speak words of Torah, prayer, encouragement, etc.

The senses are a two-way street. Using your eyes to see good brings good images into your thoughts. This in turn draws the light of the mind (i.e., the intellect) into the eyes and causes you to see even more good. "Listening to the wise" strengthens your faith and attunes your ears to the Godliness all around you. The same principle applies to the other senses. "The five senses have their source in the mind. Using them for good brings great rectification to the mind" (*Likutey Moharan* II, 5:14).

*

Rosh HaShanah: Courtrooms of the Mind

God's eyes are upon it [the Land] from the head [beginning] of the year until its end.

Deuteronomy 11:12

The Midrash teaches that the path a nation follows is determined by the person who stands at that nation's head (see *Bereishit Rabbah* 89:4). Physiologically as well, nothing happens in the body without first having been processed (at lightning speed) through one's neural synapses. Similarly, in the cycle of time, Rosh HaShanah, the Jewish New Year, is literally the "head" of the year. Nothing happens during any given year that was not destined, potentially at least, in the "head."

Let us visualize the brain as a courtroom. Testimony in this courtoom is provided by the senses, and the mind, acting as impartial judge, passes judgment.

The mind as judge makes countless, rapid decisions based on information from the senses. The more accurate this information is, the better chance the mind has of arriving at a correct decision. The amount of information which must be processed in the brain in order to cross a street or drive a car or bicycle down the road is staggering. The first few times a person drives, for example, he is more aware of this. His usual reaction is, "How do I concentrate on looking straight ahead, to the sides, behind me, and moving my hands and feet (especially with a clutch and on a steep incline) all at the same time?" After a while, the brain miraculously seems somehow to coordinate all these activities into one smooth flow. Still, any small detail that goes wrong or is overlooked can make the difference between life and death. Although we may not be aware of it, our lives are literally in danger twenty-four hours a day — and not only when we are on the road. One wrong move on our part, based on a miscalculation or a misreading of the information fed to us by our senses, can spell disaster. We can thus understand the importance of rectifying and fine-tuning the senses.

The decisions we base on information that is processed through our senses have far-reaching consequences, which may affect us directly as individuals, and which may extend to those around us: family, friends, neighbors and co-workers. In fact, the effects of our decisions may last for generations to come.

Now try to imagine the heavenly tribunal on Rosh HaShanah. Every Rosh HaShanah, according to tradition (cf. *Zohar* II, 32b), God "sits" in judgment and decides, based on how we, individually and collectively, have lived our lives over the past year, what we need, individually and collectively, to fulfill our particular missions on earth in the coming year. How does this judgment take place? Are we to be passive non-participants in a trial that will determine not only the coming year, but all the coming years of our lives and, beyond life, into Eternity? Is there anything we can do to ensure that we will be inscribed in the Book of Life on Rosh HaShanah?

There is definitely something we can do. We can purify our senses, the "lamps of our menorahs" and, through them, our thoughts. Why? Because our actions — all the actions of the past year, as well as those of all previous years — are merely manifestations of the patterns of our thoughts. The way we conduct ourselves is an outgrowth of the way we perceive both ourselves and our existence in this world. The principle determining factor which influences our judgment on Rosh HaShanah is therefore not what we have done until now, but how we *think* — which is the most powerful indicator of how we will act — from now on. On *Rosh* HaShanah, it is "all in the *head*." It is our *thoughts* which determine how we will be judged on this holy day.

This may seem unfair. What if a person can't avoid thinking certain unwholesome thoughts on Rosh HaShanah? Does that mean he is doomed forever? Of course, God takes into account the trials with which He tests each human being, and He is lenient when necessary. Yet this is not to say that we may take our thoughts any less seriously. If a bad thought comes into our minds, it is fully our responsibility to divert it and to flush it from our minds before it has a chance to develop. This is hard work at first — hard, that is, until we come to realize how easy it is. This is the "labor" of Rosh HaShanah.

Herein lies the key to Rosh HaShanah as the "head" of the year. Just as a seed may hold an entire tree, potentially contained within itself, so too on Rosh HaShanah, the stage is set for everything that will happen in the coming year. Just as every limb of the body is connected to the brain via the nervous system, so too all the days of the year can be seen as being connected to Rosh HaShanah and deriving their life force from it. In this sense, encapsulated within the essence of each Rosh HaShanah are all the lessons that we will need to learn in the coming year.

What we think on the day of Rosh HaShanah is therefore of paramount importance, for the judgment in the heavenly tribunal will be based not only on the previous year's actions; while they are important, they are not as important or as destiny-laden as the quality and subject matter of the thoughts that fill our minds on Rosh HaShanah itself. If our thoughts are holy and we know that we can change for the better, no matter what we have done in the past, this will be the deciding factor for us on Rosh HaShanah. This will "convince" the heavenly court that we are sincere in our desire that this lifetime serve as a *tikkun* (rectification), not only for the past year, but for every year of our lives and for every previous incarnation. This will align us with God's ultimate plan for all of creation.

These concepts have much broader applications. Each Rosh

HaShanah is itself only a "cell" in a larger system of New Years which ultimately connect themselves to the first New Year in the Garden of Eden. (Tradition tells us that the Sixth Day of Creation, the day on which Adam was created, was Rosh HaShanah; see *Pirkey d'Rebbe Eliezer* 8. Rosh HaShanah each year is thus called *yom harat olam*, the "birthday of the world," referring not to the world which was created five days earlier, but to the creation of Adam, the "microcosm of the world," for whose sake all of Creation came into being.) Similarly, each person on this planet is part of the greater consciousness we call Adam (mankind).

On Rosh HaShanah every creature on earth is "judged"; that is, its existence and mission are reevaluated vis-à-vis its part in the greater collective drama of life on this earth. The "verdict" that is decreed is nothing less than what is necessary to bring it back into alignment with its original purpose. Rosh HaShanah therefore involves reconnecting everything in the world to the original seed-thought of creation, in terms of why it exists and what its purpose is relative to the total picture of life.

When Rebbe Nachman speaks of Rosh HaShanah as the head, all these implications highlight his words. This is why he emphasizes thinking good and holy thoughts on Rosh HaShanah, which requires that we be cognizant of every single thought that comes into our minds and use each one to reach a greater awareness of God. Certainly we should pay attention to our thoughts and keep them pure every day of the year; however, on Rosh HaShanah, the head of the year, the power of thought is increased a hundredfold.

It is for this reason that Rebbe Nachman underscores the importance of traveling to the great tzaddikim on Rosh HaShanah. The tzaddikim are the *rosh* (head), the true leaders of Israel. On Rosh HaShanah we can rectify and fine-tune our senses through joining together three "heads":

* *Rosh HaShanah*: the head of the year.
* *The tzaddik*: the *rosh* and leader of Israel.
* *The individual's rosh*: each person's own mind and thoughts.

When these "heads" are joined together, and together they form one head, great rectifications take place and a whole new dimension of life opens up to us, where before we saw only an endless repetition of the past.

* * *

32

The Eyes: Windows to the World

The eyes are perhaps the most important of all the sense organs. Sight introduces man to colors and shapes — indeed to all the world which surrounds us. In a sense, man can hear, smell, taste and touch with his eyes, an overall sensory experience which cannot be duplicated by any of the other sense organs (i.e., through sight, one can more readily imagine the reaction of the other senses). Sight enables one to see the wonder and beauty of God's physical creation. Lacking sight, we become disconnected from reality, removed from true, definable contact with our world. Spiritually as well, "seeing" connotes looking deeply into things to discover their inner essence (see *Likutey Moharan* I, 1:2–4). Without good "eyesight," we are incapable of perceiving God's Presence all around us.

As we make our way through the routines of day-to-day living, we must guard our eyes against seeing what we want to see, as opposed to what is actually there. Ulterior motives can easily distort our perception. This is indicated in the Torah's injunction (Exodus 23:8; Deuteronomy 16:19), "Do not accept bribery. Bribery makes the eyes of the wise blind and perverts the words of the righteous." When judgment is clouded by ulterior motives, we lose our ability to discern the difference between right and wrong, between (Deuteronomy 25:1) "acquitting the innocent and convicting the guilty." Even the righteous are in danger of having their "words perverted." And if the wise, whose vision is sharp, can err in defining what they see, certainly those whose spiritual vision is weak must be especially wary (see *Likutey Moharan* I, 54:5).

Good eyesight corresponds to an expanded level of consciousness, knowledge and intellect (see *Likutey Moharan* I, 74:1). Kabbalistically, the eyes are an extension of the right hemisphere of the brain, which is associated with the *Sefirah* of Chokhmah (see *Likutey Moharan* II, 40:1). We must therefore ask ourselves, "How do we use our eyes?" Do we see the real essence of what we are looking at, or do we judge things by their outer appearances? (Recall that Chokhmah is *"ko'ach mah,"* the essence of something; see above, Chapters 14 and 17.) How can we attain that pure "Chokhmah level" of focus and concentration that will allow us to perceive the inner essence of things?

When concentrating on an object, the pupil of the eye expands or contracts to regulate the amount of light that can enter. This expansion and contraction allows the eye to focus properly without causing damage to the retina. In a comparable manner, when embarking on the search for great spiritual wisdom, it is wise to limit oneself at first to a lower level of intellect. In the early stages, focusing on gradual attainment rather than on future goals allows the intellect to "expand and contract" naturally, in order to accommodate the gradual attainment of a higher intellect (see *Likutey Moharan* I, 30:3).

Rebbe Nachman taught:

> The eyes are constantly exposed to the most amazing sights. Were a person to purify his eyes sufficiently, he would be able to see many wondrous things based solely on what he views with his eyes. Things pass before one's eyes so quickly, however, that there isn't time to focus upon and grasp all that one sees... Yet someone who is worthy can attain a higher level of sight and find himself able to glimpse exceedingly great wonders all around him. Because most people's eyes are not pure, they cannot focus properly, which precludes their seeing these wondrous, amazing sights (*Likutey Moharan* I, 254; *ibid.* I, 65:3).

Rebbe Nachman is referring here to visions that a person sees in his mind's eye. These amazing visions are not reserved only for tzaddikim, who have purified their senses and thereby attained the highest levels of consciousness. Such visions are in fact part and parcel of all our waking and sleeping lives. Tzaddikim know how to pay attention to all that transpires because they have purified their senses; they have fine-tuned themselves so that they can perceive things on a different wavelength. They therefore know how to "change channels" when a powerful visual image or a good thought comes to mind. In this way they are able to "see" what passes before their mind's eye and to grasp it before it is gone. The great tzaddikim were so proficient at this — their eyes were so pure — that wherever they looked they saw amazing visions and understood deep truths. As we shall see, in many instances, they opened their eyes to great truths by closing them!

*

Divine Providence

As noted above (Chapter 30), every eye has four colors: white, red, black and the color of the iris. These four colors correspond to four of the seven lower *Sefirot*: Chesed (Lovingkindness), Gevurah (Judgment), Tiferet (Beauty) and Malkhut (Kingship).

It is in Malkhut that all the Upper Lights converge and are perceived (cf. *Zohar* II, 204a). Chesed, Gevurah and Tiferet act in concert to draw blessing from the *mochin* (mentalities) into Malkhut, thereby revealing God's Providence and Kingship in creation. In the same way, the three colors of the eye, white (representing Chesed), red (Gevurah), and the iris, the multicolored part of the eye (Tiferet — representing the beauty of many colors), work together to regulate light and dilate the black pupil (Malkhut) so that it can focus properly and transmit images to the brain efficiently.

Rebbe Nachman often said that the main thing to look for in this world is God Himself, and for signs of His Providence and Wisdom (see *Likutey Moharan* I, 1:1; 13:4). As always, our arousal from below elicits a corresponding arousal from Above. When we use our eyes as lenses through which to see God everywhere in this world, when we begin literally to see through the veil that separates us from God, then God Himself will turn His eyes towards us. If we use our sight to focus on Him, God will look back towards us, until His sight and our sight converge and become perfectly focused. Perhaps this is the meaning of the prophecy (Isaiah 52:8), "*Eye to eye* you will see God when He returns to Zion."

Eye to eye means that our eyes parallel God's. When we speak of God's Providence we usually think of His constant "super-*vision*" and "over-*seeing*" of every detail of His Creation. This is only a "one-sided view" of things, however. When we forget or otherwise neglect to focus upon God, we "discard the image" that completes the process of God's focus. God always "keeps an eye out" for those who search for Him. "From heaven He looks down upon the children of men, to see if there is anyone who possesses the understanding to seek Him" (Psalms 14:2). We must also turn to God, for our ability to discern Divine Providence completes the cycle of sight, establishing "perfect vision," the revelation of God's Kingship (Malkhut), through us. This is the meaning of "Eye to eye you will see God when He returns to Zion."

Begin to train your eyes to see, for example, that your livelihood comes only from God. As it is written (Psalms 145:15), "The *eyes of all* wait upon You, for You dispense livelihood to each of them in his own time." Nowhere do we find the need for "focusing" on God more obvious than when we seek a livelihood. When we are properly focused, our attitude is one of absolute trust in God. This is reflected in the verse, "The eyes of all wait upon You..." The first step is to direct our eyes towards heaven for sustenance. When our "eyes" are focused on Him — when that point of contact is found — a vessel is created within which we can receive His bounty (*Likutey Moharan* I, 76:3, 4).

The way to see this Providence is by penetrating the facade of physical relationships which seem to govern your life. Look beyond all the various intermediaries that surround your livelihood. See God's Hand in your life and recognize His direct Providence upon you, never taking this Providence for granted. Pray to God for continued sustenance; pray to see His Hand in your life; pray to have total trust in Him. Learn to trust and have faith that your prayers are heard. This is your part in completing the cycle of Divine Providence. This is how you can begin to see eye to eye with God.

The most effective way to strengthen your trust in God and your faith in His Providence is through Torah study. We have seen that the Torah itself can be learned on four levels: *p'shat* (simple meaning), *remez* (allusion), *drush* (homiletical meaning) and *sod* (secret meaning) (Chapter 1). The Torah scroll itself carries another four levels: *ta'amim* (cantillations), *nekudot* (vowels), *tagim* (crowns upon the letters) and *otiot* (the letters themselves). In a Torah scroll, neither of the first of these two levels are visible; only the black letters and the mysterious crowns can be seen. Hidden within them, however, are the vowels and cantillations, which are crucial to the Torah reading. Without the vowels, there would be no way of knowing how to pronounce the letters, and without the cantillations, we would never know how to chant the words of Torah and experience its true sweetness.

Rebbe Nachman thus taught:

> When the wise man brings Torah to his people, Divine Providence is drawn down to the world. This is because the Torah contains cantillations, vowel points, crowns and letters. These are represented in the three colors of the eye and the pupil... When a wise man draws forth original Torah teachings, he brings down the "power of vision" of God's Providence upon us, and each person, based on the degree of his own closeness to the Torah, experiences God's Providence, focused on him accordingly. [He is then better able to "focus" on God.] (*Likutey Moharan* I, 13:4)

Yet one must see to it that one's sight remains "true." Rebbe

Nachman teaches (*Likutey Moharan* I, 51:1, 6), "Falsehood is damaging to the eyes, both physically and spiritually. Falsehood damages one's vision, and damaged vision creates distorted images. Falsehood fools people, causing a large object to appear small or a single object to appear as a double or multiple image. Truth, on the other hand, is unified [it is nothing less than the stamp of God's Absolute Unity] (*Shabbat* 55a). While truth is multi-faceted, it is — and can only be — one."

Falsehood is a direct affront to God's Providence. When we lie, we are in a sense pushing God out of the way in order to have our own way. In response, God acts as though He is turning His eyes away from us. The only way to reestablish our connection to God is through truth. Only by speaking truth, believing in its power and *living* it can we restore our vision, refocusing on God and His Divine Providence. His direct supervision over us is then restored in even greater measure.

*

Focus: The World to Come

As we have seen, in order to gain strong spiritual vision, we must be able to focus our sights on Godliness. This, in turn, brings us under the most direct Divine Providence. (God has no *need* for us to look towards Him in order to "take notice" of us; still, He makes the extent of His Providence dependent on the degree to which we turn to Him.)

The truth is that Godliness permeates all of Creation, for without Godliness nothing can exist. Still, as we have pointed out, we must work to concentrate our focus on Godliness to the point that we can penetrate the facade of This World and find the hidden reality of the World to Come. In a sense, we need to close our eyes to This World in order to see behind its mask; otherwise, we will live our whole lives without even guessing that God was there all the time, right beneath the surface, where we least expected to find Him.

The Talmud teaches that the "size" of the Torah is 3,200 times larger than that of this entire world (see *Eruvin* 21a). Yet you can cover your eye with your pinky and effectively block out this great light! Rebbe Nachman likened this to a person facing a lofty mountain and covering his eye with a coin. The mountain may be millions of times larger than the coin, but nevertheless the coin completely obscures it. So too, the Torah is tremendous and vast, but the "small pinky" which is This World imposes itself upon our eyes, and prevents us from seeing the great light of the Torah. True, This World is indeed a minuscule creation compared to the Torah, which is so immense, yet because the "pinky" is directly in front of a person's eye, it can block his vision so completely that he cannot see something vastly greater (*Baal Shem Tov* on *Pirkei Avot* 2:1, #49; *Likutey Moharan* I, 133:2).

"So," Rebbe Nachman explains, "when the soul of a person enters This World, he remains submerged in its empty nonsense, and it seems to him that there is nothing more to life. In this way, this small, diminutive world prevents him from seeing the great, extraordinary light of the Torah, which is many thousands times greater... Let him but remove this little obstruction from before his eyes — let him turn his eyes away from the world and cease to gaze upon it; let him but raise his head, lift up his eyes and gaze upon and consider all that is above this hindering, obstructing world — and he will merit to see the magnificent, extraordinary luminosity of the Torah and the tzaddikim... So I have heard in the name of the Baal Shem Tov, who said, 'O woe and alas! The world is full of illuminations and wondrous, awesome, mystic truths. Yet a small hand sets itself directly before the eyes and obstructs the sight of these great illuminations.'"

In keeping with the approach of the Baal Shem Tov, Rebbe Nachman teaches that if you want to attain the level of the World to Come, even in This World, just close your eyes. For a few minutes each day, close your eyes to the mundane pleasures and woes of the world, gently withdraw your mind from all that is going on around you and move yourself into another dimension.

The more you "close your eyes to This World," the more you will attain true spirituality and bring the essence of the World to Come into your life (see Likutey Moharan I, 65:3).

This is the secret behind closing our eyes and covering them when we say the *Shema* prayer. Up to a certain point the world reveals God, His Providence, His Light and His awesome Oneness. Beyond that point, however, that very same world obscures Him. We therefore close our eyes and cover them with our hand when we recite the *Shema*, in order to break through the facade of This World to reach towards the Unity behind it. We close our eyes and proclaim, "Hear O Israel, *YHVH* is our God, *YHVH* is ONE."

*

Looking Beyond

Taste and *see* that God is good.

Psalms 34:9

Since God is good, it seems logical that there should be nothing bad or evil in the world at all; there should be only good. In truth, though, suffering is plentiful, more plentiful in fact than anyone would like to acknowledge. With illness, poverty, mental anguish, family problems and countless other woes, people experience pain of some sort every day (see Likutey Moharan II, 77).

As we have seen (above, Chapter 15), "When one has Knowledge [Daat], one lacks nothing." This is because someone who has Daat is aware of God's Presence in everything he encounters. Still, the presence of pain — be it our own or someone else's — constricts our awareness of the spiritual. Our challenge in This World is to *see beyond* pain and suffering, to understand and actually feel the goodness that is there.

Rebbe Nachman taught:

> When a person is severely afflicted, the greatest anguish is due [not to the actual physical suffering, but] to the fact that Daat [Knowledge] has been taken away from him. With Daat, one understands that everything God does has a purpose and is

ultimately for the good. Without Daat, one loses sight of this basic truth and, as a result, feels anguish. This diminishing of his connection to God is the real source of his suffering.

The way to alleviate this anguish is to look beyond the suffering and to strengthen one's belief in the World to Come. Note that the natural instinct of someone experiencing intense pain is to close his eyes tightly, as if he were squinting and looking far into the distance... He does this because instinctively he is seeking Daat, the great Daat that will be revealed in the distant Future, in the World to Come, when the true purpose for everything will be revealed (*Likutey Moharan* I, 65:3; see also *Garden of the Souls: Rebbe Nachman on Suffering*).

*

The Evil Eye

He who possesses a beneficent eye shall be blessed.
Proverbs 22:9

There is a "beneficent eye" and an "evil eye." Both terms have been used for several millennia and are found in Scripture and Talmud as indicators of the measure of a man. Abraham was the paradigm of one who possesses a "beneficent eye." He always looked for good in others and felt neither jealousy of, nor hatred for, his fellow man. Bilaam, on the other hand, epitomized the possessor of an "evil eye" — one who always looks for fault or is jealous of another's possessions or status (see *Avot* 5:19).

The Talmud, when referring to the evil eye, credits it with almost mystical powers. Looking at another's possessions with jealousy in your eyes can cause evil to befall that person. For this reason Talmudic law forbids us to build our homes too close to that of our neighbors. Privacy is very important, lest we look upon our neighbors' possessions with a covetous eye. Neighbors should maintain a reasonable distance between one another, or, at the very least, homes should be built with a separation and a space between them (*Bava Batra* 3a).

Having an "evil eye" is usually understood as looking at another person with the intent that evil should befall him. It also includes coveting another's possessions, being annoyed at his success (as if his success somehow impinges on our ability to succeed in life), pettiness and so on. Rebbe Nachman teaches that an evil eye leads to an increased breathing rate. Somehow, jealousy and rage at another's success causes one to draw breath at an accelerated pace (see *Likutey Moharan* I, 55:13).

The Talmud (*Sotah* 38b) therefore teaches, "The cup of benediction at the conclusion of a meal should be given to one with a good eye. It is thus written (Proverbs 22:9), 'He who possesses a beneficent eye, shall be blessed.' Do not only read, 'shall be blessed,' but shall bless...." Conversely, one should beware of people with stingy and jealous eyes, as King Solomon cautions (Proverbs 23:6), "Do not break bread with [one who possesses] an evil eye."

It is not merely a matter of superstition. As much as a good eye blesses, an evil eye takes. The source of the power of the evil eye is greed: When one looks upon another's possessions with greed, and the other is in any way guilty of misusing his money, or is otherwise unworthy of the wealth he possesses, he might lose his possessions, God forbid. Clearly, the way we look upon another's possessions can arouse Divine judgment against him. In the same vein, when we view the possessions of others generously, we can, with the mere "look of our eyes," bring blessing upon them.

When we realize that the eyes are the "windows to the mind," the significance of the "evil eye" increases.
Rebbe Nachman taught:

Memory depends upon the eyes, as in (Exodus 13:9), "[The *tefilin* shall be as] a remembrance between your *eyes*." In order to guard one's memory, one must first guard oneself from an evil eye — from evil thoughts about others, from jealousy, and from all forms of negativity. The evil eye can cause harm not only to the one being focused upon, but also to the one who is focusing, to an even greater degree. Conversely, maintaining an evil eye goes hand in hand with forgetfulness (*Likutey Moharan* I, 54:4).

Yet we needn't live in constant fear of the evil eye, of others who may wish us harm. Rebbe Nachman teaches that if we feel incapable of guarding ourselves against an evil eye, then we should flee from it. However, if we can come to understand the essence of the evil eye, our actions can be far more effective: we can rectify it.

For example, a person might have an evil eye against another's position in life. This evil eye stems from the fallen attribute of Malkhut (Kingship, which, when blemished, leads to low self-esteem and the need to put others down in order to get ahead). To correct one's own fallen Malkhut, one should strive to elevate God's Malkhut — by learning Torah or by otherwise disseminating God's Name in the world. In this way, one demonstrates one's allegiance to God, rather than to one's own need for self-aggrandizement. This serves to rectify the evil eye of the fallen Malkhut at its root (see *Likutey Moharan* I, 54:4).

*

The Lusting Eye

The eye in Hebrew is called *ayin* (עין), pronounced exactly as the name of the Hebrew letter *ayin* (ע) is pronounced. The *gematria* (numerical equivalent) of the letter *ayin* is seventy, corresponding to the seventy souls of the House of Jacob (Genesis, Chapter 46) and the seventy facets of the Torah on the one hand, and to the seventy archetypal nations of the world and the seventy evil characteristics on the other (see above, Chapter 10).

Among all the evil characteristics of all the nations of the world, sexual immorality is the most widespread and the most damaging. The nation of Israel is therefore obligated to maintain sexual purity through overcoming lustful desires. We are thus commanded in the *Shema* prayer (Numbers 15:39), "Do not stray...after your eyes." The Talmud (*Berakhot* 12b) interprets this as a directive to guard oneself against thoughts of sexual immorality.

This is another reason why we cover our eyes when reciting the *Shema*. When we cover our eyes with the intention of overcoming our lustful desires, we nullify the powerful effects of the immorality of the seventy nations. Covering our eyes also in effect "covers" the evil *ayin* of the seventy nations, protecting us from its influence (see *Likutey Moharan* I, 36:2–3).

Another tool to protect us against sexual lust is the mitzvah of *tzitzit*; thus, during our recitation of the *Shema* we also gaze at our *tzitzit*. This is because the word *TZITZit* is from the same root as the word *TZITZ*, "to gaze." Gazing at the *tzitzit*, using our eyes, serves as a powerful protection against lustful thoughts (*Likutey Moharan* I, 7:4–5).

* * *

33

Hearing, Smell and Taste

The ears, nose and throat are closely interrelated in human physiology. The ear canal is connected to the nasal cavity, and passages link the ears directly to the throat, which is connected to the thoracic cavity. We have already discussed the close relationship that exists between the mouth, throat and lungs (Chapter 28), and the larynx and trachea that link the lungs to the throat and the breathing orifices.

Kabbalistically as well, there is a close association between the ear, nose and mouth. The ARI explains that everything in the world has its source in the four basic elements. The four elements derive their essence from the four letters of the Tetragrammaton, which in turn are rooted in the apex of the first letter, the *Yod* (see above, Chapter 4, p.34). The four letters of the Tetragrammaton, and thereby the lower *Partzufim* (or *Sefirot*) and soul levels, are also reflected in man's powers of sight, hearing, smell and speech.

Tetragrammaton	Partzuf	Soul level	Organ
Yod	Chokhmah	Chayah	eyes
Heh	Binah	Neshamah	ears
Vav	Zer Anpin	Ruach	nose
Heh	Malkhut	Nefesh	mouth

*

The Ears

Rebbe Nachman taught:

The heart "hears." Although technically speaking we hear

through our ears, the process must be completed with the heart, which facilitates one's understanding of what one has heard. Thus, a teacher must speak to his student's heart, while the student must take heed and put his own heart (through his concentration) into what his teacher has said. When the student does not take to heart his teacher's words, when he does not try to concentrate on understanding the lessons of his teacher, he is effectively separating himself from wisdom (*Likutey Moharan* II, 91:1).

A teacher must weigh his words very carefully. Those who listen to him must "hear" and accept only what is needed for their spiritual growth — no more. Each student must be particular about what he chooses to concentrate on, for not everything he hears is necessarily beneficial to him. Whatever he hears that is beyond his current intellectual and spiritual level is considered excess and should be ignored (see *Likutey Moharan* II, 47). We see, then, that it is the heart that "hears," and thus the ears are associated with Binah.

Earlier (Chapter 31) we discussed the ear in terms of its relationship to faith in the tzaddikim. An in-depth study of the ear will show us more clearly how important a part the ear plays in accepting the teachings of the tzaddikim. One must have faith in the tzaddikim in order to truly *hear* what they say, and this faith is a powerful spiritual remedy for defective hearing (cf. *Likutey Moharan* I, 21:2).

*

"He Wakens My Ear..."

We have seen that the ear plays a crucial role in one's spiritual growth. Following are several excerpts from Rebbe Nachman's teachings which deal with the importance of hearing instruction directly from the tzaddik and some advice regarding situations when this is not possible.

Hearing Torah teachings directly from a tzaddik is more beneficial by far than studying Torah alone. This is because hearing directly from the tzaddik binds one to the soul of the tzaddik (*Likutey Moharan* I, 120; *ibid.* I, 20:4).

It is very important to go to the tzaddik to hear Torah teachings from him. As for any Torah teaching that is heard from some source other than its originator, the farther removed the teaching is from its source, the less is its impact on the one who hears it. Studying from a printed book is even further removed from the source of the teaching (*Likutey Moharan* I, 19:1).

We can appreciate the importance of hearing firsthand the tzaddik's Torah, but what are we to do if we cannot travel to the tzaddik? What if we do not know to which tzaddik to travel or even who is considered a tzaddik?

As an alternative, Rebbe Nachman said (*The Aleph-Bet Book*, Torah Study, A:68), "Arising early in the morning to study Torah is beneficial to the ears." This is based on the verse (Isaiah 50:4), "God has given me the tongue of the learned, that I should know how to sustain the weary; He wakens *morning by morning*, and wakens my *ear* to hear as the learned." Rashi explains that Isaiah (a most worthy teacher) was aroused early each morning in order to receive the Divine Inspiration necessary to teach the weary and those who thirsted for spirituality. This lesson applies to anyone who seeks spirituality. Rising early to serve God, especially through Torah study, rectifies a person's hearing, enabling him to experience spiritual inspiration. And since the study of Torah involves learning the teachings of the tzaddikim, articulating their words during study is comparable to listening to their teachings directly from their mouths (see *Likutey Moharan* I, 12:1–3).

However, not everything that is spoken is worthy of being listened to; nor is every speaker to be considered a worthy bearer of the spiritual message. As we have seen (Chapter 29), Rebbe Nachman cites the verse (Psalms 19:4), "There is no speech nor words; their voice is not heard," to explain that words that are spoken do not qualify as speech if people cannot "hear" them. This refers to speech that is lacking intellectual verity, or speech that distances people from God (see *Likutey Moharan* I, 29:1). About teachers who use such speech the Rebbe said, "There are those who lecture on Torah, but they are not Torah scholars; rather they are Torah *demon*-scholars. People come to hear their lectures, assuming they will be given assistance and direction in how to serve God. However, the Torah that these teachers offer is blemished and cannot help those who hear their words. On the contrary, their lectures actually tire out their listeners, both spiritually and physically" (*Likutey Moharan* I, 28:1). The same applies to the writings of these "scholars."

To grow spiritually, it is not sufficient merely to avoid listening to slander, profanity and other offensive forms of speech. One must also be selective about *whom* one listens to. Any speech of an unworthy person, no matter what he says, can have a detrimental effect upon one's ability to strive for spirituality. It is important to note further that it is not only words that have a beneficial or deleterious effect. Rebbe Nachman teaches that "hearing songs and melodies from the wicked is harmful to one's soul, while hearing them from righteous people is very beneficial" (*Likutey Moharan* I, 3:1). Thus, one must also take extreme care in choosing the type of music one listens to.

*

Faith in the Wise

The Talmud (*Nedarim* 20b) teaches that there are five organs which are not under a person's absolute control — the two eyes, the two ears and the sexual organ — for they are all susceptible to external influences. We have seen that through the sense of hearing one can "listen to the words of the wise," and so increase one's faith in the tzaddikim. Yet, with potentially equally powerful results, the ear is always open to the sounds of destructive influences and can be easily diverted from its task of concentrating on spirituality. Thus the ear is very sensitive to strife.

Rebbe Nachman teaches that when a person is exposed to words of strife — often expressed in arguments against the Torah and the tzaddikim — he should realize that the very fact that he has heard these arguments has been orchestrated by God, solely for his own benefit. He must realize that the deficiencies he hears about are his and his alone. Someone who is exposed to argumentative talk should accept that the words he hears contain hints to the spiritual areas which he himself must rectify. By accepting anew the Torah, and by strengthening his faith in the tzaddikim, he will learn to overcome his imperfections and rectify his wrongdoings (see *Likutey Moharan* I, 5:4).

*

Shema [Hear] Israel, God is our God, God is Echad [One].
Deuteronomy 6:4

If faith is to reach the heart, one must first listen carefully to the words one hears. In fact, the most basic proclamation of our faith in God begins with the word "*Shema*" (hear). In the Torah, in the verse which opens with the word "*Shema*" (שמע) and ends with "*Echad*" (אחד, one), two letters are written larger than the others: the *Ayin* (ע) of *shema* and the *Dalet* (ד) of *echad*. These two letters make up the Hebrew word *AiD* (עד, witness); with our proclamation of faith we *testify* to God's Unity and to His Kingship over all of Creation.

If the *Ayin* and the *Dalet* were removed, the remaining letters of the opening word of the verse, *SheMa* (שמ), and the closing word, *ECHad* (אח), would comprise the word *ESMaCH* (אשמח), as in (Psalms 104:34), "*Esmach* — I will rejoice in God." This illustrates that "joy from Above is bestowed upon anyone who proclaims his faith daily" (*Zohar* III, 236b).

Reb Noson explains that our faith strengthens our joy, and our joy strengthens our faith. Joy, then, is the essence of our faith. Everyone must rejoice in God, and this joy then becomes each individual's salvation. Thus, every Jew should rejoice daily in his proclamation of the *Shema* and in the intensity of his faith. This is a Jew's eternal joy and hope, for nothing of this world remains with a person after his passing except for the joy he achieved through his faith in God and through his observance of the mitzvot (see *Likutey Halakhot, Hodaah* 6:75).

For our recitation of the *Shema* to be most effective, and in order for us to gain the maximum benefit from our words, we must attune our ears, not merely to recite the *Shema* passively, but actually to "hear" our own proclamation of faith and to inscribe it upon our hearts. This constitutes the greatest rectification of the ears.

*

The Nose

The nose is an integral part of the respiratory system. It is the major organ through which a person draws in fresh air and oxygen to sustain his body. In this section, we will study the nose both as it relates to patience and prayer, and in its importance as the organ of smell.

*

Patience and Restraint

We have seen that the nose represents both anger and patience (above, Chapter 26). Rebbe Nachman compares anger to a violent storm wind of temporary duration. One who can "wait out" the storm and fury of life's turbulent moments, through exercising patience, draws vitality from the Source of all life! (*Likutey Moharan* I, 8:3). The link between patience and rectifying the nose can be seen by the term used to describe restraining anger: *arikhat apayim*, literally, "lengthening of the nose." Anger is compared to smoke "escaping through the nostrils" (cf. II Samuel 22:9). Thus, controlling anger through patience can be compared to drawing a long, deep breath of fresh air to help one avoid the devastating effects of losing one's temper. Clearly, perfecting the attribute of patience is a means of rectifying the spiritual aspect of the nose. Rebbe Nachman taught:

> One who merits to control his temper is never afraid of missing out on anything in life. He has the patience necessary to wait for [the good] that is coming to him (*Likutey Moharan* I, 155:1).

*

A man who does not restrain his own spirit is [likened to] a breached city without a protective wall.

Proverbs 25:28

Patience is truly a virtue, whereas anger and irritability are not only harmful to one's health but to one's soul. Patience, restraint and self-control — these are the qualities which place a person at a healthy distance from his surroundings, protecting him from over-reacting or reacting impulsively in situations where mature judgment and slow, careful deliberation are called for.

The above verse teaches us that anger is also harmful to one's livelihood, one's "protective wall" of financial security. According to Rebbe Nachman, the reward of restraint is enhanced financial security. Indeed, restraint corresponds to a protective *chomah* (wall). If a person becomes angry, his *ChoMaH* is broken by his *ChaiMaH* (anger). Although people tend to consider their possessions to be their security, no one feels truly secure unless there is also a "protective wall" around their belongings. Without this protective wall, one's wealth is endangered. Here we see that the true protective wall is restraint (*Likutey Moharan* I, 59:5).

Rebbe Nachman teaches further that when the Evil One sees that a person is about to receive abundant blessings of wealth, he attempts to turn that person's *ChoMaH* into *ChaiMaH*. Therefore, if someone sees that he is about to be overcome with anger, he should realize that bounty awaits him. Let him but control his anger, and he will be able to attain wealth (*Likutey Moharan* I, 68:2).

The lust for wealth, just as anger, is compared to idolatry (*Zohar* I, 27b; *Likutey Moharan* I, 23:1), whereas patience corresponds to faith, the opposite of idol-worship (see *Likutey Moharan* I, 155:2). Faith is clearly required in areas relating to one's livelihood. Thus, where anger takes over, it precludes faith, and avarice is inevitable.

Restraining one's anger also leads to true humility (*Likutey Moharan* I, 21:6). This applies particularly to one who, in the very throes of anger, transforms that anger into compassion. He channels all the force of his accumulated anger, changing it to compassion towards those who had previously aroused his anger (see *Likutey Moharan* I, 18:2).

*

The Filter

The nose has two nostrils, which facilitate the breathing process. The Zohar (III, 224a) teaches that just as the right and left sides represent Chesed (bounty, lovingkindness) and Gevurah (strict judgment), in a similar vein, the right nostril represents the idea of a pleasant aroma, while the left nostril represents smoke and anger. Rebbe Nachman teaches that by controlling his anger a person filters out clean, pure and pleasant air from within the "smoke" of anger akin to the nose's ability to filter out pure air. Thus restraint from anger corresponds to filtering one's spirit of evil while retaining the good.

Drawing pleasantness from one's anger is accomplished by achieving self-control, which allows one to "breathe" pure air. We have seen (above, Chapter 3) that the nose corresponds to the soul level of *Ruach* (spirit). Thus, by utilizing our *ruach* — this pure spirit which we have filtered out — we can gain the ability to transform our latent intellect into effective awareness of the spiritual. We can then come to recognize the difference between "right" and "left," between good and evil (see *Likutey Moharan* I, 66:2).

*

The "Sense" of Prayer

The powerful influence of the nose becomes even more apparent in its other aspects. Rebbe Nachman teaches that prayer is compared to the nose. It is written (Isaiah 48:9), "For My Name's sake I will withhold my anger; and for My praise, *eCHToM*, [I will restrain]..." In Hebrew, the word "nose" is translated as both *af* and *CHoTeM*. Based on this, "for My praise, *echtom*" implies a connection between prayer and the nose. One who engages in sincere prayer can be assured that he will merit to partake of the "breath of life."

This also alludes to the important place prayer holds in our daily lives. Just as one cannot live without breathing, which is accomplished through the nose, so too reliance on prayer for one's salvation is of vital importance (*Rabbi Yaakov Meir Shechter*). Rebbe Nachman adds that one's physical ability to smell is enhanced by one's prayers, because prayer and the nose are conceptually one (*Likutey Moharan I, 9:5*).

Prayer is compared to the nose in another sense: As important as it is to pray continually for salvaion, we must always exercise extreme patience (as represented by the nose) while waiting for God to answer our prayers.

Mashiach corresponds both to prayer and to the nose (*Likutey Moharan II, 1:12*; see also above, Chapters 25 and 29). Scripture tells us that Mashiach's exceptional power will stem from his nose, as in (Isaiah 11:3), "He will *breathe* the fear of God." This means that his vitality will be obtained through his nose, with every breath he takes.

In addition, our Sages teach (*Sanhedrin 93b*), "Mashiach will be able to 'smell' deceit and to adjudicate by his sense of smell." As we have seen, prayer is compared to the nose; the main weapon which Mashiach will use to conquer the world and to administer true justice will be not the sword, artillery or any other physical weapon but prayer (*Likutey Moharan I, 2:1*).

Rebbe Nachman tells us that everyone has a "nose and a sense of smell" which reflect, on a personal level, the "nose and sense of smell" of Mashiach. Thus, each person has within himself a tiny portion of Mashiach, and by engaging in sincere prayer, he can arouse and cultivate this portion, thereby hastening Mashiach's arrival. This is yet another compelling reason for us to guard ourselves against immorality, for immoral thoughts and behavior lead to difficulty in prayer and thereby blemish one's aspect of Mashiach (see also *Mashiach: Who? What? Why? How? Where? and When?*, Chapter 7, for a more detailed explanation).

*

A Pure Sense of Smell

Immorality also has a basis in the nose. Anatomically, the physical sense of smell is associated with the limbic lobe of the brain, which is considered to be the link between the cognitive and emotional processes, that is, between thoughts and feelings. Since the sexual urge is undoubtedly one of man's strongest passions, which impact on his mind as well as on his emotions, physiologically the nose and sexual desire are interconnected.

In a spiritual sense, Rebbe Nachman teaches that a pure sense of smell can be attained only through sexual purity (*Likutey Moharan* I, 2:8). Where sexual purity is lacking, spiritual energy inevitably wanes. This, in turn, affects the nose, which represents one's ability to filter purity from impurity, as we have seen.

The connection between the nose and immorality is seen in the words which the Torah uses to prohibit adultery (Exodus 20:13): "*Lo tin'af*— Do not commit adultery." Our Sages comment (*Mekhilta, Yitro*) that the word *TiN'AF* is made up of a combination of the words *TeiN AF* (give the nose), implying the exhortation: "Do not even seek to *smell* the perfume of a[nother] woman," for this leads to adultery.

The Talmud (*Berakhot* 43b) teaches that smell is closely related to the soul. This is based on the similarity between the words *RuaCh* (רוח, soul; spirit) and *ReiaCh* (ריח, smell). Rebbe Nachman observes (*Likutey Moharan* II, 1:12) that as long as a putrid-smelling object is left alone, it will not emit a terrible odor, but when it is moved, it can begin to smell foul again, perhaps even worse than it did before. Similarly, if a soul has sinned, it is enveloped in a foul odor. In "moving" the soul to repentance, the tzaddik must know how to offer rebuke in such a way that the soul's naturally pleasant odor will be aroused, for abusive rebuke can cause the soul to "stink" even more (*Likutey Moharan* II, 8:1). In one's struggle for spirituality, one must always stress goodness and pleasantness, rather than stringencies and other approaches which may discourage one in the quest for Godliness. In this way one will eventually attain a level of purity, emitting fragrant odors and smelling the beauty of spiritual living.

*

Taste

Approximately ten thousand taste buds are found in one's tongue and mouth. Specific tastes are sensed more strongly in certain regions of the tongue. A sour taste is detected mainly at the sides of the tongue, while a bitter taste is felt in the back of the tongue, and sweet and salty tastes mainly at the tip of the tongue. The sense of smell also contributes much to the sense of taste, tickling the delicate taste buds and stimulating the appetite and digestive juices. It also has a good deal of influence over a person's willingness to taste his food. As we have seen, an acute "sense of smell" depends on purity, so that a person who maintains pure thoughts and deeds will experience enhanced taste in his food. (Many aspects of the sense of taste have already been dealt with earlier in our discussion of eating habits; see above, Chapter 10.)

Reb Noson speaks about "sweet and sour" tastes in a discourse dealing with eating (*Likutey Halakhot, Netilat Yadayim LiSeudoh* 6:98):

The manna contained all the tastes in the world, yet it is compared mainly to honey and oil (Exodus 16:31; Numbers 11:8). The verse states (Ezekiel 16:19), "Flour, oil and honey did I feed you..." In these three items, representing starches, fats and sugars, one has the basic ingredients and tastes which are found in most foods. This is because we need all these ingredients in order to truly experience the wonders of God's Creation. Of all these tastes, bread is the most basic and the most important. We thus find that in the Land of Israel, the taste of bread is very palatable to the tongue (cf. Deuteronomy 8:9; see also *Likutey Moharan* I, 47).

Reb Noson adds that there is a problem inherent in sweet tastes such as honey. Adam's sin of eating from the Tree of Knowledge came about because the fruit appeared *desirable* to the palate. People tend to crave sweet-tasting foods. Children in particular, and many adults as well, desire sweets. In order to rectify Adam's sin, one must curb one's appetite for sweet tastes and learn to blend all sorts of tastes. Experiencing and enjoying different types of tastes elevates man to the status of "the Holy Land," where all tastes can be experienced in bread alone.

Reb Noson concludes that it is not worthwhile to seek only sweet-tasting foods; neither is a broad variety of foods necessary. Rather, one needs only to direct one's sense of taste towards the spiritual aspects of the food, as did the Simpleton in Rebbe Nachman's story (*Rabbi Nachman's Stories*, #9, pp.160–196; see also above, Chapter 10). For every specific food the Simpleton requested, his wife would cut him a slice of bread and give it to him. Yet, when he ate it, the Simpleton tasted every possible taste. In the same way, when eating for the spiritual experience, a person can partake of all the tastes in the world in a single slice of bread!

* * *

34

The Face: The True Image of Man

The spiritual qualities of the face are remarkable. While there are many means by which to identify a person — by his gait, his build, his voice and so on — his face is clearly the most discernible feature: it is the truest portrayal of one's essential being. Reb Noson writes:

> The most important means by which to identify anything and to ascertain its value is through its "face." A person can be instantly recognized by his face. Moreover, his thoughts and speech are expressed through his face. In the same way, everything in the world has a "face," its unique identifying features, through which one can come to recognize its value, that is, its *truth* value. The face then reflects truth. This truth is actually the Godliness found in each facet of Creation, and just as God can be only One, likewise the truth can be only one (*Likutey Halakhot, Giluach* 4:1).

The face, the most outstanding and expressive aspect of anyone's appearance, represents truth. The ARI teaches that truth is the "light of the countenance," and that there are 370 radiant lights to this countenance (*Etz Chaim* 13:14). One who desires and speaks only the truth can attain these lights, and with them a shining countenance (*Likutey Moharan* I, 21:17).

But truth is not the only aspect of the face. Rebbe Nachman teaches that there is a "face of purity," which corresponds to light, life, joy, truth and faith; and there is a "face of impurity," which corresponds to darkness, death, sadness, falsehood and idolatry (*Likutey Moharan* I, 23:1).

Rebbe Nachman explains that one's worries over livelihood give one a "face" of darkness and sadness, a "face of impurity." This "face" reflects all the melancholy and worries associated with earning a livelihood; it is characterized by days filled with gloomy predictions about one's future financial well-being. Constant worries, centering around the weightiness of one's responsibilities, lead one to the belief that only through (Deuteronomy 8:17) "my power and the might of my hands have I achieved this wealth." This attitude is absolutely false. One should rather place one's faith exclusively in God as the only Provider. Then, regardless of his occupation, his efforts will lead to spirituality, as long as his work is performed with honesty.

One who believes that all his livelihood comes directly from God can attain the "face of purity," as opposed to those who believe that their livelihoods have nothing to do with Divine Providence, thus acquiring the "face of impurity." Only one who has true faith can enjoy life. He can feel secure in the knowledge that God will provide him with his needs. Faith, then, and by extension the controlling of one's avarice, can create a shining countenance. As King Solomon teaches (Proverbs 15:13), "A joyous heart illuminates the face."

Thus a shining countenance reflects the truth and faith hidden within a person. Since these truths represent satisfaction with one's lot, free of extraneous cravings, they can rectify the lusts for food and immorality (see *Likutey Moharan* I, 47:1 and 67:2; *ibid.* 23:2). This is because one who lives a life of truth needn't rely on additional experiences or possessions to make him feel fulfilled.

The Talmud also tells us that we can observe the reflection of truth in the face. "When a person is dependent upon others, his face turns all colors [in embarrassment]" (see *Berakhot* 6b). Rebbe Nachman teaches that this applies not only to those who are financially dependent upon others, but to those who crave honor,

respect or attention from others, and so create a dependency
within themselves.

Rebbe Nachman had a follower whose ambition was to
become a *rebbe* [spiritual leader]. Rebbe Nachman told him, "But
you won't even be able to recite the Grace after Meals with
proper intent!" (*Rabbi Nachman's Wisdom* #47).

The person who craves respect from others is by definition
distant from truth. He performs his devotions and expends energy
in an attempt to procure the recognition of others. His prayers can
never be truthful, for he will always feel the need to be recognized
as one who prays conscientiously. He might eventually convince
himself of the truth of his devotions; he might pray with great
fervor, thinking he is steeped in his service of God, but in reality
he craves honor and attention. This person's face also "turns all
colors," for his face reflects inner emotions that are not genuine (see
Likutey Moharan I, 66:3).

Other people often become embarrassed because of their
haughtiness. They do not feel that people of *their* stature should
have to approach others for assistance. On the other end of the
scale, there are those who become joyous when receiving help,
which also changes one's face (*Likutey Moharan* I, 251:4). In the latter case,
this "change of face" is a good sign, because joy is a positive
attribute. Nevertheless, such joy is usually short-lived, because the
individual remains needy and will soon be in want of assistance
again. As such, his level of joy is limited and therefore necessarily
incomplete. Genuine, lasting joy comes not from *receiving*
anything, but only from the inner fulfillment which rises
spontaneously from the attainment of truth. One must therefore
strive always for truth, which will cause one's countenance to truly
shine.

Rebbe Nachman thus taught:

A person should purify his countenance so that his face
shines like a mirror. With such a shining face, others will be able
literally to "see" themselves in his countenance. They will then

come to realize how their own countenance is immersed in darkness, and in this way be brought to repentance (*Likutey Moharan* I, 19:2).

*

The Forehead

A famous passage in the Zohar delves into the mysteries of the forehead, discussing every wrinkle and line, and explaining how one can "read" another person's face through the forehead (see *Zohar* II, 71b). Located between the brain and that part of the face where the senses are based, the forehead acts as an interface. Because of its prominent position on the face, it can reveal one's thoughts, simply by its movements. The forehead is associated with the *Sefirah* of Keter, alluding to the hidden powers of the mind, yet because it can be "revealing," it is also associated with Daat, for as we have seen, Daat is the external manifestation of Keter (Chapter 14).

> The gold plate [of the high priest] shall be on Aaron's forehead... *l'ratzon*, [for acceptance], before God.
>
> Exodus 28:36-38

This is the source of our understanding of the effectiveness of the forehead: the phrase "for acceptance before God" indicates acceptance of repentance and forgiveness of sin. It is "before God" because upon the *tzitz* (the gold plate) was engraved God's Holy Name, the Tetragrammaton. Now, the word *tzitz* also translates as "to gaze" (see above, Chapter 32), indicating that for the *tzitz* to effect forgiveness, one must *look* for Godliness. When can a person be successful in seeking God? When he places the *tzitz* upon his forehead — i.e., only when he connects his mind and thoughts to his search for spirituality.

The ARI writes that when a person performs a mitzvah, the letters associated with that mitzvah become inscribed upon his forehead and illuminate his face on that day. Conversely, when he commits a transgression, the letters associated with that transgression likewise appear on his forehead. Each day's mitzvot and transgressions are inscribed upon one's forehead on any given day and wiped clean for the next day's good or evil deeds. The exception to this rule is the mitzvah of charity, which remains etched on the person's forehead, as it is written, "Charity remains forever" (Psalms 111:3; *Pri Etz Chaim, Shaar Shabbat* 4, p.388). The forehead can thus convey the most awesome light of a person's good deeds, illuminating his countenance with the light of his mitzvot.

The forehead can also reveal a person's feelings. Two contrasting characteristics that are clearly "displayed" on the forehead are humility and brazenness. A modest person has a shining countenance, which reflects humility. Shamelessness and brazenness also display themselves prominently, as the verse indicates (Jeremiah 3:3), "And you had a harlot's forehead; you refused to be ashamed." Rebbe Nachman explains this verse thus:

Before committing a transgression, a person has an awareness of God and feels some measure of embarrassment before Him. If he sins, God forbid, it is because a spirit of folly has overwhelmed him. When he repents, this spirit turns into a spirit of wisdom. He then feels ashamed before God on account of his previous sins — far more ashamed than he had felt before he sinned. The sin was itself an embarrassment, but now it is his repentance which causes his embarrassment to be reflected in his face. In this sense, he now attains a higher level of awareness of God, and it is this new humility which shines upon his forehead, as opposed to "a harlot's forehead," which reflects no shame. With humility, one can attain a very high level of understanding of the fear of God (*Likutey Moharan* I, 38:5).

*

Divine Favor

The Hebrew word for forehead is *metzach*. Rebbe Nachman teaches that there is a power of impurity which is known as the *Metzach HaNachash*, the "Serpent's Forehead," which connotes the destructive forces of atheism. This *Metzach HaNachash* draws its strength from people who live long lives but do not fill their days with holiness. Atheism festers and grows stronger as life continues.

The antithesis of the *Metzach HaNachash* is the *Metzach HaRatzon*, the "Forehead of Divine Favor," which corresponds to Keter. As we have seen (above, Chapter 3), Keter corresponds to the *Partzuf* of *Arikh Anpin*, which translates as "Extended Countenance." Countering the *long* life of the *Metzach HaNachash* is the *Metzach HaRatzon*, Keter, the *Extended* Countenance, which indicates "long life" — that of the forces of holiness. Since the power of the *Metzach HaRatzon* is drawn from the "long life" which is filled with Divine favor, it can overpower the *Metzach HaNachash*, the forces of atheism.

Rebbe Nachman taught that the way to arouse the power of the *Metzach HaRatzon* and overcome the *Metzach HaNachash* is to give charity. This is because charity connotes long life, as expressed in (Ecclesiastes 11:1), "Cast your bread upon the waters, for you shall find it in *many days*." Thus, giving charity invokes "many days," meaning *Arikh Anpin*, the Extended Countenance. The *Metzach HaRatzon* then gains the power to protect a person from the challenges of atheism (Likutey Moharan II, 4:7). This corresponds with the ARI's teaching that the mitzvah of giving charity remains inscribed upon the forehead, making charity the key to the power of the *Metzach HaRatzon*.

*

Exodus and the Seder

When the moment of the Exodus from Egypt arrived, the Jews did not have time to bake *chametz*, leavened bread. Reb Noson writes that the Hebrew word *ChaMeTz* (חמץ) has the same letters as the word *MeTzaCh* (מצח), and that there is a direct connection between them.

To commemorate the Exodus, Jews celebrate the Pesach festival by eating *matzah* instead of *chametz* for the duration of the holiday. They sit down to the *Seder* on the first night and perform several mitzvot which are set out in a specific order, beginning with *Kadesh* (recitation of the *Kiddush*) and culminating with *Nirtzah* (acceptance). If the order of the *Seder* has been followed meticulously, then all one's devotions that evening are favorable and accepted before God.

Just as the story of Pesach repeats itself every year in every generation, Reb Noson applies the concept of Pesach to each individual at all times. In any journey towards spirituality, prior to one's personal exodus, one has gone through a form of slavery, a bondage that ties an individual to a material lifestyle. One must hasten to remove oneself from this bondage. In these circumstances, one hasn't time to prepare *chametz* — fully baked bread and delicacies. Due to one's hurry to flee materialism, one must make do with *matzah*.

As with everything in this world, *chametz* has its negative and positive aspects, which stem from the Tree of Knowledge of Good and Evil. For the most part, *chametz*, which ferments, is associated with evil characteristics, such as arrogance (e.g., bread "rises"), or anger and atheism, as in (Psalms 73:21), "For my heart *yitchametz* [ferments]" (i.e., is angered over the success of the wicked). On the positive side, *chametz* has the same letters as *metzach* (forehead), and its root is in the exalted level of *ratzon* (will). In this sense, *chametz* actually reflects great spiritual wisdom. In order to attain this great wisdom, one must prepare oneself with great effort and intense devotions. Since the person who seeks spirituality must first exit the slavery of materialism, he cannot presuppose that he is worthy of attaining a lofty level of spiritual wisdom immediately. Raising oneself to a high spiritual level can take a long time, and in the meantime one is not yet ready to partake of "*chametz*." It is for this reason that we are forbidden to eat *chametz* on Pesach — out of concern that we have not yet attained the necessary level of *ratzon*.

We therefore conduct a *Seder*, which means "order," through which we organize our priorities. We begin with *Kadesh*, which translates as "preparing" (Genesis 38:21, see *Rashi*), as if to say, "We are not yet ready to achieve great wisdom, but we are willing to make every effort to attain it. We must conduct ourselves properly and go from mitzvah to mitzvah, from devotion to devotion, placing our efforts in spirituality, step by step. We hope to conclude our '*seder*' with *Nirtzah*, indicating will, when all our devotions will have been accepted."

The eating of *chametz* is forbidden until the end of Pesach. This is because one must wait for the "Splitting of the Sea" (which took place on the last day of Pesach). We have seen (Chapter 19) that the Splitting of the Sea corresponds to the opening of the Gates of Wisdom (true Daat). Thus, after one has merited to enter the sea of wisdom and to pass through it safely, without having succumbed to atheistic or other harmful philosophies along the way, one can partake of *chametz*. After successfully completing all the stages of Pesach, rather than aiming one's intellectual energies towards materialism, one can be assured that one's intellectual pursuits will be directed towards faith and true spiritual desire (see *Likutey Halakhot, Birchot HaShachar* 5:16). Then one's *chametz* becomes *metzach* — the *Metzach HaRatzon* — Divine favor.

* * *

35

Hair: The Gates of Wisdom

The hair is part of the integumentary system of the human body. Integument means "outer covering," and the integumentary system generally refers to the skin and glands, hair and nails, the parts of the body that cover and protect the internal organs and limbs. We discuss the hair together with the peripheral nervous system for, like the forehead, the hair represents very lofty spiritual levels. In addition, hair responds as an organ of the senses, as for instance when it "stands on end" when it "feels" static or cold and so on.

Hair, cylindrical in form, serves as a protective covering for the body. It can grow to many lengths and comes in various thicknesses and colors. Depending upon its location on the body, the hair might be either smooth or rough. When comparing the hair of the head (for the purpose of our study, we refer to the hair which covers the scalp as "the hair of the head") with the facial hair, for example, and the hair on the head will generally be considerably smoother.

The hairs found on the head and face represent some of the highest levels of holiness. The Zohar describes many varying types of hair: long and short, curly and straight, rough and smooth, thick and thin, white, red, blond and black. The wide range of differences between one type of hair and another allude to various human characteristics. In brief, the Zohar describes the hairs as channels which allow God's light to filter from its most exalted heights down to far lower levels (see *Zohar I, 70bff; ibid. III, 129bff; Tikkuney Zohar #70, p.122aff*).

*

Hair: A Kabbalistic Introduction

The ARI explained that all hair represents judgment, and therefore constriction of light (*Shaar HaKavanot, Birkhot HaShachar,* p.3), since judgment represents restraint. This being so, would it not be beneficial to do away with hair altogether? The answer is clear: The ARI writes that judgment is an integral part of this world (see above, Chapters 18–19). Still, it must be tempered. Therefore, he writes, hair must be cut short, to minimize our exposure to judgment, but some hair must be left.

This is understood from the Torah's prohibition to shear off the *peyot,* the hair of the "corners" of the head. The singular form of the word *peyot, PeAH* (פאה), numerically corresponds to the Holy Name of God, *ELoHIM* (אלהים = 86), which alludes to Holy Judgments. Since the facial hair begins where the *peyot* terminate, this prohibition to cut the hair applies also to the beard. But, although on certain levels these hairs do represent judgment, at their source they correspond to lofty attributes of mercy, as will be explained below (see *Pri Etz Chaim, Shaar HaSelichot,* 7, p.282).

*

Gates of Wisdom

Rebbe Nachman teaches that the mind possesses great wisdom, but it is necessary to open up certain "gates" in order for this wisdom to be revealed. The hair of the head corresponds to these "gates," for they are outside the head, as if protecting all that is inside, as a gate protects a building from outsiders. This is why the Hebrew word for hair, *Sei'AR* (שער) is like the word for gate, *ShaAR* (שער), alluding to the "gates of wisdom." What exactly do these gates represent?

Rebbe Nachman teaches that the mitzvot of the Torah are gates through which one must pass in order to attain a "Perception of Godliness" — a greater intellect and a higher understanding of God. Only by observing the mitzvot of the Torah can one pass through the gates and attain true spiritual wisdom. This is because the intellect is hidden within the mind, and one can "enter" it only through its "gates" — through doing mitzvot, one can uncover the hidden intellect. Thus, a "Perception of Godliness" is that great intellect, and the mitzvot that God gave us are the gates through which we can enter in order to attain that perception. These gates are alluded to in the *SAaR*, similar to the word *ShaAR*, referring to the gates of the mitzvot (Likutey Moharan I, 30:3).

In that same lesson, Rebbe Nachman teaches that black hair corresponds to Malkhut (similar to the black pupil of the eye; see above, Chapter 32). This indicates that to attain the "Perception of Godliness," one must accept God's Malkhut, the yoke of Heaven, and perform His commandments, the mitzvot. The more complete one's mitzvah observance, the greater one's ability to attain higher "Perceptions of Godliness."

("Black hair," when mentioned in the holy writings, generally refers to an immature or early stage of intellectual development, as opposed to "white hair," which refers to a more mature stage of intellectual development [see below]. Malkhut, the lowest of the *Sefirot*, represents the beginning, or *gateway*, to greater perceptions of Godliness. Therefore, in our discussion of Malkhut as "black hair," we are referring to one's embarking on the path of spirituality.)

Rebbe Nachman points out that the Hebrew letter *shin*, with a dot on the upper right side, is pronounced with a "sh" sound; when the dot is on the left side, it becomes the letter *sin*, with an "s" sound. Thus, the pronunciation of the *shin* depends upon one's "point of view." One can either focus on the hair as a "*shaar*," and seek the wisdom it "protects," or one can focus on its external aspects, seeing it as nothing but "*sei'ar*," hair.

Everyone has some "extraneous matter" within him, the fool and the wise person alike. This extraneous matter is manifest in the hairs, which grow on the head but outside the body. The wise man "points" his extraneous matter towards spirituality — so that his *Se'ARot* (hairs) become *She'ARim* (gates), through which he increases both his wisdom and his attainment of Godliness. Thus, Elijah the Prophet is described as (2 Kings, 1:8) "a hairy man." However, the sei'arot of the fool give rise only to more extraneous matter, meaning enemies. As King David said (Psalms 69:5): "My enemies are more numerous than the hairs on my head." This is because the fool, instead of seeking the shaar of wisdom, is content to give sei'ar an important place in his life, focusing excess time and effort on insignificant outward features, such as his hair, which only leads him to more excesses. These excesses will only lead him to gain enemies. This concept is implied in the verse (Ecclesiastes 10:2), "The heart of the wise leans towards the right [Shin/SHAaR], while the fool leans towards the left [Sin/Sei'AR]" (Likutey Moharan I, 69:10).

In a similar vein, Rebbe Nachman taught that love is nurtured through a settled and clear mind (cleared of extraneous matter), while hatred develops because of a troubled mind. The more tainted a person allows his mind to become, especially through avarice, the greater will be the level of hatred that he experiences — both hatred he harbors within himself for others, and hatred others have towards him. Understandably, the longer one's mind remains in a troubled state, the longer one's enemies will have reason to maintain their hatred. This also leads to "enemies for naught" — those who never had reason to hate a person, but who hate him nonetheless. These enemies correspond to the hair. Just as hair is outside the body and draws nourishment from the "excesses of the mind," so too these "extraneous" enemies are created with excess matter of the mind. One must clear one's mind of excesses in order to attain love (see Likutey Moharan I, 69:10).

Similarly, the Talmud uses the word kluah (braided or curled hair) to describe Eve. Eve represents Binah (understanding). Thus, curled hair corresponds to understanding, which can refer either to a deeper level of understanding or to an "extraneous" one (Likutey Moharan I, 67:6). That is, one can use one's intellect either to grow spiritually or to "twist" the truth.

*

Baldness

An interesting fact about the hair is that, although it is constantly growing, the shaft of the hair that we see is composed of dead cells (which is why we feel no pain when we cut our hair). In keeping with the pattern followed by most cells in the body, hair grows quickly in one's youth but slows down, and sometimes even stops growing altogether, when one ages. The hair roots can even die, leading to baldness.

> The greater the intellect one reveals, the stronger is the opposition aroused towards that intellect (for people tend naturally to oppose any new idea). However, opposition is experienced only in the beginning, when this greater intellect is first revealed (and it is beyond the ability of most people to grasp its importance). Afterwards, when the intellect becomes fully revealed in all its profundity, then the extraneous matter, which was the cause of the strife and opposition, diminishes and disappears (*Likutey Moharan* I, 67:6).

Rebbe Nachman explains that this progression, which is associated with the revelation of intellect is reflected in the hair. When a person is young, he has a full head of hair, representing the extraneous matter that causes him to oppose new ideas. (He is also hot-blooded and ready to challenge an intellect greater than his own.) As he ages, his hair often falls out, and he may begin balding. By then, his mind is developed and recognizable as a greater intellect. This is as the Zohar teaches (III, 128b), "In elders, the mind is settled and relaxed."

*

The Beard

The number thirteen is associated with many interrelated concepts in Judaism. Thirteen is the age at which a young man becomes a *bar mitzvah* (literally, "son of the commandment"), entering the community of Israel as a peer to those much older than he, being fully accepted as one of them. The Talmud teaches that there are Thirteen Exegetical Principles of the Torah (*Safra d'Bei Rav,* Introduction) and also speaks of thirteen levels of holiness a person can attain through Torah study (*Avodah Zarah* 20b). Thirteen items were required for the building of the Sanctuary (Exodus 25). There are thirteen rivers of spices that will flow through the Garden of Eden as part of the reward of the righteous (cf. *Zohar* II, 127b). The Kabbalah speaks of the Thirteen Rectifications of the Beard (thirteen "points" or "facial features") of the *Partzuf* (Divine Persona) of *Arikh Anpin.* But perhaps the most important concept associated with the number thirteen is that of the Thirteen Attributes of God's Mercy, through which even the worst sinner, no matter how far he has strayed or how serious his transgressions, can gain God's forgiveness (see Exodus 34:6–7).

The ARI writes that these Thirteen Attributes of Mercy are rooted in the Keter and are manifest in the thirteen points of the "Beard of *Arikh Anpin,*" known as the Thirteen Rectifications of the Beard. The ARI expounds upon this subject at length, explaining many mysteries of the Kabbalah through these points of the Beard (see *Etz Chaim, Shaar Arikh Anpin* 8–11). The "Beard of *Arikh Anpin,*" as described by the ARI, parallels the human beard; thus, each person's beard corresponds to the loftiest of spiritual levels. Let us now glimpse the parallel between the Thirteen Attributes of Mercy and the Supernal Beard of *Arikh Anpin.*

> **God, merciful and gracious, slow to anger and abundant in love and truth. Keeping mercy to the thousandth generation, forgiving sin, rebellion and error, and cleansing.**
>
> Exodus 34:6–7

After the sin of the golden calf, God proclaimed the Thirteen Attributes of His Mercy to Moses. They are: (1) God, (2) merciful, (3) and gracious, (4) slow (5) to anger, (6) and abundant in love (7) and truth. (8) Keeping mercy, (9) to the thousandth generation, (10) forgiving sin, (11) rebellion (12) and error, (13) and cleansing. (This order of the Thirteen Attributes is from the ARI, as found in the *Etz Chaim, Shaar Arikh Anpin* 9. There are several other opinions; see *Rosh HaShanah* 17b, *Tosafot, s.v. Shelosh Esrei Midot.*)

The Zohar and the ARI detail each individual Attribute as it relates to a position on the face. An example is the Attribute of Truth, which corresponds to the cheeks. We saw earlier (Chapter 34) that the "countenance of the face" is truth. This is manifest in the cheeks, where one's countenance is most clearly visible. Other points of "the Beard" are the length of the mustache, the hairs below the mouth, near the ears, on the neck and so on. Thus, in total, there are thirteen points from which the beard can be discerned. Several of these points are the hairs themselves, while others are the flesh that is visible on the face, such as the lips and cheeks (for details, see *Etz Chaim, Shaar Arikh Anpin* 9).

Arikh Anpin is the level of Keter (Will or Divine favor). The term *Arikh Anpin* translates as "Long, or Extended, Face," implying ancientness. The "hair" of *Arikh Anpin* is thus depicted as the white hair of a grandfather. As we have cited above (Zohar II, 128b), "In elders, the mind is settled and relaxed." This indicates that when the concept of *Arikh Anpin* is aroused, great mercy is similarly aroused. The reason for this is that, at the level of Keter, God's mercy is unmitigated and pure. Like a grandfather, His desire is to bestow the greatest good, irrespective of how much His "grandchildren" deserve (see *Innerspace*, p.103).

Thus, although the hair, especially the facial hair, represents judgment, the hairs of the beard are still pliable — that is, though we are surrounded by judgment, it can always be softened and mitigated, resulting in a compassionate decree. This is the mystery of the Thirteen Attributes of Mercy. Even if a person has sinned and caused judgment to prevail, he can arouse God's kindness to the point that even a harsh decree can be nullified and transformed into mercy and forgiveness. Hence the human beard, paralleling as it does the awesome power of the Supernal Beard, symbolizes incredible spiritual power.

*

Beauty of the Countenance

The beard embodies the honor and beauty of one's countenance. The verse states (Leviticus 19:32), "Show honor to the countenance of the *zaken* [elder]." In its spelling, the Hebrew word *ZaKeN* is identical to the word *ZaKaN*, meaning beard. Thus, the honor of a man's countenance is manifest through his beard. The reason for this is that the Thirteen Rectifications of the Beard (Zohar III, 131a; *ibid.* 228a) correspond to the Thirteen Exegetical Principles of the Torah: the greater one's attainment of Torah knowledge, the greater one's perception of what constitutes a Godly Countenance (*Likutey Moharan* I, 20:4).

In *Likutey Moharan* (I, 27), Rebbe Nachman taught:

> Peace can be attained only through the illumination of the face, through the majestic honor of the countenance, the beard... and a majestic countenance corresponds to Torah expositions; for the Torah is expounded by means of the Thirteen Exegetical Principles that flow from the Thirteen Rectifications of the *ZaKaN* [Beard of *Arikh Anpin*], the level of the majestic countenance. It is thus written, "Show honor to the countenance of the *ZaKeN* [elder]."

> It is impossible to attain such a majestic countenance other than by rectifying one's *brit* [i.e., sexual purity]...

Rebbe Nachman here draws a connection between the beard and the sexual organs. This connection is alluded to in a number of places. The *Sefer Yetzirah* (1:3) speaks of both the *milat halashon* (circumcision of the tongue) and the *milat hamaor* (circumcision of the membrum). The Talmud (*Sanhedrin* 68b) refers to the pubic hair as "the lower beard." Similarly, the Talmud tells us that the "upper sign" of adolescence (facial hair) does not usually appear until the "lower sign" (pubic hair) has begun to grow (*Niddah* 48a). In the above lesson, Rebbe Nachman expands this connection: Just as the growth of the pubic hair must precede the growth of the beard, so too, controlling one's sexual desires must precede a revelation of the Thirteen Exegetical Principles, which flow from the Thirteen

Rectifications of the Beard. (This does not mean that until one attains sexual purity one cannot attain *any* Torah knowledge; it does, however, mean that the revelation of the Godliness that is found in the Torah will be on par with one's level of purity.) Rebbe Nachman continues:

> Commensurate to [the degree of one's sexual purity and] the refining of one's wisdom through the Thirteen Exegetical Principles is the refinement of the voice of one's song. This concept is reflected in: *"ZaKeN — Zeh KaNah Chokhmah."* ["An elder is one about whom we say, 'This one has acquired wisdom'"] (*Kiddushin* 32b). It is the *KaNeH* [trachea; windpipe] that facilitates the voice's expression...and with a pure, clear voice, one can fulfill the verse (Zephaniah 3:9), "Then I will convert all the nations to a clear tongue, that they may all call out to God to serve Him of one accord" (*Likutey Moharan* I, 27:2–6).

To summarize these ideas: controlling one's sexual desire leads to revelations of Torah teachings, which manifest in a majestic countenance. This person merits the title *"zaken,"* which implies a *kaneh*, a clear, pure voice. This voice leads to peace, for with a clear, pure voice, all will call out to God and serve Him in unity.

*

The Nine Attributes of Mercy

Arikh Anpin means literally "Long Face" or "Extended Face" and is the *Partzuf* corresponding to Keter. *Zer Anpin* means "Small Face," and is a *Partzuf* of a lower stature (see Appendix D). *Arikh Anpin*, as the greater persona, has Thirteen Rectifications of the Beard. *Zer Anpin* has Nine Rectifications (see *Zohar* II, 177b; *Etz Chaim* 13:9). These Nine Rectifications correspond to the Nine Attributes of Mercy which Moses invoked when the spies slandered the Holy Land and God wanted to punish the Jewish People (Numbers 14:18): "(1) Slow (2) to anger, (3) abundant (4) in love, (5) forgiving sin (6) and rebellion, (7) cleansing those who repent (8) and not cleansing those who do not repent, (9) but bearing in mind the sins of the fathers for their children, their grandchildren and great-grandchildren."

These nine attributes correspond to the nine points of the Beard of *Zer Anpin*. The hair of *Zer Anpin* is depicted as the black hair of a young man. Similar to the discussion regarding *Arikh Anpin*, the "color" and "size" of the hairs of the Beard of *Zer Anpin* are indicative of the nature of the mercy that can be invoked and attained at that level. *Zer Anpin* can be seen as a "parent" whose giving is dependent upon his children's merit. So too, on the level of *Zer Anpin*, the mercy is constricted; thus there are only Nine Attributes instead of Thirteen (see *Innerspace* p.103).

In one of his longest teachings about the power of a tzaddik's Torah discourse, Rebbe Nachman outlines the practical application of these Nine Rectifications. They are explained according to the Zohar's presentation (found in *Zohar* II, 177b; see *Likutey Moharan* I, 20).

- **The first rectification: Hairs upon hairs from in front of the ears to the top of the mouth** — This is the concept of *Se'ARot* [hairs], as in (Psalms 87:2), "*Sha'ARey* [the gates of] Zion," which corresponds to [the power of the tzaddik's teachings to subdue the evil inclination in the hearts of those who assemble to hear him; the idea of *shaar* and *sei'ar* (gate and hair) being interchangeable has been explained earlier in this Chapter]. "From in front of the ears to the top of the mouth," that is, prior to *hearing* [understanding] what would be expected of them if they accepted the Torah, they opened their mouths and said (Exodus 24:7), "We will *do*." This is the meaning of (Ketubot 112a) "Your mouths preceded your ears."

- **The second rectification: [The mustache above the lip] from one side to the other** — After subduing their evil, as explained above, the tzaddik takes them out from under the authority of the Other Side and brings them into the domain of Holiness. This is the meaning of "from one *side* to the other."

- **The third rectification: Below the two nostrils is a path that is full but not visible** — "Below the two nostrils is a path" refers to the nose [i.e., breath and prayer]... "A path that is full," because (Psalms

34:10) "Those who fear Him lack nothing..." "But not visible," for a person must humble himself [become invisible] and not rely on his own merits...

- **The fourth rectification: The sides [of the face] are covered [with hairs] on each side** — This is the binding of their souls [to the soul of the tzaddik]. They [who follow the tzaddik] are then said to "cover [surround] him on all sides."

- **The fifth rectification: Two *TaPuCHiN* [cheeks] are visible, red like a rose** — [When the tzaddik speaks warm words of arousal], the valves of the heart are *niPhTaCHiN* [opened]. The mercies of the Supernal Heart are then stirred, and impassioned words pour forth, like rose-red coals.

- **The sixth rectification: In one *chut* [strand] tough black hairs *TaLYan* [cascading] down to the chest** — This is the concept of drawing oneself to the Torah...for its lessons are (*Eruvin* 21b) "*TiLey TiLim shel halakhot* [heaps and heaps of laws]"... "In one *chut* [strand]" corresponds to (*Yevamot* 121b), "God is strict with the tzaddikim to a *chut hasa'arah* [hairsbreadth]."

- **The seventh rectification: Lips, red like a rose and clear of all hair** — This alludes to the creation of the angels [through words of Torah spoken in holiness], as in (Psalms 33:6), "With God's word the heavens were made, and by the breath of His mouth all their angelic hosts." "Red like a rose," as in (Psalms 104:4), "He makes winds His messengers; flaming red fire His servants."

- **The eighth rectification: Small hairs descending onto the throat and covering the back of the neck** — "Small" here is synonymous with Edom/Esau, as in (Ovadiah 1:2), "*Small* have I made you among the nations." "Descending onto the throat" is synonymous with the sword [that must be taken from Esau to punish the wicked]. It corresponds to (Psalms 149:6) "Lofty praises of God in their *throats* and a double-edged sword in their hands." "Back of the neck" refers to subduing the power of the Other Side, namely Esau, who turns his back [and refuses to accept Godly teachings].

- **The ninth rectification: Long and short hairs which end together** — This corresponds to the Land of Israel, which is divided among the tribes of Israel. Because each of the twelve tribes was likened to and given the characteristic powers of a different animal ["Judah is a lion... Naftali, a deer... Benjamin, a wolf... Dan, a snake" (*Rashi, Exodus 1:19*)], and some tribes were larger and some smaller, they are likened to (*Psalms 104:25*) "small and large animals" (*Likutey Moharan I, 20:10*).

Thus, when a person hears the Torah discourses of the tzaddikim and begins observing the mitzvot, he not only subdues his evil inclination and enters the gates of holiness himself (1), but opens the way for the tzaddik to assist others to transfer "from one side (that of evil) to the other side (that of good)" as well (2). This is accomplished through the heart-rending prayer of the tzaddik (3), which unites the congregation (4). This prayer, when said from one's heart, opens up the Supernal Heart, revealing mercy (5) and allows for the revelation of new Torah teachings of which all can partake (6). These Torah teachings create angels (7), which in turn battle the forces of the Other Side and subdue them (8). By subduing the Other Side, holiness is revealed in the world, especially the sanctity of the Holy Land (9).

Rebbe Nachman goes on to explain that this revelation of holiness is the secret of the ultimate battle against evil. Whoever strives to reveal holiness (for example, through mitzvot and prayers) creates angels and can therefore conquer any opposition to spirituality. This person is called a mighty warrior, who is able to wage a war to free the "Holy Land" from its oppressors. This mighty warrior gains the power to reveal the sanctity of the Holy Land, that is, to reveal Godliness, and so to ascend the spiritual ladder continually!

*

The *Peyot*

The locks of the hair known as *peyot* (singular, *pe'ah*) extend from the temples immediately above the sideburns to the ears. As explained earlier, the *peyot* must be neither shaved nor cut too short, even though they represent judgment, for we have seen that judgment is crucial for the existence of the world. The *peyot* are important channels through which Godly wisdom can be received. *Peah* means "corner" or "end," and the *peyot* represent the minimal revelation of the awesome sublime intellect.

We saw above (Chapter 31) that the seven orifices of the face correspond to the seven branches of the Menorah. The Menorah itself parallels the head, while the oil contained therein parallels the mind. Thus the brain corresponds to the light, and the hairs serve as channels to diffuse that light and manifest its awesome power.

There are various types of sources of man-made light. The light of a lightbulb, for instance, spreads out in a broad, general fashion, while the light of a laser beam is far more concentrated and can be directed to a specific point, either near or far away from its source, much more effectively. The light of the hair of the head can be compared to a lightbulb; that of the *peyot* would parallel the laser beam. Thus the *peyot*, though small in size, can have a great impact. Rebbe Nachman once said (*Likutey Moharan* I, 17:1), "Even the slightest of movements of one's *peyot* causes great joy Above," for the *peyot* are a visible demonstration of one's dedication to God.

Reb Noson writes that the Torah has been adhered to throughout the ages because of the beard and *peyot*. Whenever a Jew wanted to assimilate among the nations, the first thing he did was to shave off his beard and *peyot* in order to shed the signs of his Jewishness and to assume the identity of his surrounding culture. The beard and *peyot* bear such significance because they correspond to the Divine Beard and *Peyot* that channel the forces of spirituality down to man in "manageable" portions.

Thus, the beard and *peyot* are not merely "facial hair." They serve as actual barriers against the invasion of the atheistic philosophies and immoral characteristics which surround us. In this way, the beard and *peyot* serve not only as strong affirmations of our faith, but also as protectors of that faith (*Likutey Halakhot, Giluach* 3:2; *ibid.* 4:5).

*

Reb Noson offers several insights on the importance of growing a beard and *peyot*.

The Torah prohibits shaving the beard and *peyot* with a razor or other similar type of blade. Though this law is a *chok* — one for which no reason is given by the Torah — Reb Noson suggests the following thought: The beard (*ZaKaN*) alludes to *ZaKeN*, an elder, or long life. A blade is an implement which is capable of cutting life short. Concerning the prohibition of cutting the stones of the altar with metal instruments, our Sages comment (Mekhilta, Yitro), "It is unreasonable to place something that can cut life short upon something that brings long life." This idea can be similarly applied to the shaving of the beard with a blade (Likutey Halakhot, Giluach 1:1).

Reb Noson explains further that the three Festivals correspond to the "Countenance of the Face," as the joy a person feels in his heart is revealed during the Festivals. (Through one's observance of the Festivals, one elevates one's material surroundings to the service of God, which brings a revelation of joy, in the same way that joy can be observed on the countenance.) The Festivals also correspond to the intellect, which is comprised of the three columns of right, left and center (Chokhmah, Binah and Daat), upon which one can build a Sanctuary (see above, Chapter 19, and below, Part 8). In considering the significance of the number "three" in many Torah concepts, it is important to note that the two *peyot* and the beard also add up to three. The two *peyot* correspond to the right and left columns, while the beard corresponds to the center. Thus, the beard and *peyot* correspond to the Festivals, to the intellect and to the joy and beauty of the countenance! (Likutey Halakhot, Giluach 1:1).

In another discourse, Reb Noson explains why a very young child can grow *peyot*, but the growth of the beard cannot begin until one reaches puberty. This phenomenon relates to the concept of the transcendental intellect — those levels of spirituality that are currently beyond one's capacity to attain, and for which one must continually strive. The way to attain transcendental intellect is through prayer and crying out to God. Eventually, what had previously been transcendental is internalized and becomes the immanent, opening up new vistas of greater transcendental intellect. The internalization of this new intellect can be accomplished through the sanctification of one's "seven lamps" (the orifices of the head; see above, Chapter 31). As we have explained, the seven lamps reflect the mind's purity, and, by sanctifying these lamps, a person gains the ability to reach up to those levels of intellect that are as yet beyond him (see above, Chapters 15 and 31).

As a child grows, his intellect increases. Yet, no matter how much he learns, he is always limited in his capacity to absorb and internalize his knowledge. We have seen that *peah* means a "corner" or "end," which represents a minimal revelation of Godliness. It implies that the immature intellect of the child cannot absorb high levels of Godliness. Thus the *peyot*, which grow from infancy, are compared to crying out to God, pleading for revelations of wisdom and for the transcendental intellect as yet beyond one's capacity to grasp, begging God that it become internalized.

The beard, on the other hand, corresponds to the Thirteen Exegetical Principles of the Torah. This is why it begins to grow only later in life, when the intellect is more mature and is capable of absorbing great knowledge. The beard thus symbolizes the internalization of the transcendental intellect, for the main channels of the revelation of Godliness are through the beard (*Likutey Halakhot, Giluach* 5:2–3).

* * *

Part Eight

The Skeletal and Muscular System

The Torso, Arms and Legs

36

Introduction

We have seen that 613 mitzvot are divided into 248 positive commandments and 365 prohibitions. These correspond to the 248 limbs and 365 veins and sinews of the human body.

The 248 limbs enumerated in the Mishnah are actually those of a male (*Ohalot* 1:8). The Talmud (*Bekhorot* 45a) adds another four "limbs" that belong exclusively to the female reproductive system; thus a woman has a total of 252 limbs. As the Talmudic definition of a "limb" includes several organs and joints as well as bones (e.g., the four additional "limbs" attributed to the female body), there is a discrepancy between the Talmud and the contemporary scientific approach regarding this number — modern Western medicine counts some 208 limbs of the human body. This issue is dealt with in many works (see *Biblical and Talmudic Medicine* pp.60–67, by Julius Preuss, translated by Fred Rosner).

We have mentioned repeatedly the Torah's statement that man was created in the Godly image, specifically in the image of the Divine Name of *YHVH*. This is reflected in a number of ways and on various different levels. Viewed "from the inside out," the human skeleton corresponds to the *Yod*, the nerves and sinews to the first *Heh*, the flesh to the *Vav*, and the skin to the final *Heh*. Viewed "from top to bottom," the two hemispheres of the brain correspond to the *Yod* and *Heh* of the Name, the torso and arms correspond to the *Vav*, and the lower extremities correspond to the final *Heh*. This teaches us that, any way we approach it, the human body is intended to be a temple for God's Presence in this world.

There is nothing in the human body that doesn't have something to teach us about the service of God.

In this section, we will learn about the spiritual dimensions which are inherent in our bones and skin, as well as in our torso, arms and legs. As always, our study will be guided by one basic principle: that we are essentially spiritual beings inhabiting physical bodies, as opposed to physical beings possessing souls. This important distinction in the way we perceive ourselves makes all the difference in how we live in this world. It is the underlying principle that guides us in understanding "the soul of the anatomy."

Practically speaking, we arouse our souls and heal our bodies through channeling *Daat* (Godly Knowledge) into each of the 248 limbs of our bodies. This is the purpose of the commandments, specifically the 248 positive commandments of the Torah. The Torah is the Godly Light, the Universal Intelligence which is being diffused continually throughout Creation. Our job is to become aware of this light and to internalize it in every cell of our minds, hearts and bodies. In the words of Rebbe Nachman, this is what establishes our connection to Moses, the man who mastered the physical plane more than any other human being who ever lived, and who was therefore worthy of transmitting the Torah to Israel.

This connection is alluded to in Scripture's warning regarding alcoholism (Proverbs 31:5), "Lest he drink and forget that which is *MeCHuKaK* [decreed]." Rebbe Nachman reminds us that Moses is called *MeCHoKeK*, "the lawgiver" (Deuteronomy 33:21; *Bava Batra* 15a), the numerical value of *mechokek* being 248. Moses, as the lawgiver, corresponds to both the structure of the mitzvot (the decrees of the Torah) and the limbs of the body. In this sense, the power of Moses, "clothed" in the 248 limbs of the human body, instructs each and every limb, teaching it to heed the mitzvot applicable to it. Alcohol, on the other hand, addles the brain and blurs one's ability to perceive reality. When we are "drunk," that is, when our minds are blurred by the intoxicating lures of the physical world, we forget Moses, the Daat (Godly Knowledge) which is clothed in the 248 limbs (see *Likutey Moharan* II, 26; *The Aleph-Bet Book*, p. 224).

Reb Noson points out that the *Shema*, the affirmation of faith, has 248 words. These 248 words also correspond to the positive commandments, which, as we have seen, parallel the human skeletal structure. Two hundred forty-eight is also the numerical value of the word *rachem* (רחם, compassion). It must be emphasized that the most compassionate act anyone can do for someone else is to enlighten him to recognize God, thereby perfecting his Godly form (*Likutey Halakhot, Keriat Shema* 3:4).

*

The human skeleton is divided into two categories: the axial skeleton and the appendicular skeleton. The axial skeleton refers to the central column of bones: the skull, spine, ribs and sternum. The appendicular skeleton refers to the symmetrical groups of bones on either side of the central column: the shoulders, arms and legs.

The skeleton provides the framework and support for all the organs of the body. It consists of bones and cartilage, and it interacts with the limbs through tendons and ligaments. Some bones protect the vital internal organs, such as the brain, heart and lungs. Bones are also repositories for minerals, such as calcium. When the brain detects insufficient levels of calcium, it orders the bones to release measured quantities of it for absorption into the bloodstream. In addition, the bone marrow, which fills the cavities of most bones, produces essential blood cells.

The muscles are controlled by nerves, which react to the impulses of the brain. An important part of the skeletal-muscular system are the sinews (tendons and ligaments) which, together with the muscles, are found along most of the skeletal system.

The flesh, as we apply the term in this work, is that soft tissue which covers the bones and includes the muscular system (see Part 3).

The skin is part of the integumentary system (which includes the hair [discussed in Part 7], the nails and some of the glands). This constitutes the outer covering of the body. There are two main layers of skin: the outer layer is called the epidermis, and the inner layer is known as the dermis. The skin serves as a protective coating against bacteria and infection. The sweat glands in the skin rid the body of excess fluids and waste products (see also Part 3).

*

The Body: A Kabbalistic Overview

We have pointed out that the human body, "formed in the Godly image," can be seen as a reflection of the Divine Name *YHVH*. The human form also embodies the Ten *Sefirot*. The cranium corresponds to Keter, the right hemisphere of the brain corresponds to Chokhmah, and the left hemisphere corresponds to Binah. The brain stem and spine correspond to Daat. The right arm and hand corresponds to Chesed; the left arm and hand corresponds to Gevurah; and the torso corresponds to Tiferet. The right leg and kidney corresponds to Netzach; the left leg and kidney corresponds to Hod; and the sign of the holy Covenant, the circumcision, corresponds to Yesod. The space in which a person stands (i.e., one's feet) represents his or her Malkhut (Kingdom).

The seven lower *Sefirot*, therefore, correspond to the body in the following manner (see *Innerspace*, Chapters 4 and 7–9, for a detailed exposition on the *Sefirot*):

Sefirah	Physical Representation	Conceptual Representation
Chesed	Right arm/hand	Giving
Gevurah	Left arm/hand	Restraint
Tiferet	Torso	Harmony, truth
Netzach	Right leg/kidney/testicle	Victory, endurance
Hod	Left leg/kidney/testicle	Submission, majesty
Yesod	Sexual organ	Covenant, channel
Malkhut	Feet, crown of organ, mate, space	Receiving, reciprocity

*

In their ideal, "rectified" state, the Ten *Sefirot* are arrayed in three columns: right, left and center (see Appendix D). The right and left columns represent extremely powerful, ostensibly opposing, spiritual forces. The right column always represents mercy and kindness vis-à-vis the left column, which represents severity, discipline and restraint. The right column is characterized by unconditional love and acceptance, and a willingness to transcend boundaries through a merging of self and other; the left column emphasizes obligations and responsibilities, defined boundaries and self-definition. While each column alone might seem to have nothing whatsoever to do with the other, in truth, they are complementary opposites. This relationship is actualized in the center column. It is the function of the center column to synthesize the seemingly opposing forces of "right" and "left," bringing about harmony, unity and peace. When the center column functions in this manner, the Ten *Sefirot* are said to be in their rectified state.

We saw this in our discussion of Chokhmah and Binah, which define the right (intuitive, artistic) and left (analytic, logical) functions of the mind. Each alone lacks perfection. The human mind requires Daat, the confluence of Chokhmah and Binah, to achieve a perfected state of mental balance. The identical principle applies to all human forces: harmony is achieved when we learn to balance the opposing aspects of our personalities. According to the ancient teachings, this can be accomplished only when the unifying influence of Chokhmah, Binah and Daat (our Higher Godly Consciousness) is allowed to flow down into the separate, opposing "compartments" of our *midot* (personality traits and emotions).

*

The Torso

The torso embodies the concept of Tiferet, the center column of harmony and truth: it represents the ultimate goal of a harmonious life based upon truth. The torso balances the extreme tendencies of the "right" and "left" sides of our personalities.

Whereas Chesed (corresponding to the right hand) symbolizes unconditional giving and acceptance, and Gevurah (the left hand) symbolizes justice meted out on the basis of the recipient's worthiness alone, Tiferet (the torso) harmonizes these two extremes. It is for this reason that Tiferet is sometimes called *Rachamim* (mercy) and sometimes *Mishpat* (fair and proper judgment). Tiferet is thus Merciful Judgment (a judgment tempered with mercy), the ultimate blending of two seeming opposites.

This is why the Hebrew term for a judge is *ShoPheT*. His function is to adjudicate between contending parties and to help them arrive at a peaceful settlement, which is *miShPaT*. Although we as individuals may perceive truth in different ways, a truly wise judge can help us to recognize and accept the vast differences between us, and can even bridge those differences, so that we can live together in harmony. This is the manifestation of Tiferet.

Rebbe Nachman teaches that Tiferet, the central column, corresponds to prayer. Prayer is likened to (Psalms 149:6) "a double-edged sword [which cuts through the barriers between a person and God]." When praying we must be careful to direct our "sword" neither too far to the right, toward Chesed, nor too far to the left, toward Gevurah. We must keep ourselves centered and focused (*Likutey Moharan* I, 2:3).

Reb Noson explains this teaching of Rebbe Nachman: Abraham, Isaac and Jacob embody the three *Sefirot* of Chesed, Gevurah and Tiferet, respectively. Abraham is the embodiment of Chesed, as can be clearly seen through his well-known traits of kindness and hospitality. Isaac is the paradigm of Gevurah, for he was willing to make the ultimate self-sacrifice for the sake of God. It is Jacob, though, who is known as Tiferet, as he fully integrated the two attributes of his father and grandfather in his own life.

Abraham fathered two children, Ishmael and Isaac. Isaac also had two sons, Esau and Jacob. In each case, the firstborn represented a kind of genetic siphoning operation wherein *sigim* (impurities) were separated in two stages from the pure seed of the Patriarchs so that eventually, through the third generation of Jacob's sons, the holy nation of Israel, was established. Expressed in another way, Abraham and Isaac "worked together," each developing his own attribute to the fullest, until they were able to fuse these attributes together in Jacob. This is how the Jewish nation came to be.

Abraham named his firstborn son Ishmael (in Hebrew, Yishmael, literally, *Yishma El* — "God will hear"). This implies that God listens to our prayers, ostensibly because, as God's angel told Ishmael's mother, Hagar, when he informed her that she would bear a child to Abraham (Genesis 16:11), "You must name him Ishmael, for God has heard your anguish." However, in this sense, Ishmael also alludes to the notion that everything we need comes to us because of God's Chesed (Lovingkindness). Although this is absolutely true, it leaves room for great error. This attitude could lead us to the mistaken conclusion that we need not work hard to achieve anything. "God has *already* heard my prayer. Why bother praying anymore?"

Esau represents exactly the opposite approach. The name ESaU (עשו) means "finished" or "complete," from the Hebrew word ASUy (עשוי, literally, "made") (*Rashi*, Genesis 25:25). "Esau" symbolizes man with his own "self-made image" relating to the world as if he is all-important — and the final goal of life. It was Esau who asked (Genesis 25:32), "Why do I need the birthright?" indicating a denial of Divine Providence, and hence a repudiation of prayer. It is the power of "Esau" inside a person that leaves him asking: "Why pray when my prayers are useless? Since there is no providence, my prayers will not work." He is rejecting God's compassion, saying God does not listen to our prayers, as we will only get what we deserve.

These two perspectives, that of Ishmael and Esau, each of which alone must be rejected, are symbolized in the *brit milah* (circumcision) ceremony. Circumcision involves, first of all, the removal of the foreskin. The foreskin has two layers, an outer layer and an inner layer. There are therefore two stages to the mitzvah of circumcision: *milah* (literally, "cutting"), which removes the outer layer of the foreskin; and *periyah* (literally, "revealing"), which involves a peeling back of the thin inner membrane to "reveal" the corona. The outer layer of the foreskin represents a *kelipah* (husk) of unredeemable physicality. It must be totally rejected and removed. The inner layer has more subtle connotations, but is a *kelipah* nevertheless. Jewish circumcision is not complete without both. Removing the foreskin without peeling back the thin membrane to reveal the corona is tantamount to not having performed the circumcision at all (*Yoreh Deah* 264:4).

Applying this to Easu and Ishmael, the following emerges: Esau represents that part of humanity that doesn't perform circumcision at all. Esau disdains the circumcision and all that it represents, seeing no reason whatsoever to turn to God. Ishmael, on the other hand, performs the circumcision, but only partially. He removes the outer layer of the foreskin, but leaves the inner layer intact. Applying this further to prayer, Esau represents that part of us that does not want to remove the foreskin of the heart, whereas Ishmael represents that part of us that tries, but stops short of completing the process.

Reb Noson explains this concept in terms of the "double-edged sword" of prayer, represented by Tiferet, mentioned above:

> A person worthy of effectively employing the "sword of prayer" must understand how to do battle with it, deflecting it neither to the right nor to the left. For example, when a person considers the seemingly endless progression of the current exile, he must not mistakenly conclude that all the Jewish People's prayers for salvation have been for naught, God forbid. This would be wrongly and tragically inclining to the left, turning God's attribute of compassion into cruelty, as though the Holy One turns a deaf ear to our prayers. Conversely, a person should

not mistakenly conclude that, since without God's kindness it is impossible to accomplish anything through prayer, there is no point in expending effort on prayer. Relying totally on God's kindness is inclining, mistakenly, to the right.

A person must take the balanced center path. He must constantly increase his efforts at prayer, knowing that not one of his entreaties is ever in vain; yet at the same time he must bear in mind that without God's kindness he is incapable of achieving anything, regardless of all his efforts and devotions. When we do our part, constantly praying for salvation, then God surely does His part, and for His Own sake graces us with His kindness and redeems us.

The way to attain this balanced approach is through the giving of charity (the quality of Jacob as in, "Justice and *tzedakah* [charity] in Jacob; Psalms 99:4). This is why we give charity before we pray. In so doing, we distribute bounty through our own acts of charity, and this enables us to raise the quality of our prayers. So too, our prayers coupled with charity give God cause and reason to answer our entreaties and send us the bounty we seek (see *Likutey Halakhot, Nachalot* 4:23).

Jacob, the progenitor of the twelve tribes of Israel and the embodiment of the middle column, represents the middle path of truth that harmonizes the two extremes. We must follow the path of Jacob as we pray, and have faith that God has heard and accepted our prayers. Yet we must continually strengthen ourselves and intensify our prayers, for there is always much more for which we must pray.

* * *

37

Flesh and Bone

Rebbe Nachman once said, "Many people err, thinking that because someone is a tzaddik, he must look and act different from other people; this is not true. The tzaddik appears to be just like everyone else, no different from all other human beings. Yet, he is something totally different" (*Likutey Moharan* II, 116:2).

In what way does the tzaddik differ from the rest of us? Rebbe Nachman compares the soul to the Land of Israel, and the body to the Jordan River, which is the eastern border of the Holy Land. A "border" corresponds to anything that separates a person from holiness. The body can be such a border. If we allow ourselves to be drawn towards unholy things, our bodies take on the characteristics of those "borders" that separate us from the spirituality of the Holy Land. We must shed all "extraneous garments," material pursuits, before we can experience true spirituality (see *Likutey Moharan* I, 14:5).

The tzaddik is one who has "crossed the border" of physicality and entered the realm of spiritual existence. His mind is in a constant state of awareness of God, which is felt — and shared — by his body. This state can be achieved by anyone who works for it.

This, then, is the function of the limbs which make up the human form. Their job is to perform the mitzvot, thereby elevating the individual above the level of his physicality through making holy use of that very physicality.

Rebbe Nachman thus taught:

> One must have great compassion upon one's body. The soul constantly yearns to ascend to higher levels. As it grows and becomes elevated, it should be able to transmit to the body some of the illumination it attains; however, in order for this to happen, the body must first become subordinate to the soul. This is the purpose of the mitzvot: mitzvot predispose the physical body to the spiritual influx of the soul. Through observance of the mitzvot, the body becomes a clean, pure vessel which can become illuminated by the soul. This leads one to increased faith and higher levels of spirituality (*Likutey Moharan* I, 22:5, 8).

It is by no arbitrary whim that Rebbe Nachman teaches the importance of subjugating the body to the soul by means of performing mitzvot. The word *miTZVah* is from the same root as *TZeVet*, which denotes a team or unit that is joined together for a common purpose. The Torah is seen as a single unit containing many separate mitzvot, each of which corresponds to a different limb of the body (see Chapter 1; Appendix B). In the same way, the body is a single unit, albeit with many separate limbs. The body is held together by the tendons and nerves. These tendons and nerves, also represented by the mitzvot, as explained earlier (Chapter 35), are in fact extensions of the soul. Performing the mitzvot effectively binds all one's energies "together" into a single working unit, subduing the opposing forces that exist within one's being.

On the other hand, the Hebrew word for sin or transgression is *AVeiRah*, from the root word *AVaR*, to pass by or through. The term connotes disjointedness and instability (see *Likutey Halakhot, Netilat Yadayim Shacharit* 4:12). Through the observance of mitzvot, however, one is able to "pull oneself together," strengthening one's true self-identity, while transgression causes inner turmoil and a loss of identity. Thus, Rebbe Nachman taught: For a person to feel "peace in his bones" — inner peace — he must possess the awe of Heaven. This leads to perfection of both the body and the soul (*Likutey Moharan* I, 14:8–9).

*

Rebbe Nachman thus taught:

> The word *aveirah* [עבירה; transgression] implies *OVeR* [עובר, crossing over] within his bones, from *AiVeR* to *AiVeR* [עבר, side to side]. The word *mitzvah*, however, connotes joining together. When a person performs bundles of commandments, he binds together the shattered fragments of his bones, as it is written (Psalms 34:21), "[God] safeguards all his bones; not one of them is broken" (*Likutey Moharan* I, 4:6).

The verse states (Ezekiel 32:27), "Their iniquities will be engraved upon their bones." The meaning of this, Rebbe Nachman teaches, is that each *aveirah* (sin; transgression) has its own combination of letters. For example, if a person transgresses the prohibition (Exodus 20:3), "You shall have no other gods besides Me," he destroys that prohibition's positive letter combination and forms of it a negative letter combination. This negative letter combination becomes engraved upon his bones, in fulfillment of the verse (Jeremiah 5:25), "Your iniquities have turned away these [good, positive] things; your sins have withheld bounty from you."

How can this process be reversed? Rebbe Nachman reveals that the mitzvah of *vidui lifnei HaShem* (usually translated as "confession before God") is the most powerful method of removing the "engraved sins" from one's bones, for, he says, speech itself emanates from the bones, as it is written (Psalms 35:10), "All my bones will *say*..." That is, when all my bones will *say* their confessions, the letter combinations engraved on them will be rearranged and rectified.

The fact is that very few people understand what confession is. They think of it as some kind of "guilt trip," and so lose out on its positive benefits. The Hebrew word *vidui* (וידוי, confession) shares its root with the verb *lehodot* (להודות) meaning to thank, or to admit. Indeed, the reflexive form of this verb, *lehitvadot*, although usually translated as "to confess," in fact literally means, "to admit to oneself." *Vidui lifnei HaShem* involves speaking directly to God in our own words, calling out and giving expression to our pain and our struggles, telling Him everything we have done — in short, a catharsis (i.e., "coming clean"). Such articulation of our shortcomings involves the profound realization that we always stand before God.

An *aveirah* blocks this crucial realization. When we repent and turn to God, speaking directly to Him, we are able to remove that block (and its negative letter combination) which the *aveirah* has formed and achieve a consciousness of being in God's Presence. Through this special form of communication with God, we are able to reestablish our connection with ourselves, to recognize who we are as opposed to what we have done and what has been done to us. This frees us from our own inner distortions and imperfections, which have been caused by our sins, thus allowing us to attain an objectivity that is impossible while our struggles remain locked up inside us. Only when we are free to be *who we are* can we truly recognize God and praise Him (see *Likutey Moharan* I, 4:5).

Rebbe Nachman points out that in order for confession to be most effective, it should be done in the presence of a Torah Sage who has reached very high levels of humility and piety. This is the meaning of the verse (Proverbs 16:14), "The King's wrath is a messenger of death, but a wise Sage can pacify it." The negative letter combinations that sin produces are the "messengers of death" — the destroying angels that attack the sinner. The "wise Sage" refers to Moses, about whom it is written (Numbers 12:3), "The man Moses was very *anav* [humble]." Such a Sage can pacify God's wrath, because his *ANaVah* (ענוה, humility and self-effacement) nullifies the negative effect of *AVoN* (עון, sin) (*Biur HaLikutim ad. loc.*).

Based on this teaching, Rebbe Nachman's followers used to confess before him, but at his request they curtailed this practice some three years before he passed away (*Tzaddik* #491). Breslover Chassidim to this day still confess (i.e., articulate in words everything that they have done) in their daily sessions of *hitbodedut* (private, secluded prayer before God).

*

Rebbe Nachman teaches further about the importance of confessing:

All the mitzvot combined create a complete structure, which parallels the 248 limbs and 365 sinews. Joy as well comprises a complete structure, which permeates the entire form of the Torah, as it is written (Psalms 19:9), "The precepts of God are upright, bringing joy to the heart!" By performing the mitzvot with joy, one can extend that joy so that it is felt throughout the entire body. When some specific limb does not "feel" joy, it is a sign that that organ has been blemished by sin. As we have pointed out, the act of confession clears away the obstruction or the blemish caused by sin. This allows a feeling of complete joy to flow throughout the entire body (see *Likutey Moharan* I, 178).

The Rebbe further teaches that "each type of physical joy has its own boundary, whereas spiritual joy is limitless. Someone who can take himself beyond the limitations of materialism, through using his body to perform mitzvot and thereby to attain spirituality, can achieve unbounded, complete joy" (*Likutey Moharan* II, 33).

*

Prayer and Resurrection

Rebbe Nachman taught:

Praying with concentration expands the mind and refreshes the soul. This brings fresh life to the bones. A blemish of the soul is also a blemish of the bones, as it is written (Psalms 6:3, 4), "My bones shudder; my soul is frightened...." This fright results from not having prayed with concentration. In order to remove any blemish from the soul and, in turn, the bones, one should pray so that one's very bones *feel* the words, as in (*ibid.* 35:10), "All my bones shall say, 'God! Who is like You?'" This is because concentration is a function of the mind, and bone marrow is the "mind" and "soul" of the bones. When we concentrate our minds on our prayers, our "bones' mind" [the bone marrow] carries out its functions properly and refreshes the bones and limbs (*Likutey Moharan* I, 67:9).

The bones are likened to a *SuKkah*, as in (Job 10:11), "You have clothed me in skin and flesh; within bone and sinew *t'SoKh'kheini* [You have concealed me]." Praying with all one's strength and concentration corresponds to the verse (Psalms 35:10), "All my bones shall say, 'God! Who is like You?'" Since the bones correspond to a sukkah, such prayer is likened to entering a sukkah and fulfilling the mitzvot associated with it, totally surrounding oneself with the mitzvot.

*

The Flesh

Man is of flesh, while the angels are of fire; but man is superior.
Likutey Moharan II, 1:2

The human body is composed largely of flesh and bone. Flesh is composed of basically the same type of tissue as the internal organs. As we have discussed (above, Part 3), the organs give rise to man's evil inclination and his undesirable characteristics. Yet the flesh, composed of the very same tissue, can be transformed into a formidable opponent against the evil characteristics.

Rav Amram Chasida experienced a serious battle with his evil inclination. When he finally prevailed, his evil inclination appeared to him as a pillar of fire. Rav Amram said to his evil inclination, "You are made of fire, while I am made of flesh. But I am superior to you!" (*Kiddushin* 81a).

Though a great tzaddik, Rav Amram was also a human being. He nearly succumbed to temptation and came extremely close to committing a grave sin. Yet he took hold of himself and conquered his evil inclination. His mere flesh, so easily tempted, had gained superiority over even the fire of an angel! Such is the power of striving for spirituality.

The Kabbalah tells us that humans inhabit the Universe of *Asiyah*, while the angels inhabit the Universe of *Yetzirah* (see Appendix

D). It would seem, therefore, that the angels are higher than humans in the spiritual hierarchy. Our Sages teach, though, that the souls of humans are rooted in the Universe of *Beriyah* (see Zohar I, 125b), which is above the Universe where the angels reside. For this reason a human being, though formed of flesh and bone, can reach levels which even angels cannot attain! This is what is meant by, "Man is of flesh, while the angels are of fire; but man is superior."

Rebbe Nachman explains that the challenges posed to man by the angels stem from the attribute of jealousy based on the angels' desire to maintain their higher status. Man's goal should be to ascend to *his* source, which is higher than the angelic Universe. When man controls himself against sin, he is in effect controlling the "angels," more specifically, his evil urge, and that is how he ascends beyond even the level of the angels. This human victory causes the angels to be jealous of man and incites them to try even harder to cause him to fall. Rebbe Nachman adds that even holy angels, whose job it is to assist people in their service of God, become jealous of the man who ascends above them (see Likutey Moharan II, 1:2).

*

If even angels can succumb to the rage of jealousy, how much more susceptible is man? A great degree of self-control is necessary to rise above the evil characteristic of jealousy.

The Talmud discusses jealousy at length (see Shabbat 152b). Jealousy causes the decay of the bones and flesh. One who conquers this evil characteristic can transcend the material limitations of his flesh and bone and attain a "spiritual body" that is immune to the natural ravages of physical decomposition. Reb Noson writes:

> It is common knowledge that after death the body decomposes. The flesh, no longer nourished by the soul, has no means of sustenance and necessarily decays. Still, King David said (Psalms 16:9–10), "Therefore my heart is joyous...even my flesh

will dwell securely. For You will not relinquish my soul to the pit; You will not let Your devoted one see destruction." To what is King David referring? He is speaking of one who recognizes his Creator while he is still alive, and therefore merits to illuminate his body with the attainments of his soul. To the degree that he accomplishes this, he transforms his physical aspect into a spiritual entity, so that even after death his "flesh will dwell securely" (*Likutey Halakhot, Hashkamat HaBoker* 4:4).

The more we seek God (according to the advice and teachings of the great tzaddikim), and internalize the higher levels of spirituality in our daily lives, the more we will be able to rise above our petty jealousies, and so be certain that even our flesh will endure after death.

*

The concept of transcending our physical limitations can be applied as well to the skin that covers our bodies. Skin "hides" man's inner essence. The First Man was created with a different kind of covering. It was radiant in and of itself, and was able to diffuse this inner, spiritual radiance. After his sin, Adam's covering became skin as we know it, the leathery "hide" we have today.

Reb Noson writes that the transformation of man's radiant skin into its current properties resulted from Adam's having eaten from the Tree of Knowledge of Good and Evil. Thus, the skin corresponds to the *kelipat nogah*, which is an admixture of both good and evil. This *kelipah* is akin to the imagination, or illusory powers, through which one can conjure up both good and evil; the image which one pictures is actually a "coating" over reality. Our task is to peel off all the coatings of the mind that conceal the radiant good within, and also to distinguish between good and evil (*Likutey Halakhot, Tefilin* 5:34). It is through seeking spirituality that man can enable his skin to radiate the good that God created to all other sectors of His Creation. This is part of the "aura" one feels when in the presence of a holy person.

In a separate discourse, Reb Noson carries this concept a step further. He parallels the "skin" to faith and encourages us to cultivate our powers of imagination in order to strengthen our faith. Even our ability to relate to God, he says, is based on imagination, for we cannot actually conceive of God. God gave us permission to call Him by certain names that depict Him, but in reality they are nothing more than representations.

Had Adam not eaten from the Tree of Knowledge, then he, as well as all of mankind, would have been able to attain an actual perception of God through the "radiant garment" of his skin. But Adam transgressed and so forfeited this ability. Only after he ate from the Tree did he realize he was naked — divested of his radiant garments (Genesis 3:7). He had lost the ability to experience God directly, and could now grasp Him only through his imagination, represented by the *kelipat nogah* (skin). This has become the essence of faith: man can grasp God only through the "clothing" (i.e., skin) which represents faith. Strengthening one's faith can enable one to achieve a higher awareness of God and a stronger relationship with Him (*Likutey Halakhot, Tzitzit* 5:10).

*

The Sense of Touch

The sense of touch is present throughout the body. Feelings of pain are also associated with the sense of touch. This physical sensitivity is a necessity for survival for, were it absent, we would never realize if we were cut, burned or otherwise injured.

In the same way, our *spiritual* sense of touch and our connection to spirituality are crucial to our existence. When we perform the mitzvot, employing our physical bodies for spiritual pursuits, we become *spiritually* sensitive. Everyone has sensitivities, but these are generally limited to certain specific areas of life. In the spiritual realm, taking charity as an example, we find that some people are interested in helping the homeless and destitute, and others the handicapped; others support institutions of education, health care and so on. Everyone who gives charity favors his own area of interest. No one can say that other areas are unimportant; nevertheless, a particular charity tends to interest certain individuals more than others. Their sensitivities are simply more attuned to these specific areas.

In similar fashion, certain parts of the body perform one mitzvah especially well, while others succeed better in some other mitzvah, and so on. When a person develops his entire body through all the mitzvot he can possibly perform, he attunes himself spiritually to additional areas, and becomes generally more sensitive and empathetic. Even his physical touch becomes a "touch of sensitivity," deeply appreciated by everyone with whom he associates.

* * *

38

The Arms and Hands

Hands are called *yadayim* in Hebrew. Each hand has five fingers, which together contain fourteen bones — four of the fingers each have three bones, equaling twelve, and the thumb has two, bringing the total to fourteen. The Hebrew word *YaD* (יד) is numerically equivalent to fourteen, alluding to the fourteen bones of the fingers. (The significance of this will be explained later in this chapter.)

When the average person extends his arms, the entire span is equal to his height. The arms and hands thus correspond to the outer range, or overall limitations, of one's potential.

The same dynamic can be applied to our spiritual reach. In the *Sefirotic* tree, Chesed (Love and Kindness) and Gevurah (Judgment and Restraint) correspond to the right and left arms (and hands) respectively. Just as our arms' reach corresponds to our physical limitations, Chesed and Gevurah can be said to represent the boundaries of our spiritual reach. Chesed would describe the farthest point we can currently reach on the side of loving, giving and accepting, while Gevurah represents the extreme boundary of our ability to make proper judgments.

Since Chesed and Gevurah are the *Sefirot* that interface directly with the *mochin* (powers of intellect), they express thoughts. The current level of a person's thoughts represents the extent of his spiritual capacity, his reach. His thoughts will determine how much Chesed and Gevurah he will use, depending on the current level. Hands, represented by Chesed and Gevurah, also express thoughts, through the hand motions and movements that tend to accompany speech. The hands are always moving; *which* way they move depends on one's intentions. For this reason the Talmud declares (Shabbat 14a), "Busy hands!" for they are constantly disclosing one's inner emotions. Thus the hands express not only one's physical outer reach, but one's spiritual capacity. Nowhere is this more evident than in prayer and faith, as we shall see.

*

"Hand-y" Weapons: Prayer and Faith

Rebbe Nachman taught:

> Hands are compared to prayer, as when Moses raised his arms in supplication during the battle with Amalek; and prayer and faith are synonymous (*Likutey Moharan* I, 7:1).

We know that one who believes sincerely in God will, more often than not, move his hands during prayer, as if to give emphasis to his words. However, there are many people who consider themselves "sophisticated" and are too self-conscious to display any public expression of their inner feelings. This inability to bring heartfelt emotion into one's prayer demonstrates a shortcoming in one's faith.

When the Jews battled Amalek in the desert, Moses ascended a nearby mountain and prayed for their success. While praying, the Torah tells us, "His *hands* were *faithful*" — spread out in supplication (Exodus 17:12; Rashi). His faith in God fueled his prayers and gave him the strength to raise his hands to God. As long as his hands were raised — as long as he expressed his faith in God — the Jews triumphed. This was the perfect weapon to be used against Amalek, the paradigm of sophistication and atheism (see *Likutey Moharan* II, 19:2; see above, Chapter 17). Thus, the hands, prayer and faith are, on one level, synonymous.

Rebbe Nachman teaches that "one's prayers must be offered as supplications, as requests for mercy, not as demands" (see *Likutey Moharan* I, 20:5). One's attitude in praying becomes apparent through one's hands, for one's "demands" or "requests" are often disclosed by the hands' movements.

Rebbe Nachman also teaches that the manifestation of speech through the hands is alluded to in (Ecclesiastes 10:20), "That which has *KeNaFayim* [wings] will tell." These "wings" are actually the hands, which "deliver" speech to its destination, revealing and perfecting one's expressions.

In a sense, the hands function in similar fashion to the *KaNFei rei'ah*, the lobes of the lung. Note that the arms extend from the body directly opposite the lungs, and both correspond to the location of the wings on a bird. Just as the lobes of the lungs assist in the passage of air, thus enabling speech, so too, the hands assist in bringing forth one's verbal message. Therefore, when a person is aroused to clap or move his hands in other ways in the course of expressing himself to God, his prayers are more effective (see *Likutey Moharan* I, 45).

Rebbe Nachman taught that expressing oneself with one's hands during prayer is a level of (cf. Numbers 12:8) "seeing God." The Hebrew word for a prophet (*NaVi*, נביא) — one who "sees" an image of God — is related to the Hebrew term for speech (Isaiah 57:19), "*NiV sefatayim* [ניב, motion of the lips]." Another verse states (Hosea 12:11), "Through the *hand* of the prophets, I cause an image to be seen." Thus prayers, combined with hand movements, enable one to perceive an "image of God" (*Likutey Moharan* I, 212:1).

*

Blemished Hands, Blemished Faith

We know that faith is an important element in sincere prayer, and that the hands express one's faith — or lack of it. The hands, and faith, can be blemished through avarice as in (Deuteronomy 8:17), "My power and the might of my *hand* have brought me this wealth." This is because both the hands and faith provide a person's livelihood: his hands toil, and his faith in God causes God to provide for him. An obsessive pursuit of wealth shows that he lacks faith in God's ability to give him his sustenance.

Rebbe Nachman teaches that today idolatry (the opposite of faith) is basically found in the worship of money. Idolatry is so closely associated with money because silver and gold represent Chesed and Gevurah respectively, which together reflect the beauty (i.e., Tiferet) of the supernal colors (each *Sefirah* corresponds to a different color; see *Zohar* II, 148a; Appendix D). As we have seen, the "hands" — represented by Chesed and Gevurah (silver and gold) — represent faith. When faith is present, the real beauty of money becomes revealed, for then it is used to support the pursuit of Godliness. When there is faith, even the money spent on one's mundane requirements reflects spirituality (see *Likutey Moharan* I, 25:4). When one lacks faith, when money is not used for spiritual purposes, the beauty of these "colors" (reflecting Chesed and Gevurah) becomes concealed. Men then become dissatisfied with the wealth they possess and seek more.

For this reason (though they may be unaware of it) people are eager to get their "hands" (i.e., Chesed and Gevurah) on money. For it is the hands that reflect both one's livelihood and one's ability to turn and direct one's toil into faith. Rebbe Nachman thus teaches that "so great is the value of living from the fruits of one's own labor, that a person who does so can recognize God's glory in a way which even angels cannot perceive!" (*The Aleph-Bet Book, Mamon* B:11).

One way to rectify blemished hands, and thereby faith, is by receiving advice and rebuke from the true tzaddikim. The reason for this is that the tzaddikim instill people with faith in God through their teachings (*Likutey Moharan* I, 22:2-3; *ibid.* I, 23:2).

*

The Power of Creation

In the beginning, God created the heavens and the earth.

Genesis 1:1

We have seen how prayer and faith can be powerful weapons through the hands — as long as prayer is sincere. But that is not all. Through prayer, hands have the ability to arouse the power of Creation. This is explained as follows:

Rashi comments that the verse "In the beginning..." reveals the *ko'ach* (strength) of God. The world is His Creation and He can give any land therein to whomever He wishes. Originally, He gave the Holy Land to the Canaanites. Then He took it from them and bequeathed it to Israel (*Rashi* on Genesis 1:1).

Furthermore, when speaking about the Act of Creation, the verse states, (Isaiah 48:13), "My Hand founded the earth; and My Right Hand spanned the heavens." Our Sages tell us that the first "hand" mentioned in the verse refers to God's left hand. This teaches us that both the "Right and Left Hands" were instrumental in creating heaven and earth (*Menachot* 36b).

Now recall that the hand is called *yad* because of the fourteen bones it contains. The number of Hebrew letters found in the first verse of the Torah is twenty-eight. The Hebrew word for strength is *ko'ach*, also numerically equal to twenty-eight. Since each hand has fourteen bones, both hands together contain "twenty-eight bones," representing the *ko'ach* of God. Based on this, Rebbe Nachman teaches that every person has within himself the ability to arouse the power of Creation with his hands (i.e., his prayers). He taught:

> Some people make motions with their hands during their prayers — some even clap hands — to help them intensify their concentration. Doing so is very beneficial, because it connects one to the Creation. The account of Creation is Israel's deed to the Holy Land, for the purpose of beginning the Scriptures with the story of Creation was to reveal the sanctity of the Land. Praying to God shows one's acceptance of God as the One Who created the world. There are a total of twenty-eight bones in the fingers of a person's two hands. These twenty-eight bones correspond to the twenty-eight letters in the first verse of the Torah describing the Creation of the world. Movement of one's hands during prayers arouses the forces of Creation, drawing

upon one the sanctity of the Holy Land! Drawing the holiness of the Holy Land upon oneself helps to defeat the evil thoughts that invade one's mind while praying (*Likutey Moharan* I, 44).

(This does not imply that one should clap hands and make motions that disturb others who are praying in the vicinity. One should use prudence, always being considerate of others.)

Once, when speaking of movements of the hands that people make during their prayers, Rebbe Nachman said that this is the intention of the Zohar (*Tikkuney Zohar* #21, p.44b) when it speaks of "hands that write secrets": Hand movements during prayers can actually inscribe secrets on High! (*Rabbi Nachman's Wisdom* #75).

*

The "Three Hands"

When describing the Exodus and the Splitting of the Red Sea, the Torah mentions "three hands," which correspond to Chesed, Gevurah and Tiferet (*Zohar* III, 246b):

Hebrew	English	*Sefirah*
Yad HaGedolah	Great Hand	Chesed
Yad HaChazakah	Mighty Hand	Gevurah
Yad HaRamah	Exalted Hand	Tiferet

(Scripture's references to the three hands are found in the Book of Exodus: *Yad HaGedolah* [14:31], *Yad HaChazakah* [6:1], and *Yad HaRamah* [14:8].)

Chesed, Gevurah and Tiferet are the *Sefirot* that transmit divine life force from the *mochin*. Stated differently, Chokhmah, Binah and Daat are revealed via Chesed, Gevurah and Tiferet respectively. Rebbe Nachman thus teaches that through the "hands" we can grasp the Torah, the *mochin* (*Likutey Moharan* I, 101:2).

This is better understood in light of the fact that Daat is actually formed by the unification of Chokhmah and Binah. Chokhmah and Binah correspond to the first two letters of the Tetragrammaton, *Yod* and *Heh*. Numerically, *YH* (יה) is equal to fifteen. The letter *Heh* itself can be expanded in three different ways (see Appendix D), and three times fifteen is forty-five. This is the numerical equivalent of *ADaM* (אדם), man. By fully utilizing one's mind (Chokhmah and Binah) for holiness, one assumes the identity of man. The verse (Numbers 19:14), "This is the Torah — man," indicates that the way to gain the identity of *man* is through the Torah, specifically the *mochin* of the Torah. Still, one must get a "handle" on the Torah in order to grasp it properly and understand how to implement its teachings to attain spirituality. Only then does one truly become man. This is achieved through the "three hands" — Chesed, Gevurah and Tiferet.

The power of the "three hands" can mitigate harsh decrees. Rebbe Nachman teaches that hand-clapping can negate strife. A separation of right and left connotes strife. When one "claps" one's hands, bringing together the Great Hand (right) and the Mighty Hand (left), one makes "peace" between them (the Exalted Hand). Peace brings about the mitigation of all painful decrees (*Likutey Moharan* I, 46).

The ARI teaches that, aside from reaching out towards higher levels (to the *mochin*, in order to grasp Torah), the hands represent the ability to reach down into the lower worlds and raise them up. The hands have a unique ability to extend in both directions, raising and uplifting that which is "below" as well as reaching upwards to bring down bounty from Above.

The ARI writes further that the Holy Name which God used to create the world is known as *Shem Mem-Bet*, the Holy Name of Forty-Two Letters. This Name is associated with the realm of Binah. Just as hands are necessary to pick up and elevate something from a lower level, all elevations of the lower realms to those above them are performed through this Holy Name of Forty-Two Letters (*Shaar HaKavanot* p.95ff). The reason for this is that, as we have seen, the Hebrew word for hand is *YaD* (numerically totaling fourteen), and there are "three hands": the "great hand," the "mighty hand" and the "exalted hand." Three times *yad* (fourteen) is forty-two, corresponding to the Name of Forty-Two Letters and to Binah.

Rebbe Nachman taught:

It is customary, when one is ill or in need, to bring a *pidyon* [redemption money] to a tzaddik. The tzaddik places his hands upon the money to mitigate these decrees. This is effective because money corresponds to the "feet" [i.e., livelihood] that support a person. The "feet" also represent judgments (see below, Chapter 39), and one must mitigate judgments at their root, which is in Binah. Thus, the "three hands," when placed upon the money (judgments), correspond to the elevation of the judgments (feet) into the realm of Binah (the intellect), the source of judgments, where they are mitigated and also sweetened (*Likutey Moharan* I, 180).

*

Left-handed?

We have seen how the *Sefirot* line up in three self-complementary columns. Furthermore, we have explained that the right hand represents Chesed (Abraham), the left Gevurah (Isaac) and the center column, where they are joined together, represents Tiferet (Jacob; truth) (see above, Chapter 36).

Rebbe Nachman teaches that at their source the "three hands" are actually one hand. The right hand, as the greater power, represents the potential to act. The left hand, being subordinate to the right, represents the actual accomplishment. However, at the start of a given process, there is no visible activity — it is just a thought, lacking even a concrete idea, let alone an accomplishment. This is compared to "one hand." At that point, the hands appear as one, with nothing to differentiate the right from the left. One must "separate the hands" — by first defining the underlying thought and then developing it. Only then can one actualize that thought (*Likutey Moharan* I, 66:2). Connecting this to Chesed, Gevurah and Tiferet, we should recall that the ideal state of rectification of the *Sefirot* is when they are aligned in three columns (see Chapter 36). The value of having "three hands" — not just a single hand — is that we can invoke the unique power of each "hand" to help develop our potential.

Reb Noson explains that the main catalyst for bringing any potential into being is truth (Tiferet), for "truth endures and falsehood does not" (Shabbat 104a). If a person is bound to truth, his ideas will eventually be actualized, and they will endure. Lacking truth, his deeds, though they may come to fruition, will eventually turn sterile (Likutey Halakhot, Matnat Shkhiv Mera 2:4). It is clear that we must first seek truth in our endeavors. Then, when we begin to formulate our thoughts and take steps to make them happen, they can endure.

What if one strays from the truth?

Rebbe Nachman spoke about the effects of falsehood and strife. He said, "A liar is reincarnated as a left-handed person" (The Aleph-Bet Book, Truth A:48). Reb Noson explains that this is based on the verse (Psalms 144:8), "Their mouths speak vanity; their right hand is a right hand of falsehood." When one speaks untruths, one separates the left hand from the right and fails to differentiate between right and wrong. As a consequence, he has a "false right hand" — his left hand becomes the stronger hand (Likutey Halakhot, Matnat Shkhiv Mera 2:4).

Rebbe Nachman also taught, "One who engages in strife is reincarnated as a left-handed person." We learn this from Korach, who sought to separate himself from Aaron. The Jewish people are divided into three groups, representing the "three columns" of Chesed, Gevurah and Tiferet. The Kohen represents Chesed, the Levite Gevurah, and the Israelites represent Tiferet. Korach (a Levite) sought to make the left dominate the right (he wanted to gain status over Aaron, the high priest, a Kohen). Therefore, the punishment of one who engages in strife is to have his right hand subjugated to his left (Rabbi Nachman's Wisdom #152).

The ARI writes that when a person finds himself overly inclined towards a certain characteristic, it is an indication that he must work to rectify this trait in his current incarnation. The few teachings of Rebbe Nachman which have been mentioned above do not necessarily dictate the reasons for any given individual's sojourn on earth; still, they can serve as a helpful guide to someone who finds that he tends towards falsehood or strife.

*

The Priestly Blessings

The hands are basic to the process of bringing blessing into the world. For instance, one of the Biblical commandments is that the *Kohanim* [priests] bless the nation of Israel daily. The priests are required to extend their hands while reciting their blessings, which cause the Presence of God to rest with the nation (see Numbers 6:22–27; *Sotah* 38a).

Rebbe Nachman teaches that performing the mitzvot with joy elevates the feet, for a happy person feels like dancing. As the feet ascend, the hands move upwards as well. When the hands reach an "elevated" position, blessings are drawn into the world, as in (Leviticus 9:22), "Aaron *raised his hands* and blessed the people." One who receives blessings from Above is able to transfer their bounty to others, even to those on lower levels. As we have seen, Rebbe Nachman emphasizes that the greatest blessing is Daat, a greater awareness of God (see *Likutey Moharan* I, 24:4-5).

A person's hands thus represent his ability to draw blessing into the world through drawing himself closer to a spiritual life. By "raising his hands" to God, he demonstrates his recognition of God. Furthermore, since the hands represent the ability to "extend outward," one who raises his hands to God is able to transmit his own recognition to others.

Reb Noson adds that raising one's hands in supplication to God arouses God's compassion, to the point that His Thirteen Attributes of Mercy are revealed. The priests must raise their hands, for they must draw this abundant blessing down upon every Jew. Yet it is not only the priests who possess the ability to arouse the Thirteen Attributes, for each and every individual can also arouse the full measure of God's mercy. The more people raise their hands in prayer and supplication, the more bounty is bestowed. With increased blessing for all, people will be free to use their hands solely for prayer, instead of using them to toil for their material sustenance. Hands will then be used to attain spirituality, and to assist in bestowing it upon others! (*Likutey Halakhot, Birkhot HaShachar* 5:98–100).

In one of the last lessons he gave in his life, Rebbe Nachman spoke at length about the importance of the hands in one's daily spiritual quest. He explains how one can use one's hands to bring down heavenly wisdom to help one serve God.

The hands allude to "hints" [i.e., through their motions] which one must "receive" and understand in order to know how to fulfill one's mission in life. Heavenly wisdom, being a very bright light (see above, Chapter 15), cannot always be revealed clearly and directly to man. A person must observe the hints sent to him from heaven, and then understand how to apply them in his daily life. His hands can then open to receive [the Godly wisdom, which as it descends materializes as] sustenance, as in (Psalms 145:16), "You open Your *hands* and satiate all living things according to Your Will." Someone who understands the allusions which have been revealed to him can aspire to a lofty aspect of God's Will — to serve God beyond any human limitations or physical boundaries (*Likutey Moharan* II, 7:10).

*

The Fingers

Rebbe Nachman taught:

The five fingers correspond to the five phonetic families: gutturals, labials, palatals, linguals and dentals (see above, "The Respiratory System," Chapter 26; see *Likutey Moharan* I, 38:3).

We have seen that the hands are similar in their function to speech, in that the hands portray the workings of the mind and convey ideas. Rebbe Nachman taught that this function is particularly evident in one's fingers. Each finger is shaped differently, to perform the task for which it is best suited.

The twenty-eight bones in the fingers (fourteen in each hand) represent the twenty-eight "times" that a person experiences in the course of his lifetime. King Solomon describes these times as (Ecclesiastes 3:1-8), "A time to be born...to die, to cry...to laugh; to embrace...to distance; a time of war...of peace..." (see *Tikkuney Zohar* #69, p.101b). Reb Noson adds that each of these times and concepts of life contain the potential for "hints," and through them one can come to recognize God (see *Likutey Halakhot, Netilat Yadayim Li'Seudah* 6:54). Thus the fingers are closely akin to the power of speech since it is the mode through which the concealed becomes revealed, as the fingers represent the "times" in which God can be revealed.

The five fingers allude to another kind of revelation: The Talmud speaks of Fifty Gates of Binah (*Rosh HaShanah* 21b), the Fiftieth Gate being the level which was revealed by God in order to bring about the Exodus. This is the very same level that will be revealed at the time of the coming of the Mashiach. It is this level that is alluded to in the five fingers of each hand.

Rebbe Nachman taught:

> Each hand has five fingers. When two hands clap against one another, the five fingers of the right hand meet with those of the left hand, and vice versa. When right hand meets left, "five meeting five" makes a total of twenty-five, and in the reverse meeting, when the left hand meets the right, it brings the total to fifty. This "fifty" corresponds to the Fiftieth Level, which is the source of salvation. Therefore, clapping our hands during our prayers (see above) arouses the power of salvation and hastens the Redemption (*Likutey Moharan* I, 45).

*

Healing is in the Hands

Rebbe Nachman taught:

> [The Torah opens with a description of how God first created the world with Ten Utterances (*Rosh HaShanah* 32a; *Bereishit Rabbah* 17:1).] An angel was created with every one of these Utterances (*Chagigah*

14a). As God expanded Creation, each Utterance divided and subdivided into many "sparks" [i.e., smaller utterances]. This is the meaning of the verse (Jeremiah 23:29), "Behold, My words are like fire, and like a hammer that shatters rock." Similarly, many angels were created of every angel, exactly according to the number of sparks. Then an angel which had been created from an original Utterance became an archangel over entire camps of lesser angels, which were created from the sparks.

Each and every one of these [lesser] angels is given "responsibility" for a particular aspect of Creation. Even trees and plants [especially those with healing properties] have their angel guides supervising their growth, as the Sages said (*Bereishit Rabbah* 10:6), "There is nothing below, not even a common herb, which does not have an angel on high that strikes it and tells it to grow." Each of these angels receives its life force from the particular Utterance which is the source of its creation. It then transmits a measured amount of this life force to its particular charge.

This power of the angels to receive and transmit life force is referred to as the power of the "hands." [The Hebrew word for power is *ko'ach* (כח), numerically equal to twenty-eight, the number of bones contained in the fingers of both hands.] With its "right hand," an angel receives life force. With its "left hand," it dispenses the exact amount needed to its charge below. This is the meaning of the Sages' statement, "he strikes it and tells it to grow." "Striking" is done with the angel's left hand [for the left side represents Gevurah, judgment].

The Torah bids us (Proverbs 4:20-22), "My son, attend to my words; incline your ear to my utterances... For they are life to those who find them and healing to all their flesh." We learn from this that all healing flows from God, through His Torah. The Torah is the source of the [healing] power of the angels, who in turn transmit it to all the various herbs in their charge. This power is manifest when one accepts the Torah and has faith in the Sages who reveal it; for the Torah was given over to the Sages, and one who deviates from their teachings is called "he who causes a breach in the wall [of faith]." This is the meaning of the injunction (Deuteronomy 17:11), "Do not deviate, neither to the right nor to the left, from what they [the Sages] teach you." If you deviate to the right [i.e., tending towards unnecessary zealousness], your angel's "right hand" [ability to receive from its corresponding archangel and Utterance] will be hindered. If you deviate to the left [by transgressing the Torah], the angel's "left hand" [ability to transmit] will be hindered. Of course, the removal of your angel's hands means that you cannot receive your healing, for without an angel to bestow the life force upon it, the herb upon which your healing depends loses its power to heal (Likutey Moharan I, 57:1).

Thus, the degree to which a person is attached to Torah determines the degree to which he is able to be healed.

* * *

39

The Legs

The legs are part of the appendicular skeleton. Extending downwards from the lower extremity of the torso, they are the main pillars which support the body, as well as the principal means of human locomotion. Spiritually, the legs represent the lower and outer reaches of man. With his legs man makes contact with the physical ground. When he pushes his legs against the earth, he is able to lift himself and rise up above that very earth.

The legs correspond to the *Sefirot* of Netzach and Hod. Together with the sexual organ, which corresponds to Yesod, they comprise the lower triad of *Sefirot*. *NeTZaCH* comes from the root of *l'NaTZeaCH*, which means to gain dominance, or victory. *HOD* means splendor, but also relates to the term *HODa'ah*, admission, which connotes a state of submission. Netzach is an extension of Chesed, the attribute of giving. Only one who is "in control" is able to extend benevolence to others. Hod is a manifestation of Gevurah, the characteristic of restraint. Both attributes are necessary in order to achieve a balance in life, for one must know not only how to hold back, but also when to acquiesce to others. Using both "legs," one can move forward, confident of "victory" and success in one's endeavors, while at the same time balancing this with a healthy awareness that there are times one should hold back and submit to forces stronger than oneself.

Rebbe Nachman emphasized how important it is to balance these two opposite forces. In many places (see for instance *Likutey Moharan* I, 6:4) he uses the expression, being adept at "running and returning." This is based on Ezekiel's vision in which he saw (Ezekiel 1:14) "the *Chayot* running and returning, as the appearance of a flash of lightning." In our service of God, the skill of "running" is necessary for those times when we wish to "rise up to heaven" (Psalms 139:8). The skill of "returning" is required when we must perforce (*ibid.*) "make our bed in hell."

This means that if, on the one hand, you are worthy of ascending to a certain level, you must not allow yourself to remain at your current level. No matter where you stand, never be content with your present level. You are capable of more, you are therefore obligated to develop and use that capability. This is Netzach. This is the skill you need to allow yourself to believe and know that you can constantly advance further and further.

On the other hand, if you should fall, God forbid, then regardless of how far and to what depths you have fallen, even if it is to the very depths of depravity, God forbid, you must never give up hope. Whatever happens, search out and entreat God to help you. Remain strong in whatever way you can, in whatever position you find yourself. Even in the lowest pit, God can be found. There, too, you must attach yourself to Him and not let go. This is Hod. This is the skill of returning, of finding God even when "your bed is in hell," of submitting, even in the most unfavorable circumstances, to His Will and to His Will alone.

Your legs have tremendous strength. Learn how to use them. Practice standing firmly on the ground. When you decide to move forward, do so with conviction. Assert yourself. When you must stop and give way, do so without hesitation and without regrets.

Giving way entails understanding the secret of self-effacement. The right leg corresponds to self-assertion, the left leg to self-effacement. Walking requires a combination of the two. When you assert yourself, don't push God out of the picture. When you must efface yourself, don't be fooled into thinking that you are any less of a person. The greatest tzaddikim knew the secret of self-effacement, and therein lies their very greatness. Even concerning God it is said that:

> Wherever you find mention of God's greatness and omnipotence, you also find mention of His humility. This idea is written in the Torah, repeated in the Prophets, and repeated again in the Sacred Writings.
>
> In the Torah it is written (Deuteronomy 10:17), "God your Lord is the Supreme Being, and the Highest Authority. The great, mighty and awesome God, He does not give special consideration or take bribes." Immediately following this, it is written (*ibid.* 10:18), "He upholds justice for the orphan and widow, and loves the foreigner, granting him food and clothing."
>
> This is repeated in the Prophets, as it is written (Isaiah 57:15), "For thus says [God], High and Exalted, dwelling in eternity, whose Name is Holy: 'I dwell lofty and transcendent, but I am with those with a broken and humbled spirit. I revive the humble spirit and give new life to the brokenhearted.'"
>
> It is repeated again in the Sacred Writings, as it is written (Psalms 68:5), "Sing to God; chant praises to His Name. Soar up to the One Who rides over the heavens with His Name, *Yod-Heh*, and exult greatly in His Presence." Immediately following this, it is written (*ibid.*, 68:6), "[Even] in His holy abode, God is a Father of orphans and a Defender of widows" (*Megillah* 31a).

Emulate God; emulate the tzaddikim; emulate the angels. Know when to run forward and when to give way and take every step with the certitude of faith. In this way you will establish your life on "solid footing." Indeed, balancing these two forces of Netzach and Hod leads to the establishment of a solid Yesod (foundation) for life. Just as Chesed and Gevurah achieve perfection when combined in Tiferet, in the same way, Netzach and Hod merge and find perfection in Yesod. The ARI thus teaches that the spiritual energy that descends from the eight higher *Sefirot*, from Keter through Hod, all merges in Yesod, which is a "comprehensive *Sefirah*." This is because Yesod corresponds to the organ of procreation, where all the channeled energy converges, and can be shared with Malkhut in the final stage of developing one's spirituality. This concept is reflected in the seed which is transferred from Yesod to Malkhut (see Part 9). In this sense, Malkhut also becomes a "comprehensive *Sefirah*," for it receives *all* the energy and bounty of the higher *Sefirot*, through Yesod.

The interaction between Yesod and Malkhut completes the process of the descent of the life force through the system of the *Sefirot*. We may therefore derive that when a person has attained a life of *balanced* spiritual aspirations — through rectifying his own Godly image — he is then ready to channel that stability to others. The completing of this cycle requires Malkhut, represented in one's mate. This aspect of human purpose will be discussed in Part 9, "The Reproductive System."

Throughout the holy writings we find that the "feet" correspond to Malkhut; though, as we have pointed out, they also represent Netzach and Hod. Netzach and Hod merge in Yesod, which then merges with Malkhut. Since Malkhut is inclusive of all the *Sefirot*, and also represents the lowest level, specific reference will determine whether the legs and feet will be identified with Netzach and Hod or with Malkhut.

*

The ARI teaches that Hod, being the lowest extreme of the body on its left side (which represents judgments; see Appendix D), is the location of the source of potential evil. For this reason, when Jacob fought with Esau's guardian angel, the angel smote him on his left thigh, indicating a weakening of Jacob's ability to battle evil during the exile (see Genesis 32:26; *Chullin* 91a).

As we have seen, the legs and feet represent the very lowest extreme that man can reach and, as such, his continuous contact with the material world. Spiritual existence is called "life," whereas focusing solely on the material leads to insensitivity and spiritual death. Rebbe Nachman therefore teaches that the feet, representing Malkhut, are closest to the side of death, to the realm of the "Other Side," as the verse states (Proverbs 5:5), "Her feet descend unto death." Therefore, one who has blemished the "feet" not only binds himself to a material existence, but actually gives over his spiritual strength to the Other Side and enables the forces of evil to draw nourishment through him (*Likutey Moharan* I, 67:4), may God save us.

In the same vein, Rebbe Nachman teaches that the entire physical world is comparable to the "feet," the lowest extremity of the universes of holiness. This is the meaning of (Isaiah 66:1) "The earth is My footstool." Clearly, one can find God anywhere, even in the most mundane of environments. Nevertheless, holiness found in the lowest levels cannot be nearly as powerful as that which is discovered at higher levels. Furthermore, intense exposure to the material world can overwhelm a person, distancing him from the very holiness he is seeking. Rebbe Nachman therefore strongly recommends that we seek God through Torah study and prayer, rather than having to descend to the lower levels in order to realize our spiritual quest (see *Likutey Moharan* I, 54:2).

*

Walking Tall

Rebbe Nachman taught:

> In order to be able to walk on the path of repentance, one must know *Halakhah*, the Codes (*Likutey Moharan* I, 6:4).

The Hebrew term for walking is *HaLiKHAh* (הליכה), which is closely related to the word *HaLaKHAh* (הלכה), the Codes of Law. Since the word for "walking" is similar to that of the Codes, we deduce that knowledge of the Codes is the knowledge necessary to succeed on the path of life. The Codes state what is permissible (referring to the *Sefirah* of Netzach, for they instruct us as to when and how to go forward) and what is forbidden (referring to Hod, for they instruct us as to when to refrain from going). Such knowledge "brings peace" into an otherwise divided heart (see *Likutey Moharan* I, 62:2; see also above, Chapter 22). Knowing what to do in any given situation creates a secure and healthy attitude (foundation or Yesod) towards life.

Rebbe Nachman also taught that prayer corresponds to the feet (*Likutey Moharan* I, 55:5). Praying to God constitutes a recognition of His dominion, and this is the essence of "standing firm." Furthermore, awe corresponds to the feet, as in (Ecclesiastes 12:13) "The end of all...is to fear God." Fear is the "end," which indicates the lowest levels. One must begin one's spiritual quest on "solid footing," with awe of God. When the "feet" are "solid" (when the fear of God is established), they create a channel through which one may receive bounty from God.

Rebbe Nachman taught:

> The Three Festivals are called the *Shalosh Regalim* [literally, "three legs"], because they reveal the awe of God (*Likutey Moharan* II, 4:6).

Each of the Three Festivals commemorates numerous miracles. Pesach commemorates the Exodus and the Splitting of the Red Sea. The Revelation at Mount Sinai took place on Shavuot, when the Torah was given. Sukkot bids us to remember the Seven Clouds of Glory that protected Israel in the desert. By observing the Three Festivals, we reconnect to the miracles they commemorate, and so reveal the awe of God (see *Likutey Moharan* II, 4:4).

*

However, not everything that corresponds to the "feet" is necessarily positive. Since man always has free choice, the potential for evil must also exist.

Rebbe Nachman taught:

> ReGeL [foot] corresponds to RaGaL [slander], for the slanderer "walks" from place to place, spreading his slanderous tales (*Likutey Moharan* I, 14:12).

Of all forms of evil speech, slander is by far the worst. The Talmud (Erkhin 15b) equates slander with murder, for slandering another person can cause him untold damage, be it financial, emotional, spiritual or even physical. One who engages in slander also weakens his own "foundation" — his "legs" — and leaves himself nothing firm to stand upon. Conversely, when people desist from engaging in slander and gossip, peace is increased in the world (*Likutey Moharan* I, 14:12). (Peace, *shalom*, corresponds to Yesod — the "foundation" — the perfect balance of Netzach and Hod; cf. *Likutey Moharan* I, 33:1.)

Arrogance is also associated with the feet, as it is written (Psalms 36:12), "Let not the foot of haughtiness overcome me" (*Likutey Moharan* I, 22:13). An arrogant person often suffers from an inferiority complex and feels that in order to gain recognition he must boast. But arrogance is a despicable trait, and it is because of arrogance that the Jewish People are forced to remain in exile and cannot return ("go" back) to their Land (see *Likutey Moharan* I, 11:8).

Atheism is likewise represented in the "feet." We learn this from Psalm 73, in which King David describes how the success of the wicked almost caused him to veer from the path of truth. He thus wrote (Psalms 73:2-3), "But as for me, my feet almost turned away; in an instant my steps would have been swept aside. For I envied the arrogant when I beheld the peace of the wicked..." (See the entire text of this psalm.)

*

Earning a Living

One's livelihood is compared to the feet, as we are taught (*Sanhedrin* 110a), "A person's money stands him on his feet [gives him financial security]."

Rebbe Nachman taught:

> It is important to elevate one's livelihood to the level of the *Lechem HaPanim* [the shewbread of the Temple]... It was baked on Friday afternoon and miraculously remained fresh until the following Shabbat, nine days later. Thus, the shewbread signifies an easy livelihood, one that comes directly from God (similar to the manna). When a person can elevate his livelihood to this level of "the face" [*panim*], that is to say, when he has complete faith in God that He will provide, then through his

livelihood he brings about forgiveness for sins and reveals Godliness in the world (*Likutey Moharan* I, 31:9).

Earning a living is not a simple matter. It requires persistence and hard work. One can never really know if any of one's efforts will succeed. Rebbe Nachman teaches that all forms of work are rooted in the thirty-nine archetypal forms of work which were performed in the building of the Sanctuary (see *Shabbat* 73a). This indicates that, for one who has faith, even mundane work becomes spiritual in nature, as if through his work he is building a Sanctuary (for that is in fact what he is doing when he provides for his household with faith). If a person lacks faith, however, he engages in the "thirty-nine forms of work" in vain (see *Likutey Moharan* I, 11:4). Only those who realize that it is God alone Who provides do not need to worry about their livelihood. Thus, man must always work on building his faith, which also corresponds to the legs.

Rebbe Nachman further teaches that the need to travel for business purposes results from a blemish in faith (*Likutey Moharan* I, 40). Reb Noson explains that exile in general is the result of blemished faith. Just as Adam and Eve were expelled from the Garden of Eden because they ate from the Tree of Knowledge, and the Jewish nation as a whole was exiled to Babylon to rectify the sin of idolatry, so too all the travels that one undertakes are necessary for the sake of rectifying one's faith. Conceptually, traveling from place to place involves using one's feet to locate and elevate all the sparks of holiness spread throughout the world. Thus, though the original blemish of faith is what caused our national pattern of "travel and exile," people can use their travels for spiritual benefits — for themselves and, in fact, even for the entire world (see *Likutey Halakhot, Pikadon* 5:19). Since much travel is for the sake of business, the belief that it is only God Who provides livelihood is an area in which one must strengthen one's faith.

The Talmud teaches (*Sukkah* 53a), "Man's legs are his guarantors: wherever he must go, they will take him." This means that when a person's "feet" are strong, they keep him firm and guarantee that he will not descend into the realm of evil and impurity (see *Likutey Moharan* I, 10:9). People today are constantly on the move — going to work, to a store, to visit, to learn Torah and so on. Contemporary man has open to him horizons that were not even dreamed of centuries ago. Thus, man's ability to bring about rectifications nowadays is far greater than it ever was in previous generations; and every person, through his travels, has the ability to accomplish this. Rebbe Nachman teaches that everywhere a person goes he can bring about rectifications, for wherever he goes he can perform some good deed. If he will but guard himself from sin, he will automatically rectify sparks of holiness wherever he visits (*Rabbi Nachman's Wisdom* #85).

*

Dancing

One who feels happy may become "uplifted" to the point that his feelings beg expression through dance and bodily movements. Rebbe Nachman teaches (*Likutey Moharan* I, 169:1), "One should strive for joy, so that even one's heels *feel* this joy. Then, through dance, one is able to mitigate judgments." We have pointed out that both the arms and the legs correspond to faith. Let us examine the strength of the two working in unison.

Rebbe Nachman taught:

> Dancing and hand-clapping emanate from the spirit in one's heart. As can be readily observed, when a person's heart is happy, he dances and claps his hands...

The arms, in particular the hands, come together in clapping; the legs, in particular the feet, move together in dance. The spirit which brings the arms and legs together is happiness and joy. This spirit comes to the person through the tzaddik, who is called "a man who has spirit" (see Numbers 27:18). That is, the tzaddik corresponds to the spirit because he inspires people to seek Godliness. The Rebbe continues:

Through the tzaddik, who corresponds to the spirit of the heart, haughtiness is eliminated, as it is written (Psalms 36:12), "Let not the foot of pride come against me." Idolatry is also eliminated, as it is written (Genesis 18:4), "'...and wash your feet' — this alludes to idolatry" (*Bava Metzia* 86b) [and haughtiness is equated with idolatry; see *Sotah* 4b]. Thus, when the feet are lifted up in dance [through the tzaddik, the spirit in the heart], haughtiness, which is in fact idolatry, is eliminated. Through this, divine judgments and harsh decrees are mitigated, for (*Sifri* 13:18) "as long as idol worship exists, divine anger visits the world." When idolatry disappears, Divine anger disappears and *chasadim* [kindnesses] are drawn to the world. Then the feet are (I Samuel 2:9) "the feet of *ChaSiDav* [His pious ones]" — alluding to the aspect of *ChaSaDim*. This corresponds to (Isaiah 55:3) "...*ChaSDei* [the kindnesses of] David are faithful"; they are described as "faithful" because [through the tzaddik's "spirit" and influence] heresy and atheism are eliminated...

This [spirit] also corresponds to hand-clapping for, through the spirit, the *illumination* of the hands is revealed, as in (Songs 5:2), "The call of my Beloved *dofeik* [pulsates]." *Dofek*, as the *Tikkuney Zohar* (#25, p.70a) teaches, is an aspect of spirit [the breath/spirit that causes the heart to beat and pulsate, and is the source of the pulse of the hands]. A verse that follows this (Songs 5:4), "My Beloved put His hand in through the hole," alludes to the revelation of the hands' illumination, which is hand-clapping. At that point, idol worship — which refers to heresy — is eliminated. It is thus written (Exodus 17:12), "And his [Moses'] hands were faithful" (*Likutey Moharan* I, 10:6).

The hands and feet, when they are rectified, correspond to faith. When blemished, they correspond to haughtiness, idolatry and heresy. Haughtiness is likened to a foot. Just as a person relies on his feet to support his body physically, so too he depends on his haughty spirit to hold him up emotionally. Such haughtiness can be countered and negated by means of "dancing feet" —

provided the spirit that moves them is drawn from the heart and from the tzaddik. Rebbe Nachman continues:

> We find therefore that through the tzaddik — that is, through the spirit in the heart — the illumination of the hands and feet (i.e., clapping and dancing) is revealed. Haughtiness and atheism are thereby eliminated, and faith is increased. It is then that the verse (Psalms 26:12), "My foot stands in an even place," is fulfilled. "My foot stands" is a reference to faith, whereas heresy is called "a foot that turns away" (see Psalms 73:2).
>
> The Torah, too, corresponds to hands and feet, for the Torah consists of both revealed and hidden teachings. The revealed corresponds to the hands, as in (Songs 5:4), "My Beloved put His hand in through the *chor* [hole]." The "*chor*" alludes to (Exodus 32:16) "*ChaRut* [engraved] on the tablets," this being the revealed Torah. The hidden Torah corresponds to the feet, as our Sages explained the verse (Songs 7:2) "The rounded thighs" — "Just as the thigh is hidden, so too are the words of Torah" (*Sukkah* 49b; see *Likutey Moharan* I, 10:6–7).

Heresy engenders harsh decrees, whereas the Torah and the tzaddikim bring spirit and life force. When we are joyous, we dance and clap our hands, drawing this *spirit* into our entire body. Drawing the joyous spirit of the Torah into our limbs cleanses our systems through strengthening our faith. It eliminates heresy, and thus mitigates harsh decrees. Since the tzaddik also corresponds to the enlivened spirit, associating oneself closely with the tzaddik also mitigates harsh decrees.

Dancing is so effective in mitigating judgments because Malkhut, the lowest of the spiritual levels, is where judgments are manifest. In fact, judgments are also called "feet," for they too *run* to fulfill their mission (see *Likutey Moharan* I, 169:1).

Rebbe Nachman taught:

> All blessings descend from Chokhmah, while all judgments originate in Binah. Chokhmah and Binah are *mochin*. The energy or bounty they deliver descends and ultimately reaches the

Sefirot of Netzach and Hod, then flows through Yesod into Malkhut. The Hebrew word for knee is *BeReKh* [ברך], which shares the letters of *BeRaKhah* [ברכה, blessing] and *BeKhoRah* [בכורה, the right of the firstborn]. *Bekhorah* alludes to Chokhmah, the first of the *Sefirot*. When blessings emanate from Chokhmah, they pass through Binah and then descend, through the *birkayim* [knees/legs], to the lower realms, where judgments reign. Blessings, drawn from Chokhmah to Malkhut, can mitigate the judgments of Malkhut (see *Likutey Moharan* I, 41).

Furthermore, Netzach and Hod are at the source of both prophecy and song (*Tikkuney Zohar* #21, p.49a). A person who rejoices earnestly and dances with joy can reach a level of prophecy, which corresponds to song and true joy. All those who support Torah (through charity) are also elevated by joy, for support of Torah corresponds to the feet, which support man. In fact, joy elevates everything associated with the feet (*Likutey Moharan* II, 81).

*

Yesod, the Tzaddik

We have seen that the legs and feet correspond to Netzach and Hod, which merge in Yesod. As we shall see in the next section, "The Reproductive System," the *Sefirah* of Yesod corresponds to the sexual organ. It also corresponds to the tzaddik, the righteous person, for it is he who overcomes the most difficult test of this world, that of controlling one's sexual urge.

Many of Rebbe Nachman's lessons refer to the tzaddikim as "the feet," for they are the principal support of the Jewish nation. Yet we also find that the Jewish People are connected to the tzaddik as the feet are connected to the body (see *Likutey Moharan* I, 20:10). Thus the tzaddik is referred to as both "feet" and "body." This apparent contradiction can be explained when we realize that the tzaddik is on a higher level than the average person, as the trunk and upper extremities of the body are higher than the legs. Nevertheless, it is the feet and legs which *support* the body. In the same way, the tzaddik's greatness is due, in a sense, to the Jewish People — those who depend upon him and to whom he must relate. He supports them, and they support him. Thus, when the Jews sinned with the Golden Calf, God told Moses (Exodus 32:7), "Go down," and our Sages explain (Berakhot 32a), "Go down from your level. I gave you greatness only because of Israel."

As we have pointed out, the spiritual energy that descends through Netzach and Hod is channeled through Yesod into Malkhut. Therefore, these four *Sefirot* combined are referred to as the "feet" of the Divine Persona. Let us examine in what way the tzaddikim correspond to the legs and feet, in order to better understand why Netzach and Hod are said to merge in Yesod. We must also understand why the Jewish People are considered the "feet" of the tzaddik — why they are compared to Malkhut in respect of the tzaddik, who is compared to Yesod. This will help us to understand the meaning of leadership and who is worthy of the task.

Rebbe Nachman taught:

> The generation's leaders are represented by the feet, because advice corresponds to the feet, as in (Exodus 11:8), "The people who are at your feet." Rashi explains this phrase to mean "those who follow your advice." When the Jews were preparing for their Exodus from Egypt and all that it represented, they had to leave behind their material surroundings and embark upon the ultimate spiritual journey to Sinai and the Land of Israel. Their most basic need at that point was for a devoted leader who could advise each individual according to his own requirements. This leader they found in Moses, whose self-sacrifice for the sake of his people is well documented. It is this combination of self-sacrifice and the God-given wisdom to advise which established Moses as the paradigm of leadership. Thus, leaders are those who can give truly beneficial advice which will help their people advance spiritually. Because these leaders *go out* among the people and mingle with them, *advising* them on how

to repent and serve God, they are compared to the feet (*Likutey Moharan* I, 22:1).

The verse in Deuteronomy (7:12) states, "And it shall come to pass, *ekev*, if you shall hear these judgments..." The term *ekev* literally means the heel of the foot, which corresponds to judgments. One who *hears* and heeds the "feet" of the nation, indicating the true leaders who give rebuke, can know when judgments are about to descend upon the world, and can help mitigate them by repenting (*Likutey Moharan* I, 22:15). Thus we see that the interaction between the leaders and the people occurs at the level of the "feet." The reason for this is that humility plays a crucial role in the relationship between a leader and his followers. The legs represent humility and modesty, for they are limbs that are generally concealed and are "beneath" the body. When a person is humble, he is willing to hear others and listen to their advice and, based on this advice, he is able to work on improving himself.

Rebbe Nachman teaches that even more than a worthy generation, a generation which is on a lower spiritual level needs a leader who can instill in it very great wisdom and intellect. Those who are on lower levels, especially in the era prior to Mashiach's coming, represent the "feet," that is, the lower extremities.

The ARI writes that every soul in every generation is rooted in the soul of Adam, the first man. The souls of the earlier generations were rooted in Adam's upper extremities. As the generations approach the days of Mashiach, the new souls which arise are rooted in Adam's lower extremities (*Tikkuney Zohar* #70, p.138b; see *Shaar HaGilgulim*, #30–31). It is for this reason that the time preceding Mashiach's coming is known as "*Ikveta d'Meshicha*" (Footsteps of the Messiah), for these last generations stem from Adam's heels and feet. The ultimate leader necessary for such a generation can be no less than someone like Moses, who parallels Mashiach (*Likutey Moharan* II, 39:1). May he come speedily, in our days. Amen.

* * *

Part Nine

The Reproductive System

40

Introduction

The reproductive system highlights the anatomical differences between a male and a female. These differences are outwardly visible and reflect the amazing, God-given qualities that enable a human being to bring new life into the world.

We open this section with an overview of the male and female reproductive organs. After having apprised ourselves of some of the most wondrous aspects of our biological organs, we will be better able to appreciate their spiritual counterparts. Although reproduction involves the entire array of ten *Sefirot* from Keter through Malkhut, we will concentrate in particular on the last two *Sefirot*, Yesod (Foundation) and Malkhut (Kingship).

*

Reproduction is made possible when a male and female cohabit. In the process, the male delivers semen, a jelly-like fluid containing several million sperm cells, into the female reproductive tract. When a single sperm cell fertilizes an ovum (egg) of the female, an embryo is formed, which develops throughout pregnancy and results in a newborn infant.

A male reaches puberty, that stage of his development at which he becomes capable of sexual reproduction, at around the age of thirteen. (That is why, according to Jewish law, he is considered a "man" at this age.) The male reproductive system, which is external to the body, consists of the scrotum, testes and sexual organ. The sperm, or seed, is produced and developed through a multitude of internal glands and ducts in the testes, which also produce male hormones. When the male is aroused, the organ becomes erect, enabling ejaculation, or the discharge of semen, to occur. The reason the main male reproductive organs lie outside the body is that the internal body temperature is too high to sustain the development of the sperm. The scrotum is designed to maintain the sperm cells at a temperature slightly lower than that inside the body.

The female reproductive system, which is housed within the body, includes the ovaries, which produce ova, or eggs, as well as female hormones; the uterine tubes (also called the oviducts or the fallopian tubes); and the uterus, or womb. At around the age of twelve, when a female reaches puberty, she begins her menstrual cycle — the process that prepares the uterine lining to receive the fertilized eggs. With the marital union, the reproductive fluids of both partners unite and fertilization can take place, usually within the uterine tubes.

The fertilized egg divides to form an embryo, which is implanted in the wall of the uterus, there to develop until it is able to survive outside the uterus. Throughout its development, the embryo (the child in its very earliest stages of development in the uterus) and the fetus (the term given to describe the developing child after the first three months following conception) is nourished through the placenta, which enables the exchange of nutrients, oxygen and waste products between the mother and the developing child.

Childbirth begins when the fetus reaches "maturity." During labor, the uterine wall begins contracting rhythmically, slowly at first, and then with increasing frequency and intensity (causing labor pains), until the miracle of childbirth occurs.

After childbirth the mother has the natural ability to provide nourishment for her infant in the form of human milk through lactation, a process for which her body has been preparing throughout pregnancy.

*

The ARI offers several explanations for the fact that puberty begins for the female at the age of twelve, while it takes an additional year for the male to develop. Essays on this topic are scattered throughout several chapters of the *Etz Chaim* and are too lengthy to discuss here. The reader is encouraged to research this topic independently (see *Etz Chaim* 25:8; *ibid.* 35:2).

Reb Noson explains that this difference between the male and female ages of maturation is due to the fact that the male corresponds to Zer Anpin — which, in turn, corresponds to the Written Torah, which is expounded through the Thirteen Exegetical Principles. He therefore becomes an "adult" at the age of thirteen. The female corresponds to Malkhut, which is conceptually the embodiment of the Twelve Tribes, the kingdom of holiness and faith (the Kingdom of Israel, who accepted the Torah at Sinai, is comprised of the Twelve Tribes; see also *Likutey Moharan* I, 36). She therefore reaches adulthood at twelve years of age (*Likutey Halakhot, Dayanim* 3:26).

As the physical dimension mirrors the spiritual, the perfection of the union between Zer Anpin and Malkhut is reflected in the union of a husband and wife. The "seed" of the spiritual plane is the spiritual energy which descends directly from God through the *Sefirot*, from the highest levels downward, until it reaches the *Sefirah* of Yesod. This energy is referred to as *shefa* (usually translated as "life force," "effulgence" or "bounty"). As *shefa* descends and passes through the entire array of *Sefirot*, each *Sefirah* contributes its own unique characteristics. By the time it reaches Yesod, the "seed" is fully developed and ready to be transferred to Malkhut. It is within Malkhut that the "fruits of Yesod" are deposited, so that God's Kingdom can be revealed and established on earth.

In a similar manner to the way in which each of the *Sefirot* contribute their unique characteristics to Yesod, each part of the human body contributes its unique characteristics to the seed which is needed for the formation of the human child. We learn this from the Talmud which teaches (see *Niddah* 43a) that the sperm is drawn from the entire human body, from *all* the organs, glands and hormones (for they all contribute to an individual's state of health). In addition, the Zohar teaches that the semen, white in color, originates in the "white matter" of the brain; hence the mind is the *true* source of human seed (*Zohar* III, 235b; see *Likutey Moharan* I, 29:4). (On a practical level, a person about to cohabit has first had some *thought* of marital relations, no matter how fleeting, which precedes his actions.) Comparable to the system involving the interaction of the *Sefirot*, which begins in the *mochin* (the intellect) and descends to Yesod before being transferred to Malkhut, so too, the *thoughts* of a person during cohabitation have an enormous effect on the formation of the unborn infant's characteristics, since the seed originates in the mind.

The transfer of the spiritual "seed" from Zer Anpin to Malkhut, corresponding to the fertilization of the egg within the female, results in what could be seen as Malkhut's "pregnancy," and to the revelation (birth) of new *shefa* in the world. In the same way, the entire array of one's "personal *sefirot*" (manifest in one's intellect and character traits), from Keter and Chokhmah downward, all contribute to the development of one's physical seed (see *Likutey Moharan* I, 10:5, note 35).

*

Yesod and Malkhut: A Kabbalistic Introduction

Many of the concepts related to Yesod and Malkhut, which correspond to the union between male and female, will be discussed in the coming chapters. Here we present only a brief introduction to these topics.

Zer Anpin comprises six *Sefirot*, starting with Chesed, Yesod being the sixth. Specifically, the energy of Chesed, Gevurah and the *Sefirot* that follow are all contained and remain within Zer Anpin until they reach the *Sefirah* of Yesod. (Thus, the revelation of Chesed, etc., takes place only on the level of Yesod.) It is through Yesod that Zer Anpin transmits *shefa* (bounty) to Malkhut.

Malkhut receives that *shefa* and gestates with it, until it is ready to be transferred to the world for the benefit of mankind.

Sefer Yetzirah explains that the six directions of space (north, south, east, west, up and down) correspond to the six *Sefirot* of Zer Anpin. For one standing in any given location, the six directions point *outward*. This actually defines the masculine aspect, for a male relates to the world and expresses himself with an "outward" orientation. Malkhut, the feminine aspect, on the other hand, is a single *Sefirah* and is the center point which draws towards itself all the six directions of Zer Anpin. The feminine aspect of Creation is thus represented in an introspective mode and is the ultimate focus of Zer Anpin.

Expanding on this point, we can view Zer Anpin and Malkhut as the six weekdays and Shabbat. The six days of the week correspond to the six *Sefirot* of Zer Anpin, the male aspect, when we go out and about our business — whether our material needs or our spiritual struggles. On Shabbat, we are on the female level, because we can now absorb the fruits of all we have done during the week. Thus, a person could work very hard, physically or spiritually, all week long, but without Shabbat he has no way of *receiving* the benefits of his efforts (see *Innerspace*, p.75).

Zer Anpin and Malkhut have a very special relationship as they correspond to the final *Vav* and *Heh* of the Tetragrammaton. This relationship is an extension of the relationship between *Abba*/Chokhmah (Father/Wisdom) and *Imma*/Binah (Mother/Understanding), which correspond respectively to the *Yod* and the first *Heh* of the Tetragrammaton (see Appendix D). The difference is that, whereas Chokhmah and Binah (as Father and Mother) are considered to be of "equal status," Zer Anpin and Malkhut are not — at first — equals; rather they are depicted as "son" and "daughter." Zer Anpin is Malkhut's "older brother," and she is his "younger sister." As "children" they are separate and different, and must *grow into* the roles of equal partners. Only when they both mature does Zer Anpin unite with

Malkhut and call her (Songs 4:9, 4:10, 4:12, 5:1, 5:2) "my sister, my bride." Nearly three quarters of the ARI's writings deal with the "growth and maturation" of Zer Anpin and Malkhut.

In the human growth process, the development of the ability to reproduce signals a major milestone in maturation. Maturation and reproduction go hand in hand; they both involve Daat. In observing the growth of a child, for instance, we find that a certain level of intellect is apparent at birth; it is clear that a new mind has come to the world. The healthy infant is immediately sharply aware of his environment and responds to it in his own way; his interrelated central and peripheral nervous systems are functional from the start. Within a few months, the infant gains some control over his arms and hands, while his legs gain strength and coordination several months later. At this point, the child's intellect is extremely limited. He has yet to grow, studying and storing information in his developing mind, learning and understanding. By the time he reaches puberty, we begin to see that he has acquired his own body of knowledge. This knowledge is his level of Daat. When a child matures to the point that he is ready to procreate, he is able to bring additional revelations of intellect into the world.

Yesod, as we have seen, corresponds to the sexual organ, which becomes the focal point of the release of both the spiritual and physical energy which stems from the combined powers of the entire body and all the *Sefirot*. It can thus be said that a person's approach to marital relations is the primary indication of his innate character, of how much he has worked on developing himself and to what extent he has attained psychological maturity. That is, character and self-development go hand-in-hand with the growth of one's intellect. This is true for both men and women.

Specifically, the nature of one's Chesed (ability to love and care for another) or Gevurah (sense of judgment and restraint), in whatever manner and to whatever degree it has been developed, will find its expression in the way one relates to one's spouse before, during and following marital relations. Here it is extremely important for each partner to develop the sensitivity to know how to include God in the relationship. This in turn establishes the Kingdom of Heaven in this world. Only when peace reigns and people interact with each other with the utmost respect and love can the full glory of God become revealed.

*

Male and female He created them.

Genesis 1:27

The Zohar teaches that every soul actually contains both "male" and "female" characteristics. When the time comes for a given soul to descend to the physical world, it separates and its characteristics become a "dual entity," one part being male and one part female. This is the great significance of marriage and the marital union: it brings the "two halves" of a soul back together again (see *Zohar* III, 283b).

We can thus better understand an interesting teaching of the ARI: Each of the Ten *Sefirot* corresponds to one of the Holy Names of God, each of which expresses a specific power of God. The Holy Name which corresponds to Yesod is *Shadai* (שדי), which translates as, "There is enough!" This name implies that God has the full ability to bestow upon each and every person all his needs. The Holy Name corresponding to Malkhut is *Adonay*, which connotes "Master," for He is the Master of the Universe and *King* over all (see Appendix D).

The verse states (Genesis 35:11), "I am *El Shadai*; be fruitful and multiply..." Expanding the letters of the Holy Name *SHaDaiY* (שדי) (*Shin Dalet Yod*) yields the letters שין (*Shin, Yod, Nun*), דלת (*Dalet Lamed Tav*), and יוד (*Yod, Vav, Dalet*). If we eliminate the initial letters of each of these, we are left with the "hidden letters" of *Yod, Nun* (numerical value is 60), *Lamed, Tav* (430), and *Vav, Dalet* (10). Together, the numerical values of these letters is equal to 500.

We have pointed out (above, Chapter 36) that a male has 248 limbs, while a female possesses 252 limbs. The sum of the limbs of the unified entity which is formed by the joining of two separate individuals, a male and a female, is 500 (see *Baal HaTurim* on Genesis 35:11). As marital relations are to be performed modestly, *hidden* from the eye, these "hidden letters" (which are not pronounced) correspond to the special relationship between male and female, which unites them in holiness so that they can procreate. When a couple recognizes the importance of the marital act — the beauty and intimacy that exists when two opposites merge into one unit — then peace is attained, and the Kingship of God is established ever more firmly.

*

Yesod

The ARI speaks of *Or Yashar* (Direct Light) and *Or Chozer* (Reflected Light). God sends us His direct bounty, and we are sustained by it. Through it we live and are able to perform good deeds. Reciprocally, these good deeds bring God a certain pleasure. Like a father and mother, God loves it when His children "grow up" and become capable of emulating Him. This is the *nachas* (pleasure) He receives from our good deeds. When we strive to emulate God, it is considered as if we are giving something back to Him.
Rebbe Nachman taught:

> The benefactor corresponds to the masculine aspect, while the beneficiary corresponds to the feminine aspect. Whoever *gives* to others corresponds to the male. Whoever *receives* corresponds to the female. This principle applies to all Universes, on all levels. Even God, when He receives pleasure from the performance of good deeds by His creations, is considered, as it were, a Beneficiary, reflecting the Feminine Aspect (*Likutey Moharan* I, 73:2).

This concept may be viewed in terms of man's interaction with God through the Ten *Sefirot*: God's bounty extends from Above, down through the path of all the *Sefirot*, through Yesod and into Malkhut. Malkhut, as we have often mentioned, is the lowest of the *Sefirot* and the principal point through which man can come to recognize and serve God. Accepting God's Kingship is the first step in approaching Him. Thus, initially it is through the *Sefirah* of Malkhut that we interact and establish a fundamental relationship with God. (Remember that Malkhut corresponds to the female, which is in keeping with the role of *accepting* the yoke of God's Kingdom.) Only after we have accepted the yoke of His Malkhut (Kingdom) can we begin to relate to Yesod as the bridge to the loftier realms. Just as God takes pleasure in sending us bounty, He also gains pleasure from His creations as they advance to ever higher levels in their recognition and service of God.

The *Sefirah* of Yesod corresponds to the *brit*, the male reproductive organ; in the Kabbalah, Yesod is referred to as *Chai Olamim* — the "Life of the Worlds" (*Zohar* I, 193b): "Life," both because it serves the very essence and purpose of life, and because it is said to be "alive," that is, instrumental in bringing forth life; and "Worlds," because Yesod acts as the catalyst, allowing for the interaction between the Upper Worlds and this world (Malkhut). Just as the *Sefirah* of Yesod transfers *shefa* from the upper *Sefirot* to the *Sefirah* of Malkhut, Yesod is the relay point where Malkhut, having derived its life force and bounty from Above, can return to God the pleasure of His creations serving Him.

"Yesod thus represents one of the greatest human pleasures that exists. It is a type of pleasure that involves the deepest levels of the human psyche. Pleasure can be either good or evil, as it can lead one in either direction" (*Innerspace*, p.69). One's personal level of Yesod (Foundation) can indeed be one of holiness, and can propel one to search for ever greater levels of Godliness. On the other hand, sexual desire can be used (and often is) to lead one away from spirituality. In the coming chapters we will discuss the significance of the fact that both lust and spirituality emanate from the same source.

* * *

41

The Covenant of Abraham

Abraham's father, Terach, was preeminent among the idolators of his day. Growing up in idolatrous surroundings, Abraham always felt a void in his life. Seeking and searching for fulfillment, he found God; through incredibly difficult periods of famine, war and childlessness, he remained faithful to Him. Ultimately, God made an everlasting covenant with Abraham and his descendants.

> God appeared to Abraham and said, "I am *El Shadai*; walk before Me and be perfect. And I will make My Covenant with you...I will establish My Covenant between Me and you and your offspring...I will be your God...and you will inherit this land...This is My Covenant...All your male children shall be circumcised..."
>
> Genesis 17:1–14

The Covenant (*brit* in Hebrew) is the pact which God made with Abraham and the Jewish nation.

We must appreciate the significance of the fact that God, the King of kings, has made a pact with His People. Is it possible that simply by undergoing circumcision in infancy, we have done our part in the fulfillment of the Covenant? Could it be that from the moment of circumcision we are absolved from *guarding* the Covenant and all that it stands for? Were any mortal king to make a Covenant with a people, would they not honor and cherish it, and do their utmost to fulfill it at all times? They would certainly make every effort to safeguard it from being violated! How much more should a Jew feel obligated to constantly honor, fulfill and guard his Covenant with God, throughout his life!

What, then, is the substance of this Covenant? What exactly is required of a Jew who would heed this pact? In fact, where are we told that the Covenant must be cherished and guarded throughout life, beyond that which is actually written in the account of the pact God made with Abraham, that is, the *act* of circumcision?

The specific sign of God's Covenant, the sexual organ, has been empowered with the ability to initiate new life. But procreation can be accomplished only through a sexual union. The Talmud teaches that there are three partners in the formation of a child: "The father contributes the white of the body [bones, tissues, etc.]; the mother contributes the red [skin, flesh, etc.]; and God breathes life into the child..." (*Niddah* 31a). A child enters the world only when these three partners function together. How is this accomplished?

The Hebrew word for marriage is *KiDduSHin*, which stems from the word *KoDeSH* (holy). When the union between husband and wife is a holy one, the Divine Presence, the Third Partner, resides with them (cf. *Sotah* 17a). Thus, the sexual union, when performed in holiness, is a reflection of the couple's attitude of respect for the God-granted powers of procreation. Living within the guidelines of permissible sexual relationships ensures the guarding of the sign of the Covenant, and hence the safekeeping of the Covenant itself.

Rebbe Nachman taught:

> As long as a person marries according to Torah law and maintains his marital behavior within the Torah's boundaries, he is reckoned as one who cherishes the Covenant of Abraham (*Likutey Moharan* I, 11:7). The principal means of drawing near to God is through guarding the Covenant (*Likutey Moharan* I, 29:5).

*

The Circumcision

The physical aspect of our commitment to the Covenant between God and Abraham is circumcision. A male is born with a foreskin covering the glans, the tip of the organ. This foreskin is superfluous, and, as with other "excesses" of the body, it can be removed without adverse effects. The *brit milah*, the Covenant of Circumcision, makes its removal a requirement. The process of the circumcision involves the removal of the foreskin, called *orlah*, to reveal the glans.

There are actually two layers which cover the glans: the first is the foreskin itself, which must be removed, and the second is a thin membrane, which must be opened and peeled back from the glans. During the circumcision the *orlah* is cut off completely; this part of the process is called the *milah*. However, *milah* leaves the tip of the organ still covered by the membrane, and so *periyah* is performed. *Periyah* means to uncover or reveal, and this process involves the opening of the membrane in order to reveal the tip of the organ. Removing the foreskin while leaving the membrane would render the circumcision invalid.

The ARI writes that the mitzvah of *brit milah* corresponds to the prophetic vision of the Holy Chariot that Ezekiel witnessed. "And I saw a storm wind from the north, a great cloud and a flashing fire; a *Nogah* [glowing radiance] was about it, and a *Chashmal* appeared in the fire" (Ezekiel 1:4). Rebbe Nachman offers an interpretation of this vision as it applies to the human condition (see *Likutey Moharan* I, 82; *ibid.* 19:3–5): The storm wind can be said to represent the obstacles presented by family, friends and financial difficulties that one faces in one's spiritual quest. The great cloud represents doubts and confusion, such as questions of faith. The flashing fire alludes to avarice, sexual lust, arrogance and uncontrolled bursts of temper. The *nogah* is a brightness which is composed partially of good and partially of evil. The good of the *nogah* must be reincorporated into holiness, so that the evil, deprived of its life source, will wither and die. The *Chashmal* serves as a barrier, preventing the evil of the *nogah* from penetrating the realm of holiness.

The foreskin represents the three totally evil *kelipot* (literally, "husks") — represented by the storm wind, the great cloud and the flashing fire in Ezekiel's vision. It completely covers the glans, which is called *Ateret HaYesod* (the Crown of the Yesod) and prevents Divine *shefa* (bounty) from passing through Yesod to Malkhut as it should. Removing the "foreskin" — *milah* — conceptually removes these three *kelipot* from Yesod, allowing for a free transfer of bounty. Still, unless the Yesod is *fully* revealed, this transfer cannot take place properly.

The thin membrane around the glans, corresponding to the fourth *kelipah, Kelipat Nogah,* must be peeled back. We are thus commanded to perform *periyah*, the peeling back of the membrane and the revealing of the glans. Once the *periyah* is performed, the evil element in *nogah* is prevented from entering the realm of holiness.

When discussing the removal of the foreskin, Reb Noson speaks of other applications of the terms:

> There is an injunction known as *orlah*, which prohibits the eating of the fruits of newly planted trees for the first three years. During the fourth year one may partake of the fruits, but only after they have been redeemed. From the fifth year onward, one can enjoy the fruits of one's labors without restriction (see Leviticus 19:23–25). This teaches us the value of humility and of rejecting arrogance. Corresponding to the first four years, there are four levels of humility. A person should be humble before those who are greater than he, before his peers, and even before those of lesser status than himself. When he reaches that third level of humility at which he considers himself to be lesser than all others, then he must strive for an even higher degree of humility.
>
> The first three levels of humility contain a measure of arrogance; these levels correspond to the three evil *kelipot* — for on each of these levels a person refuses, to some degree, to humble himself before others. Even someone who acts with "total humility" — a humility that places him beneath the norm of human esteem — can also possess some arrogance, because he may not feel that it is fitting for him to be so humbled. This is the subtle evil of *nogah*. Only when he realizes that before the

Creator he must always be completely humble does his *nogah* become a totally positive force (see *Likutey Halakhot, Orlah* 5:1–2).

Man's single most evil characteristic is arrogance, and it must be eradicated. It is this characteristic which corresponds to the foreskin. Arrogance is a trait that tends to sabotage itself: it is its own primary source of humiliation, for an arrogant person is despised, and it is his very arrogance that causes people to seek to discredit him. By his actions as well he brings humiliation upon himself, expecting and demanding that things go his way, when too often they don't (see *Likutey Moharan* II, 82).

Nowhere is this particular shortcoming more evident than in people's attitude towards their sexual prowess; some people tend to "show off," yet, when they do it generally becomes a source of humiliation. Conversely, he who seeks the spirituality of the Covenant of Abraham removes his foreskin — his arrogance — which is the source of his humiliation and shame. Rebbe Nachman thus taught that "shame and embarrassment coincide with sexual immorality, and sexual immorality is synonymous with a blemished Covenant" (*Likutey Moharan* I, 19:3).

Rebbe Nachman also taught:

The *brit* corresponds to the *CHaSHMaL* which protects one from evil [as above], for *CHaSH* carries the meaning of "silence" and *MaL* suggests the *MiLah* [circumcision]. We have already seen that the foreskin corresponds to humiliation. When a person is insulted or otherwise embarrassed, yet remains silent and controls his natural desire to retort to the point that he bears no malice even in his heart, then that person reveals the qualities of the *brit*, thereby gaining tremendous merit (*Likutey Moharan* I, 82:2).

Thus the Covenant of Abraham cultivates within a person the characteristic of self-control; though humiliated, he is able to restrain himself from responding. This behavior cleanses his own heart (see also above, Chapter 9, "The Bloodstream"). It is most significant that the heart is also said to have a foreskin, and one who turns to

God is able (and in fact required) to "circumcise" his heart (cf. Deuteronomy 10:16).

(It is interesting to note that there is an anatomical foreskin of the heart which is known as the pericardium. There are certain conditions which Western medicine treats by surgically removing the pericardium.)

*

Rebbe Nachman teaches that the *brit* parallels the concept of "be fruitful and multiply." By guarding the Covenant one can merit an easy livelihood, and one's income can be "fruitful" (*Likutey Moharan* I, 23:4; *ibid.* 34:4). The *brit* is also referred to as (Numbers 25:12) "the covenant of peace," because a person who guards his Covenant will succeed in finding that elusive blessing of peace — within his home, within his body and within his soul. Where there is peace, there is bounty and blessing, as we are taught (Psalms 147:14), "[God] makes your borders peaceful; He provides bountiful crops."

The prophet (Ezekiel 36:30) speaks of "the shame of hunger." This corresponds to a reflection of the shame of the foreskin, as in (Joshua 5:8–9), "After Joshua had circumcised all the people...God said, 'Today I have removed the shame of Egypt from you.'" Removing the foreskin, that is, eliminating the *kelipot* surrounding the brit, which are represented by "hunger" and "famine," opens the channels for bounty to reach a person (see *Likutey Moharan* I, 39). Thus, denigrating the Covenant in any way can lead to poverty (*Likutey Moharan* I, 7:7).

*

A Good Deal

God informed Abraham that He was making a Covenant with him and with all his offspring after him. This Covenant is the sign that God will be true to the Jewish people, and that the Jewish People will be true to God. This is the Covenant of (Genesis 17:10): "You shall circumcise every male child." Rebbe Nachman thus teaches: All Jews are called tzaddikim, in that they are circumcised (*Likutey Moharan* I, 23:10). In other words, the merit of the *brit milah* is very great: it is sufficient to earn a person the distinction of holiness

and the accolade of "tzaddik." The Zohar illustrates this with the
following story:

> In fulfillment of God's commandment, Abraham
> circumcised his eldest son, Ishmael (Genesis 17:25). As a result, for
> four hundred years, Ishmael's guardian angel presented his
> claim for reward before the Heavenly Court.
>
> "Is it not true that whoever has undergone a *brit milah* has a
> portion in Your Name?" the angel questioned.
>
> "Yes," God answered.
>
> "If so," the angel asked, "why has Ishmael not been given a
> portion of holiness equal to that of Abraham's other son, Isaac?"
>
> "Ishmael's circumcision was not performed for the sake of
> the mitzvah" was God's reply.
>
> "Nevertheless," the angel demanded, "he was circumcised."
>
> To this God answered, "Ishmael will indeed be given a
> portion of holiness as his reward. However, just as his *brit milah*
> was empty and void of deeper meaning, so too, the portion of
> holiness which he will receive will be empty and void. The Holy
> Land will be Ishmael's reward, but his possession of it will come
> only when it is empty of Jews."

Indeed, the Zohar continues, Arab occupation of the Holy
Land will be the major factor that will prevent the Jewish people
from returning to their homeland, until such time as the merit of
the mitzvah of Ishmael's circumcision will terminate (Zohar II, 32a).

If this is the reward for *brit milah* when it is not performed for
the sake of the mitzvah, devoid of meaning, how much greater
must be the reward for those who perform the *brit milah* for the
sake of fulfilling God's will!

Furthermore, the Midrash states that Abraham sits by the
entrance to Gehennom and protects anyone who has been properly
circumcised, effectively preventing him from entering.
Nevertheless, if one has willfully abused his *brit*, then Abraham
will not defend him. How does Abraham know whether or not a
soul had guarded the holiness of his *brit* during his lifetime? If he

has not, a foreskin will grow back to identify him as one who abused its gift through sexual misconduct. One who sincerely tries to safeguard the Covenant will be recognized by Abraham and saved from Gehennom (*Bereishit Rabbah* 48:8).

*

Love and Marriage

Abraham is the paradigm of *chesed* (acts of kindness). His love for his fellow man was so great that he was constantly seeking ways to help others. He therefore merited to be the first person commanded to perform the mitzvah of *milah*. What is the connection between Chesed and *milah*?

As we have seen, the energy of Chesed can be revealed only through Yesod. In Abraham's time the Torah had not yet been given; by what means was his devotion to God manifest? Through his great yearning and desire to serve God. Abraham felt it was his life's mission to reveal the Chesed, the Lovingkindness, of God and His Kingdom to the world. He also had an overwhelming desire to share his own love and kindness with others. In order to succeed in bringing so much love into the world, he needed to be circumcised. The circumcision removed any *kelipot* that might prevent him from transferring God's Chesed and *shefa* to others. Spiritually, of course, this meant he had to banish any negative traits, symbolized by the foreskin. Rebbe Nachman taught:

> *Chesed* — love — is displayed through the desire and yearning that a person has. One who has great love will yearn deeply to attain that which he desires. This love is manifest in the *brit* (*Likutey Moharan* I, 31:6).

Love, like *chesed*, means giving unreservedly of oneself to others. This defines the goal of marriage: Each partner must be committed to giving fully and unconditionally of him/herself to the other. The marriage bond is essentially a spiritual one, a bond that transcends the physical desires and material needs of either partner. One who focuses on the spiritual bond that exists between male and female realizes that there is a spirit which surrounds their love, one which far surpasses their physical bond. Couples who approach marriage with this attitude can weather the trying times that they inevitably encounter, for their Covenant centers around the greater needs of their partners — their spiritual needs.

When, on the other hand, misguided couples marry solely on the basis of physical attraction, the marriage deteriorates with the passage of time; their relationship wears itself out, and they begin to drift apart. If their approach to life tends to be somewhat old-fashioned, they may feel a responsibility to stay together, perhaps for the sake of the children, but neither partner will relish the relationship any longer. If they are "in tune with the times," they may become entangled in illicit, extramarital relationships. Falsehood makes its way into their lives and becomes part of their daily routine. Fear of discovery then corrodes whatever is left of a dying relationship.

If the *chesed* (i.e., the feelings of love and kindness) in a relationship is blemished, then the *brit* is blemished, for the manifestation of Chesed is Yesod. That is, if Chesed is already blemished at the source, it will be blemished when it is manifest as the Yesod, and the physical relationship within the marriage will reflect that. In most cases, the love had been blemished to begin with, never having been a *true* love, based on a spiritual bond. Furthermore, as we have already explained, Chesed is the first revelation of the *mochin* (above, Chapter 36). As such, a deceitful or broken Covenant is a sure sign of a blemished mind (see *Likutey Moharan* I, 34:7).

Rebbe Nachman thus teaches:

> The prophet foretells (Isaiah 11:9), "They shall neither destroy nor harm in all My holy mountain, for the earth will be filled with Daat [Knowledge] of God as the waters cover the sea." The attributes of compassion and kindness depend wholly on Daat, and in the Messianic Future, Daat will be very great. For this reason, when Mashiach comes, there will be no cruelty or desire to harm others. Compassion will spread far and wide.
>
> Nowadays, however, there are times when the forces of evil

can suck nourishment from compassion... Then compassion becomes distorted. When compassion is distorted, it turns into cruelty, and Daat itself is blemished... When Daat is blemished, passions for illicit relations [such as adultery] are aroused. This is in keeping with what the Sages said (*Sotah* 3a): "No man sins unless a spirit of folly enters him [and distorts his Daat]." When, on the other hand, Daat is perfected, one is protected from these passions (*Likutey Moharan* II, 8:2).

Rebbe Nachman is telling us that not all love and compassion are what they seem to be. One may, for example, forgo reprimanding a child out of "compassion," but that child will lose a chance to learn what is expected of him. At other times, one might act with apparent cruelty in disciplining a child, yet this may serve to strengthen the child's character. The lack of adequate discipline may be a reflection of blemished Daat, where compassion is misplaced. Thus a perfect balance, as reflected in Tiferet and Yesod (the center column; see Appendix D), is a necessary element of any relationship. This balance in relating to others displays a balanced mind, a well-developed Daat, where love and compassion are true and beneficial, and where one can relate to others with honesty.

Someone whose Daat is balanced has the ability to maintain a mature, loving, fruitful marriage. This is because his Daat will filter down to his Yesod, to every aspect of his personality and character traits (reflected by his personal array of *sefirot*). Eventually, it is manifest in a healthy relationship with his spouse, which involves giving, as well as honesty and faithfulness. In turn, guarding the covenant and establishing a trustworthy relationship will contribute to a well-developed Daat.

However, one whose Daat is blemished will come to have illicit relations. He will not be faithful to his spouse because his intentions behind the relationship are not healthy or, in all probability, honest. In fact, our Sages refer to an illicit relationship as falsehood and idolatry (*Zohar* II, 87b; see also *Likutey Moharan* I, 36:8), for one who is involved in an illicit relationship is living a lie. Such a person cannot discover spirituality. Through his own actions, he has removed himself from truth, which is Godliness. Thus he will in turn blemish the Daat which would normally bring him closer to God.

We thus find that the *brit* and faith are interdependent (see *Likutey Moharan* I, 31:3). Being a loyal and faithful spouse is the result of guarding one's sexual conduct which, in turn, is the result of a balanced Daat. Controlling one's lustful desires establishes one on a path of honesty and truth.

Interestingly, the attribute of faith was also the hallmark of Abraham, as Scripture declares (Genesis 15:6), "He believed in God." Based on this verse, the Midrash teaches that "Abraham was the first of the believers and the first to circumcise himself" (*Esther Rabbah, Pesichta* 10; *Shir HaShirim Rabbah* 4:19; see *Likutey Moharan* I, 31:6). The connection is intrinsic to both faith and the *brit*: Since Abraham was the first in his era to have faith in the True God, it was he who was given the mitzvah of circumcision.

Amalek, on the other hand, represents atheism. This was manifest when the Amalekites battled against the Jews: they castrated their victims (see Deuteronomy 25:18, Rashi; *Likutey Moharan* II, 19:3). Rebbe Nachman thus teaches that "faith can be kept only when one guards the Covenant" (*Likutey Moharan* I, 31:3).

The concepts are closely related: one who guards the Covenant is (or becomes) an honest and trustworthy person. Furthermore, as we learned above, through guarding the Covenant a person is able to attain true Daat, an expanded consciousness, for through the Covenant his mind is shielded. Conversely, someone who blemishes the Covenant is "wasting his mind" and reduces his intellect to the level of his biological urges (see also *Likutey Moharan* I, 29:4).

Thus, true Daat goes hand in hand with the guarding of the Covenant (see *Likutey Moharan* I, 177:2), as do love and compassion, the manifestations of that intellect. And adultery, being untrue to one's partner, blemishes the Covenant. It is the equivalent (on a human level) of idolatry, disloyalty to the Divine.

However, Rebbe Nachman teaches that there is recourse. The Kabbalistic meditations for the month of Elul correspond to the guarding of the Covenant. These meditations include learning how to "travel along the path of repentance." Anyone who strays from his ordained path and becomes enticed by immorality blemishes the paths and byways upon which he must travel throughout his life. Repenting and beginning anew to guard the Covenant can rectify one's misdeeds and lead a person back to the proper path (*Likutey Moharan* II, 87).

*

Shadai: "There is Enough!"

We can now better understand how the Holy Name *Shadai* (see above, Chapter 40) is related to the concept of the *brit*, and how one who guards the Covenant can draw spirituality from this Holy Name and thereby come to recognize God.

The Name *ShaDaI* is an acronym for *Sheyesh DaI*, "there is enough!" God possesses sufficient resources to be able to sustain each and every facet of Creation. This Holy Name reflects the idea that one need not look beyond one's own boundaries — whether intellectual, emotional, material or financial — in order to find satisfaction. One who seeks spirituality will invariably be sustained with "enough" by He Who sustains all.

Consider the following teachings:

Shadai indicates contentment with one's lot in life. This is reflected in one's faith, for one with a strong measure of faith does not lust after material possessions. Guarding the Covenant and, in so doing, breaking our lust draws upon us the power of this Holy Name of God (see *Likutey Moharan* I, 23:12).

Haughtiness leads one to blemish the Covenant. Guarding the Covenant reflects both restraint and humility. Restraint is an acknowledgement that God's resources are sufficient to provide for all one's needs (*Likutey Moharan* I, 11:3).

* * *

42

Yesod: The Tzaddik

Throughout the Talmud and Midrash we find references to the tzaddikim and their greatness, yet we do not find any concise description of what qualifies one to be called a tzaddik. How do we define a tzaddik? Clearly the reference is to a spiritual person. But is this "spiritual person" someone who is knowledgeable in Torah or someone who prays fervently? Is he one who is very attentive to certain mitzvot, or does he fulfill *all* the mitzvot to the fullest possible extent? The Kabbalah is very explicit about what a tzaddik is. "Who is a tzaddik?" the Zohar asks. "He is one who guards the Covenant" (Zohar I, 59b).

In the Kabbalah, Yesod corresponds to the level of tzaddik, the righteous person. Joseph is presented as the paradigm of the tzaddik: because he stood firm in his greatest trial, when he rejected the sexual advances of Potifar's wife (Genesis 39). Since, generally speaking, the male sexual drive is far stronger than that of the female (see Ketubot 64b), the focus of this chapter will relate mainly, but not exclusively, to the challenges faced by the male. However, many of the concepts discussed will apply equally to women.

Zer Anpin, which is composed of six of the lower *Sefirot*, represents a higher level than Malkhut, the lowest *Sefirah*. The nature of this relationship will be explained in greater detail below (Chapter 44). At this point, we can understand that Yesod, which is incorporated in Zer Anpin, implies a higher level which is the root or source of Malkhut, the level below it.

Rebbe Nachman teaches that there are two levels of the *brit*. The higher level refers to the level of tzaddik, guarding one's covenant. The lower level corresponds to Torah knowledge, which differentiates between the pure and the impure, the permitted and the forbidden, the fit and the unfit (*Likutey Moharan* I, 31:5). The higher level of the *brit* was achieved by Abraham, whose characteristic attribute was Chesed. As we have seen, the energy of Chesed becomes revealed only in Yesod; therefore it was to Abraham that the commandment of circumcision was given. The secondary, lower level of *brit* was achieved by Abraham's servant Eliezer, who mastered Abraham's teachings (*Yoma* 28b). Those who attain these two levels of *brit* are known as *tzaddik* and *lamdan*, a righteous person and a learned person, respectively. The learned person is necessarily on a lower level than the tzaddik, as one's knowledge must be subordinate to one's good deeds, for knowledge alone can mislead a person (see *Avot*, 3:17).

One who attains the more exalted level of *brit*, as Abraham did, can be very "fertile" indeed. Abraham is called (Genesis 17:5) "father of a multitude of nations": in addition to his own children, he "fathered" the souls of many converts. The person who ascends to a high level of righteousness can teach other souls to serve God (see *Likutey Moharan* I, 31:5–8).

We see, then, that to be a tzaddik is to have reached a most awesome level; it ranks above even the level of those who have mastered the entire Torah. Guarding the *brit* — observing those laws that pertain to the Covenant — enables even the simplest person to attain a level of tzaddik, though he may not be on the highest level of tzaddik. Many people may be skeptical of this concept. Is this *all* that is required to become a tzaddik? The answer, Rebbe Nachman tells us, is yes. "One can be a tzaddik even without being a scholar... Even the simplest person can be a tzaddik" (*Rabbi Nachman's Wisdom* #76).

The numerical value of the Hebrew word *brit* (ברית) is 612, for this one mitzvah is inclusive of all the other 612 mitzvot. The word

Torah (תורה) on the other hand is numerically equal to 611, as it too is included in the mitzvah of *brit*. We may thus conclude that guarding the *brit* is equivalent in value to all the other mitzvot combined. Any attempt we make to guard the Covenant by attaining sexual purity will automatically propel us towards Torah and holiness.

Furthermore, Rebbe Nachman teaches that one cannot even begin to grasp the teachings of a tzaddik unless one's mind is cleansed of lustful thoughts. Even if someone is learned, that is, he has mastered the lower level of *brit*, his studies can still mislead him. One must always strive to attain the higher level of *brit*, by cleansing oneself of lust. Only then can one understand the tzaddik's teachings (see *Likutey Moharan* I, 36:5). This is a basic doctrine for everyone, at every stage of life.

This discussion seems to imply an inherent contradiction: How can one ever hope to learn about spirituality if one's Covenant is blemished? A person cannot rectify that which is blemished until he first learns — from the tzaddik — how to rectify his wrongdoings. Yet one cannot grasp the tzaddik's teachings until one's wrongs have been rectified! This paradox is resolved through the principle that any individual is able to grasp the tzaddik's teachings according to the degree to which he is *willing* to rectify his wrongs. If a person accepts that his shortcomings are in fact shortcomings, that they stem from some flaw within *himself*, and that he must ultimately rely on the tzaddik's advice to help him correct that flaw, then he will be able to benefit from the tzaddik's teachings (*Parparaot LeChokhmah* I, 36:5).

Understanding this teaching is of fundamental importance when embarking on a spiritual quest. The Covenant is *the* foundation upon which one can truly begin to build one's spiritual life. Yet considering the temptations that exist, as will be discussed shortly, how can one ever hope to surmount the obstacles? The ideas of accepting responsibility for one's shortcomings and being *willing* to accept guidance from the tzaddik teach us that the option for Godliness is a real one, and *can* be attained by anyone, based on the *efforts* he puts into his search. Just as one can hope to reach the upper rungs of a ladder only if one first climbs up the lower rungs, so too, each individual's efforts to begin slowly and work steadily will contribute to an ever-increasing level of spirituality, enabling him eventually to enter the Gates of Holiness and actually taste the true sweetness of the tzaddik's teachings.

*

A Solid Foundation...

The tzaddik is the foundation of the world.

Proverbs 10:25

How does one attain the level of a tzaddik? How can one guard one's *brit*? What are the benefits of being careful to guard and cherish one's reproductive faculties, and what pitfalls does one face if one succumbs to the ever-present temptations?

Both the Talmud (*Gittin* 52a) and the Zohar (II, 203a) speak about a "storm wind" that can cause an upheaval in a person's home before the onset of Shabbat. The six weekdays parallel the six *Sefirot* of Zer Anpin, while Shabbat parallels Malkhut (see above, Chapter 40). Thus, when Yesod (the sixth *Sefirah*, paralleling the sixth day) is ready to transfer its seed to Malkhut — conceptually the onset of Shabbat — a "storm wind," that is, a sudden onslaught of obstacles, rages to prevent this transfer, by tempting one to succumb to anger or transgression. Temptations, just like the weekdays, are a constantly recurring cycle.

Since Malkhut corresponds both to one's mate and to speech (see above, Chapters 26, 29), a person can overcome temptation by sanctifying his speech. He thus "sanctifies" his relationship, giving due respect to his partner in marriage, and never engaging in prohibited relationships. Sanctifying Malkhut gives rise to a desire for spirituality, diminishing one's evil desires (see *Likutey Moharan* I, 19:3).

Rebbe Nachman teaches that there is a "dew of holiness" whose drops descend into the world, bringing with them abundant blessing and prosperity. This dew corresponds to the "drops" of seed which, as we have seen (above, Chapter 40), emanate from a person's mind. Someone who conducts himself with a focus on spirituality draws blessing into the world through his "drops." However, engaging in prohibited sexual acts is a waste of seed, a weakening of the mind and a squandering of bounty — an impudent rejection of all the good that God offers us. Thus, defiling the Covenant, like wasting seed, dissipates all blessings and bounty, which then become nourishment for the unholy powers of the Other Side (see *Likutey Moharan* I, 11:4).

So we see that guarding the Covenant is a process of sanctification. Defiling the Covenant through sexual impurity constitutes the reverse of this sanctity. The most basic level of guarding the *brit* is adhering to the Torah's laws of marriage and family purity. Following are the most common examples of defiling the Covenant:

- Relations with a woman who does not adhere to the laws of family purity
- Relations with a woman whom the Torah forbids one to marry (such as a *Kohen* marrying a divorcee; or worse still, adultery, incest or marrying out of the faith)
- Relations out of wedlock
- Homosexuality
- Masturbation

Committing any of these acts is a defilement of the Covenant and the very opposite of honoring and sanctifying the God-granted powers of procreation. Each involves wasting seed and the transference of all blessing and bounty to the Other Side, to the forces of evil that are parasites on holiness.

*

Rebbe Nachman taught:

A burning lust in one's heart is likened to a storm wind. Such a lust can be "cooled" through holy speech. If a person does not take the initiative to "cool it," the storm wind itself will "cool him" — by causing him to have a nocturnal emission (*Likutey Moharan* I, 19:5).

The Hebrew word for such an emission is *KeRIy*, which is similar to the Hebrew word *KeRIrut*, meaning cold. A nocturnal emission is called *miKReh lailah*, for the raging storm that burns within, which causes the emission, in turn leads the individual to become cold and indifferent to the influences of spirituality. When someone succumbs to temptation and wastes his seed, this "cools" his spiritual aspirations. If, however, he controls his temptations, he can "calm down" and find physical and spiritual satisfaction within his permitted relationship.

Unfortunately, truly guarding the Covenant is never an easy level to attain. The world we live in offers countless enticements; every man is exposed to all sorts of temptations long before he even considers marriage. The longer one waits to marry, the harder it becomes to guard the sign of the Covenant in purity. Rebbe Nachman therefore advises his followers to marry as young as possible, before being overcome by temptation. Our Sages have taught: One who marries before the age of twenty can be saved from lustful thoughts (*Kiddushin* 29b). Though marriage at this age isn't realistic in every case, people should certainly marry as early as possible.

Even after marriage, however, various complications are bound to arise which can cause all sorts of problems in guarding the Covenant. Work and financial pressures, problems with one's children, excessive travel, and many other circumstances that arise often pose severe challenges. When one adds to the list of daily temptations the increasingly noticeable presence of the media, one faces a formidable task indeed. Still, the institution of marriage is so basic to maintaining one's emotional and spiritual equilibrium that Reb Noson once remarked, "If you are married and tell me you are devoted to the service of the Almighty, I will believe you. If you are not married and tell me that you are devoted to God's service, I won't believe you!" (*Aveneha Barzel* p.85).

*

Rebbe Nachman teaches that immorality can destroy one's body (*Likutey Moharan* II, 107). This is in line with the Talmud's teaching (*Sukkah* 52b), "A man has a small organ [the *brit*]: If he starves it, it will be satisfied; if he feeds it, it will never be satisfied." The more a person engages in sexual activity, the more his appetite for it grows. The more respect he gives to his procreative faculties through restraint, the greater will be his satisfaction when engaging in marital relations. This is because exercising control brings one to clarity of mind. One who constantly seeks increased sensual pleasures eventually squanders his vital energy and beclouds his mind, thus causing harm to himself as well as to others.

This concept is clearly demonstrated in modern society, in the increase of homosexuality, pedophilia, sexual abuse and violent sexual crimes. All these are the actions of people whose minds have been violated and defiled through incessant exposure to seductive movies, fiction, advertisements, and so on.

Homosexuality and masturbation, for example, are the most blatant forms of wasting seed, yet many contemporary professional counselors advocate these activities as helpful releases from emotional stress. When people in need of therapy seek help in order to gain emotional stability, they are often encouraged to engage in behavior that promises instead to sap their energy and waste their minds. This is a devastating approach which sets the unfortunate client on a path of ongoing sexual abuse — of himself, no less — with little hope for improvement, until he wakes up one day and realizes that he has been misguided and misled.

This is why the first phase of *teshuvah* (repentance) usually involves a complete change of lifestyle — a swing from one extreme to another — in order to make a clean break from a negative form of habitual behavior and give oneself time to adjust to and create a new pattern of living. For example, it is known and understood that the only way to get over alcohol or drug addiction is through complete abstinence. An alcoholic who says "Just one more little drink..." will never overcome his addiction. The same goes for sexual promiscuity. The only difference between the two is that, in the case of alcohol or drug addiction, one may never return to one's previous ways. In the case of sexual relations, however, *teshuvah* will entail a second phase called "sanctification of that which is permitted." In other words, according to Judaism, healthy and loving sexual relations within the sacred precincts of marriage and according to the laws of family purity are, by far, a greater rectification for past wrongdoings than any form of abstinence.

In general, however, as we said, the first phase of *teshuvah* must involve restraint and self control. Until a person learns restraint, he has no "Yesod" in his life, no solid foundation upon which to stand. After one has practiced restraint, and learned its precious lessons, he or she can then move on to a healthy new life.

What about a person who fails to do *teshuvah* for past wrongdoings; is there no hope for them? This brings us to the divine gift of reincarnation. All Kabbalistic sources are in agreement: The soul (or the portion of the soul that requires it) will be reincarnated to rectify any wrongdoings committed in its previous lifetime. To facilitate this, the reincarnated individual will be drawn to the specific areas which require rectification. According to the ARI, the Talmud (Shabbat 118b) alludes to this when it tells us that Rabbi Yosef was asked about his father Rabbah, "Which mitzvah was he most careful to perform?" The questioner knew that every Jew is required to fulfill all the mitzvot to the best of his ability. Clearly, however, he was asking a deeper question: if a person is inordinately connected to a particular mitzvah, it indicates that his entire mission in being born was to rectify that mitzvah. According to this, the questioner was asking which particular mitzvah had Rabbah's soul been lacking in his previous incarnation. The ARI writes that the same applies to every single individual. The main characteristics of one's spiritual weaknesses are the specific areas one must rectify (see *Sha'ar HaGilgulim* 16).

Thus, if a person is born with a tendency to shed blood, he should harness this trait to be in the service of God, i.e., becoming a *shochet* (ritual slaughterer) or a *mohel* (circumciser). Everyone has difficulties in their character traits which God gave them to work on in this life. If they were given a problem, it is their task to find out how to use it in a way that serves God, rather than going against His directives. The same is true of one's sexual urges, the desire for material possessions and so on.

Rebbe Nachman teaches that blemishing the Covenant brings the "sword," as in (Leviticus 26:25), "I will bring a sword upon you, that shall execute the vengeance of the Covenant" (*Likutey Moharan* I, 20:10). This sword is manifest in the various kinds of suffering that people endure. Conversely, the *brit* represents peace (see above, Chapter 41). Guarding the Covenant literally brings peace to a person's home, enabling husband and wife to learn to communicate with one another in a holy Yesod/Malkhut relationship. In this way, a couple can build a home upon a solid foundation. Where there are violations of the Covenant, the very foundation upon which they build their life is shaky. Their relationship is unstable; insecurity fills their lives.

Yet this is not a hopeless situation. Reb Noson writes that even a small measure of intellect is sufficient to counter the worst attacks on a person's mind — and Yesod — so that he can emerge victorious. Rebbe Nachman writes that everything happens "in the mind" (see *Likutey Moharan* I, 72). The seed emanates from the mind because that is where all the "action" is taking place. If a person feels an urge which would draw him away from spirituality, his mind *can* control that urge. The urge may return, but someone who cares can again redirect his mind. As we have seen (Chapter 18), one who seeks spirituality is open-minded and is always able to turn to other thoughts in order to change his focus. One who does not seek spirituality, on the other hand, is narrow-minded, and his thoughts may easily become fixed on a single track.

Rebbe Nachman adds that a person's seed is indeed very precious. The Hebrew word *YaKaR* (יקר, precious) has the same letters as *KeRiY* (קרי, emission). One who elevates God's honor through proper moral conduct makes himself very precious. He achieves the power to elevate even those who have fallen through wasted seed. The Glory of God is then revealed and elevated, even by those who are just beginning to recognize Him! (*Likutey Moharan I, 14:1, 13*).

Even if a person has actually blemished his *brit*, there is always hope. The *brit* is called a *chotem* (seal), for the Covenant of Abraham is God's seal upon man's body. A blemished Covenant corresponds to (Leviticus 15:3) "*heCHTiM besaro* — his flesh is sealed [i.e., his organ has been blocked up with seminal discharge]." By learning to restrain oneself in guarding the Covenant, one can elevate oneself from a state of "*heCHTiM besaro*," bringing oneself to the state of *CHoTeM* (the seal of the Covenant) and thereby rectifying one's blemishes (*Likutey Moharan II, 5:11*).

*

...Brings Contentment in Life

Were it not for salt, the world could not bear the bitterness.
Zohar I, 241b

Salt is unique in that, despite its bitter taste, it serves as a condiment for nearly all types of food. In this sense, salt contains two opposing properties — it tastes sharp, yet it sweetens other foods, making them palatable to the tongue. In a deeper sense, the "dichotomy of salt" represents both the suffering a person endures and the solace he finds in confronting his suffering. Indeed, the Talmud finds a parallel between salt and suffering, in that God made a covenant with both of them.

There is a covenant with salt, as in (Leviticus 2:13) "Do not allow the salt of the eternal Covenant of God to be lacking [from the sacrifices]...”; and there is a covenant with suffering (see Deuteronomy 28:69). Just as salt softens meat, so too suffering [softens the person, for it] effects forgiveness for sin (*Berakhot* 5a).

The sad fact of life is that suffering visits everyone. Some people suffer from little nuisances, others from financial difficulties, and yet others from serious illness or domestic problems. Some people suffer daily, others intermittently; but everyone suffers. Yet nearly all who endure suffering will admit that things “could still be worse.” The Talmud equates salt with suffering, for “just as salt softens meat, so too, suffering effects forgiveness for a person’s sins.” While there is always the pain of suffering, within that suffering there is a built-in “sweetener” — for it causes man to recognize his errors and helps him to direct his life towards rectifying his shortcomings. (This is also alluded to in the gallbladder: the bile it contains is very bitter, yet its function is to “sweeten”; see above, Chapter 11.)

The Talmud’s use of the word “covenant” with regard to salt and suffering is explored by Rebbe Nachman to reveal yet another dimension of how the Covenant can bring a person to a life of sweetness and contentment.

Rebbe Nachman taught:

> The tzaddik corresponds to *brit*. He sustains the entire world, bearing all its blessings, as we are told (Proverbs 10:6), “Blessings upon the head of the tzaddik.” For the tzaddik [i.e., Yesod] holds the “seed” of all souls, from which emanates all bounty to the world (*Likutey Moharan* I, 54:3).

Rebbe Nachman continues, explaining that the concept of tzaddik alludes to guarding the Covenant. Anyone, to the extent to which he guards his covenant, can merit the title of “tzaddik.” A guarded Covenant helps a person to bear suffering and to receive blessings, and also helps him to earn an easier livelihood. Thus a guarded Covenant, indicating both the level of the tzaddik and the covenant of salt, helps to alleviate the other covenant, that of suffering.

How is this effected? The seed, which originates in the brain, is compared to *tal*, the holy dew of God's Light which flows from the Upper Worlds. This is based on the following teaching from the *Tikkuney Zohar* (Second Introduction, p.17b):

> Rabbi Shimon arose and began his discourse. He said (I Chronicles 29:11): "Yours, O God, are the Loving Greatness and the Power. [Yours is] the Harmony [of both these extremes]. [Yours is] the Dominance and the Empathy over all that is in heaven and earth. Yours, O God, is the Kingship and the Absolute Sovereignty over everything!" Hear, you supernal ones, slumberers of Hebron, and [Moses] the Faithful Shepherd. Wake up from your sleep! "Awake and sing, O you who dwell in the dust! *For Your dew will be a dew of lights* and the earth will spew forth its dead" (Isaiah 26:19). These are the righteous ones, concerning whom it is said (Songs 5:2), "I am asleep but my heart is awake; the voice of my Beloved knocks. Open your heart to Me, My sister, My friend, My dove, My perfect twin, for My head is filled with dew and My locks with the drops of the night." For in truth, the righteous are not dead. For this reason it is said concerning them, "Awake and sing, O you who dwell in the dust!"
>
> Faithful Shepherd, you and the Patriarchs must awake and sing in order to arouse the *Shekhinah* [literally, "Indwelling Presence of God"]. For as long as mankind is unable to perceive God's Presence in Creation, the *Shekhinah* is said to be asleep in exile! Until now, all the righteous have rested in a deep slumber. [But when the time of the Redemption arrives,] the *Shekhinah* will suddenly give forth three cries in order to awaken the Faithful Shepherd! She will say to him: Rise up, O Faithful Shepherd, for concerning you it is written, "I am asleep, but my heart is awake; the voice of my Beloved knocks" [reprimanding me lovingly] with the Four Letters of His Name. And He says: "Open up to Me, My sister, My friend, My dove, My perfect twin." For (Lamentations 4:22) "the punishment for your sin has been

terminated, O daughter of Zion; no longer will I carry you away into exile." "For My head is filled with *tal* [dew]."

What does "filled with *tal*" signify? It refers to the Blessed Holy One. He says: From the day that the earthly Temple was destroyed and I sent Israel into exile, you thought I was dwelling peacefully in My Heavenly House. No! The fact is that I have not entered [My House] Above since the day you went into exile. To show you that I have not entered during the entire long night of your exile, I give you a sign: "My head is filled with *tal*, and My locks with drops of the night." The numerical value of *TaL* [טל, the Hebrew letters *tet-lamed*] is 39. This is equivalent to the numerical value of the first three letters of My Name [when each letter is "expanded" with *Alephs*]: *Yod-Vav-Dalet* = 20, *Heh-Aleph* = 6, and *Vav-Aleph-Vav* = 13 (totaling 39). The fourth letter, *Heh-Aleph*, is equal to 6. This represents My *Shekhinah* in exile. When all Four Letters of the Holy Name are added together, they equal 45 (see Appendix D). When the last letter, *Heh-Aleph* (הא), is separated from the others [i. e., when My Presence is hidden from mankind], they equal only 39. The final letter thus represents the *Shekhinah*, which is unable to receive the *tal* [dew] of the first three letters, for It is in exile. However, when this *tal* will flow down to "fill" the *Shekhinah* from the flow of all the Supernal Springs, She will be revived and the Redemption will have arrived. At that time, the Faithful Shepherd and the holy Patriarchs will immediately rise up. This is the mystery of the unification of God's Four-Letter Name, *YHVH*.

The basic *gematria* (numerical equivalent) of the Tetragrammaton, *YHVH* (יהוה), is 26. The second, third and fourth letters of the Name can be "expanded" in four different ways, yielding four different numerical equations (see Appendix D). One of these is obtained by spelling out the Name with *Alephs*; thus, as the Zohar states, *Yod-Vav-Dalet* = 20, *Heh-Aleph* = 6, *Vav-Aleph-Vav* = 13, *Heh-Aleph* = 6, yielding a total of 45. The final letter, *Heh-Aleph*, corresponds to the *Shekhinah* and to the *Sefirah* of Malkhut. The dew (i.e., bounty) of God that descends to Malkhut comes from the first three letters, *YHV*, יהו [when expanded: יוד, הא, ואו]), which equal 39, having the same value as *TaL* (טל).

    TaL corresponds to the thirty-nine forms of work which were employed in the building of the Tabernacle. As is well known, all bounty and goodness come to the world through the Tabernacle (i.e., the Temple, where there is a revelation of Godliness). One who guards the Covenant draws upon himself the *tal* of bounty. When he engages in the thirty-nine forms of work in seeking his livelihood, his efforts are thus an aspect of the Tabernacle — referring to the Tabernacle when it is built, which corresponds to the thirty-nine lights of *tal*. His livelihood comes easily and is always sweet. When a person defiles his *brit*, on the other hand, his work is an aspect of the Tabernacle in its state of destruction. His livelihood comes with difficulty and is full of bitterness. This is equivalent to receiving the thirty-nine lashes prescribed by the Torah as punishment for various infractions (*Likutey Moharan* I, 11:4).

    Guarding the Covenant helps a person live a life of contentment and happiness, and also protects him from falling prey to the idolatry of avarice. Nothing causes man to lose his vitality and virility like worry and sadness. This leads to depression, which brings in its wake further worries, *ad infinitum*. Thus, worry over one's finances (which, as has been explained [above, Chapter 41], stems from blemishing one's *brit*) can actually shorten a person's life. Similarly, one who rebels against the tzaddik, the true guardian of the Covenant, is punished and plagued by an avaricious discontent. Guarding the Covenant and listening to the tzaddik helps one to overcome such worries, and leads one to joy (*Likutey Moharan* I, 23:3-7).

*

Noah and the Rainbow

    The rainbow as a Covenant is another symbol of guarding the *brit*. As has been stated earlier, the Torah reflects the ongoing saga of mankind. When we analyze the story of Noah and the Flood, we can see how it reflects the universal battle against immorality (see Genesis 6–9).

The souls of the Generation of the Flood were steeped in immorality. They practiced adultery, homosexuality, masturbation and bestiality (see *Bereishit Rabbah* 26:5). Their wanton waste of seed invoked terrible judgments, to the point that mankind had to be wiped out completely.

This generation's punishment "fit their crime." The principal sin of the Generation of the Flood was wasted seed. The Talmud states that one who wastes seed is considered as if he himself brought a flood to the world (*Niddah* 13a). We can better understand this when we realize that a single discharge of semen contains *several hundred million* sperm cells, each of which holds the potential to fertilize a female ovum. This seed is "alive" with life-providing power, and therefore any waste of seed is nothing less than a loss of life — just as a flood causes loss of life.

Only one man of the whole generation, Noah, was deemed worthy to be saved from the Flood that God brought upon the world. He was the only Biblical figure to carry the title of tzaddik. For a tzaddik is a person who guards his Covenant, and Noah was singled out in his generation of immorality as the only guardian of the *brit*.

In order to escape the Flood, Noah had to build an Ark to protect himself, his family and at least two of each animal species. Rebbe Nachman teaches that the Hebrew rendering of "Ark" is *teivah*, which also translates as "word." The "word" of Noah was prayer. Essentially, this "word" of prayer, the most sacred and effective use of speech, was all that protected those in the Ark from the destructive waters of the Flood (see *Likutey Moharan* I, 14:10).

Thus we see that, as the tzaddik of his generation, Noah's only option for salvation was to properly direct his prayers to God. The tzaddik, as we have seen, is so called because he guards his Covenant. This enables him to unite with Malkhut, which represents speech (see above), and so to strengthen prayer and to direct it properly. It is because of his prayers that Noah himself was saved from the destruction of the Flood. As a tzaddik who could strengthen his prayers, he was able to save his family as well.

When Noah left the Ark after the Flood had subsided, he was overwhelmed by the sight of the world's destruction. Noah prayed to God, Who promised him that He would never again bring such a flood upon the earth. As a token of this promise which precluded another flood, God gave Noah, as His Covenant, the sign of the rainbow.

When God offered His Covenant, He expected that in return for his protection man would follow suit and behave with respect for human morality. But before long, Ham (Cham), Noah's youngest son, caused untold damage in his sexual transgression. Noah cursed him harshly, telling him, (see Genesis 9:18–29), "You shall be a slave."

Noah's son Ham transgressed against the very force that allowed Noah to survive — the *brit*. Ham translates as "hot," indicating the "hot blood of lust" that leads a person astray (*Tikkuney Zohar* #18, p.37a). For the untempered "heat" of this transgression, Ham was cursed to be a slave. Because he allowed himself to be enslaved to his desires, his curse was ultimate servitude. This is the fate of one who does not control his lust.

Bringing into these concepts a more practical application, Rebbe Nachman teaches that the *brit* of Noah and the *brit* of Abraham have much in common: The rainbow, which signifies God's *brit* with Noah, is called *keshet*, which also translates as a bow. The Covenant of Abraham is similarly referred to as the *keshet habrit*, the bow of the Covenant; it alludes to the *brit* when it functions in purity. The organ of the *brit* is seen as a bow; the seed, as the arrow (*Zohar* III, 272a; *Likutey Moharan* I, 29:6). Through guarding the *brit*, one gains the power of effective prayer; through rectifying the Covenant (bow), one can become an "archer of arrows," successfully directing one's prayers most effectively to their "target" (*Likutey Moharan* II, 83:1).

The reason prayer is affected by the *brit* is because Zer Anpin corresponds to the voice and Malkhut to speech (see *Zohar* II, 230b). Yesod, which represents the *brit*, is a manifestation of Zer Anpin, and Malkhut receives from Yesod. Therefore, one who guards the *brit* rectifies the voice and gives speech, or prayer, power. On the other hand, one who blemishes his *brit* blemishes his voice, thereby losing his feeling for prayer; blemishing the *brit* diminishes the power of one's prayers (see *Likutey Moharan* 27:6; *ibid.* II, 1:10).

This is also alluded to in the fact that the trachea has six cartilage rings supporting it (see above, Chapter 26). Yesod is the sixth *Sefirah* of Zer Anpin. Thus, through blemishing Yesod, the "sixth" aspect of Zer Anpin, the voice becomes blemished.

We have already seen that the seed is drawn from one's entire body (above, Chapter 40). Rebbe Nachman teaches that one who guards the Covenant merits to feel the sweetness of his prayers throughout his body. All his bones feel this sweetness, as King David sang (Psalms 35:10), "All my bones shall say: 'O God, who is like You!'" His prayers are like arrows that shoot unerringly, straight and true, to their destination (*Likutey Moharan* I, 50:1).

* * *

43

The General Remedy

Once, when speaking on the topic of the Covenant, Rebbe Nachman remarked that perhaps as much as three-quarters of the world's male population experiences nocturnal emissions. Sometimes this results from overeating, sometimes from illness. But for those who experience it as a result of their sinful thoughts, the ramifications are truly frightening (cf. *Rabbi Nachman's Wisdom* #141). With this in mind, Rebbe Nachman revealed the *Tikkun HaKlali* (General Remedy).

We know that for each sin there is an appropriate *tikkun*, a specific action which can rectify the spiritual harm incurred by that sin. However, what *tikkun* can there be when we need to rectify many sins, or to rectify even one sin whose ramifications are many? Is it necessary to enact all the many specific *tikkunim* (rectifications)? Is such an approach really viable? Because it is not, Rebbe Nachman tells us that there exists a concept of general rectification, a General Remedy for all sins.

Rebbe Nachman taught:

There are 365 prohibitions in the Torah, corresponding to the 365 sinews and blood vessels of the body. Transgressing any single commandment corresponds to blemishing the specific vein or sinew which is associated with that commandment. To rectify each transgression is practically impossible, for each mitzvah has many offshoots, just as each blood vessel and vein has many capillaries. Where, then, can one turn for full rectification? Here the concept of a General Remedy applies; it is one remedy which stands above all and which can rectify all. This can be achieved with the rectification of the *brit*. [The Torah has a total of 613 mitzvot. The word *brit* is numerically equal to 612, and adding one for the mitzvah of *brit* itself makes it numerically equal to 613. Thus, the observance of this one mitzvah encompasses all the others.] Through rectifying the Covenant, one can rectify all of one's sins.

This is effective because the *brit* is associated with the Holy Name *Shadai*, "There is enough!" (as above, Chapter 40). God has *enough* — sufficient kindness and ability — to rectify even the worst sins, the most evil transgressions. If, after improperly ejaculating and so wasting seed, one begins to guard the Covenant and to seek the General Remedy, one actually reaches towards *SHaDaIy*, the Lovingkindness of God. By repenting, one gains the ability to *SHaDI* [which translates as "putting in place"] all the necessary rectifications to all the various veins and sinews, rectifying even the most complex areas (*Likutey Moharan* I, 29:4).

As we have seen (above, Chapter 42), the *brit* is inclusive of all levels of Torah and spirituality. Through guarding the *brit*, one is able to "put" rectifications in place in those areas which, under other circumstances, would have been impossible to reach. Thus, even the gravest of sins can be rectified when one attains the general rectification of the Covenant of the brit.

*

The General Remedy (Tikkun HaKlali)

The General Remedy which Rebbe Nachman revealed parallels the Ten Types of Song with which the Book of Psalms was composed (see *Pesachim* 117a; *Zohar* III, 101a). We have discussed the power of song (Chapter 29) and have seen that it is a profound expression of one's inner being. Rebbe Nachman teaches that the Ten Types of Song bring vitality to the ten modes of pulse (see above, Chapter 24). When joy is blemished, the pulse becomes impaired. The

General Remedy invokes the level of song and joy which are able to overpower the melancholy and depression which cause one to experience emissions. Song has the power to rejuvenate one's blemished veins and sinews, bringing rectifications to even the most remote capillaries (see also *Likutey Moharan* II, 24:1). Song has the power to sift the good from the bad, and to obliterate the spiritual blemishes which are the products of sin.

Therefore, to effect this powerful rectification, Rebbe Nachman advised us to recite ten chapters from the Book of Psalms. Although any ten psalms can correspond to the Ten Types of Song, Rebbe Nachman disclosed which specific ten comprise the General Remedy. They are chapters: **16, 32, 41, 42, 59, 77, 90, 105, 137, 150.** These chapters together constitute a very effective rectification and should be recited as soon as possible after one has experienced a nocturnal emission, preferably on the same day (see *Likutey Moharan* II, 92:1–2).

Since these ten chapters of the *Tikkun HaKlali* serve as a special remedy for the sin of wasteful emission of seed — the all-encompassing sin of defiling the sign of the Covenant — they also serve as a general rectification for all other sins. We know that guarding the Covenant demands sexual purity, and that the guarding of the Covenant is equivalent to all the other mitzvot combined. It follows that defiling the Covenant through sexual impurity causes a spiritual blemish which is much more serious than that caused by any other single sin. Blemishing the *brit* is therefore a specific transgression with very wide-ranging ramifications. This is exactly why it requires a General Remedy — a *Tikkun Klali* — in order to rectify it.

Rebbe Nachman said, "Reciting these ten chapters from the Book of Psalms is a very wonderful remedy and a most powerful rectification. It is entirely original; from the time of Creation, tzaddikim have sought the remedy for this sin. God has been good to me, granting me this understanding and allowing me to reveal this remedy to the world" (*Rabbi Nachman's Wisdom* #141).

Rebbe Nachman teaches us that by reciting the ten psalms of the General Remedy, we can rectify all the blemishes caused by wasted seed — and by all our sins — and in this way come to true repentance (*Rabbi Nachman's Wisdom* #141).

*

It must be emphasized that Rebbe Nachman recommended the recital of the General Remedy as a rectification for an *accidental* nocturnal occurrence, not for the deliberate wasting of seed (cf. *Rabbi Nachman's Wisdom* #141). We should not mistakenly assume that knowledge of the General Remedy renders intentional sin inconsequential. Indeed, the Zohar teaches that for the willful emission of seed there can be no effective repentance (*Zohar* I, 188a).

And yet, despite the severity of the sin of willfully defiling the sign of the Covenant, the Rebbe emphatically insisted that this teaching of the Zohar should not be taken literally. He argued that repentance helps for *all* sins, even one as severe as this. True repentance involves never repeating the sin: encountering the same situation, facing the same temptation, and withstanding it (*Rabbi Nachman's Wisdom* #71). As Rebbe Nachman said: "Never give up!" (*Likutey Moharan* II, 78).

Reb Noson writes:

> There is a spark of eternal holiness that exists within each and every Jew. One who spills his seed needlessly damages this vital spark, bringing evil and even death to the world (see above, Chapter 42). Nevertheless, he can repent. He must take steps to repair and rectify his "spark of holiness." The way to do this is to attach himself to the tzaddik — to one who guards his Covenant completely. In this way, he becomes worthy of revealing additional levels of God's Lovingkindness through his repentance. Logically, one who has forfeited this spark ought not to be entitled to repent; but if in fact he does repent, he causes new levels of Lovingkindness to be revealed (*Likutey Halakhot, Tefilin* 2:11).

*

Helpful Hints

It is no simple matter to overcome the sexual urge. One needs as much assistance as possible to prevail over this compelling inclination. Rebbe Nachman therefore offered several suggestions which can be most helpful in conquering lust.

In a general sense, Rebbe Nachman teaches that performing the mitzvot corresponds to rectifying the *brit* (*Likutey Moharan* II, 1:11). *MiTZVah* stems from the root *leTZaVot*, "to bind" or "to gather." It is through the performance of mitzvot that one is able to recall one's "losses" and to collect one's "wasted" seed in order to rectify it.

Rebbe Nachman also teaches: "When you merit true joy to the point that you are joyous enough to dance, God Himself will protect your Covenant and help you guard its purity" (*Likutey Moharan* I, 169). Depression is called the "Serpent's bite"; it leads to defilement of the *brit*. Joy, on the other hand, is the most effective weapon against depression, and hence it is the best method by which to overcome lust and guard the Covenant.

Torah study is another tool which is essential for guarding the Covenant. Rebbe Nachman said that Torah study has enormous power. It can raise a person out of any abyss into which he has fallen. When asked about a blemished *brit*, Rebbe Nachman answered, "Torah [in the *Sefirah* of Tiferet] stands higher than *brit* [Yesod]!" (*Tzaddik* #573).

(We mentioned earlier that the *brit* is inclusive of all the other mitzvot of the Torah [see Chapters 42–43]. That apparently contradicts what the Rebbe teaches here, that the level of Torah is higher than the level of *brit*. However, we must understand that the Torah is actually God's Thought which He revealed to us so that we can know which path to take in order to come close to Him. As such, the *brit* is rooted in Torah. However, on our level it encompasses the other mitzvot.)

Rebbe Nachman also taught:

- Truth protects the sign of the Covenant from blemish (*The Aleph-Bet Book*, Truth A:24; see also above, Chapter 41, on the topic of truth and the Covenant).

- Inspiring others to serve God is a rectification for having blemished the Covenant (*Likutey Moharan* I, 14). (Those whom one has inspired were also "outside the realm of holiness," as is the wasted seed, and all are now returned to holiness.)

- To rectify the Covenant, pursue peace (*The Aleph-Bet Book*, Immoral Behavior A:30; see above, Chapter 41, on the topic of peace).

- Earning money in order to give charity serves to rectify one's *damim* [money], which effectively cleanses *damim* [the blood of immorality and impurity]. Charity is compared to seed, as in (Hosea 10:12), "Sow charity for yourselves." Rectified seed — guarding the Covenant — purifies the mind and cleanses the veins. Thus charity can rectify the mind (*Likutey Moharan* I, 29:9).

- Whoever performs kindness and charity rectifies his Covenant (cf. *The Aleph-Bet Book*, Charity, A:54).

- Charity is a rectification for blemishing the Covenant. Blemishing the *brit* by wasting "seed" causes spiritual bounty to be transferred to the Other Side. Giving charity returns this bounty to the realm of holiness. However, this is so only if the recipient is worthy. Giving charity to an unworthy person or cause directs additional bounty to the Other Side, compounding the gravity of one's sins (*Likutey Moharan* I, 264).

- The Holy Land can help purify one's *brit* (*Likutey Moharan* I, 44). At the time God made the Covenant with Abraham, He promised him the Holy Land. The two are implicitly related.

Prayer and *hitbodedut* are also helpful. Prayer plays a major role in the quest for purity, as we shall see in the following chapter. In addition, as outlined above, Rebbe Nachman revealed the General Remedy as a means by which to combat lust and to rectify the spiritual damage incurred through sexual transgressions. All these concepts may be studied in greater detail in the book entitled *Rabbi Nachman's Tikkun* (published by Breslov Research Institute).

* * *

44

Malkhut: The Female Principle

Malkhut is Kingship. It is the last of the *Sefirot*, representing the completion and culmination of Creation, which is the revelation of God's Kingdom. In the human physiology, the "energy" of Malkhut is contained in the female reproductive organs. Spiritually, as well, Malkhut is considered a "feminine principle," for it benefits from the flow of spiritual energy which emanates from Above. As we have seen, Malkhut also returns that which it has received in a more complete and refined form. In the marital union, the male gives hundreds of millions of sperm cells, of which only one generally succeeds in fusing with the nucleus of the female ovum. From her single fertilized egg she returns a complete infant. Before discussing the female organs in detail, let us review some of the principles and manifestations of Malkhut.

Zer Anpin and Malkhut are two Divine Persona that act independently; yet they are interdependent (see Appendix D). Each denotes a *separate* individual — yet each is incomplete on its own. Each must interact with the other. As we have mentioned (Chapter 40), Malkhut represents introspection, the ability to look within and to direct oneself. This is seen more clearly in the way Malkhut manifests as the Oral Law, as prayer and faith.

*

The Written and Oral Law

The Zohar teaches that the Written Law (the Torah) corresponds to Zer Anpin and the Oral Law to Malkhut. While the

Written Law is the primary source for every law, as well as for every point of spirituality, it does not provide clear guidelines for *how* to put these laws into effect. The verses of the Written Law are far too terse to be interpreted at face value. This is also the case regarding Zer Anpin: complete on its own, yet beyond reach. When, however, we join the Written Law to the Oral Law, we have a perfect combination. The Written Law states a verse, and the Oral Law expounds it. Accordingly, we can see how all the laws are outlined in just a few words of the Written Law, and we begin to view the Written Law with a deeper respect for its abundant treasures. If, on the other hand, the Written and Oral Laws are viewed as separate entities, we remain with two separate units, neither of which alone can direct us to spirituality.

Thus Malkhut (the Oral Law) stands as the completion of Tiferet (i.e., Zer Anpin, the Written Law). Indeed, the Oral Law discloses the deeper connections between the various parts of the Written Law. It is for this reason that we must not observe the commandments of the Torah without the "wise counsel" of the Oral Law. Attempting to follow any particular commandment or ruling of the Written Law without seeing it in relation to other parts of the Written Law, as explained in the Oral Law, can lead to serious distortions. As an aspect of Malkhut, the Oral Law has the unique ability to receive from the higher level, from the Written Law, and to transform it into a practical form, thus enabling it to interface with all the levels that lie below it. If a person follows the "dictates of Malkhut," the Oral Law, even without possessing any knowledge or understanding of the Written Law, he will fulfill his basic obligations. As has been indicated, the reverse does not hold true.

*

Torah and Prayer

Zer Anpin and Malkhut also represent Torah (both the Oral Law and the Written Law) and prayer, respectively. From the Torah we know *what* to do, but translating that knowledge into deeds requires prayer. We can study and become knowledgeable in the science of how to seek a spiritual life, but only by praying to God can we truly merit to realize and internalize the aim of our studies. Here we see again how Malkhut serves as a reflector for Zer Anpin, prayer being the perfect complement to the Torah. By praying for the ability to fulfill the Torah, a person can succeed in ascending to higher spiritual planes, from which he will be able to search for greater and deeper perceptions of Godliness. Thus Malkhut, which was originally the recipient of the Torah of Zer Anpin, in turn becomes the catalyst through which one can transform one's intellectual attainments into far greater accomplishments.

Malkhut facilitates the revelation of the Kingdom of God. It is the *Sefirah* through which we can interact with Him. When God sends us bounty, and we acknowledge that it comes from Him, that acknowledgement demonstrates our submission to His Kingship. In this way, we become the significant factor in the revelation of His Malkhut. Our participation in this dynamic relationship requires that we take all that we have received and return it to God in a more complete form, which, as we have seen, is the function of Malkhut. We can accomplish this through prayer.

In our prayers, we often ask God to do things for us. We may find ourselves beset by problems, with no apparent way out of a difficult situation. When we pray to God, we request a solution or a salvation which requires God's intervention, in ways that may be above and beyond the normal, "natural" course of events. When we persist, our prayers are likely to be answered. *This* is the true manifestation of Malkhut — *our* ability to rule. In fact, it is in a sense, the ability to rule over God Himself, to "force" Him, as it were, to alter "natural" circumstances and to improve our lot for the better. This defines the reciprocal relationship of Zer Anpin and Malkhut, in which we can take the spiritual energy invested in us by God and use it to serve Him, to the point that we become, so to speak, the "benefactors," while God is the "Beneficiary."

Reb Noson points out that Zer Anpin and Malkhut together comprise the seven lower *Sefirot*. The Torah is called "seven," as in (Proverbs 9:1; see *Rashi*), "It is hewn of seven pillars." Prayer is likewise called "seven," as in (Psalms 119:164), "Seven times a day I praise You..." Thus Torah and prayer each represent the array of the seven *Sefirot* of Zer Anpin and Malkhut when the two are united. The nature of Malkhut is reflected by King David, who is known as the personification of Malkhut. The numerical equivalent of *DaViD* (דוד) is 14, representing the combination of the seven pillars of Torah and the seven praises of prayer. One who combines the two devotions, that of Torah study and that of prayer, perfects his aspect of Malkhut, as did King David (see *Likutey Halakhot, Birkhot HaShachar* 5:60).

In the current era, Zer Anpin and Malkhut are unequal, for the one is mostly giving while the other is almost exclusively receiving. That is why, in this world, inequality is prevalent. The ARI teaches that when Mashiach comes, Malkhut, the feminine aspect, will be equal to Zer Anpin, and in certain respects even greater. Reb Noson notes that nowadays, a person who is serious in his Torah study and prayers — especially in his *hitbodedut* — and who makes them "equal partners" by investing the same amount of effort into both, attains a level of the equality of Zer Anpin and Malkhut that will exist in the Messianic era (see *Likutey Halakhot, Rosh Chodesh* 5:4; *ibid., Matanah* 5:8).

*

Faith

Another fundamental concept of Malkhut is faith. Faith is based on the idea that there exists something that transcends *my* knowledge: I am aware that it is there, yet at present I cannot grasp it. Rebbe Nachman teaches that Malkhut functions, in this sense, as a funnel — large at one end and tiny at the other. The minuscule opening at the bottom is the point through which all heavenly wisdom filters, and without which we would never be able to grasp the higher intellect, on any level (see *Likutey Moharan* I, 30:3).

Malkhut is thus the "funnel" through which Chokhmah can pass so that it can be imparted to mankind. (This concept was also explained earlier with regard to the *mochin*; see above, Chapter 14.)

Conversely, faith must be directed towards the search for Godliness, the higher, true Intellect. One whose faith (Malkhut) is a "separate entity," not directed towards Zer Anpin (i.e., the Torah) and those levels above it — towards God Himself — cannot attain spiritual intellect. They separate Malkhut from its spiritual energy source, preventing the transmission of true intellect to Malkhut and thereby fostering a faith that is misplaced or unattached to any true intellect. Similarly, people who are in thrall to "foreign intellects," such as atheistic wisdoms and other foolish ideas that masquerade as wisdom, may have faith in the existence of vast knowledge, but their intellect is misplaced.

*

Speech

As we have already seen (Chapter 29), speech is also related to the concept of Malkhut. No leader can rule without speech. His edicts must be revealed in order for his subjects to obey them. In the same way, Malkhut, through the aspect of speech, *proclaims* God's will and reveals His sovereignty.

Rebbe Nachman thus taught:

> Malkhut corresponds to the Divine Presence. One who rectifies his speech merits the ability to make intimate contact with Malkhut, God's Divine Presence (*Likutey Moharan* I, 12:1).

Malkhut, represented by the mouth, is the point through which the most sublime thoughts are channeled downwards until they are revealed on this gross physical plane. While no one can ever know what another is thinking, through the aspect of Malkhut that is seen in speech, those thoughts can be revealed. Malkhut thus represents the culmination of the entire process of thought, as well as the trigger for new thoughts (which could not have been called to mind had other thoughts not been expressed and heard).

*

All the "pairs" we have discussed here are as inseparable as they are interdependent. Thought and speech, though distinct, are inseparable. The same is true of intellect and faith, Torah and prayer, the Written and Oral Torah, Tiferet and Malkhut, male and female. In each case, it is precisely *because* of their differences that the two complement each other and interact. Each is a full partner, though each has a totally different function. Just as various hormones influence different parts of our bodies in different but necessary ways, so too these diverse spiritual forces educe different, though equally important, manifestations of spiritual concepts. This unique distinction is precisely what makes interaction between various forces possible, in order for new ideas and concepts to be revealed — for new life to be created!

* * *

45

Eve

J ust as Adam is the paradigm of men, Eve (Chavah) is the paradigm of women. The Hebrew word *CHAVaH* carries the connotation of speech, as in the verse (Psalms 19:3), "Night to night *yeCHAVeH* [expresses] knowledge." Eve is thus the speech of Malkhut that perfects man and differentiates him from animals for of all of Creation it is only the human being that possesses the power of speech. This is particularly significant in light of the fact that one of the root meanings of the name *ADaM* (man) is *DoM* (silence)! This meaning refers to the silence of meditative thought, the activity of thought before it is expressed. Eve is thus the creative speech that issues forth from this deep silence of meditation.

There are two traditions as to how Eve was created. One is that a rib was extracted from Adam, and from that Eve was created. The other is that Adam and Eve were created back to back and were then split down the middle. These two opinions are indicated by the very names Adam and Eve when compared to the Tetragrammaton.

The numerical equivalent of the name Adam is 45 (אדם, *Aleph*=1, *Dalet*=4, *Mem*=40), which is the same as that of the Tetragrammaton, *YHVH*, when each letter is spelled out in full, using *Alephs* (יוד הא ואו הא, *YOD*=20, *HEh*=6, *VAV*=13, *HEh*=6; see Appendix D).

When the initial letters of the Tetragrammaton are calculated alone, they equal 26 (י=10, ה=5, ו=6, ה=5). When these initial letters are omitted from the fully spelled out name (whose numerical equivalent is 45), the remaining letters (וד=10, א=1, או=7, א=1) yield a total of 19, the numerical equivalent of ChaVaH (Eve) (חוה, ח=8, ו=6, ה=5).

These same equivalents are obtained when the Tetragrammaton of 45 is split down the middle. The first two letters spelled out (יוד=20, הא=6) equal 26. The second two letters spelled out (ואו=13, הא=6) equal 19.

Thus, through two highly significant methods of calculation, the Tetragrammaton of 45 is a special combination of 26 plus 19, which equals 45, ADaM. The first method, whereby we *extract* the "fill-in" letters of the female (19), leaving over the initial letters of the male (26), is the parallel or inner counterpart of the tradition that Eve was *extracted* from Adam's side or rib. In this sense, the male aspect of Adam (45) is the actual Name *YHVH* (26), while the female, inner aspect is Chavah (19).

The second method of calculation, whereby the Tetragrammaton is split down the middle, is the parallel or inner counterpart of the tradition that Adam and Eve were themselves created back to back, and only afterwards separated by being split down the middle (see *Berakhot* 61a).

*

The Treasure

Vayiven, and God *built* her....

Genesis 2:22

After God separated Eve from Adam, He *built* her into a complete form. According to the Talmud, this means that He "constructed" the female form as an *otzar*, a storage house or silo, a structure narrower at the top and wider at the bottom, for the explicit purpose of being able to carry within her a fetus (*Berakhot* 61a). The woman's body begins to adopt this form when she reaches puberty and her pelvis begins to widen, because at that point she has reached the age when conception can take place.

Rebbe Nachman teaches that the word *otzar*, to which woman

is compared, also bears the meaning of a "treasure." The treasure inherent in woman is the fear of God, as in (Isaiah 33:6), "The fear of God is His treasure," for one who lacks the treasure of awe of God cannot enter the gates of holiness. This is also seen from the woman's correlation to the *Sefirah* of Malkhut, which corresponds to fear and awe (see *Likutey Moharan* I, 60:9; see also above, Chapter 40, that Malkhut is the gate of awe and fear of God; see also Chapters 32 and 35).

One might think that even without actual fear of God, one's devotions can be performed out of love, but the truth is that a love that lacks awe and respect is virtually meaningless. As in a physical relationship, love wanes. Indeed, what reason is there for it to continue? However, in a relationship based on *both* love and respect, each aspect strengthens the other. God created within man the ability to love and to give of himself, yet without the personification of awe, the aspect of woman, man would be unable to reinforce and renew himself when he found himself overwhelmed by the many and varied vicissitudes of life. Awe and fear of God instill within a person the necessary restraints which enable him to continue on a clear path when things look bleak. Fear of God can always bring a person back to his former level — and forward to levels he has not yet attained.

*

Bounty

The realm of Malkhut is where man interacts with God. Because of this, it is important to know the nature of this *Sefirah*, in order to interact with God more effectively.

The ARI teaches that all the Universes are in a state of continuous motion. Each point in time is different because the balance of energy in each Universe is perpetually changing moment by moment (*Etz Chaim* 1:5). Reb Noson adds that this is precisely why repentance is effective for everyone; for each moment begins a fresh life in a totally new situation which has never before existed (*Likutey Halakhot, Tefilin* 5:5). Nowhere is this change more evident than in Malkhut, the *Sefirah* which reflects the feminine aspect.

The most unique and continual changes are those that occur in a woman's body. Each month, for example, the menstrual cycle affects both a woman's body and her mental and emotional states. The transformations within a woman's body that take place throughout pregnancy are even more remarkable than those physiological differences which exist between man and woman.

These changes were not always part of a woman's life. They began only after Adam and Eve ate from the Tree of Knowledge of Good and Evil. Before their sin, Adam and Eve cohabitated, and their children, Cain and Abel, were born immediately. After they ate from the Tree, Adam and Eve were each punished in different ways. Instead of remaining in the Garden of Eden, free of concern over his livelihood, man was forced out and cursed with having to work hard and sweat to provide for his physical needs. The woman, for her part, was punished with the discomforts of menstrual cycles, pregnancy and the pain of childbirth (*Rashi* on Genesis 3:16–19).

The broader concept of "immediate childbirth" which existed in the Garden of Eden was reflected on a conceptual level as well, so that in man's state of existence before he ate from the Tree, a person would have been able to conceive new ideas, and could immediately see the outcome. The transgression of Adam and Eve resulted in the need for all of humanity to experience the painful processes of experimentation and trial and error, and the heartache of having to wait helplessly before being able to enjoy the results of or to experience their rewards.

Although we must live with a certain level of tribulation as a consequence of the First Man's deeds, this can be of benefit to our spiritual growth. One advantage, as we said above, is that repentance is more effective. For this reason, one must realize that one's prayers must always be different, constantly adjusting to meet the changing needs and new challenges that arise. This is because all interaction with God takes place in the realm of Malkhut, which corresponds to speech and prayer. Both aspects of Malkhut — change and prayer — must be incorporated for effective repentance, since this is the realm in which one communicates with God.

Another benefit of Adam and Eve's punishments applies to the changes a woman undergoes and how they manifest in Malkhut. The changes seen in Malkhut are compared to the human stages of infancy, maturity, marriage and childbirth. In terms of the relationship between man and God as manifest in Malkhut, we must realize that, in accordance with the constant transformations which occur within Malkhut, man's ability to exercise control over God's bestowal of abundance to this world is regulated. Thus the various stages — infancy, maturity, marriage and childbirth — that are represented within the realm of Malkhut correspond to the levels of man's performance of good deeds.

God will send bounty to the world in accordance with one's efforts to attain knowledge of Him. If man employs all his strength in the performance of mitzvot, God bestows plentiful bounty. If man sins, either bounty is withheld, or it is sent in abundance, only to be sidetracked through the winding paths and "back alleyways" to the Other Side, which then penetrates Malkhut and draws the *shefa* (bounty) to itself, God forbid.

It is important to note, as the ARI explains (*Etz Chaim* 35:1), that the Hebrew word for woman is NeKeVah (נקבה). These letters stand for the three stages of development of the female: *K'tanah* (child), *Na'arah* (puberty) and *Bogeret* (maturity). The final letter *Heh* of *nekevaH* represents the final letter *Heh* of the Tetragrammaton. A woman will never revert to childhood once she has reached puberty, and will never revert to puberty once she has reached adulthood; the *Sefirah* of Malkhut, however, *is* always changing. After Malkhut attains a level of maturity and "mates" with Zer Anpin, *shefa* descends. But since mankind is not yet ready for the Redemption, Malkhut must revert to a stage of immaturity, beginning the whole process again. With the turn of the whole of mankind to God, in Messianic times, Malkhut will mature fully and remain at that level. *Shefa* will then abound, good health and prosperity will be everyone's portion, and all suffering will be removed from the face of the earth.

*

A Pure Foundation

One of the differences between the male and female physiology is that when the male reaches puberty, without major apparent changes to his body, he is able to procreate. His foreskin, representing various evil characteristics, was removed long before, at his circumcision (see above, Chapter 41). The female body, on the other hand, begins to undergo several noticeable changes at puberty: her pelvis and hips widen and her breasts develop, to cite some examples. Unlike the male, the female Yesod still has a *kelipat nogah*, reflected in the hymen, which must be penetrated in order for her to procreate.

A woman's development parallels the changes undergone by Malkhut as it reaches its own stages of maturity. Only when Malkhut has "matured" is it ready to unite with Zer Anpin, and so to receive Divine *shefa*.

Our Sages teach that a woman's virginity denotes purity (Niddah 65b). The ARI deals extensively with this subject, though his teachings are beyond the scope of this work. Basic to the ARI's general approach, however, is that the existence of the hymen enables a woman to safeguard herself from exposure to unworthy forces, until she is ready to engage in pure marital relations for the sake of procreation. At that point, the Yesod of the male combines with the Yesod of the female, establishing a solid "foundation," in which conception and childbirth can occur.

This concept teaches us that each individual is equipped by God with a means of safeguarding himself against atheism and immorality. Anyone who wishes can protect himself from these forces and build a spiritual life, with his own God-given resources, for everyone possesses the ability to lay solid moral foundations for the generations to come.

*

Renewal: The Monthly Cycle

Malkhut corresponds to the moon. We view the moon in a monthly cycle, gradually waxing from the beginning of each month, becoming full at mid-month, and then beginning to wane. When it reaches the point where it seems to disappear, it is immediately renewed, waxing again. Thus the moon is an ever-changing entity, as is woman, who experiences the monthly cycle of menstruation. Both are manifestations of Malkhut.

When the menstrual cycle begins, various hormones are released which stimulate the development of the ova (eggs). About fourteen days later, an ovum is mature and ready to be fertilized. This state of maturity lasts for only a few days. If fertilization does not occur during this time, the ovum begins to degenerate, and shortly thereafter the inner lining of the uterus, together with the ovum, is expelled from the body in menstruation. This cycle is strikingly similar to that of the moon, which waxes to "maturity" at mid-month, remains full for just a few days, and then diminishes.

Reb Noson writes that these cycles can be seen to correspond to human existence in general. Each person has his constant ups and downs, his "waxings and wanings," which today we might refer to as biorhythms. The ARI writes that every person has at least one day in each month when everything goes "just right," as well as various other successful days at specific times of the month (see *Shaar HaGilgulim* #38, p.135). But how should one deal with the more difficult times, which are also scattered throughout each month?

The message is inherent in the physical cycles found within nature — the lunar cycle and the menstrual cycle — that everything that happens, whether good and bad, is part of the ongoing cycle of life. When some time or event brings with it success, relief or happiness, we must try to use the situation to our best advantage. However, when difficult moments inevitably arrive, we must overcome any tendency towards pessimism or negativity, drawing strength from the good times, aware that just as the moon wanes, it also waxes. This is why the "New Moon" is called *Rosh Chodesh*; the word *CHoDeSH* has the same letters as the Hebrew word *CHaDaSH* (new). The renewal of the moon each month teaches us that a person can always renew himself, no matter what situation he finds himself in. In fact, Reb Noson continues, a person can renew himself each and every day (*Likutey Halakhot, Tefilin* 5:19).

King David reflects all the qualities of Malkhut, as manifest in the moon (as above, Chapter 40). Our Sages teach (*Zohar* I, 55a) that King David should not have survived, for he was destined to be stillborn. God allowed Adam to be privy to this bit of information and so, in order to save the great potential he recognized in the soul of David, Adam granted him seventy years of his own life. (Adam thus lived only nine hundred and thirty years, instead of the thousand years he had originally been destined to live.) In keeping with the cyclic pattern that can be found within Malkhut, King David always renewed himself. He, more than any other Biblical personality, suffered terribly throughout his entire lifetime. Yet he constantly revitalized and reinvigorated himself. Thus, even though he originally had "no life," he was able, with the energy he generated within his soul through his own efforts for renewal, to create for himself a full life! (*Likutey Halakhot, Tefilin* 5:21).

*

Family Purity

The Torah prohibits a woman from having marital relations during and immediately following her menstrual period, and after she has counted seven clean days without seeing the slightest trace of blood upon examination. After that time has elapsed, she enters the purifying waters of the *mikvah* (ritual bath) and becomes permitted to her husband. This is all part of the mitzvah of family purity.

During menstruation, a woman's uterus is considered to have an "open wound." Any abrasive contact with a foreign object at that time is liable to produce irritation, which could lead to serious health problems. This is but one explanation for abstention from marital relations during and immediately after the menstrual period.

(Studies have shown that where families observed the mitzvah of family purity, the rate of cancer of the cervix and/or the uterus was far lower than when family purity laws were not heeded. Some of these studies were released by Dr. Hiram Wineberg, head of Gynecology of Mount Sinai Hospital of New York in 1919, and have been followed up by Dr. M. Smytlin of Brooklyn and Professor L. Duncan Bulkley of the New York Skin and Cancer Hospital among others. The material is beyond the scope of this book but is cited as additional examples of the physical advantages of observing the Torah laws of family purity. For more information on family purity and the importance of immersing in the *mikvah*, see *The Waters of Eden*, by Rabbi Aryeh Kaplan, published by NCSY.)

The Talmud offers another important reason for the limited interlude of abstention imposed by the Torah: were the couple to have the opportunity for constant intimate relations, this might lead to excessive familiarity, causing their love and respect for one another to wane. The Torah's injunction for the couple to abstain from intimacy for part of the month keeps alive the feeling of freshness in the relationship (*Niddah* 31b).

The Hebrew term for menstruation is *nidah*, stemming from the roots *nad* and *nadad* (wander; in exile). The concept of exile is thus inherent in the phenomenon of menstruation. After Adam ate from the Tree of Knowledge, part of his punishment was exile from the Garden of Eden. Eve, too, ate from the Tree, and part of her punishment was the phenomenon of menstruation — a type of "banishment."

Rebbe Nachman taught:

There are 365 Torah prohibitions, corresponding to the 365 sinews and blood vessels of the human body. One who guards himself from sin, especially from sexual sin, keeps his vascular system clean and healthy. However, those who commit sins, particularly sexual sins, render all their blood impure in the same way that menstrual blood is considered impure. This corresponds to the concept of the "menstrual blood" of the Divine Presence. It represents Malkhut in exile, whereby She (Malkhut) is "separated" from Her "Husband" (Zer Anpin). Our actions relative to God's commandments elicit a responsive reaction in God's relationship towards us. Thus, human failure to avoid sin is the reason for Israel's and mankind's continued exile from the Garden of Eden (*Likutey Moharan* I, 29:3).

The greatest tragedy of exile occurs when Jews forget the wealth of their own culture and become assimilated within their host nations. Their sensitivity to spirituality becomes dulled, and they begin to strive for the same material comforts that their neighbors possess. Yet this situation need not be irreversible.

Menstruation is a monthly cycle, and immersing in the *mikvah* serves as the "gate" through which one emerges from impurity into purity. The sins that cause one to descend from spirituality, to be forced into exile and to be distanced from Godliness, can be removed and cleansed through the purifying waters of the *mikvah*.

Reb Noson explains how immersing in the *mikvah* can cleanse one of sin:

> Immersion in the *mikvah* is an act of self-nullification before God, for no human being can survive in water. By immersing one's body completely in water, one is demonstrating a willingness to sacrifice one's very life in order to cleanse oneself completely of sin. This form of self-nullification indicates a state of "nothingness," which in Hebrew is referred to as "*mah*." The numerical equivalent of *MaH* is 45, the same as that of *YHVH* (when expanded with *Alephs*; see Appendix D). Repenting and returning to God is the rectification and purification of spiritual "menstrual impurity," and effectively allows the aspect of Adam and the aspect of Eve to unite as one in holiness (*Likutey Halakhot, Mikvaot* 1:1).

Rebbe Nachman compares the fluctuating, cyclic relationship of Jewish married life — the times of togetherness and the times of abstention — to the movement of the angelic creatures of the Holy Chariot of God, who were (Ezekiel 1:14) "running and returning." We may infer from this that the attainment of spirituality requires both times of physical closeness and times of abstention (cf. *Likutey Moharan* I, 265). Hence, one who practices the laws of family purity can remain pure even in times of impurity, if the *desire* for purity is foremost in one's mind. But the reverse is equally applicable: Those who refuse to negate themselves before God will remain impure, even in times of apparent "purity."

Rebbe Nachman also taught that the hands correspond to faith (see above, Chapter 37). The numerical equivalent of *NiDaT* (נדת [menstrual blood], 454) is equal to the *gematria* of *YaD* (יד, hand) when its letters (*YOD DaLeT*) are expanded (*Yod Vav Dalet* יוד=20, plus *Dalet Lamed Tav* דלת =434). The imperfection created when one blemishes one's hands, meaning one's faith, is compared to the impurity of menstruation. Rectifying faith is the true purification from "menstruation" (*Likutey Moharan* I, 22:1–2, notes 22, 33).

*

Nurturing

Breast-feeding is a natural function that generally only a mother can perform after she has given birth to a child. During the course of pregnancy, the fetus draws its sustenance from the food which the mother eats. Lactation begins after birth, when hormones suppress the menstrual flow and stimulate the production of breast milk for the infant to suckle (see *Bekhorot* 6b). As Rebbe Nachman describes it, during lactation the menstrual blood, a sign of impurity, is transformed into a substance of absolute purity, providing a means of life support for those too weak to fend for themselves (see *Likutey Moharan* I, 9:3).

King David said (Psalms 103:2), "Bless God, my soul; do not forget His *gemul* [benefits]." The Talmud remarks that the word *gemul* refers also to breast-feeding. King David was expressing thanks to God that, as human beings, our mothers' breasts are located in the region of the heart, the seat of Binah, unlike the mammary glands of other mammals, which are located in the region of the genitals. A human child is created to serve God and to live a spiritual life, and therefore, unlike animals, is not forced to view the genital area. King David's gratitude was further inspired by the fact that a human infant does not nurse from the general area from which waste matter is excreted (see *Berakhot* 10a).

The ARI writes (*Shaar HaKlalim* 3) that the Holy Name of God associated with Binah is *Elohiym*. Since human breasts are situated in the area in which Binah is based, close to the heart, this Holy Name alludes to the function of breast-feeding. The Hebrew word for breasts is *dadim* (singular *dad*). There are two breasts, a right and a left. Of the five letters of the Holy Name *ELoHiYM* (אלהים), the first two letters on the right are *EL* (אל) and the last two letters on the left are *YM* (ים), with a *Heh* (ה) in the center.

When God extended Moses' spirit of prophecy to the seventy elders, the Torah relates (Numbers 11:27), "Eldad and Meydad are prophesying in the camp." When one combines the right and left breasts with the right and left letters of the name *Elohiym*, that is, when one puts a *DaD* with *EL* and a *DaD* with *YM*, the words ELDaD and MeYDaD are formed. The breasts, placed in the region of Binah, therefore allude to the source from which one can draw prophecy. The letter *Heh*, which is in the center of the Holy Name *Elohiym*, corresponds to the milk, and supplies both breasts. *CHaLaV* (חלב, milk) is numerically equal to 40, and there are three expansions of the letter *Heh* which, when added together with their constituent letters, also equal 40 (see *Etz Chaim, Shaar HaKlalim* 3, pp.7–8). Thus the breasts allude to some of the highest levels of spirituality, from which a person can draw spiritual nourishment to sustain himself.

Rebbe Nachman taught:

> There is a spiritual source of bounty which is known as Eldad and Meydad. These names correspond to the breasts.

Bounty itself is associated with the letter *Heh*, as in (Genesis 47:23), "*Hei lakhem zera* [here is seed for you]." Thus, the letters which form the names of Eldad and Meydad, implying bounty, together with the letter *Heh*, which means bounty, comprise the Name of *ELoHiYM*, an endless source of bounty.

When a person sins, he blemishes the letter *Heh*, such that the leg of the letter is removed, leaving the form of a *dalet*. (The "leg" is the letter *yod* which connotes Chokhmah, Wisdom. A person sins due to a spirit of folly [as above, Chapter 41], hence his leg-wisdom is "removed"). *DaLet*, associated with the Hebrew word *DaL* [poor], denotes poverty. *Dalet* thus also denotes Malkhut, because it is the *Sefirah* that possesses nothing of its own — it has only that which it receives from Zer Anpin. Thus, when one sins, the letter *Heh* of *ELoHiYM* is converted to a *Dalet* to read "*EL DaMiY* — God is silent," meaning "prophecy is withheld." In order to change this situation, one must pray. Prayer "opens" Malkhut to receive the *shefa* of prophecy that has been diminished as a result of sin. Rectifying one's sins and drawing bounty to oneself requires both humility and fear of God. With these attributes, Malkhut is rebuilt, and *shefa* can be drawn into it (*Likutey Moharan* I, 97:1-5).

A mother who eats a balanced diet will be able to provide sufficient healthful nourishment for her child. The same applies to the spiritual nourishment an infant absorbs from its mother. Rebbe Nachman teaches that a brazen woman imparts her quality of impudence to her suckling infant. A modest woman likewise transfers to her infant her own refined attributes. Thus, the physical act of breast-feeding passes crucial spiritual influences to an infant (*Likutey Moharan* II, 1:4; see also *Avodah Zarah* 10b, *Tosafot, s.v. Amar*).

Reb Noson writes in one of his classic discourses about the nurturing of the human being: Man is unique among all animal life forms in that the human infant suckles from the breasts, which are in the area of the heart, the home of Binah. Animals, on the other hand, suckle near the region from where waste matter is excreted. In a broader sense, we may learn from this that each individual has his or her unique place from which to derive nourishment and no one should ever attempt to infringe on another person's livelihood. Doing so creates a situation that forces the one who has been wronged to rise up and defend himself against those who have encroached upon or in some way violated his life or livelihood.

Reb Noson goes on to apply this concept to national patterns of Jewish assimilation. To ensure that the non-Jew acts as a human being towards him, the Jew must act characteristically as a Jew and follow Torah law. When the Jew attempts to act like a non-Jew, he is in effect invading the non-Jew's territory and threatening him. This causes the non-Jew to react violently and inhumanly toward the "Jewish invaders" (*Likutey Halakhot, Mekach u'Memkar* 4:9).

*

We have seen that the breasts symbolize a deep spiritual sustenance which is at once tremendously powerful yet individual. In a broader sense, each person must draw sustenance on his own level and must not seek a lifestyle that is inappropriate to his current abilities. The breasts are also termed *shadayim*, which contains the word "*DaI* — enough!" for there is no need to look beyond one's own source of bounty to fulfill one's needs; there is ample spirituality available for everyone.

* * *

46

"Be Fruitful and Multiply"

What brings more joy to our hearts than a wedding? Reb Noson writes that the joy of a wedding is comparable to the joy of the World to Come (*Likutey Halakhot, Birkhat HaReiach* 5:20). Yet even Reb Noson himself was known to question this joy, just as King Solomon expressed (Ecclesiastes 2:2), "Of joy, what does it achieve?" In truth, what reason have the couple to be joyous? What guarantee is there that this relationship will be firmly established and that it will endure? Will they cope with their financial responsibilities? Will their children thrive? (The rate of infant mortality was quite high in Reb Noson's day.) What of the problems inherent in raising one's children — childhood diseases, the challenges of adolescence and all the other "normal" problems that accompany growing children?

The Midrash expresses a similar thought. Commenting on the verse (Ecclesiastes 7:1), "A good name is better than fine oil; and the day of death is better than the day of birth," the Midrash offers this analogy: One ship was departing on its voyage at the same time that another was docking, having completed its trip (in the days before radio communication, it was impossible to know how a ship was faring at sea or when it would arrive). The departing ship was seen off by many well-wishers shouting *"Bon voyage!"* The incoming ship, however, had no one to welcome it home. A wise man observed this scene and commented, "The opposite reactions would seem far more appropriate. The ship setting off on its journey should arouse a great deal of concern. What kind of winds and other conditions will it encounter? What trials await the departing ship? It is rather the incoming ship that should be cheered, for it has safely completed its voyage."

In the same manner, everyone rejoices at a birth; but who can tell what awaits that infant as he grows to maturity and encounters the inevitable difficulties of life? It is rather the person who has already completed the journey of his life and has passed away with a good name for whom we should rejoice (*Kohelet Rabbah* 7:4).

And yet Reb Noson compares nuptial joy to that of the World to Come!

Rebbe Nachman teaches that the union of a couple is very precious (*Likutey Moharan* II, 32:4). Reb Noson explains that this union is rooted in the loftiest of levels of God's plan for Creation, a level which no mind can conceive. The human soul is rooted in the very first inspiration — the "thought" which preceded any act of Creation. It was God's *thought* to create souls that afterwards "caused" Him, as it were, to bring the remainder of the universe into existence. All of Creation thus serves as a framework for the existence and activity of human souls, and the sole purpose of Creation is the revelation of Godliness. This purpose is fulfilled through our performance of good deeds during our sojourn on this earth, while we are still clothed in physical bodies.

But the descent of any soul into this physical world is possible only through the union of man and wife. This union makes it possible to draw exalted souls down to this earth, for in their very union, man and wife reach up to that highest of levels (*Likutey Halakhot, Minchah* 7:93).

We have already seen that the main test of one's spirituality is the control one exercises in overcoming one's physical lust. Let us now explore how spirituality and sexuality — by definition, apparently contradictory terms — join together in holiness to bring forth a new soul.

At its source, the soul is a single unit. When it enters this world, the soul is divided into two separate bodies, which parallel two opposing forces — the male and the female — both of which must be harnessed in order to strive for Godliness. Each "half" must at first undergo a great deal of individual growth, and each must eventually seek out the other. The two can then be reunited, this time in marriage.

Reb Noson writes that what is most singular about the conception of a child is that the process must be initiated through the organs of the excretory system, in order to draw a holy soul down from the loftiest of levels! (Although the female reproductive system is not part of the excretory system as we find in the male, it may be viewed as such, since the sperm enters the same passage through which the menstrual blood exits.)

The reason the soul must first descend through the excretory organs is that, at its source, it is a most awesome entity (see Chapter 3), and thus its ability to reveal Godliness is extremely powerful. The forces of evil necessarily oppose the descent of the soul to this world, for each soul would be able, through its innate composition, to overcome temptation easily. This natural ability of the soul would preclude the free will of a human being, for a balance between the forces of good and evil must be equal in order for free will to exist. The forces of evil only agree to the entry of the soul into this world when it is a result of arousal of sensual desire, manifested in the baser organ, for then it is considered to be "tainted" with physicality, and the balance between spirituality and materialism can be maintained.

Reb Noson goes on to explain that a soul on its way to this earth passes through all the Supernal Universes, before reaching the parents through whom, when their sensual lust is aroused to its highest pitch, conception occurs. Then, after a pregnancy, culminating in labor, pain and blood, that soul finally enters into human form. From this we can see that a person who wishes to seek spirituality finds himself in a quandary: On the one hand, he seeks his source, at the loftiest of levels. On the other hand, he was born of lust and so embodies some of man's basest characteristics (*Likutey Halakhot, Minchah* 7:20). It is therefore puzzling that the institution of marriage is so highly regarded in Jewish tradition and literature, and we must attempt to understand what makes the union between male and female so significant.

*

Daat

In the Bible, marital relations are referred to as Daat, as in the verse (Genesis 4:1), "And Adam *knew* his wife, Eve." When a husband and wife join together in purity and sanctity, their souls join to form a vehicle for the revelation of that Daat of Godliness. Their kiss represents the unifying of the *Yod* and *Heh*, the first letters of the Name (יה), corresponding to the Divine *Partzufim* (Persona) of Abba and Imma (Father and Mother). Through their sexual union which is rooted in the level of Yesod, they represent the unifying of the *Vav* and the *Heh*, the final letters of the Tetragrammaton (וה), which correspond to Zer Anpin and Malkhut, respectively. Like the two Cherubim in the Holy of Holies, they together constitute a *mishkan* (tabernacle) or a *merkavah* (chariot) for the Divine Name of YHVH. These are the lofty thoughts and intentions a couple should have when they join together to bring new life into the world.

The *Partzufim* of Abba and Imma correspond to the *Sefirot* of Chokhmah and Binah. The confluence of Chokhmah and Binah brings about a revelation of Daat. The confluence of Zer Anpin and Malkhut, which takes place in the *Sefirah* of Yesod, brings this revelation to its full fruition. This double confluence which occurs through the marital union must be a positive experience in order for it to be effective in bringing down the highest souls into earthly bodies. The Talmud therefore teaches that anger and idle thoughts must always be removed before engaging in marital relations, so that the union can take place in a peaceful and harmonious atmosphere of love. Relations should be conducted with modesty and with an appreciation for the awesome power that the couple together are able to generate (cf. *Nedarim* 20a–b).

Rebbe Nachman adds that acting with modesty in marital

relations is compared to fulfilling the mitzvah of sukkah, and also that this level of modesty allows one to merit the sanctity of the Holy Land (*Likutey Moharan* I, 48:3). This is because the fulfillment of each of these two mitzvot (the sukkah and being in the Holy Land) requires one's being completely within and enveloped by the mitzvah. By remaining covered (by a sheet or quilt) during marital relations, a couple is likewise enveloped within the mitzvah in which they are engaged.

Marital relations may take place at any time, but since modesty dictates that the couple be hidden from view (darkness and concealment actually accentuate the auditory and tactile experience), nighttime is preferable. Shabbat represents peace, as has been explained (above, Chapters 10–11); therefore Friday night is considered the most propitious time for marital relations.

Rebbe Nachman taught:

> Guarding the *brit* has two levels. The person who engages in marital relations during the six days of the week is considered to be one who guards his *brit*, since he is careful not to transgress the Torah's laws. However, the person who guards the *brit* through engaging in marital relations [only] on Shabbat eve attains a higher level.
>
> The first [lower] type of union corresponds to *halakhah* [the revealed law], and the second to Kabbalah [the concealed tradition]... Whoever fulfills his marital obligations according to Torah Law, even during the six weekdays, attains a level from which he can reveal Godliness to all, for this level corresponds to the level of the revealed Torah, the *halakhah*. The higher level of engaging in marital relations only on Shabbat corresponds to the deepest mysteries of Torah, the Kabbalah, wherein a more intimate relationship with God is engendered (*Likutey Moharan* I, 11:5–6).

Rebbe Nachman teaches that the desire for marital relations begins in the mind. Thus it is crucial that one's mind, as the source of desire, be connected to God while one is engaging in marital relations. This enables one to draw down a pure, illuminated soul for the child then conceived. Of course, conception does not always result from marital relations. Nevertheless, by attaching themselves to Godliness in their intimate relationship, a couple can arouse and elevate the souls at their source level (the level of thought, as above) and bring them to repentance (see *Likutey Moharan* I, 14:3–4). Thus, focusing one's mind upon one's relationship with God during marital relations is a source of true Daat, for whether or not conception results, the world becomes imbued with knowledge of God.

The marital union of a couple generally begins with an embrace and a kiss. Just as in the physical realm, where these acts arouse feelings of strong attachment to one another, they also create a parallel spiritual connection. The Kabbalistic principles of *chibuk* (embracing), *nishuk* (kissing) and *zivug* (intimacy) refer to spiritual relationships in the Upper Worlds. *Although these Kabbalistic concepts have no connection whatsoever to any physical actions*, they are embodied in the actions of a husband and wife involved in marital intimacy in purity.

Pure acts of physical intimacy are in fact described as a bonding together of souls. This is because Chokhmah (corresponding to the first Divine thought) is the source of all souls, just as thought — being the beginning, and in fact the source, of the marital act — is also the source of the conception of a soul (*Sha'ar Ma'amarei Rashbi* p.32; see *Likutey Moharan* I, 12:4, nn.80–82). Thus the arousal of Chokhmah, the male aspect, is one element of Daat. The response is the arousal of Binah, the female aspect, which is another element of Daat. The actual act of intimacy *is* Daat, the joining of the two very different elements (as discussed above, Part 4).

When a couple engages in the act of sexual intimacy, they are literally bonding themselves together. The different forces within them can then merge and blend together to form a single unit, a manifestation of Daat, which is the fruit of their combined intellect (which can be actualized in the form of a child). If, however, one binds oneself in a prohibited relationship, the result is totally unrelated to Daat. In such a case, the elements of Chokhmah and Binah which are forced into close proximity are not of the same form and can never truly blend. Just as anyone would be disgusted to relate sexually to a person who is physically repulsive to him, so too the soul feels disgust at being bound to another soul which it finds detestable.

This is one of the reasons for the Torah's strict injunctions regarding sexual relationships. Prohibited relationships include cohabitation with a menstruating woman or with a woman who has not yet immersed in the *mikvah*, even one's wife; adultery; incest; and homosexuality. Several of these are referred to in the Torah as "abominations." The soul was created to seek spirituality. Any sexual activity prohibited by the Torah, because of the nature of the bonding that takes place between two consenting individuals in such a relationship, will raise a spiritual barrier. Bonding one's soul to the soul of another in a prohibited relationship creates an attachment to the Other Side — and reversing that attachment by breaking off the relationship isn't that easy (see *Bereishit Rabbah* 80:11).

As we have seen, seed originates in the mind (Keter), "travels" down the spine (i.e., Daat) until it reaches Yesod, and is then transferred to Malkhut, its final destination. When properly understood, this process can encourage us to distance ourselves from prohibited sexual activities and to exercise modesty in our marital relations. When traveling, any deviation from an established route can lead a person astray. In the same way, any minor deviation from the Torah's prescribed path of morality can seriously mislead the one who seeks the road to spiritual perfection. For this reason, although the Talmud teaches that a married couple may engage in any form of intimacy, the Sages nevertheless strongly recommend staying within certain parameters (see *Nedarim* 20b). Experimenting with nonstandard practices in marital relations can lead to fantasies, which in turn may lead to other aberrations, manifestations of the troubled mind, which can prove very difficult to keep in check.

This same ethical approach applies to all sorts of prohibited relationships. At first, a relationship may seem to be just a step beyond what is acceptable, but, as one thing leads to another, these "almost acceptable" relationships may lead to more deviant acts. The increase in homosexuality, pedophilia and rape in the world today bears witness to the extreme callousness that has developed in modern sexual attitudes which plagues our society. A sure indication of a society's dementia is the extent to which it rationalizes and justifies the afflictions which lead to such behavior. We must pray hard to be protected from becoming ensnared in these attitudes. And all those who are involved in sexually deviant behavior must pray incessantly to extricate themselves from that lifestyle and regain a reasonable level of moral stature.

This was the challenge of the protagonist in Rebbe Nachman's story of "The Exchanged Children," where the prince became the slave, and the slave, the prince. A prince is one who should *act* like royalty, stately in his attitudes towards life and fully in control. Instead, the prince in the story became a slave to his lusts. In the same way, morally misguided individuals attempt to conduct themselves as if they are in charge of their lives, but in reality they are slaves to their own neurotic cravings and erotic fantasies.

*

Marital Relations

One should not conclude, because of the strong injunctions against prohibited relationships, that the Torah views marital relations in a negative light. On the contrary, Judaism perceives marital intimacy as a very important and positive facet of married life and strongly encourages it (within reasonable limits). The Talmud teaches (see *Eruvin* 63b) that in one instance Joshua caused the Jews to abstain from marital relations for only one night, and for this he was punished. In fact, Talmudic and Kabbalistic literature use metaphors based on the union between husband and wife to explain many teachings. For example, "Why is rain called *ReViAH?* Because it *RoVeAH* [impregnates] the ground" (*Yerushalmi, Shevi'it* 9:8; cf. *Taanit* 6b). Such metaphors are used because a union in holiness between husband and wife is considered one of the most beautiful and powerful acts of which man is capable. Indeed, our ultimate goal on this earth is for each individual to strive for that same level of intimate connection with God. Thus, it is one's *approach* to marital relations that marks the difference between a spiritual act and a lustful one. Rebbe Nachman teaches that a person must strengthen himself and muster all his inner powers to elevate his lusts (cf. *Likutey Moharan* I, 253; see also *Sotah* 47a: "One should push away one's lust with one's left hand, but draw it near with one's right").

*

Conception

We saw above (Chapter 20) that the air one breathes is influenced by one's desires. The arousal for sexual relations begins with one's desires, and, according to the nature of that desire, one creates an atmosphere for holy unification. One who is on the level of a tzaddik directs his desires to unify the letters of Torah, bringing about new Torah revelations and in that way "creating souls" (see above, Chapter 27). This effects greater revelations of Godliness in the world. Yet the average person can also reveal Godliness through the marital union, for he has the ability to bring to the world a new soul (see *Likutey Moharan* I, 31:14). Thus, in marital relations, nearly everything depends upon the attitude of the couple; both their mental orientation and their physical state contribute to the formation of the child. Rebbe Nachman thus taught that it is very important to direct one's thoughts to spirituality during marital relations. These thoughts will not interfere with the body's physical responses, nor will they in any way detract from one's ability to bring children into the world. On the contrary, spiritual thoughts during physical intimacy are extremely beneficial, both for the child that is conceived and for the couple engaged in relations (*Likutey Moharan* II, 106).

On a more practical note, since the menstrual cycle and the phases of the moon are conceptually related (see above, Chapter 45), Rebbe Nachman recommends that every couple, before engaging in relations, recite the biblical passages which refer to the New Moon (Numbers 28:11–15; see *Likutey Moharan* I, 151).

*

Since sperm cells cannot develop at the standard body temperature, their development takes place within the scrotum, where a cooler temperature is maintained. When the male is ready to perform his role in the marital union, the sperm is drawn into the body, heated to body temperature and then discharged. Rebbe Nachman taught:

A man "holds his breath" during marital relations for two reasons: First, this allows the sperm to maintain the warm temperature of the body so that it can succeed in fertilizing the female ovum. Second, the body cannot expel fluid and inhale at the same time (*Likutey Moharan* I, 60:3).

In this lesson, Rebbe Nachman also speaks of "pure, cool air" and associates it with wealth and bounty. As we have pointed out, a person's desires influence his approach to marital relations, and these desires actually circulate in the air he breathes. This air also influences the purity of one's seed. One who breathes unpolluted air enhances his body's state of health, so that his seed is enhanced by a "clean system," which is most beneficial for the child conceived in that union. Just as this is true on a physical level, so does it apply in the spiritual realm: A state of spiritual purity during relations positively influences the character of the child. This purity brings with it wealth and bounty, which are symbolized by the seed.

* * *

47

The Godly Image

The purpose of man's creation was to reveal the "Godly image." As we have seen throughout this work, man was endowed with a body that parallels the Supernal Universes and the *Sefirot*, in order to attain spirituality. The First Man was to have attained that level, but he sinned, "shattering" his Godly image and spreading sparks of holiness all over the world (see above, Chapter 8). Since then, all his descendants, each and every individual, according to his or her efforts to attain spirituality, "collects" those sparks and rebuilds the Godly image that was lost. As we know, man must ultimately die, bringing to a halt his efforts to rectify Adam's sin. Thus, the very first mitzvah in the Torah is to "be fruitful and multiply" — to bear children — so that the process of "rebuilding" the "Godly image" can continue steadily, until it is completed. This is the importance of having children.

Children are called *BaNim* in Hebrew, with a root related to the word *BiNyan*, "a building," for children are the building and foundation of the world. Without them, the world would have no enduring existence. This idea is explicit in the Torah and is illustrated by the desire of Abraham and Sarah to conceive a child. After long years of childlessness, Sarah said to Abraham (Genesis 16:2), "Perhaps I will be *built* through her [Hagar]." Rashi comments on her words, "From here we learn that not only is a person who has no children 'not built,' he is actually in a state of ruin." For indeed, what will remain after his life is over? Who will bear his name and continue his life's work after he has gone?

Children hold the key to something more basic than their parents' means for building the future; they can also help to rectify the past. Reb Noson writes:

> Having children to whom one tries to impart the recognition of God is itself a very great rectification of the *brit*. A person can never know what sort of offspring he may father; from his seed may issue a tzaddik, perhaps even a very great tzaddik. Among the ancestors of even the great Rabbi Shimon bar Yochai, the author of the Holy Zohar, there were very simple and ordinary people. Yet from them descended this great tzaddik, who revealed such awesome levels of Godliness and holiness in the world. Rabbi Shimon in his greatness was able to rectify the shortcomings of all his ancestors. Indeed, with his far-reaching merits he assumed responsibility for the rectification of the entire world (see *Sukkah 45b; Likutey Halakhot, Shabbat* 6:23).

Having children is the first mitzvah recorded in the Torah, and this mitzvah has great implications that apply to each and every person, each day. One is the concept of renewal: a person should never allow himself to become a "dried-out tree" that does not bear fruit. He must try to grow each day, to "give birth" to new ideas, new ways with which to find God, even in this world of mundane existence. Another is the necessity to share one's wisdom and awareness of the spiritual with others — "planting seeds" of Godliness in their minds and hearts. But, aside from its many broader conceptual applications, this mitzvah requires of us the actual fathering of children, literally, to "be fruitful and multiply."

*

The Mission

The very day on which they cohabited for the first time, Adam and Eve brought Cain and Abel into the world. This phenomenon of "instant development" was possible for them at that point in time, because the souls of Cain and Abel only needed to descend from the lofty spiritual levels in which they had originated into the spiritual existence of the Garden of Eden. The transgression of Adam and Eve created the need thereafter for a waiting period of nine months before a fertilized egg could become a fully developed child. This is due to the fact that the descent of the lofty human soul from the Supernal Worlds into the current status of this material world is a drastic change for that soul to face. Time is needed for the soul to adapt to its new surroundings.

The Talmud gives us a hint of what transpires during that waiting period (*Niddah* 30b): "When the infant is in its mother's womb, an angel teaches it the entire Torah. When it is born, the angel strikes the infant above the lip [apparent in the indentation between the lip and the nose], and all the angel's teachings are forgotten."

The obvious question which presents itself here is, Why study if one is inevitably going to forget all that one has learned? The commentaries state that without the study of Torah prior to birth, no one would ever stand a chance against the blinding forces of materialism. The studies, though forgotten on the level of conscious memory, leave a powerful impression upon the soul, and anyone who so desires can draw from and build upon that impression, and so develop a mighty awareness of spirituality. Rebbe Nachman taught:

> Before a person is born, he is taught all that he must work towards and accomplish through the course of his lifetime. The moment he enters the world, he forgets this entire body of knowledge. His mission in life is to seek what he lost. His "lost articles," his forgotten mission, may be found with the tzaddik (*Likutey Moharan* I, 188).

"During the Revelation at Mount Sinai," the Talmud tells us, "each Jew was adorned with crowns [of spiritual lights]. When the Jewish people committed the sin of the golden calf, the crowns were taken away from them, and Moses merited to have all those crowns" (*Shabbat* 88a). This teaching implies that the "lost articles" — the spiritual lights of the Jews — can be found with the tzaddikim. Seeking out the true tzaddik, the one who has a clear spiritual outlook, will help a person discover his true path, for the tzaddik understands the various paths of spirituality and can direct the person on the path that is proper for him.

*

The Purification Process

The spiritual concept of "pregnancy" which is referred to in the Holy Writings can be compared to an "embryo" which forms in the *Sefirah* of Malkhut. All that exists in the physical dimension mirrors that which is found in the spiritual; thus the same terminology is applied to two separate phenomena — one physical and one spiritual.

We are aware that all interaction between man and God takes place in the realm of Malkhut. Just as a mother seeks what is best for her children, Malkhut always attempts to elevate her "children." One who is worthy can readily benefit from this relationship and can ascend quite easily; but how does Malkhut relate to someone who was remiss and has gone astray during his life, one who has allowed himself to come to a state that requires rectification before he can again move forward and up?

The ARI teaches that the function of Malkhut in this world is more than simply to receive the *shefa* from Above and transmit it to this world. Malkhut also seeks out those souls that have become disconnected from their source, that have so descended that they have become trapped in the lowest realms, and it tries to elevate them as well. God's master plan for the world is that all people come to recognize Him, and it is through Malkhut (which represents acceptance of the Kingship of God) that God takes the steps necessary to implement this plan.

One who does not recognize God on his own, however, requires outside assistance. Since a tzaddik is able to achieve a high level of recognition of God, this assistance can be rendered by the tzaddikim, the righteous personifications of Yesod, who have remained faithful to God. Since Malkhut receives its energy from Yesod, the tzaddik, Malkhut acts as the interface between the tzaddik and those souls which require purification. In this way, they can relate to and benefit from the tzaddik's teachings, which are on a very lofty spiritual level. The light of the tzaddikim (i.e., their teachings and advice) is filtered through Malkhut to the broader population. Similarly, the good deeds of people who follow the advice of the tzaddik filter back to the tzaddikim (i.e., Yesod) through Malkhut. Alone their deeds could not reach the higher realms; they are not yet pure enough. Malkhut elevates and helps purify their deeds so they can reach the tzaddik, who further elevates them. In this way, each time anyone performs a good deed, that deed can be taken up by the tzaddik and incorporated within the spiritual "buildings of holiness" (*Likutey Halakhot, Minchah* 7:11–12).

(The reason Malkhut is the *Sefirah* which seeks out lost souls is that, as the interface between God and mankind, it is considered the source of the souls. Furthermore, Malkhut is the lowest of the *Sefirot* and is therefore closest to the realm of the Forces of Evil. We have seen (Chapter 28) that there are sparks of holiness [i.e., souls] which fall prey to the forces of materialism and become trapped in the realm of evil. Since their original misdeed distanced them from God, their personal blemish is considered a blemish in Malkhut, i.e., in the acceptance of God's Kingship. These souls must therefore pass through Malkhut for their rectification. It is a fact that no matter how low any sparks have fallen, they will eventually regret their circumstances and begin to seek their source. The ARI delved into this topic in many of his essays, discussing, for example, the descent of Malkhut into the lower realms to effect rectification, but these discussions are beyond the scope of this book.)

Thus, with the help of the tzaddik, Malkhut seeks out those souls who have fallen into error or transgression, building upon every positive vestige. Each good deed a person performs becomes a beacon of light upon which Malkhut can focus in order to help draw him back towards spirituality.

Still, if someone has remained distant from Godliness for an extended period of time, how can he be expected to be capable of receiving and benefiting from this bright spiritual light? It is in such an instance that the concept of Malkhut's "pregnancy" is crucial. The souls which had been distant from God experience a period of "gestation," during which they are slowly introduced to the opportunity to develop and grow into spirituality. Without this intermediate stage, the gap between the soul's current level and the road to spirituality would be too wide to bridge. Malkhut's "pregnancy" is thus a purification process, which corresponds to the trials and tribulations a soul must endure before being "born" into spirituality.

*

Pregnancy and Birth

When conception has occurred, the fertilized egg forms an embryo which implants itself in the wall of the uterus. Gradually, a more defined form begins to take shape, and the embryo becomes a human fetus. The Talmud teaches (Niddah 38b) that the Hebrew word for pregnancy, HeiRaYON (הריון), is numerically equivalent to 271 — the number of days which elapse from the moment of conception to full prenatal development. Modern medicine assumes that 266 days are required for this development. (When this seeming contradiction was presented to an obstetrician in a leading New York hospital, his response was, "The Talmud has been at it a lot longer than modern medicine. They must know better!")

But even after conception has taken place, there are times when a pregnacy terminates unexpectedly. This may be due to an imbalance in the hormones or to other problems, excessive physical or emotional stress, for example, which cause the fetus to be aborted.

Pregnancy has its parallel in the spiritual realm, as Rebbe Nachman taught:

> Revealing a new idea or a new path in serving God is comparable to a pregnancy. One must wait, allowing this idea to "gestate" until the time is ripe for it to be "born." Through strife, however, one might cause a "miscarriage," forcing an underdeveloped idea out before its time, thereby destroying any "life" it might have brought into the world (Likutey Moharan II, 20).

If the pregnancy is healthy and reaches full term the mother goes into labor: When birth is imminent, her uterine contractions gently turn the fully developed fetus so that it can enter the narrow birth canal head first. As the moment of birth approaches, the contractions intensify. With the onset of actual labor, each contraction can cause severe pain. The mother's legs begin to feel heavy and cold. Blood flows from the uterus, and the amniotic sac opens. The child begins to emerge, and, with God's help, a healthy child is born.

We have seen that the transfer of seed from Yesod to Malkhut symbolizes the transfer of bounty to the world. The bounty "gestates" in the *Sefirah* of Malkhut, after which it is given to the world. The reason for this "pregnancy" is to guard God's bounty from the forces of the Other Side, until such time as it is "fully developed" and people are ready to receive it.

It is written (*Zohar* III, 249b) that a woman cries out "seventy times" before giving birth. The reason for this is that each of the seven *Sefirot* of Zer Anpin and Malkhut is comprised of ten *Sefirot* of its own. In order for Malkhut to "give birth," that is, to reveal *shefa* on one's current level, it must reach through the entire range of the *Sefirot* of Zer Anpin and Malkhut. Thus, it must go through all the seven *Sefirot*, multiplied by the ten *Sefirot* contained within each, seventy *Sefirot* in all (*Zohar* III, 249b).

Rebbe Nachman taught:

> The painful contractions of labor correspond to the pain one must endure before "giving birth" to new ideas that hold the potential for success, or to new knowledge of spirituality. A woman in labor cries out with seventy cries of anguish before her child is born. So too, one who desires new levels of Godliness to be revealed to him must cry out again and again in prayer, in order to be able to "give birth" to these new, exalted ideas (*Likutey Moharan* I, 21:7).

Rebbe Nachman also taught that just as childbirth is accompanied by much pain and many cries, so can the performance of mitzvot be a painful process. Each time a person attempts to do a mitzvah, he may find the way fraught with difficulties. At that point, he must cry out to God to help him.

Charity acts as a powerful catalyst to help open wide the "narrow" doors that seem to hold one back from one's ability to "give birth," that is, to perform the mitzvot properly (Likutey Moharan II, 4:2). It is likewise very beneficial to give charity for the sake of a woman who is about to give birth.

Rebbe Nachman also said that it is worthwhile to recite Psalm 100 (Mizmor L'Todah) for a woman who is in labor so that she may have an easier childbirth. The first letters of each of the two first words of that psalm, ML (מל), together add up to seventy, the number of the cries of a woman in labor. The first words of the psalm itself correspond to Lovingkindness.

There are also forty-three words (numerically equivalent to MG, מג) in Psalm 100, which serve to negate the effects of the kelipot. These kelipot seek to prevent the birth of the child, for that child might come to recognize God. Therefore they (the kelipot) say (1 Kings 3:26), "GaM li, GaM lakh, lo yihiyeh — Neither for me, nor for you, shall there be [a child]." The forty-three (MG, מג) words found in the psalm are able to nullify the power of GaM (גם, 43), which encapsulates the desire of the kelipot to prevent the child's birth (Likutey Moharan II, 2:12).

*

The Zohar teaches that the blood of childbirth corresponds to the sustenance that is given over to the Other Side, which is manifest in severe judgments. The coldness a woman feels in her legs with the interruption of the normal flow of blood during childbirth is an indication of the presence of judgments. The concept of childbirth as the revelation of new ideas corresponds to the restriction of the mind, that is, judgments, prior to the attainment of knowledge. This is because judgments are based in Malkhut, which is manifest in the feet. For this reason, judgments are felt mainly in the legs and feet, and they cause one to feel "heavy" and lethargic. After the birth, the normal flow of blood resumes. Childbirth is thus considered a mitigation of judgments (*Likutey Moharan* I, 169:1; see also *Likutey Moharan* II, 2:3).

Rebbe Nachman taught:

> "*Mizmor l'todah hari'u laShem kol ha'aretz*" [A thanksgiving praise: Sing to God, all the world] (Psalms 100:1). This psalm alludes to childbirth, as well as to the "bearing" of new laws and to the understanding of new concepts in the *halakhah*. The word *L'ToDaH* [thanks; praise] contains the same letters as *ToLaDaH* [birth]. The word *HaLaKhaH*, referring to Jewish law, is the acrostic of *Hari'u LaShem Kol Ha'aretz*. To come to understand the Halakhic Codes, one must endure difficulties to the same degree as does a woman in childbirth. When that "child" is finally born, one can praise God with a new understanding, a new level of recognition of Him and His Malkhut (*Likutey Moharan* II, 2:2).

*

Exile and Exodus

> **Just as there are *tzirim* [hinges] and *d'latot* [doors] to a house, so too a woman has hinges and doors.**
>
> *Bekhorot* 45a

The Hebrew word for contractions is *tzirim*, which also translates as "hinges." When a fetus is ready to be born, the mother's cervix dilates, the contractions of the uterus push out the baby, and the cervix opens, as would a door, to accommodate the passage of the newborn child into the world.

Rebbe Nachman taught that the *Sefirah* of Malkhut corresponds to the letter *dalet* (see above, Chapter 45). The word *DaLeT* has the same letters as *DeLeT*, "door," which must be opened to allow for birth (*Likutey Moharan* I, 135:4–5). The letter *dalet* is numerically equal to four, and conveys the idea of the four exiles of the four kingdoms of evil (see *Bereishit Rabbah* 2:4). It is thus the task of mankind to "cut through" the kingdoms of evil in order to release the holiness of Malkhut trapped within them. This "cutting" is represented in the opening of the cervix during labor.

We know that man comprises four elements which are all based in one source element (see above, Chapter 4). In the same way, the power of evil has four kingdoms and a source kingdom of evil, which is manifest in Amalek, as in (Numbers 24:20), "Amalek is the first of nations." Thus, Amalek stands in the way of the holiness of Malkhut and tries to overpower it. The Prophet Samuel realized this, and therefore, when he avenged the Jews against Agag, the king of Amalek, he "cut him" into *four* parts (1 Samuel, 15:33; Rashi). This is the same idea. The holiness of Malkhut was released by "cutting" Agag, corresponding to the opening of the cervix.

Reb Noson writes that the battle of Amalek against faith is symbolized by a difficult childbirth. Malkhut corresponds to faith, its desire being to "be born," to arouse faith in the world. This is precisely what Amalek opposes.

At the time of the Exodus, God performed awesome miracles, bringing faith even to those who were extremely distant from Him. The Egyptian exile of Abraham's descendants is compared to the plight of a woman in hard labor, unable to give birth. With the Exodus, the Nation of Israel (faith) was born, but immediately Amalek reared its head, with the intention of ensuring the "newborn" would not survive for long. Ultimate salvation therefore requires the complete removal of Amalek, the elimination of all forms of atheism, so that the *d'latot* (doors) may be opened, and the "newborn" (renewed faith) may grow to full maturity (Likutey Halakhot, Tefilin 5:30–34).

*

Mashiach or Abortion?

The Talmud states (Yevamot 63b), "Mashiach cannot come until all the souls which have been created are born." It further states, "Whoever does not procreate is considered as though he has committed murder!" The reason for this extremely sharp analogy is that the whole purpose of man's existence is to reveal Godliness. Since every human being is created in the "image of God," it follows that every child born increases the revelation of Godliness in the world. Thus, one who does not propagate actually diminishes the revelation of God in this world. This is tantamount to murder (see *Tur, Even HaEzer, Piryah V'Rivyah* 1).

If failure to engage in procreation is equivalent to murder, how much more must this be true of abortion? The human soul, whether born or unborn, is certainly a Godly portion (see above, Part 2). As we have pointed out, pregnancy is the beginning of a revelation of Godliness. Any attempt to abort a pregnancy is an attempt to diminish God's Presence in this world. Abortion is permitted only in cases where it is necessary in order to save the mother's life, for her life is itself a revelation of Godliness. (Should the fetus in some way endanger the mother's life, there is no question that the life of the yet unborn child must be ended in favor of the mother who is already living in the world.)

Abraham and Sarah were the first to succeed in properly and fully revealing the Kingdom of God in this world. Abraham was the paradigm of Chesed, which is revealed in the *Sefirah* of Yesod. The name *SaRah* shares the same root as *S'raRah* (authority, power); thus Sarah personifies Malkhut. The confluence of Yesod and Malkhut reveals Godliness in the world. However, Abraham and Sarah were barren. After much prayer (which is itself a manifestation of Malkhut; above, Chapter 44), children were born to them. Ishmael, Isaac, Jacob and Esau are all considered their offspring. (Ishmael was born to Abraham after Sarah had given him her maidservant Hagar for a wife. He is thus considered "their" child. Jacob and Esau were Isaac's children.)

In the Passover Haggadah, we speak of the representative four sons: the wise son, the wicked son, the simple son, and the son who does not know how to ask. Rebbe Nachman teaches that these "four sons" encompass all the children of Abraham and Sarah. Isaac represents the wise son; Esau, the wicked son; Jacob, the simple son (see Genesis 25:27); and Ishmael, the son who does not know how to ask (there is no mention in the Bible of Ishmael ever speaking). These four "sons" — including even the wicked son —

parallel *dalet* (numerically four), the manifestation of Malkhut; for children, no matter how they turn out — for better or worse — contribute in some manner to the rectification of Malkhut (see *Likutey Moharan* I, 30:6).

As mentioned earlier in this chapter, children are often the redeeming factor in the lives of their parents and ancestors. Yet in other instances, children themselves may require redemption — even the Patriarchs and Matriarchs did not have only perfect children. Rebbe Nachman commented on these two opposite types of offspring: "Good children are the best medicine for their ancestors" (*The Aleph-Bet Book* Children, A:42).

Regarding children who have strayed from the proper path, Rebbe Nachman said (*Aveneha Barzel*, p.21, #4), "A person should pray to have many children, no matter how they turn out. Eventually Mashiach will come, and he will rectify the entire world, bringing it back to the spiritual state it enjoyed on the day of the creation of Adam and Eve!"

*

E Pluribus Unum

Shema Yisrael! [Hear Israel!] The Lord our God is One!
Deuteronomy 6:4

Man was created to "be fruitful and multiply." The reason, as has been stated above, is to bring forth new revelations of Godliness continually. Yet why must man be "*so* fruitful?" Wouldn't it be enough if every set of parents had only two children, so that the world's population could remain constant? Why should any couple have more than two children, and why, even if parents opt for more than two children, should they have large families?

The Talmud teaches (*Yevamot* 63b), "Whoever does not populate the world is considered to have diminished the Godly image therein." This is because each individual child is born with his own mind. He (or she) brings to the world his very own intellect, a specific intellect which has never before existed in the world. (This is why children do not always listen to their parents — every child's mind is absolutely individual.) Every single mind, each new intellect, is capable of recognizing God and can reflect His greatness in its own way. Rebbe Nachman thus teaches that "an increased birthrate will reveal more of God's honor" (*Likutey Moharan* II, 71:8).

Those who seek a materialistic lifestyle may tend to view children as little more than a physical addition to the family, not to mention the additional drain on the family budget. In some homes, children are altogether unwanted — they put a crimp in the family's lifestyle. Other families feel that children are all right, and after having an "addition" or two, they graciously set aside some "quality time" for their children, offering them a few hours a week — whether or not the children are interested in spending those particular hours with their parents.

More spiritually inclined families also have material needs which must be met, but for them life's objectives are altogether different, far more meaningful and enduring. One need only observe a spiritually oriented family to witness the warmth, respect and closeness that pervades their lives. This does not mean that they are angels, nor does it mean that rifts do not occur. Nevertheless, for the most part, the spiritually inclined have a broader view of life and manage to provide for their families — with spiritual largesse.

This is implied in the Holy Name of God that is associated with Yesod — *ShaDai* — which combines the two words "*yeSh Dai* — "There is enough!" (see above, Chapter 40). Ultimately, those who live a spiritual life find the resources necessary to raise their larger families. It is these families that increase God's honor and glory.

*

It is a wonderful thing for each and every person to arrive at a personal recognition of God, from his own individual perspective. However, when people realize that everyone is worshiping the One God, then they find another, even more beautiful concept.

Rebbe Nachman taught:

> Every person understands life in a manner which is different from that of his peers. No two people are alike. This is why God is very pleased when, from among a variety of opinions proffered regarding a specific halakhic issue, one of them is accepted by the majority. When the *many* agree to *one* idea, this is very precious in God's eyes (*Likutey Moharan* II, 2:6).

No two people are alike; there have never been, in the history of humankind, two people who were alike in every detail — nor will there ever be. People might be similar, but never exactly alike. Thus, every person has his or her own understanding of God — each views Him from a different perspective. When we recite the *Shema*, the affirmation of faith, we are each, from our varied perspectives, recognizing the universal truth that God is One.

This concept is tremendously significant. Though each person possesses a different view, all can *agree* on "One" thing. This is the perfected state of peace, of "pluralism grounded in the most exalted Unity," which allows people to overcome their differences and to achieve true peace.

Reb Noson writes that this is the true meaning behind the mitzvah to have as many children as possible. Bringing more and more people into the world, each with his own mind, each with a different perspective of God, yet each serving the One God in the best way he can, reflects the Glory of God most powerfully. How beautiful will it be, when Mashiach arrives, to see so many *different* people with a *common* goal! At that time, *true* peace will reign (*Likutey Halakhot, Prikah u'Teinah* 4:23).

*

Rebbe Nachman taught:

> *Sefer Yetzirah* (4:12) tells us that two stones build two houses, three stones build six houses and four stones build twenty-four houses... That is, with two "stones," A and B, one can make two

combinations (AB and BA); with three "stones," A, B and C, one can make six combinations; with four, A, B, C and D, one can make twenty-four combinations, and so on. Each additional stone increases the product exponentially.

The "stones" referred to above are souls (cf. Lamentations 4:1). Thus, a simple quorum of ten people yields 3,628,800 combinations! Imagine the increase in the number of combinations with every single "stone" — every soul — which is added to the population. Imagine the number of combinations produced by 100 people...or by 1,000...or by 2,500 people...or more. The possibilities are staggering!

Rebbe Nachman explains that every one of these "stones" — these souls — becomes a part of the "building" of holiness. Each and every person, in becoming part of this "building," increases the "world community" of holiness (*Likutey Moharan* II, 8:6).

Herein lies the vital importance of having children. The more children one has, the more one increases the structure of holiness in the world (*Likutey Halakhot, Piryah v'Rivyah* 5:2).

*

Peace on Earth

> **Rabbi Elazar said in the name of Rabbi Chanina: Learned men bring peace to the world, as the verse states (Isaiah 54:13), "All your children [*banayikh*] will have been taught about God; and for your children there will be abundant peace." Do not read *BaNaYiKH* [children], but rather *BoNoYiKH* [builders].**
>
> *Berakhot* 64a

Rabbi Yoshiyahu Pinto comments on this passage: Those who seek spirituality through Torah study are engaged in building solid foundations for the world (just as children are the foundation of the world). The verse states (Isaiah 48:22), "There is no peace for the wicked"; only those who seek spirituality can attain peace. Furthermore, the learned men, those who study and teach others, bring peace to those who were originally distant from spirituality. Even more directly, they bring peace to those who support them.

This is alluded to in the repetition of the word *banayikh* in the verse, "All your children will have been taught about God; and for your children there will be abundant peace" — "Do not read *BaNaYiKH*, but *BoNoYiKH*." The words *BaNayikh* and *BoNoyikh* are both related to the word *BiNah* (Understanding). Those who devote themselves to seeking an understanding of the spiritual are the true builders of the world. They spread the knowledge of God to all, thereby filling the entire world with peace and harmony.

* * *

Part Ten

Life and Death

48

"And It Was Very Good"

Life as we know it begins with conception and ends with death.
Between those events come infancy, childhood, puberty,
adolescence, maturity, middle age and, if we merit it, old age. Of
life, King Solomon wrote (Ecclesiastes 1:2), "Vanity of vanities, says
Kohelet; vanity of vanities, all is vanity." As the Sages comment,
if each singular use of "vanity" in the verse represents one, and
each plural use of "vanities" represents two, this verse contains a
total of seven "vanities!" The Midrash therefore asks (*Kohelet Rabbah*
1:3), "Why seven times vanity? They correspond to the seven
phases through which a person lives during his lifetime." The
Midrash illustrates these phases:

- The infant is like a king: he is placed in a royal "carriage," and
  everyone hugs and kisses him.
- During childhood, he is compared to a swine, always getting
  himself dirty.
- When he reaches puberty, he is compared to a jumping goat.
- In adolescence, he loves exhibiting his prowess and showing off,
  like a stallion.
- Upon reaching maturity, when he assumes the responsibility of
  marriage and must earn a livelihood, he is likened to a mule.
- In middle age, he marries off his children. He is then compared to
  a brazen dog, who must boldly seek the means to do so.
- Finally, in old age, when he can only "ape" what the young do, he
  is likened to a monkey.

The Midrash adds that King Solomon, the wisest of all men, used the term *hevel* (vanity; mist or steam) to teach us that life passes by very quickly, holding nary a benefit for the individual. Life is a "mist of mists" — it is soon gone, dissipated before you know it. While this is not a very encouraging summary of the life span of a human being, it is quite accurate.

How can one escape this cheerless cycle?

When King Solomon made this statement, he was clearly referring to a materialistic life, for he continues (Ecclesiastes 1:3), "Of what avail is all of man's labor under the sun?" The Midrash comments, "Of no avail — under the sun. But above the sun? This has value!" What is "above the sun?" What is above the material world? Spirituality (*Kohelet Rabbah* 1:4).

Someone who desires a materialistic life will easily recognize himself or his loved ones in one of the stages listed above. However, one who attempts to live a spiritual life — on whatever level he can — will find himself "above" those descriptions. Spiritual aspirations bring respite from the daily grind of life and are accompanied by rewards that are beyond the reach of the "benefits" offered by a material life. Once, when conversing with his followers about life, Rebbe Nachman remarked, "It is not how long a person lives, it is how *well* he lives, that counts." The Rebbe, who himself lived only thirty-eight years, was referring to how much spirituality a person can attain during his lifetime.

Reb Noson, throughout the *Likutey Halakhot*, writes again and again that spirituality is most definitely accessible to everyone, even to those who are most distant from God. In fact, the deeper one has become "buried" in a life of materialism, the greater will be the revelation of God's glory when one turns to Him. Jethro was a high priest of idolatry. When he came to the Israelite camp and said (Exodus 18:11), "Now I know that God is above all gods," the glory of God was elevated in *all* the worlds — in this world and in all the Supernal Universes (Zohar II, 69a).

Jethro had been steeped in idolatry. As an idolator he was on the lowest of spiritual levels, and yet his recognition of God caused a tremendous revelation of the glory of God — a revelation even into the darkness of his former life! (see *Likutey Moharan* I, 10:2). Everyone has the ability to create such a revelation. A person must only be careful not to "bite off more than he can chew" (see *Likutey Halakhot, Kriat Shema* 1:2).

We have seen throughout this book that, in all aspects of life, we are only a small step away from spirituality. God created man in a form which can reflect and radiate the Divine at a moment's notice — at any time, in any place — if one but desires it. Reb Noson once said, "If a person is not able to perform a whole mitzvah, should he then not perform half a mitzvah?" Every good deed — even an incomplete one, if done with sincere intent — creates an angel which acts as an advocate before the Heavenly Tribunal on Judgment Day! (see *Avot* 4:13).

*

Judgment Day

> **The days of our lives are seventy years, if with special strength, eighty years; most of them are troubled, and then they are cut...**
> Psalms 90:10

As a person ages, death becomes ever more imminent; but death can occur at any age — in middle age, youth, childhood or even infancy. The day of one's death is one's personal Day of Judgment, when one's deeds, both good and evil, are scrutinized. The Zohar (II, 199b) teaches that it is a day of *seven* judgments:

- The actual death
- Announcement of one's deeds, whether good or evil
- Placement in the grave
- The judgment of the grave
- The decaying of the body
- Gehennom
- The interval before the soul is completely purified

The ARI teaches that these various judgments are not intended as punishments so much as they are meant to cleanse a person from sin. Thus, Gehennom — and Reincarnation, when it is imposed — are means by which one's sins are purged. Death, too, is an integral part of this cleansing process.

The accounting system which God uses when drawing up our final balance sheet is far beyond the level of man's understanding. In His unfathomable mercy, God adds to the credit column *all* mitigating circumstances — one's upbringing, environment, community, financial resources and so on. Nevertheless, the judgment is real; we are held fully accountable. The main question that we must answer is: Have I tried hard enough?

Reb Noson writes that a person's most important advocate for mercy on the day of judgment is the "will factor," the degree to which he or she *wanted* spirituality. If our will was strong throughout life, even if we were remiss, our credit is greatly increased. This does not imply that a weak effort can suffice. "I just couldn't do it" is not an acceptable excuse. Reb Noson's "will factor" involves making every possible effort. If our efforts prove unsuccessful, then what are we to do? We must try again, and again, and again. As Rebbe Nachman used to say: "*Gevalt*! Never give up!"

*

Reward and Punishment

> **And God saw that it was *tov m'aod*, very good...**
>
> Genesis 1:31

Each day of the First Week of Creation, God brought forth another facet of the world. Each day, upon surveying His handiwork, God said "It is good." On the sixth day, after having created the entire world, including man, "God saw everything He had made, and behold it was *very* good." The Midrash asks "Why did God add the word 'very' on the sixth day: 'very' good?" Several opinions are cited: "'Very good' — this is death!"; "'Very good' — this is beneficence and compassion towards others!"; "*Tov M'AoD*, 'very good' — this is ADaM!" (*Bereishit Rabbah* 9:10–12).

We have discussed in various contexts that man must struggle through life. Ask any rational person, "To where does life lead?" and his answer will likely be, "To the grave!" This being the case, of what value is a person's life? Physical existence is necessarily limited. Sometimes one is fortunate to live long enough to reap at least some benefits, but there is no one who has not had to contend with adversity in life. What has he to show for it?

Someone who seeks spirituality knows that life does not come to an end with death. Moreover, he can experience the exalted spiritual existence that awaits him, even in this world, while still limited by his physical body. The Mishnah teaches (*Avot* 4:21), "This World is compared to an anteroom of the Palace [the World to Come]. Prepare yourself in the anteroom so that you may enter the Palace!" But This World is more than a *preparation* for the World to Come. A sensitive, thinking person will realize that once he enters the anteroom of the Palace, he is *already inside* the Palace itself. If we live our lives with this knowledge, we are uplifted by the awareness and will be spurred to act accordingly, making careful, calculated efforts to perfect ourselves while we have the opportunity. Perhaps the actual joys and comforts of the Palace are currently out of reach; still, we are not that far from them and can always bear them in mind. Just as the anticipation of a planned wedding brings joy to a person's heart, so too the anticipation of the joys of the World to Come can be glimpsed and even experienced before we have reached them.

Before we can experience the World to Come, we must first pass through the entrance to the Palace. This "entrance" is the process of death. While death may be a terrifying thought, for the average person it is actually a "*very* good" and important process. Had history unfolded differently, had Adam not sinned, man might have lived forever. He was created in a spiritual body which was to have lived eternally. This was not to be, however, for man did not stand up to the test and instead descended into materialism — a condition that cannot last forever.

But suffering and death are to man's advantage, for one who tries to live a spiritual life is cleansed, for the most part, while still alive, and death becomes the final stage of this rectification process. In death, the body decomposes, and all the physical pleasures in which we delighted are obliterated. Yet, when the time of the Resurrection finally arrives, we who have suffered will be "reborn"; the physical body will be recreated in a physical — yet spiritual — state. We will then live forever, in the way God originally intended man to live (*Likutey Halakhot, Tefilin* 5:18).

This is the meaning of the teachings cited in the Midrash: "'Very good' — this is death!"; "'Very good' — this is beneficence and compassion towards others!"; "'*Tov M'AoD*, very good' — this is ADaM!" Death is *very good* because in death man can cleanse himself from all impurities. *Very good* is beneficence, because these deeds bring us to the World to Come.

And, "Very good is Adam!" The word *M'AoD* (מאד) contains the same letters as the word ADaM (אדם), because, through the world as we know it, one can become Man in the most exalted sense: a totally spiritual individual, the climax of Creation.

*

May we all merit to witness the Revelation of God, with the Rebuilding of the Holy Temple, the Ingathering of the Exiles, and the Coming of the Mashiach, speedily in our days, Amen.

* * *

Appendix A

The Exchanged Children

The Exchanged Children

This story was told by Rebbe Nachman on Saturday night, October 14, 1809. Rebbe Nachman's followers were discussing with him the Napoleonic Wars, which were then sweeping the European continent. Reb Naftali, a close follower of the Rebbe, said that Napoleon's career was surprising, for although not born into royalty he had risen to become emperor. It is significant that the day Rebbe Nachman told this story was the same day the Treaty of Schönbrun was signed, giving Napoleon control of Austria's share of Poland.

Rebbe Nachman said, "Who knows what sort of soul he has? It is possible that it was exchanged. There is a Chamber of Exchanges where souls are sometimes exchanged."

The story, according to Reb Noson's interpretation in *Likutey Halakhot, Birkhot HaShachar 3*, forms the basis of our discussion of body and soul. We present the story here in its entirety. For those interested in a deeper study of the story with running commentary, see *Rabbi Nachman's Stories*, Story #11, pp.231–277.

* * *

Once there was a king, who kept in his palace a maidservant to wait on the queen. She was not a simple servant, who would not have had access to the king, but rather a lady-in-waiting.

When the time came for the queen to give birth, this maidservant was also ready to deliver a child. They both bore sons and the midwife exchanged the babies, to see what would happen and how the situation would develop. She exchanged the infants by placing the king's son next to the maidservant and the servant's son next to the queen.

The two boys began to grow up. The one who was assumed to be the king's son was given greater and greater status, and continued to advance, becoming highly talented. The one who was assumed to be the maidservant's son, but who was actually the king's true son, grew up in the servant's house. The two of them studied together in the same school.

The king's true son was called "the servant's son," but he was drawn by his nature to the ways of royalty, even though he was raised in the servant's house. Conversely, the maid's son, who was known as "the king's son," was drawn by his nature to different conduct, not to the ways of royalty. However, since he was growing up in the king's palace, he was raised in the royal manner and learned to behave accordingly.

The midwife, finding it difficult to keep her secret, told someone of how she had exchanged the boys; and since one friend has another to confide in, and that one has yet another, so in the usual manner the secret was revealed until everyone was speaking about how the king's son had been exchanged.

Of course, people did not speak about it openly, since it would not have been desirable for the king to find out about it — for what could he have done. There was no remedy. He could not believe the rumor, since it might have been false, and how could he then exchange the boys again? No, the report could not be revealed to the king. Still, the people whispered freely about it among themselves.

One day someone revealed the secret to the king's false son, telling him that people were saying that he had been exchanged with the servant's son at birth. "But," the informant added, "it is impossible for you to investigate this matter, since that would be beneath your dignity. Besides, there really is no way to ascertain the truth. I am only telling you this, since there may be a rebellion against the king someday, and the rebels' hand could be strengthened if it could be claimed that they are proclaiming the king's true son king. I am speaking of the one whom they claim is the king's son in their rumors. Therefore, you must devise some sort of plan to do away with him."

The king's false son began to persecute the father of the other son, who was in truth his own father. He was always looking for ways to do him harm. He caused him one injury after another, trying to force him to flee the kingdom together with his son. As long as the king was alive, the son did not have much power. Still, he managed to make the servant miserable.

After some time, the king grew old and died, and the servant's son inherited the kingdom. He then did much greater harm to the father of the other son, oppressing him time after time. He would do this with cunning, so that people would not trace the evil back to him, since it would not be proper for the masses to realize what he was doing. Nevertheless, in his secret ways, he caused the father constant misery.

The father of the true prince understood that the new king was persecuting him because of the rumors. He told his "son," who was actually the king's true son, the entire story, saying: "No matter what the truth is, I have great pity on you. If you *are* my son, I certainly have great pity on you. If you are really the king's son, the pity is even greater. He wants to destroy you completely, heaven forbid! Therefore, you must get yourself far away from here."

This upset the youth greatly, but the king continued to direct persecutions at him, one after another. The son therefore made up his mind to leave. His father gave him a considerable amount of money, and he went on his way.

The king's true son was extremely upset at having been exiled from his land for no reason. He thought about his situation and tried to understand why he was being banished. "If I am really the king's son, I certainly do not deserve to be treated like this; and if I am not the king's son, I also do not deserve to be compelled to flee for no reason. What have I done wrong?"

He became very bitter, and took to drinking and visiting brothels. He decided to spend his life doing nothing other than getting drunk and following his heart's desires, since he had been exiled without reason.

Meanwhile, the new king reigned over the kingdom with a firm hand. Whenever he heard people spreading rumors of the exchange, he would punish them harshly. He ruled strictly and arrogantly.

*

One day, the king went hunting with his royal ministers. They came to a pleasant area where a river was flowing, and stopped there to rest and stroll about.

The king lay down and began thinking about how he had exiled the servant's son for no reason. No matter what the truth was, it was not fair. If the other was actually the prince, then not only had he lost his position because of the exchange, but he had also been banished without reason. If he was not the king's son, he certainly did not deserve to be exiled, since he had done nothing wrong. The king thought about it, and regretted his sin and the great injustice for which he was responsible, but he did not know what to do for himself or what advice to follow. He could not consult with anyone in this matter. Worrying about this, he became very depressed. He told his ministers to return home; he was beset with worry and had no desire for sport. The entire group left for home. When the king returned, he obviously had many other interests and concerns. He busied himself with his affairs and soon forgot the entire matter.

*

Meanwhile, the exiled son continued his activities and squandered his money. One day he took a stroll by himself, and on the way he lay down to rest. He started thinking about what had happened to him. *What has God done to me?* he thought. *If I am the king's son, then it is certainly not right. And if I am not the king's son, I still don't deserve to be an exiled fugitive.*

Then he began to look at the matter in a different light. "On the other hand, if it is so, if God can do such a thing, to exchange a king's son and cause all this to happen to him, does my behavior make sense? Has it been proper for me to act as I have?" He began to grieve and greatly regretted the evil deeds that he had done; but afterwards, he returned to his dwelling and to his drinking again. However, since he had already begun to entertain thoughts of regret and repentance, these thoughts constantly disturbed him.

One night he went to sleep and dreamed that there was a fair in a certain place on a certain day that he was to attend. There he was to accept the first job offered him, even if he felt that it was beneath his dignity. When he awoke, the dream was imbedded firmly in his mind. Sometimes thoughts like these are immediately forgotten, yet this dream was constantly on his mind. Nevertheless, since he felt that it would be very difficult for him to do, he just made himself all the more drunk.

The dream, however, recurred a number of times, and it disturbed him greatly. Once he was told in the dream, "If you want to have any pity on yourself, do as you have been told." He then realized that he must obey the dream.

He gave what remained of his money to his host, and he also left all his fine clothing with his host, and went to the fair wearing only the simple garb of a peddler.

He arrived at the place and awoke early to attend the fair. When he got to the fairgrounds, he met a merchant who asked him, "Would you like to hire yourself out for a job?"

"Yes," he replied.

"I am driving some cattle," said the merchant. "Hire yourself out to me."

Because of the dream, he did not take any time to think the matter over, but instantly said: "Yes."

The merchant took him on and immediately gave him work to do. He ordered him around as a master orders his servants.

The young man began to appraise his situation. This type of servitude was certainly not befitting his station, for he was a delicate person, and now he would have to drive cattle, walking on foot alongside the animals. Still, he could not change his mind.

The merchant was ordering him around like a master.

The young man asked the merchant, "How can I drive the animals all by myself?"

"I have other drovers for my cattle," replied the merchant. "You can work alongside them."

With that, the merchant gave him some cattle to drive, and he brought them outside the city. There the other drovers were gathered, and they all set out together.

The young man drove the cattle, while the merchant rode alongside on horseback. The merchant rode the horse cruelly, with anger and arrogance, and treated the young man especially cruelly.

Seeing how cruel the merchant was, the young man was very frightened. He was afraid that the merchant would strike him with his staff. He was so delicate that such a blow would surely kill him. He thus drove the cattle with the merchant alongside them.

Finally they came to a stop, and they took the sack of bread that the merchant had given the drovers to eat. They gave the young man some of this bread, and he ate it. Afterwards, they passed close to a thick forest, where the trees stood very close to one another.

Two of the cows that the young man was driving for the merchant strayed. The merchant screamed at him, so he ran to catch them, but they ran further away, and he continued to pursue them.

The forest was so dense and thick that as soon as he entered the forest, he lost sight of his companions. The more he chased the cows, the further they fled. He continued chasing them until he was deep in the forest.

He thought over his situation. *No matter what I do, I will die. If I go back without the animals, the merchant will kill me.* For in his fear of the merchant, it seemed to him that he would be killed if he returned without the animals. *But if I stay here*, he thought, *I will be killed by the wild beasts in the forest. Why should I go back to the merchant? How can I confront him without the animals?* He was deathly afraid of his employer.

He continued pursuing the animals, but the more he chased them, the more they fled.

Meanwhile, it became night. He had never before spent the night deep in a forest like this. He heard wild animals howling and decided, *I will climb a tree and spend the night there.* All night he heard the sound of wild animals roaring.

In the morning, he looked and saw his cattle standing nearby. He climbed down from the tree, but when he tried to catch them, they again took flight. Again the more he chased them, the further they fled.

Whenever the cows found some grass and stopped to graze, he tried to catch them, but they bolted and ran away again. On and on he chased them, and on and on they fled, deeper and deeper into the forest. They were so deep in the forest, and so far from civilization, that the wild beasts there had no fear of man at all.

Night fell again, and when he heard the beasts roaring, he was extremely frightened. Then he saw an immense tree, and began to climb it. When he got high up in the tree, he found another person lying there and became very frightened. At the same time, though, he was somewhat comforted, since he had found another human being there.

They began questioning one another. "Who are you?" he asked.

"A human being. Who are you?"

"A human being."

"How did you get here?"

The young man did not want to tell him all the details of what had happened, so he answered, "Because of the cows. I was tending cattle, and two animals strayed. This is how I got here."

He then asked the stranger whom he found in the tree, "How did you get here?"

"I came here because of a horse," replied the other. "I was out riding, and when I stopped to rest, the horse strayed into the forest. I tried to catch him, but he fled further and further, until I came here."

They decided to join forces and remain together. They spoke about how they would remain together even when they reached civilization.

The two of them spent the night in the tree. They heard the wild beasts howling and roaring and making a great noise.

In the morning, he heard the sound of very loud laughter, "Ha! ha! ha!," resounding over the entire forest. The laughter seemed to spread out all over the forest. It was such loud laughter that the sound made the tree tremble and sway. The young man was very alarmed and terrified by the sound.

The stranger he had discovered in the tree told him, "I am no longer afraid of this, because I have already spent a number of nights here, and each night just before daybreak I hear this sound of great laughter, which makes all the trees tremble and shake."

The young man was still very upset, and he said to his companion, "This seems to be a place of demons; such laughter is never heard in civilized places. Who has ever heard laughter resounding all over the world?"

Then the day quickly dawned, and they saw their animals standing nearby. The young man's cattle were there alongside the stranger's horse. They climbed down and began to give chase, one after the cows, and the other after the horse.

The cattle fled further, and the young man ran after them as before. The other also ran after the horse, which also ran further away. Eventually they became separated and were far apart from one another.

While chasing through the forest, the young man found a sack full of bread. This was a very precious commodity in the wilderness. He took the sack on his shoulder and continued after the cattle.

Suddenly he encountered another stranger. At first he was very frightened, but he was also somewhat comforted for having found another man here.

"How did you come here?" asked the stranger.

He responded by asking the stranger, "How did *you* come here?"

The stranger replied: "I, my forefathers and their ancestors were brought up here. But you? How did you come here? No human from civilization ever comes here."

The young man was very alarmed. He realized that the stranger was not a human being. He had said that his ancestors had grown up here, and that no human from a civilized area ever comes here, so he was obviously not a human being. Still, this stranger from the forest did nothing to harm him and was behaving in a friendly manner.

"What are you doing here?" asked the forest man of the king's true son.

He replied that he was chasing his cattle.

"Stop chasing your sins," said the stranger. "These are not animals at all. They are your sins, and they are leading you on. Enough now! You have already received your due punishment, and now you can stop chasing. Come with me, and you will receive what is due you."

The king's true son went with him, but he was afraid to speak any further with him or ask him any questions. He realized that one who is inhuman like this could open his mouth and swallow him.

*

While he was walking after the forest man, he encountered his companion chasing his horse. As soon as he saw him, he signaled him: *This stranger is not a human being. Don't talk to him. Don't have any dealings with him at all, since he is not human.* He then whispered all this in his companion's ear, telling him how he knew.

His companion, the man with the horse, saw the sack of bread on his shoulder. He began to plead, "My brother, I have not eaten for days! Give me some bread."

He replied, "Here in the wilderness such pleas are of no avail. I must look out for my own life first; and I need the bread for myself."

The other began to plead and beg. "I will give you anything I have."

The king's true son, however, realized that here in the wilderness no gift or bribe is worth as much as bread. He replied, "What can you give me that would compare in value to bread in the wilderness?"

"I will give you my entire self," replied the man with the horse. "I will sell myself to you for bread!"

The man with the cattle decided that it would be worthwhile to buy a person for some bread. So he bought the other as a servant for life. The other made an oath and swore that he would be his eternal slave even when they returned to civilization. The king's son would give him bread: that is, they would eat together from the sack until the bread was finished.

They followed the forest man. The owner of the horse, who was now the true prince's slave, followed the drover of the cattle and the two of them walked behind the forest man.

Things were now somewhat easier for the king's son. If he had to lift something, or needed something else to be done, he would order his slave to do it for him.

They followed the forest man until they came to a place of snakes and scorpions. The king's son was very much afraid. Out of fear, he asked the forest man, "How can we get across?"

"If you think that's hard," replied the other, "how can you get to my house?"

With that, he pointed to his house, which was standing in midair. "How can you get into my house?" he asked.

They went with the forest man and he brought them safely across, and then brought them into his house. He gave them food and drink, and then went away.

The king's true son made use of his servant for all his needs.

Meanwhile the slave was very bitter. He had sold himself as a slave because of one occasion when he had needed bread; now they had plenty to eat. For an hour's worth of food, he would be a slave for the rest of his life. He moaned and sighed, *How did I come to such a state — to be a slave?*

The king's true son, who was his master, asked him, "What great status did you have before, that you are groaning for having come to this state?"

He answered, telling him the whole story of how he had been a king, and that people had spread rumors that he had been exchanged as an infant. He related how he had exiled his friend. Then one day it had occurred to him that it was not a good thing that he had done, and he regretted it. After that, he had constantly regretted the vile deed and great injustice that he had done to his friend.

Then one night he dreamt that he could correct this wrong by abdicating his kingdom and going wherever his eyes led him. This would be an atonement for his sin; but he had not wanted to do it. However, the dreams continued to torment him and urge him to do it, until he finally decided to obey. He abdicated his kingdom and wandered about until he came here. Now he had become a slave.

The king's true son listened in silence to everything that his newly obtained slave said. He thought to himself, *I will see what happens. Then I will decide how to deal with him.*

That night, the forest man returned. He gave them food and drink, and they spent the night there. Just before morning they heard the tremendous laughter, which made all the trees shake and tremble.

The slave urged the king's true son to ask the forest man the meaning of this.

The king's son asked the forest man, "What is this sound of tremendous laughter every day before dawn?"

He replied, "This is the sound of the day laughing at the night. The night asks the day, 'Why is it that when you come, I have no name?' Then the day laughs with this loud laughter, and it becomes day. This is the significance of the sound of laughter."

The king's son found this very astonishing, for it is a very wondrous thing that the day laughs at the night.

In the morning, the forest man once again departed, while they remained there, eating and drinking. At night he came back, and they ate, drank, and again spent the night.

That night, they heard the sounds of the wild beasts. All of them were howling and roaring with different calls. The lion roared, while the leopard growled, and the birds whistled and screeched with their own sounds. All of them made loud noises, and at first, the young man and his slave trembled in fear. They were so afraid that they could not concentrate on the sounds.

Afterwards, however, they began to attune their ears, and heard the sound of music, an awesomely beautiful song. They listened more intently and heard that it was an extremely amazing song. It was a wonderfully great joy to hear it. All the joys of the world were as nothing — other joys became meaningless when compared to the wondrous delight of listening to this song.

They discussed the situation and agreed that they would remain there. They had enough food and drink, and they could enjoy this wonderful delight, compared to which all other enjoyments were worthless.

The slave urged his master, the king's true son, to ask the forest man the meaning of this song and he asked.

The forest man replied that this song was composed because the sun made a garment for the moon. All the animals of the forest said that the moon does them a great service; for their dominion is at night. Sometimes they must enter an inhabited area, and they cannot do this by day, so their main time is the night. By shining for them at night, the moon does them a great favor. The wild animals therefore agreed that they would compose a new melody in honor of the moon. "This is the melody that you are now hearing. All the animals and birds are singing a new song in honor of the moon's having received a garment from the sun."

When they heard that this was a melody, they listened even more attentively to it. They heard that it was a very wonderful and beautiful song.

The forest man continued, "Why do you find this so novel? I have an instrument that I received from my forefathers, who in turn inherited it from their ancestors. The container is made with special leaves and colors. When this instrument is placed on any animal or bird, the creature immediately begins to sing this song."

Just then, the laughter was heard, and it was day. The forest man went on his way, as before. The king's true son went to look for the instrument. He searched the entire room, but could not find it, and he was afraid to go any further.

The king's true son and his slave were afraid to ask the forest man to bring them back to civilization.

*

Afterwards the forest man returned and informed them that he would lead them back to civilization. When he brought them to an inhabited area, he presented the wondrous instrument to the king's true son and said, "I am giving you this instrument." Then, referring to the serving woman's son, who had become king and was now a slave again, he told the young man, "You will soon know how to deal with him."

"Where shall we go?" they asked.

The forest man told them that they should inquire and seek a land known as "The Foolish Land with the Wise King."

"In which direction shall we begin inquiring about this land?" they asked.

The forest man pointed out the direction and said to the king's true son, "Go there, to that country, and you will achieve your greatness."

They set out on their journey. They very much desired to find an animal, either wild or domestic, on which to try out the instrument to see if it would produce the wondrous song, but they did not encounter any animals at all.

Then, when they came to a more densely inhabited area, they found an animal. They placed the instrument on it, and it began to sing the song of the forest.

They continued traveling until they came to the country the forest man had described. There was a wall surrounding this country, and it could be entered only through one gate. One had to walk several miles around the wall to arrive at this gate. They walked around along the wall until they finally came to the gate.

When they got there, the guards did not want to let them enter; the king of the land had died, and his son was now the new king. The king had left a will declaring that although the land had previously been called "The Foolish Land with the Wise King," after his death it would be called "The Wise Land with the Foolish King." The man who undertook and succeeded in restoring the land's former name — that is, "The Foolish Land with the Wise King" — would become the new king.

Therefore no one was being allowed into the land unless he was prepared to undertake this. They did not want the king's son to enter. They said to him: "Can you undertake the task of restoring the land's original name?" It was certainly impossible for him to attempt it; therefore they could not go in.

The slave urged the king's son to return home, but he did not want to leave, since the forest man had told him to go to this land, and here he would come to his greatness.

Just then, another man arrived riding a horse, and he wanted to enter the gate, but the guards would not let him in for the same reason. Seeing the stranger's horse standing there, the king's true son placed the instrument on it. It began to play the wonderful melody of the forest.

The horse's owner begged him to sell him this instrument, but he did not want to sell it. "What could you give me for such a wonderful instrument?" asked the king's son.

The horseman said, "What can you ever do with this instrument? It has no real use. At best you can make a show with it and earn a gulden. I have knowledge that is better than your instrument. From my forefathers, I have inherited the knowledge of how to understand one thing from another thing. If someone makes any statement, through the tradition that I have, I can understand one thing from another. I have never revealed this to anyone in the world. But if you give me your instrument, I will teach you this knowledge."

The king's son decided that it would be very wonderful to understand one thing from another. He gave the horseman the instrument, and the other taught him the method through which he could understand one thing from another.

*

Now that the king's true son could do this, he went to the gate. He understood that it would be possible for him to attempt to restore the land's original name, since he understood one thing from another, even though he did not know how, or by what means. Nevertheless, understanding one thing from another, he understood that it would be possible.

He therefore made up his mind that he would tell them to let him enter, since he would now make an effort to restore the land's original name. After all, what had he to lose?

He asked the men at the gate to let him in and told them he would attempt to restore the land's original name.

They let him enter and informed the ruling ministers that a man had been found who was willing to undertake to restore the land's original name. He was brought to the ministers of the land, and they told him, "You must realize that we are not fools, heaven forbid. However, the late king was so extraordinarily wise that, compared to him, we were all considered fools. It was for this reason that the land was called 'The Foolish Land with the Wise King.' When the king died his son took his place. He is also wise, but compared to us, he is not wise at all. The land therefore now bears the opposite name, 'The Wise Land with the Foolish King'.

"The king left a will stating that when a wise person was found who could restore the original name to the kingdom, that person would be king. He likewise ordered his son to abdicate in favor of such a wise person when he was found and let the wise person be king. This person would have to be so extraordinarily wise that compared to him everyone else was foolish. This man would be king, and then the name of the land would once again become 'The Foolish Land with the Wise King,' since compared to him everyone else would be fools. Now you know what you are getting yourself into."

The ministers continued, "We have a test to see if you are so wise. There is a garden here which was left by the late king, who was an extremely wise man. This garden is a great wonder. All sorts of metal instruments grow in it, silver instruments and golden instruments. It is an awesome wonder. However, it is impossible to enter the garden. As soon as anyone enters it, he is pursued and begins to scream. He does not know who is chasing him and sees nothing. Still, he is pursued until he is chased out of the garden. Let us see if you are wise enough to enter this garden.

The king's son asked them if the person who enters the garden is beaten in any way.

506 / Anatomy of the Soul

They answered, "Primarily, he is chased and he does not know who is chasing him. But he flees in great terror." This is what they had been told by people who had entered the garden.

The king's true son went to the garden. He saw that there was a wall around it and an open gate. There were no guards there, since such a garden obviously did not need to be guarded.

He went nearer to the garden. Next to the garden, he saw a statue of a man. Looking more closely, he saw a tablet above the man. The inscription on it said that this man had been a king many centuries ago, and during this king's reign there had been peace. Before this king's reign there had been wars, and after it there had also been wars, but during his reign there had been peace.

He contemplated the situation. He already could understand one thing from another, and understood that everything depended on this man. When a person entered the garden and was pursued, he did not need to flee at all. He had only to stand next to this man, and he would be saved. Furthermore, if the statue of this man was placed *within* the garden instead of next to it, then anyone would be able to enter the garden safely. The king's son was able to understand all this, since he could understand one thing from another.

The king's son entered the garden. As soon as he was pursued, he walked over and stood next to this statue of the man, which stood just outside the garden. He was thus able to leave safely, without being harmed. Others who had entered the garden had fled in such terror when they were pursued that they had injured themselves; however the king's son had emerged safely and calmly since he had stood next to the statue. The ministers were amazed to see him come out safely.

The king's true son then ordered that the statue be placed inside the garden. When this was done, all the ministers were able to enter the garden. They entered the garden and went out in peace, without being harmed in any way.

The ministers said, "Nevertheless! Even though we have seen such an accomplishment from you, nevertheless for one accomplishment you do not deserve to receive the kingdom. We shall test you once more."

They explained, "The late king had a throne. The throne is very tall, and next to it stand many species of animals and birds carved out of wood. In front of the throne stands a bed. There is a table near the bed, and on the table stands a lamp.

"From the throne, various paved, walled paths go forth. These paths extend from all sides of the throne, but no one knows the relationship of the throne to these paths.

"At a certain distance down one of the paths stands a golden lion. If any person comes near that lion, it opens its mouth to devour him. However, the path extends far beyond the lion. The same is true of the other paths which extend from the throne; they are very much the same. Standing on each one is another type of wild beast, such as a leopard made of another kind of metal. It is also impossible to come close to that leopard. The path then extends beyond where the leopard stands. This is the pattern of all the paths.

"These paths extend throughout the entire land. No one understands the relationship of the throne with all its details to the paths. This, then, will be your test. See if you can understand the significance of the throne and everything associated with it."

They showed him the throne and he saw that it was extremely high. He came nearer to the throne and gazed at it. As he contemplated the throne, he realized that it was made of the same type of wood as the box of the instrument that the forest man had given him.

He looked further and saw that a rose was missing from the top of the throne. If the rose were in its place on the throne, then he understood that the throne would have the same power as the box, and would produce music whenever it was placed on any animal or bird. Then he gazed longer and noticed that the rose, missing from the top of the throne, was lying at the bottom of the throne. He would have to take it and place it back on top, and then the throne would have the same power as the box.

The late king had devised each detail with such wisdom that no person could understand its significance until an extraordinarily wise person who would understand the concept came along. He would then know how to exchange and correctly arrange all the objects associated with the throne.

He then saw that the same was true of the bed. He understood that it had to be moved slightly from the place where it stood. The table also had to be moved somewhat, and the lamp likewise had to have its position adjusted. The birds and animals as well had to be shifted to different places. Thus, a bird would have to be taken from one place and set in another place. The same was true of all the animals. The king had cleverly disguised everything so that only a very wise person would be able to rearrange it all correctly.

The same was true of the lion which stood by the path: it had to be stood in a different place. This was also true of all the beasts on the paths.

The king's son gave instructions that everything be rearranged properly, and that the rose be taken from the foot of the throne and inserted at the top. Everything was rearranged in the proper order.

All the animals and birds then began to sing a very wonderful melody. Each one functioned properly.

The king's true son was awarded the kingdom.

The king's true son, who had now been crowned king, said to the son of the maidservant, "Now I understand that I am actually the king's son, and you are actually the maidservant's son."

* * *

Appendix B

The Body and the Mitzvot

Sefer Charedim

Sefer Charedim

Man was created in a Godly image, that is, in an image which reflects spirituality (for God has no physical image whatsoever). Reb Noson writes that anyone with an understanding of the Kabbalah — the Zohar, the writings of the ARI and their commentaries — will realize that every mystery of Torah that they speak about reflects the "Godly image" in which man was created. This includes the concepts of the Vacated Space, the Shattering of the Vessels, the Supernal Universes and all the other mysteries of the Torah. Every concept applies to each and every individual, male or female, young or old, for (Numbers 19:14) "this is the Torah — man..." The Torah reflects man; and man can reflect the spirituality of the Torah and the holiness of God Himself (see *Likutey Halakhot, Minchah* 7:22).

The Zohar teaches that man is a microcosm. Each organ or limb reflects a different facet of Creation. Therefore, if through one's actions one draws spirituality into each of one's organs, one is, in a sense, revealing God throughout the entire world! Each person is an entire world and, by drawing Godliness to oneself, God is revealed everywhere. Conversely, one who lacks the rectifications which are accomplished by those mitzvot which parallel a given limb is considered "handicapped," and finds the revelation of Godliness difficult. This is why, when people call out to God, He seems at times not to "hear." This is not the case, though; the absence of a Godly response is just a sign that God has not been welcomed into that particular *place* (*Tikkuney Zohar* #70, p.130b). The way to draw Godliness towards ourselves is to perform the mitzvot, thereby rectifying the "limbs and organs" to which each mitzvah applies.

But how is one to do this? Which mitzvah rectifies the eyes, which the arms, the head, the legs and so on? There are 248 positive commandments and 365 prohibitions. If we could know which mitzvot correspond to which organs, would it influence people's attitude towards the mitzvot? Rebbe Nachman taught:

> All the mitzvot together form a complete structure, just as the body is a complete structure. Each mitzvah corresponds to a different organ, limb or vessel of the body. For example, performing mitzvot that correspond to the head helps to rectify one's head. Moreover, the greater one's joy in performing the mitzvot, the greater is the rectification that can be achieved (*Likutey Moharan* I, 5:2).

*

While we do not know exactly which mitzvah corresponds to which organ or limb, we are aware that, in a general sense, those mitzvot which are more closely associated with certain organs have a stronger tie to them. In his classic work, *Sefer Charedim* (Book of the Pious), Rabbi Eliezer Azkiri (d. 1600) extolls the observance of the mitzvot and the benefits man can derive from them, physically and spiritually. He divides the mitzvot according to the structure of the body by explaining which mitzvot are performed by which organ.

Following is an abridged version of the *Sefer Charedim*. Some mitzvot can be performed by several organs, and often several limbs perform a single mitzvah. We have listed the mitzvot according to the main organ involved in each, both the positive commandments and the prohibitions. As in the *Sefer Charedim*, we have listed the positive commandments first and the prohibitions afterwards.

Several mitzvot apply to specific times or places and cannot currently be performed. Others apply to specific individuals or groups (*Kohen Gadol*, *Kohanim*, Levites, men or women). Still others apply only to the Holy Land or to the Temple. Listed here is a selection of those mitzvot which can apply to most people, at most times and most places.

*

The Heart

The heart is the seat of the emotions, passions and thoughts, as we have seen in our text (Part 5). It is therefore obvious that certain mitzvot listed here can be applied to the mind as well as to the heart.

Positive

- Faith: to believe in God; to believe that He created the entire Universe and guides it with Divine Providence; to believe that He gave us the Torah — Written and Oral — at Sinai; to believe in the tzaddikim; to believe in the Exodus, in Mashiach, in the Resurrection, and other basic principles of faith

- To recite the *Shema*, the affirmation of our faith

- Fear of God: to maintain constantly an attitude of respect, fear and awe of God, which includes showing proper respect in the synagogue

- To pray

- Love of God: feeling love and showing honor for God, through the mitzvot, Shabbat, the Festivals and every other aspect of one's relationship with God; to draw oneself towards God and to the tzaddikim

- Rejoicing on the Festivals and when performing all the mitzvot

- To sanctify God's Name

- Repentance

- Respect and love for parents, friends, converts, all Jews

- Modesty, humility and controlling anger and other potentially evil characteristics

Prohibitions

- Eradicating heresy and idolatry

- Not coveting others' possessions; avoiding jealousy

- Not forgetting God, the Revelation at Sinai, the wickedness of Amalek

- Eliminating one's arrogance, anger, hatred of other Jews and similar characteristics

- Banishing evil thoughts

- Not to waste pity on those who are unworthy

*

The Eyes

Positive

- To look at the *tzitzit*, to read Torah from texts
- To cry over the loss of a worthy person, to bemoan the loss of the Temple

Prohibitions

- Not to look lustfully or arrogantly, not to look at idolatry, not to read books that speak about atheism...

*

The Ears

Positive

- To involve oneself in Torah study, to hear the *shofar* on Rosh HaShanah, to hear the *Megillah* on Purim
- To listen to the tzaddikim and to the righteous judges
- To hear the words of one's own prayers and blessings
- To listen to the Torah being read, to hear the *Kaddish* and blessings in order to answer "Amen"

Prohibitions

- Not to listen to an inciter against Torah and/or against faith in God
- Not to listen to falsehood, slander or other prohibited forms of speech

*

The Nose

- The nose corresponds to purity (see Chapter 34); thus one should take care not to become enticed by forbidden smells.

*

The Mouth: Speech

Positive

- To speak respectfully at all times to parents, grandparents, teachers and all others to whom respect is due

- To recite the blessings, the *Shema*, the prayers, the *Kaddish* for the deceased, *Kiddush*, *Havdalah*, *Hallel*, the Pesach Haggadah, the Counting of the Omer and related "verbal mitzvot"; to listen to the *Kaddish* and blessings in order to answer "Amen"

- Verbal confession of one's sins before God

- Studying Torah and teaching Torah to others

- To speak only words of truth, peace and positive influence; to speak softly and respectfully to others

Prohibitions

- Not to speak God's Name in vain; not to cause others to mention God's Name in vain — such as in an oath, in unnecessary blessings, cursing others, and so on

- Not to swear falsely or in vain, not to bear false witness

- Not to speak profanity, falsehood, slander, mockery, flattery, idolatry, deception; not to insult or embarrass others; not to hurt others in any way through one's words

- Not to instigate or in any way create strife, whether directly or indirectly; not to advise others improperly

*

The Mouth: Eating

Positive

- To eat on Shabbat, the Festivals, Rosh Chodesh and other feasts associated with mitzvot (such as weddings, circumcisions, redemptions of firstborn); to eat matzah on Pesach; to eat in the *sukkah* on Sukkot

- To eat only kosher food; to eat foods which have been properly tithed (this mitzvah applies to foods grown in the Land of Israel)

Prohibitions

- Not to eat on Yom Kippur, not to eat *chametz* on Pesach, not to eat outside the *sukkah*

- Not to eat nonkosher food: improperly slaughtered kosher animals, nonkosher animals (e.g., pork), nonkosher fowl (e.g., ravens), reptiles, nonkosher fish (e.g., shrimp, lobsters, clams); not to eat meat and dairy together

- Not to eat foods which have not been properly tithed, not to eat from fruits that were not harvested according to the laws of the Sabbatical Year (these mitzvot apply to foods grown in the Land of Israel)

*

The Hands

Any mitzvah that can be performed by use of the hands. Some examples:

Positive

- Honoring one's parents, rabbis and elders; putting on *tzitzit* and *tefillin*; lighting candles for Shabbat and Festivals; lighting Chanukah candles

- Washing one's hands upon rising and before eating as prescribed by law; holding the *lulav* and *etrog* on Sukkot; writing or buying Torah-related books

- Placing the *mezuzah* upon the door, returning lost objects to their rightful owners, building safeguards into one's home so that people are not harmed (e.g., building a wall or railing around a flat roof)

- Paying one's workers on time, giving charity, tithing foods

- Assisting others when necessary, helping to save another's life

Prohibitions

- Not to form any object of idolatry, not to commit murder, not to strike another person, not to steal, not to borrow another's possessions without permission, not to act deceitfully
- Not to destroy fruit-producing trees or foods or other useful items, not to stand by idly and watch another person about to be harmed, not raising dangerous animals
- Not to accept bribery, not to shave off one's *peyot*, not to use the hands for lustful purposes
- Not to use the hands for forbidden work on Shabbat or on Festivals

*

The Legs

Any mitzvah that can be performed by use of the legs. Some examples:

Positive

- To stand up before one's parents and elders, to stand up when one sees a Torah scroll or a Torah scholar, to walk (or travel) to a synagogue or to perform other mitzvot
- To visit the sick, to attend a funeral
- To comfort the bereaved (this mitzvah can also apply to the mouth)

Prohibitions

- Not to walk further than the permitted distance on Shabbat and Festivals
- Not to bow down to idolatry, not to walk in an arrogant manner

*

The Brit

Positive

- Circumcision according to the Codes

- To marry; to have a minimum of two children, one male and one female

- To fulfill one's marital obligations, to sanctify oneself and to cohabit in a modest manner

Prohibitions

- To purposely refrain from marrying and procreating

- To abstain from marital relations during a woman's menstrual period until her immersion in the *mikvah*

- Not to force one's wife into marital relations, not to act lewdly

- To refrain from any incestuous or adulterous liaison or otherwise prohibited relationship, not to engage in homosexual or bestial relationships, not to engage in promiscuity, not to masturbate

Sefer Charedim depicts many varied reincarnations as punishment for sexual sins and strongly advises against committing them, since the punishments are far more severe than one would imagine.

*

There are many other mitzvot which a person can perform with his various organs; only a few illustrations of the more commonly applicable mitzvot have been cited here. The crucial lesson to be gleaned from these examples is that by doing one's best to serve God, one can illuminate one's body with spirituality. Then one can truly merit a Godly image!

* * *

Appendix C

The Sefirot and the Characteristics

Tomer Devorah

Tomer Devorah

Rabbi Moshe Cordovero (1522–1570) authored many important works in Kabbalah and headed the Safed school of Kabbalah before the ARI's arrival there. Among his writings is the *Tomer Devorah* (Palm Tree of Devorah), which explains the major "Characteristics" of God, which man should work to emulate, and how they are alluded to in the Ten *Sefirot*. He shows in this important work how man can attain these lofty levels. He opens his first chapter with an explanation of his objective in the book:

> It is proper for man to resemble his Creator, for then he becomes worthy of his "Godly image." If he were to resemble a spiritual image in his body alone, while lacking the development of the related spiritual characteristics, he would be falsifying the exalted form he possesses and would earn the title, "a nice form with despicable deeds," for the spiritual form and Godly image consist of man's deeds. To what avail is the physical "Godly image" of man if in deeds he does not resemble his Creator? It is therefore fitting for man to be similar in his actions and deeds to [the *Sefirah* of] Keter...

Rabbi Moshe Cordovero proceeds with a study of how the Characteristics are alluded to in each of the Ten *Sefirot* and how man can attain these characteristics on each of the Supernal Levels. He also explains (Chapter 2) that man cannot succeed in attaining all these attributes at once, but must strive to develop and internalize them at a steady pace. Following is a summary of the *Tomer Devorah's* teachings.

Keter

The Thirteen Attributes of Mercy are rooted in the *Sefirah* of Keter (see Chapter 34). Striving to attain these attributes rectifies one's level of Keter. Rabbi Cordovero bases his list of the spiritual characteristics on the verse in Micah (7:18–20) in which the Thirteen Attributes of Mercy are enumerated. These attributes, which man can strive for, are:

(1) Tolerance; (2) Patience with others; (3) Forgiveness of others; (4) Seeking good in others and for others; (5) Not maintaining one's anger; (6) Seeking acts of kindness; (7) Loving and seeking the benefit of someone who has hurt you and now wishes to rectify that damage (forgiving him is not sufficient); (8) Remembering another's good deeds and forgetting his evil deeds; (9) Feeling compassion for others, even for evil people; (10) Acting with honesty; (11) Acting with kindness and leniency towards others (not insisting upon "the letter of the law" where others are concerned); (12) Assisting others to repent and not bearing a grudge against them; (13) Seeking ways to show mercy and compassion to others, even if one does not find any redeeming factor in them.

Additional attributes and deeds which parallel Keter and are found in the "Godly image" of the human body are:

• Humility; keeping one's mind free from any evil thoughts; always showing favor to others; noticing manifestations of good while rejecting evil; avoiding looking at anything improper or indecent; assisting the indigent; not becoming angry; exercising patience; receiving every person joyfully; never speaking evil, cursing or engaging in idle chatter; always speaking good.

To attain the attribute of humility, one should flee from honor and never seek it. One should recognize one's shortcomings, continually remember one's sins and seek ways to rectify them. This will keep one on the road to attaining humility. Additionally, one should try to honor everyone and to love others.

Chokhmah

One must look towards God to impart of His knowledge to man, in order that man may attain clearer perceptions of Godliness. Furthermore, a person should always be willing to share his knowledge with someone else.

The verse states (Psalms 104:24), "Everything was created with Chokhmah." Thus, everything in the world reflects God's wisdom. With this awareness, a person must focus his thoughts on how to benefit others, seeking ways to help them. Just as a father has compassion upon his children, it is the responsibility of each person to be compassionate towards others, as well as towards all levels of Creation — mineral, vegetable and animal. One must care for one's environment and surroundings, since they all reflect God and His Wisdom.

Binah

To perfect the attribute of Binah, one should continually repent. Repentance is associated with Binah, the heart and the blood system, as discussed in our text in Chapter 9.

Chesed

Chesed is associated with love, and thus a person must cultivate love for God and for mankind. There are many ways to cultivate this love:

- Taking care of one's own children and providing for their needs;
- Visiting the sick and tending to their needs; likewise performing the mitzvah of burying the dead and comforting the bereaved;
- Giving charity to the poor;
- Being hospitable to guests and making peace between people.

Gevurah

Gevurah denotes restraint, and this attribute has been discussed throughout our text. One must always exercise restraint when faced with temptation to sin.

Tiferet

The Torah corresponds to Tiferet; thus Torah study is the principal method by which to develop one's attribute of Tiferet. However, if a person acts haughtily regarding his knowledge, looking down upon his students, upon his friends and upon others less fortunate than himself, he deprives himself of truly benefiting from his Torah knowledge. One must also use one's Torah knowledge to reach consensus with one's colleagues, and not to engage in strife or in unwarranted arguments.

Netzach and Hod

Netzach and Hod correspond to the feet, which support the body. The way to attain these attributes is by furthering the influence of spirituality in the world, namely, by respecting and maintaining Torah study, the foundation of the universe. The study of the Chumash (Bible) strengthens Netzach, the study of Mishnah strengthens Hod, and the study of Talmud strengthens both.

Yesod

To strengthen Yesod, one must guard oneself from immoral thoughts and immoral speech. One must also guard one's Covenant from immoral deeds (see Chapter 41).

Malkhut

Since Malkhut is associated with "poverty" (as it has no light of its own; see Chapter 44), to develop the attribute of Malkhut one must humble oneself. This includes maintaining a humble lifestyle, avoiding ostentatiousness.

Also important for perfecting Malkhut is to strive for the fear of Heaven, since Malkhut represents the acceptance of the yoke of Heaven.

To attain any level of Malkhut it is necessary to be married and to conduct oneself according to the Torah's dictates of family purity (see Chapter 44).

*

May it be the will of the Almighty that we merit to go only in His ways, to perfect our "Godly image," and to become worthy of reflecting the awesome powers of the Ten Sefirot all the days of our lives. Amen.

* * *

Appendix D

Charts and Diagrams

THE ORDER OF THE TEN SEFIROT

כתר
KETER

חכמה
CHOKHMAH

בינה
BINAH

חסד
CHESED

גבורה
GEVURAH

תפארת
TIFERET

נצח
NETZACH

הוד
HOD

יסוד
YESOD

מלכות
MALKHUT

THE STRUCTURE OF THE SEFIROT

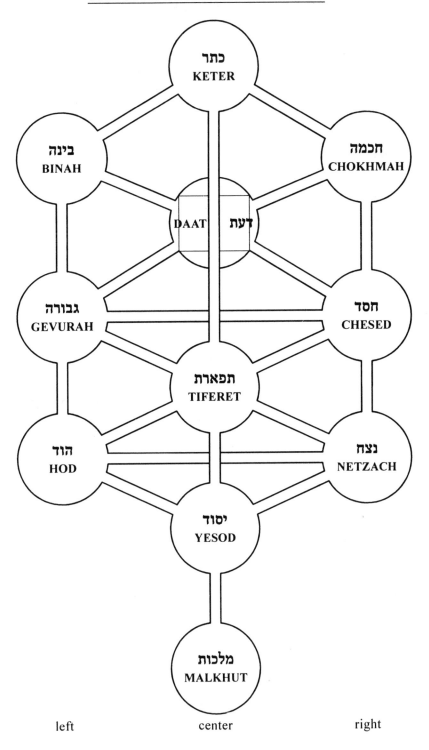

left   center   right

THE PARTZUFIM - THE DIVINE PERSONA

Sefirah	*Persona*
KETER	ATIK YOMIN ARIKH ANPIN
CHOKHMAH	ABBA
Daat	
BINAH	IMMA

	Chesed	
	Gevurah	
	Tiferet	
TIFERET	Netzach	Z'ER ANPIN
	Hod	
	Yesod	

MALKHUT	NUKVA of Z'ER ANPIN

EXPANSIONS OF THE HOLY NAME OF GOD

Expansion	Partzuf	Value	Expansion

YHVH - Expansion of the Tetragrammaton - יהוה

Expansion		Partzuf	Value		Expansion
YOD HY VYV HY	AB	Chokhmah	72	עב	יוד הי ויו הי
YOD HY VAV HY	SaG	Binah	63	סג	יוד הי ואו הי
YOD HA VAV HA	MaH	Z'er Anpin	45	מה	יוד הא ואו הא
YOD HH VV HH	BaN	Malkhut	52	בן	יוד הה וו הה

ÆHYH - Expansion of the Holy Name EHYeH - אהיה

Expansion			Value		Expansion
ALePh HY YOD HY	KSA		161	קסא	אלף הי יוד הי
ALePh HH YOD HH	KNA		151	קנא	אלף הה יוד הה
ALePh HA YOD HA	KMG		143	קמג	אלף הא יוד הא

ÆLHYM - Expansion of the Holy Name ELoHIM - אלהים

Expansion		Value	Expansion
ALePh LaMeD HY YOD MeM		300	אלף למד הי יוד ממ
ALePh LaMeD HH YOD MeM		295	אלף למד הה יוד ממ
ALePh LaMeD HA YOD MeM		291	אלף למד הא יוד ממ

THE SEFIROT AND ASSOCIATED NAMES OF GOD

Sefirah	Holy Name
Keter - Crown	*Ehyeh Asher Ehyeh*
Chokhmah - Wisdom	*YaH*
Binah - Understanding	*YHVH* (pronounced Elohim)
Chesed - Lovingkindness	*El*
Gevurah - Strength	*Elohim*
Tiferet - Beauty	*YHVH* (pronounced Adonoy)
Netzach - Victory	*Adonoy Tzevaot*
Hod - Splendor	*Elohim Tzevaot*
Yesod - Foundation	*Shaddai, El Chai*
Malkhut - Kingship	*Adonoy*

HEBREW LETTER NUMEROLOGY - GEMATRIA

100 = ק	10 = י	1 = א
200 = ר	20 = כ	2 = ב
300 = שׁ	30 = ל	3 = ג
400 = ת	40 = מ	4 = ד
	50 = נ	5 = ה
	60 = ס	6 = ו
	70 = ע	7 = ז
	80 = פ	8 = ח
	90 = צ	9 = ט

LEVELS OF EXISTENCE

World	Manifestation	Sefirah	Soul	Letter
Adam Kadmon	Nothingness	Keter	*Yechidah*	Apex of Yod
Atzilut	Thought	Chokhmah	*Chayah*	Yod
Beriyah	Speech	Binah	*Neshamah*	Heh
Yetzirah	Action	Tiferet (six sefirot)	*Ruach*	Vav
Asiyah		Malkhut	*Nefesh*	Heh

World	Inhabitants	T-N-T-A
Adam Kadmon	Tetragrammatons	
Atzilut - Nearness	Sefirot, Partzufim	*Taamim* - Cantillations
Beriyah - Creation	The Throne, Souls	*Nekudot* - Vowels
Yetzirah - Formation	Angels	*Tagin* - Crowns
Asiyah - Action	Forms	*Otiyot* - Letters